S0-ACI-321
3 0301 00086553 1

# OUT OF BOUNDS

# OUT OF BOUNDS

## Male Writers and Gender(ed) Criticism

EDITED BY
Laura Claridge
AND
Elizabeth Langland



The University of Massachusetts Press
AMHERST

Printed in the United States of America
LC
ISBN 0-87023-734-9 (cloth); 735-7 (paper)
Designed by Jack Harrison
Set in Sabon by Keystone Typesetting, Inc.
Printed and bound by Thomson-Shore, Inc.

Library of Congress Cataloging-in-Publication Data
Out of bounds : male writers and gender(ed) criticism / edited by
Laura Claridge and Elizabeth Langland.
p. cm.
Includes bibliographical references.
ISBN 0-87023-734-9 (alk. paper). — ISBN 0-87023-735-7
(pbk. : alk. paper).
1. English literature—Men authors—History and criticism.
2. American literature—Men authors—History and criticism.
3. Masculinity (Psychology) in literature.
4. Femininity (Psychology) in literature.
5. Feminism and literature—Great Britain.
6. Feminism and literature—United States.
7. Patriarchy in literature.
8. Sex role in literature.
9. Men in literature.
I. Claridge, Laura P.
II. Langland, Elizabeth.
PR120.M45098 1990
810.9'9286—dc20 90-35674
CIP

British Library Cataloguing in Publication data are available.

*To*
*Jon Palmer Claridge*
*and*
*Jerald Jahn*

To imagine a language means to imagine a form of life.
LUDWIG WITTGENSTEIN

# Contents

# Acknowledgments

We welcome the opportunity to acknowledge those whose ideas helped inspire this project and those whose encouragement helped bring it to fruition. Specifically, we thank Carolyn Heilbrun, Sandra Gilbert, Susan Gubar, Marianne Hirsch, Catharine Stimpson, Paul Smith, and Gerhard Joseph for comments and criticisms that made this a better volume than it would otherwise have been. More generally, we owe a debt to the feminist and gender critics who have preceded us and so paved the way for the issues and questions we engage here. We would also like to thank our contributors, who made our editing task pleasant and helped to teach us about our subject in the process.

But most of all we take pleasure in acknowledging the support—manifested in so many different forms—of our families: Jon, Ian, and Devon, and Jerry, Erika, and Peter. They create a richness of lived experience that reminds us of the compelling truths motivating ideology and feminist inquiry.

# Contributors

**Donald Ault,** Professor of English at the University of Florida, is the author of *Visionary Physics: Blake's Response to Newton* and *Narrative Unbound: Revisioning William Blake's "The Four Zoas."* He has written on comics, animated cartoons, and movie serials and is a contributor and scholarly adviser to *The Carl Barks Library of Donald Duck and Uncle Scrooge.*

**Joseph A. Boone,** Associate Professor of English at the University of Southern California, is the author of *Tradition Counter Tradition: Love and the Form of Fiction* and coeditor of *Engendering Men: The Question of Male Feminist Criticism.* He is currently working on a book entitled *Sexuality, Narrative, and Modernity: Experiments in the Psychology of "Sex" and "Self" in Fiction.*

**Laura Claridge,** Associate Professor of English at the U.S. Naval Academy, has recently completed a study entitled *Romantic Potency: The Paradox of Desire in Wordsworth, Shelley, and Byron.* She has published articles on Pope, Mary Shelley, and Faulkner. Currently she is working on the "beautiful" as the neglected supplement to studies of the sublime.

**Deirdre David,** Professor of English at the University of Maryland at College Park, is the author of *Fictions of Resolution in Three Victorian Novels* and *Intellectual Women and Victorian Patriarchy: Harriet Martineau, Elizabeth Barrett Browning, George Eliot.* Her work in progress, "Grilled Alive in Calcutta: Victorian India, Victorian Women," deals with issues of race and gender in writing about the nineteenth-century British Raj.

**Margaret R. Higonnet,** Professor of English at the University of Connecticut, has published on feminist theory, romanticism, and children's literature. She has coedited *The Representation of Women in Fiction* and *Behind the Lines: Gender and the Two World Wars.*

**U. C. Knoepflmacher** is Professor of English and Paton Foundation Professor of Ancient and Modern Literature at Princeton University. Among his more recent publications are a book on *Wuthering Heights* in Cambridge Landmarks of Literature series and articles on Dickens's "bruised femininity" and on female spaces in Hardy's poetry.

**Elizabeth Langland,** Professor of English at the University of Florida, is the author of *Society in the Novel* and *Anne Brontë: The Other One.* She has also coedited two collections: *The Voyage In: Fictions of Female Development* and *A Feminist Perspective in the Academy: The Difference It Makes.* She is currently working on a study of domestic ideology and middle-class women in the Victorian novel.

**Frank Lentricchia** is Professor of English at Duke University and the editor of the *South Atlantic Quarterly* and the Wisconsin Project on American Writers. His books include *The Gaiety of Language* (1968), *Robert Frost: Modern Poetics and the Landscapes of Self* (1975), *After the New Criticism* (1980), *Criticism and Social Change* (1983), *Ariel and the Police* (1988), and, most recently, an edited volume, *Critical Terms for Literary Study.*

**Melvyn New,** Professor of English at the University of Florida, has been writing on fiction for the past twenty years, most often on the work of Laurence Sterne. His present projects include an edition of Sterne's forty-five sermons for the Florida edition of the *Works of Sterne,* for which he is General Editor, and a volume on *Tristram Shandy* for the Twayne World Masterpiece series.

**Karen Oakes** has taught American literature and women's studies at Brandeis University and at Colby College in Waterville, Maine, where she is currently Visiting Assistant Professor. Her essay in this volume derives from the chapter on Whitman in her book manuscript, *Reading Femininity: Gender Gestures in Poetic Intercourse.*

**James Phelan,** Professor of English at Ohio State University, has written *Worlds from Words: A Theory of Language in Fiction*; *Reading People, Reading Plots: Character, Progression, and the Interpretation of Narrative*; and *Living with Tenure.* He is the editor of *Reading Narrative: Form, Ethics, Ideology.* His essay is part of a larger study of narrative discourse now in progress.

**Marlon B. Ross** is Associate Professor of English at the University of Michigan in Ann Arbor. He is the author of *The Contours of Masculine Desire: Romanticism and the Rise of Women's Poetry.*

**Judith L. Sensibar,** Associate Professor of English at Arizona State University, is the author of *The Origins of Faulkner's Art* and the editor of Faulkner's *Vision in Spring.* She is currently at work on a narrative about the Faulkner family for which she received an ACLS grant in 1988–89. She has also written on Edith Wharton, Henry James, and T. S. Eliot.

**William Veeder** is a Professor of English at the University of Chicago and a Visiting Scholar at the Institute for Psychoanalysis in Chicago. He has written books on W. B. Yeats, Henry James, and Mary Shelley, coauthored a history of Anglo-American feminism, and coedited a selection of James's literary criticism and a collection of essays on *Dr Jekyll and Mr Hyde.* He is presently working on a study of Ambrose Bierce and San Francisco gothic fiction.

**Joseph Wittreich** is Distinguished Professor of English at the Graduate School of the City University of New York. His most recent books are *Interpreting "Samson Agonistes"* and *Feminist Milton.* He is currently at work on a project entitled *Wars of Truths: Milton and the New Criticisms.*

# OUT OF BOUNDS

# Introduction

LAURA CLARIDGE and ELIZABETH LANGLAND

THIS COLLECTION grew out of a special MLA session which the editors organized in 1986. Called "Male Feminist Voices," it aimed to articulate the special problems confronting male literary figures who wanted to escape patriarchal language. At the early stages of the thinking represented by that panel, we posed the problem in this way:

> Luce Irigaray asks, "what can be said about a feminine sexuality 'other' than the one prescribed in, and by, phallocratism? How can its language be recovered, or invented?"[1] Historically, it may well be time to push her question further: "what can be said about a *male* sexuality 'other' than the one prescribed in, and by, phallocratism?" That is, it is not enough to locate woman on the other side of a maleness that is assumed to coexist with patriarchy. For there is at least the possibility that maleness exists in a relation to patriarchy as a third term of gender discourse, whose terms are woman, man, and patriarchy. Even as we (under)mine patriarchy to expose its spurious claims to universality, so must we be vigilant against the error of equating it with man.

The central insight that we must consider patriarchy a gender-complicated term—not conflated with the concept "male" alone—has held up and has been further supported, in fact, by other feminist discourse emerging since that session two years ago. We had, however, initially defined a male writer's resistance to and defiance of the phallic mode and a patriarchal ideology as "feminist." That is, our original, unexamined assumption was that antipatriarchal activity would necessarily encompass feminism.

Thus one unexpected result of this collection of essays is our conclusion that no such generalization can be maintained. For to write against patriarchy as a male fettered by it does not necessarily result in writing for liberation of gender bondage, a primary aim of philosophical and practical feminism. "Feminist" tends to imply a political agenda—the granting of full economic, political, and social equality to women. It implies as well a commitment to woman's autonomy and a recognition of her individual and independent importance. Although many male writers are interested in a space or possibility for expression coded as "feminine," they are not necessarily interested in particular women and their plights—or even the general plight of the generic "woman." A male writer may simply need the space of what he or his culture terms the feminine in which to express himself more fully because he experiences the patriarchal construction of his masculinity as a constriction. He may, that is, appropriate the feminine to enlarge himself, a process not incompatible with contempt for actual women. Thus it is possible for the male writer wrestling with patriarchal language to be antifeminist or, at least, to sidestep totally the issue of gender equality.

These conclusions motivated us to reformulate the focus of our project in the following way in order to encourage our essayists to grapple with what might seem to be the ineffable:

> We hope that in exploring male writers trying to work their way out of a constricting male-inflected language, we do not end up claiming that the movement away from patriarchy necessarily culminates in the feminine. In fact, any success in escaping the bondage of language will inevitably be qualified. The challenge of this collection lies in avoiding the easy binary opposition of masculine versus feminine that literary criticism has too often sustained through its concept of patriarchy.

And here we have a second, more subtle reason for disavowing a necessary symmetry of men-against-patriarchy with male feminists, one which takes us to the heart of a general problem with inquiries into gender issues: their bipolarity. We remain locked in binary oppositions when we speak of gender: man/woman, male/female, masculine/feminine, patriarch/feminist. Such a realization forced us to conclude that to find oneself on the side of the "feminine" (whatever that might be) or to "write as a woman" (whatever that might mean) increasingly seems a problematic objective of feminism. To aim thus would merely sustain patriarchy by perpetuating the polarization undergirding it.

Yet, viable as this conception is, it began to sound as if we were participating in one more celebration of the canonical male writers for their power of vision as they leapt, with superior male muscularity, over the old problems of masculine and feminine in which, we feared we might seem to imply, women writers became mired. The danger of this new emphasis, then, lay in losing what had energized our inquiry initially, that which had impelled us to call our session as well as our projected volume "Male Feminist Voices."

What underlay that choice was a conviction that recognizing the ways in which man, as well as woman, is constructed by patriarchy has feminist implications, that it is a *line of thought* which, in conceptualizing the constructed nature of male as well as female experiences, begins to free us from the binary thinking responsible for imprisoning both women and men even as it initiates one significant goal of feminism, the liberation of both sexes from gender proscriptions. To represent better the achievements and insights of our essays, our title evolved into its present form, *Out of Bounds,* but with the ubiquitous convention of an explanatory subtitle: "Male Writers and Feminist Inquiry." Still, mirroring the slipperiness of any discourse about gender, that subtitle insistently proclaimed its ability to mislead. For, after all, no one (least of all the editors) claimed that all the essays proceed from a methodology consistently identifiable as "feminist." Troubled and complex as such a critical description would be, we were sure that our contributors were complicating our thesis from various critical strengths with their attention to male gender within patriarchy (terms which themselves are hardly trouble-free). And therein lies our attempt in a revised-yet-again subtitle to allude to what really takes place in our text: "Gender(ed) Criticism" foregrounds our thesis—gender in the writings of male canonical authors sensitive to the limitations of language in their culture—as well as reminding our readers of the context of our project: criticism offered up by women and men inscribed, inevitably, by the same conditions they seek to question.

Must male authors, as they attempt to subvert the "masculine" subjective configurations available to them at a particular moment in history, initially if briefly align themselves with what their society codifies as the female? If antipatriarchal movement is assumed always to be at least in part toward a recuperation of the female, because her oppression is central to patriarchal structure, then a severe and oft covered or ignored contradiction inheres in the implication that the female can define her "authentic" self best outside of patriarchy, uninscribed by it. For, in fact, "female" as an organizing principle is deeply imbedded, in spite of feminist inquiries (always conducted from within, too, as Derrida has asserted for any would-be subversive intellectual activity), in the very patriarchy constitutive of gender. So do we merely mean that the male literary figure moves from the gendered male position in society to the gendered female position—and that that movement is in and of itself liberating? This is, of course, far too easy and, again, finally reductive in its logical end as a categorical construction of reality and identity. One important goal of this collection lies in challenging the easy binary hierarchy of masculine versus feminine that has thus far beleaguered literary criticism of patriarchy.

The *écriture féminine* of the French feminists has provided generative insights and has made cogent the imperative to dismantle a phallocentric ideology. But to code a language that is playful, open, disruptive, nonhierarchical, and antitheoretical as "feminine," and one that is logical, closed, rigid, hierarchical, and theoretical as "masculine," preserves the very binary oppositions a Cixous or an Irigaray means to dismantle, as critics such as Toril Moi and Domna Stanton have pointed out.[2]

For what, exactly, does it mean to speak in terms of male or female—readers, texts, writers, or contexts? If we speak of women's writings, or men's writings, aren't we really just refusing to call the emperor on his nakedness? Such ultimately naive assumptions that we can separate gender so neatly beg the very question feminist theory at its strongest would raise: Is there such a thing as a predictable norm for man or woman? Don't many of the assumptions that underwrite *écriture féminine,* for example, or the variations on the theme of reading as a woman, or writing as a man, imply a deeply held belief that at some level a universal, totalizing opposition is in place that makes such generalizations valued?

In addition, this attribution of traits to gender makes easier the appropriation of language for political means. Certain gender-identified constructions (e.g., "a text trying to close itself is 'male,' whereas a text striving to remain open is 'female' ") can be seen as fictions of an era, shrewd political gestures in which, as Melvyn New argues in this volume, "heretofore marginalized forms were appropriated by the heretofore marginalized readers . . . as the genres of their own voices." The tendency to take what Gerald Graff has called "two paradigmatically opposed 'world-hypotheses' " and then "to assign honorific and derogatory gender labels to them" has disturbed many critics on the contemporary critical scene. Graff is himself critiquing Ellen Messer-Davidow's endorsement of what she terms a "feminist" theory. He moves New's point on "male" and "female" writing to the level of theory, called "male-traditional" and "feminist" in Messer-Davidow's paradigm. Graff notes that

> Male-traditional has simply been made synonymous with the technological or instrumental rationality that has been a target of social critics from the early Romantics to the Frankfurt School. The dispositions Messer-Davidow classifies as feminist do not correspond so clearly with a single preestablished term, but they are generally reminiscent of the world view which has been called "contextualism" (in Pepper's typology) or "historicism" and is exemplified in such tendencies as modern pragmatism, existentialism, and post-structuralism.[3]

And, as we have seen, the overarching problem of such gender typologies, despite their political expediency, lies in the way they preserve the gender distinctions they are meant to subvert.

Yet it is true that many male writers have recourse to something culturally coded as the "feminine" in their search for an escape from a logocentric and phallocentric discourse. Attraction to and demystification of the feminine is perhaps a necessary first step in exploding the patriarchal structuration of language. The allure, the fear and the hatred of the feminine, which are generated by patriarchal binary thinking, must be overcome before we can confront the deep-seated polarization of Western thought itself. We would suggest interpreting this process in a new way—not as a liberation inherent in a movement from a culturally contaminated space of the "masculine" to a pure creative space of the "feminine." Both terms, we have recognized, are implicated in patriarchy. Rather, the movement suggests the first step in a Derridean deconstruction in which the hierarchies are reversed preliminary to dismantling the hierarchical structure. That is, writers work through the coded oppositions to deconstruct them, in a gesture reminiscent of the Derridean space of writing as *différance* where signification is produced not through opposition alone but through an interplay between presence and absence and through the endless deferral of meaning. The question that remains—and that we hope our book *opens*, though not answers—is how to proceed from this first deconstructive moment in gender demystification.

Such exploration is not without its pain: Suspicion greets heuristic attempts to turn the lens of gender onto male literature and linguistic analysis. After all, we say, hasn't most literary criticism traditionally dealt with men, under the guise of "man"? Yet when Freud directed his attention to the specifics of *female* sexuality, making male the norm, maleness became occluded as a discrete object of analytic rigor, placed in the shadows. Thus, oddly enough, it is the male who becomes the other in Freud's explorations of sexuality. Much has rightly been made of Freud's disservice to women in terms of socially constructed gender models of identity, but even here, we have underestimated the psychoanalytic injustice to men in failing to address specifically, rather than implicitly through universality, what it means to be a man, posed against as well as within patriarchy, just as we must explore what it means to be a woman both as a term anterior to and complicitous with the normative social constructs.

It is precisely from this juncture, this confusion of man with a myth of a universal (paradoxically) gendered/gender-free pronoun, that our study takes its justification. We maintain that, whereas the position "man" has indeed functioned as the nodal point for traditional literary criticism of the past centuries, man as a gendered, cultural creature has received precious little attention. And to take feminist criticism seriously as a method that places gender at the heart of things is to insist that to ignore the question "What is it to be a man?" is to imperil both the rigor and the integrity of feminist theory and practice. Judith Fetterley's generative *Resisting Reader*,[4] for instance, takes as its basic assumption that everyone learns to read as a man, when, in fact, it is far more accurate to claim that everyone learns to read from the perspective of patriarchy. Surely, some men read no more knowingly from gender—no more "at home"—the cultural works Fetterley designates as constructed for male readers than do some women. "Universality" is no gender for either sex.

By now it is obvious that at the heart of this collection lies the editors' deep conviction that any definition of patriarchy is fundamentally flawed "insofar as it fails to take into account the extent to which patriarchy operates as a system within which our language and logic, and therefore our very understanding and experience of human subjectivity, are formed."[5] That is, we recognize that female and male are imbricated in maintaining the dominant class ideology, one powerfully dependent upon gender stereotypes for its sustenance. This is not to deny the obvious inequities between the positions women and men have occupied. But it is to insist that the question be nuanced far beyond defining men as the villain and women as the victim. The term cannot be unraveled thus, for we know too much of the complexity of assigning simple guilt and innocence: There are men more innocent of the power politics of "patriarchy" than some women; there are men as resistant to it, as confined by its assumptions, as women, who at least can take comfort in being empowered by marginalization.

And, after all, what is it like to be a symbol of a power group, yet to find oneself self-alienated as the result of belonging to, of being constructed by, such a group? We have written and read much on what it is like to work from the outside as an obviously peripheral class, but what about those who work from the outside even as they live on the inside? What different dynamics occur; what economies drive the literature of men who write from such a place? What does it mean not to belong to that which it is assumed one belongs to? To ask this question, albeit a question for a different study, is implicitly to interrogate the benefit of speaking a priori symbolically (and usually in reality) from outside a power base and from writing, self-consciously, against it, as women marginalized by patriarchy have had to do.

Clearly, the organizing principle for this collection, men against patriarchy, assumes a certain theoretical framework on gender, sex, and the concept of patriarchy itself as knowable. For though these issues are not engaged explicitly as the hermeneutical enterprise of the following essays, readers deserve the framework from which the editors' (and most contributors') convictions proceed. To enter this domain therefore demands that we define our terms. Of course, it is precisely through definitions that so many of our current sexual/gender problems have arisen. For example, Eve Kosofsky Sedgwick's *Between Men* demonstrates that the mutual exclusiveness of "masculine" and "feminine" does not hold for all class and political structures, that sexuality (homo- and hetero-) and gender are both strongly materially conditioned. By emphasizing Marx's position that ideology functions as a mechanism for concealing or rationalizing contradiction within a status quo,[6] Sedgwick therein reminds us that the lack of discretion between gender terms, such as male/female, masculine/feminine, woman/man, is covered over in/by society in order to maintain the hierarchy at work in the binarism. How can we discuss masculine/feminine, female/male, male feminist/female feminist, homosexual/heterosexual without reinforcing, at however covert a level, a dualism that always, in the end, keeps people in their place? Do we abolish these words? Can we coin exemplary words such as *Ms.*, which does so much more than oppose *Mr.:* It conflates *Miss* and *Mrs.;* it is both less and more than either; it carries with it the reminder of woman as property but, therefore, also a reminder of the materialism, not transcendence, of language that defines us all.

As soon as we fix the potential flow of meaning, as soon as we stop the continuum of gender and sexual difference as we name the moments female and male, masculine and feminine, we are reabsorbed into the ontological hierarchy upon which sexual prejudices are founded. Thus we allow to stand, in this volume, multifarious uses of these gender/sexual terms, pinned down through the context of each individual essay; in the process, the essayists reveal themselves often struggling against the terms that would succeed in polarizing—or simplifying—their arguments. In one sense, failure is almost the operative assumption, since the word "gender" itself is already a bifurcated signifier, dependent upon the binary positions for its very protest against them. If Freud is right about the indiscriminate sexual satisfactions initially available to the libidinous subject, then social categorization of those satisfactions—because so often covert—becomes immediately dangerous. The bracketing of totality, of unity, is pertinent to the analysis of sexuality and gender. We are questioning the unity of the terms male and female, of masculine versus feminine, of woman versus man. As Jacques Derrida has stated in reference to the idea that any writing can be a totality, such "implications concern the entirety of our culture, directly or indirectly."[7] Of course, deconstruction has taught us, paradoxically, the historicism of these gender terms—the imperialism inherent in any attempt by us to fix these categories, to define *other* races, classes, and, perhaps this is the point, other sexes or genders. Thus we cannot define even patriarchy—a key term in this volume without succumbing to the historical naiveté that would make of an unending network of intersections a monolithic construction instead. We have therefore encouraged our essayists to work pragmatically and indirectly, allowing the terms of each canonical writer's embattlement to emerge from the contours of his particular text.

But what is typical of ways in which today's writers use these terms? Female and male most often are invoked as a biological, sexual category, seemingly stable in a way that other terms cannot claim. Yet even here there is slippage, as such "scientific" measurable qualities as estrogen, testosterone, body fat, and so on, divide far less discretely in terms of physical definition than we once thought. That is, while few would deny the ability to define sex, it may be harder in certain cases than others, calling into question the ease with which even this opposition is maintained. Confused primary or sexual apparatus, bodily contours that trick the viewer whose gaze would at least lay claim to deciding biological discriminations—all complicate what is the easiest of our inherited taxonomies. And, of course, the bogey, the question that makes us queasy, goes unanswered, maybe best untackled forever: What does culture rightly extrapolate from sex to encode gender identity? Broadway's hit *M. Butterfly* dramatically captures possible confusions. The play retells the true story of a Frenchman attached to the Chinese embassy who "believed" he was having an affair with an Oriental woman—who was, in fact, a man—and who even believed that his "mistress" bore him a child. His conviction was difficult to unsettle and, when dislodged, his resulting agony provoked a suicide attempt. This romance demonstrates that when men look at women (or women at men) they see what they expect to see. Moreover, it suggests that, in playing roles, individuals become what they have acted. The real-life model for the Chinese mistress, Shi Paipu, commented of his experience playing women on stage that "the men who played the roles would begin to think of themselves as feminine."[8]

With Freud and Kristeva, we hold that the body and the culture that conditions it are the material basis for subjecthood; and if we as feminist theorists are to intersect as many defining structures as we can, we must include the material. Yet, though theorists have been fairly comfortable of late dealing with the cultural, historical, economic, realities, we shy away from the body for fear that there the bottom-line threat to feminism confronts us—sexual, not cultural, difference. We construct sophisticated, satisfying explanations of gender identities, but what does it mean to be biologically female or male—to produce more estrogen than testosterone, to have testes rather than ovaries? If hormonal quantities can affect human behavior, does this imply a sexual class inflection? Beyond psychological variations, what does the physical reality of having breasts, a penis, a vagina, a hairy chest mean for the "possessor"? We socialize all this, quite rightly, but is the physical experience interpreted only through cultural experience—or should "essence" be added to what would see itself as a truly thoughtful analysis? Is the material of biology totally irrelevant, or merely highly dangerous to encounter, since it has been the stuff of such oppression in the past? It seems as if the moment that the body is invoked in gender studies, the new heuristic tool reinforces our insistence on organizing experience through privileged terms.

It is impossible to separate the various real dynamics that constitute one's psyche or self: Even to catalogue gender, race, class, religion begs the question, for none of these categories exists discretely from the others. But this very complex intersection makes uncertain that two women readers bring to bear more significant equal assumptions and shared expectations than a man and a woman whose psychological developments intersect at more points than do the two women's. For to say anything else suggests one of two positions: Biology is our destiny (hence, biological givens always make women closer to each other than to men), or cultural gender is totalizing and predictable above and beyond all other combinations of psychological developments. Though we would certainly claim a priority to the role that sex and gender play in one's identity, we simply believe that identity is too complex and individual to generalize about without doing great damage to the intellectual rigor of feminist theory—to furthering, under new names, old forms of stereotyping, the charge, of course, routinely leveled against French feminist essentialism.

The problem implicit throughout in this collection is an apparently intractable one: an allocation of blame and responsibility for one's participation in patriarchy. The questions of female versus male (biology), of masculine versus feminine (gender), of witting versus unwitting participation, all come into play. Our major concern, finally, is to call attention to the dangerous simplicity of aligning patriarchy with male categories—or, to put it another way, of assigning misogynistic women to a category of women-as-men, women who have simply identified with and internalized male values. We are suggesting that patriarchy is as complex in gender construction as it is in terms of class and race structure, that both men and women have felt constricted and confused by its paradigms. Particularly, in this collection of essays, we address the issue of these men: What do male writers who feel fettered by the patriarchal literary tradition do to escape a language implicitly—and often explicitly—defined as their own? That is, what "right" do men have to complain against a male-inflected language? Is it possible that the adversarial, agonistic position that many women writers adopt linguistically engenders narratives whose vitality exceeds a poetics of male at-homeness in language? And if so, is such a position merely a writing strategy or an ideological commitment?

It is well to be forthright about what we hope is evident at this point: This volume is not interested in a thematics of feminism. We asked our authors to concentrate on language, voice, and form and to avoid studies of feminist themes in men's writings, studies of male writers depicting sympathetic female characters, and studies of political problems faced by male feminist writers. Indeed, one difficulty we confronted immediately was that many of the writers considered in this volume have been termed misogynist for their *images* of women. That recognition forced us to consider the tension between a mimetic and a discursive approach to gender in literature. Attending to the mimetic or representational aspects of literature, we easily discover in the authors we examine image after stereotypical image of both women and men, images that reinscribe the patriarchal status quo. In fact, one answer these writers might make to our critical quarrels with their representations of women is that their representations of men are equally culture-bound. Of course, since male is the privileged term in patriarchy, the images seem less restrictive, but they are, nonetheless, confining. Even with all these qualifications, however, a thematics of feminism has not allowed us a very rich confrontation with male writers—or as innocent a one with female writers as we might wish. As Domna Stanton reminds us, "The adoption of the mimetic function, traditionally assigned to woman, may freeze and fixate the feminine at the mirror stage, rather than lead to a difference beyond the same old binary plays."[9] The generative—we would call it "feminist"—act for the male writers of our study, then, is not *representing* what is not and never has been, but breaking down or dismantling the terms and forms that have preserved the status quo of two genders, a feminist act we wish to continue as critics of their products. "It is only through a creative use of anxiety that we can start to look forward again," conclude Juliet Mitchell and Ann Oakley in their own exploratory volume *What Is Feminism?*[10] We enlist their courage to embolden our own enterprise, since it risks by its very nature alienating "traditional" feminist critics as well as, on the other side, "traditional" humanists.

The novelists and poets investigated in this volume are central to our traditional literary canon, which is seen, almost automatically, as patriarchal. From Milton, who stands at the head of this "canon," through Sterne, Blake, Shelley, Keats, Thackeray, Browning, Whitman, Collins, Hardy, James, Forster, Frost, Faulkner, and Durrell, previous feminist analysis has tended to align these writers with male authors in general as resting complacently on their patriarchal laurels. They have been contrasted in their procedures to women writers who define, it is argued, an alternative tradition. Brilliant as such studies of the women's tradition in literature have been and important as they continue to be in generating new questions, they have depended upon sustaining a clear opposition between the insights available to men's and women's literature. Indeed, such studies have illuminated the binary nature of inquiry. It is that opposition we now wish to complicate.

Thus, we have sought to apply a range of exegetical approaches to a variety of male authors who write on or out of the relationship of man, woman, and patriarchy. What we conceived originally as a dual-authored study seemed more generously executed as a collection of essays meant to stimulate a plurality of critical voices comparable to the diversity represented by the poets and novelists: Multiple approaches to various minds suggest the rich range of inquiries possible and desirable. In addition, this collection inevitably reminds us to what extent the act of interpretation bears upon all "objectivity" of a text, particularly as the heuristic act is engaged with something as pertinent to everyday life as is gender. One writer uses tools of formal analysis to investigate gender issues in a male's text; does such a critic unfailingly uncover something left veiled by psychoanalytic inquiry operating under the same rubric that the editors imposed? A book such as ours might seem to reinscribe an authority for these canonical writers that would otherwise have been repudiated. Our thesis—that male writers are themselves embattled with the patriarchal terms of their gendered construction—undermines the very premise on which these canonical writers have previously held their authority: that is, that they speak a universal and timeless truth. Though the individual writers still emerge as worthy, the terms of their valuation have changed. The essays focus on the degree and complexity of personal embattlement, an emphasis that aligns these male writers with female writers, that allows one to perceive that some men feel more oppressed than women, and that precludes a simple recuperation of authority.

We have named above the writers treated in this volume. They are all British or American, an emphasis that is both a strength and a limitation of our volume. If we are going to investigate male responses to patriarchal language, then it seems especially challenging to look anew at some of those whom the academic community has assumed to be particularly comfortable with that tradition and its prerogatives. And it makes sense to engage writers with whom most readers will be familiar, those, indeed, whom we have learned to see as central to the "canon" and the system of beliefs that canon embodies. At the same time, we recognize that, by concentrating on canonical writers in the British and American tradition, we are undoubtedly missing some eloquent and innovative male responses to the triad of man, woman, and patriarchy. For, as we all know by now, patriarchy, as a term of power, encompasses issues of class and race as well as gender. On these questions, our volume is largely silent, although Joseph Boone's discussion of Lawrence Durrell's *Quartet* accommodates an interest in the ways race and gender intersect, and Frank Lentricchia's reading of Robert Frost insists upon class structure interacting with male anxiety as a component of the gendered literary history of modernism. Still, we lay no claim to having reflected, as a volume, on the complication of class and race as an ideological dimension of a male-inflected response to a patriarchy constituted, in fact, through these categories as well as gender. Nor have we analyzed the enormously important and subtle topic of men reading men versus women reading men—a subject implicated in our inclusion of both male and female critics responding to canonical male authors. Although these perspectives are crucial to feminist inquiry—to any intellectual worrying of epistemological categories—in the end they are not our subject, and they *are* the emphasis of several books, for instance, already cited in our notes. Based upon the responses to our call for papers, we simply decided that our audience would benefit most from a tightly controlled focus on gender as the primary term in our examination of an antipatriarchal position in male-written literature. Consequently, we do not want to argue that the writers included are necessarily the most significant or the most interesting available for study. Together, however, they all generate a range of compelling issues and raise a number of important questions.

We had initially planned to group the essays according to similar central insights that their analyses yielded. Our own vigorous discussions and disagreements over what paper belonged under which heading persuaded us to adopt another course, which recognized that such groupings tended rather to limit than to illuminate, because each paper engages several major questions. To help forestall editor-inspired biases in the reader, we have arranged the essays chronologically by author. Happily, since most subsequent male writers have had to confront him as the patriarchal bogey, Milton begins our collection, with Joseph Wittreich complicating the varying historical perspectives that have been imposed upon readings of *Paradise Lost.* Wittreich reveals a Milton far more subversive of traditional hierarchical gender positions than has been previously allowed. In fact, if Harold Bloom is correct in positing Milton as the father figure against which all the later sons, at least, must react, it would be interesting—in another study and another time—to question to what extent these indebted male authors spin gender paradigms from their period's particular historical understandings of gender in Milton.

Just as Milton, by virtue of writing a new form of epic, immediately gains access to a novelty of gender presentation, so several of the other writers explored herein question gender constructs as they experiment with the pressures of plot upon theme. Elizabeth Langland, for instance, opens her essay on E. M. Forster with the arresting observation that the most "obvious" formal element of *Howards End,* the presence of a controlling narrator, has been almost universally misidentified as male. Langland rereads the "traditional" Forster to suggest instead an author intent upon eluding the tendency of plot (as patriarchal form) to overthrow the innovation of theme. Through a process of linguistic subversion, Forster thwarts the impetus toward closure and seeks an evaluative term that is coded as neither masculine nor feminine. Melvyn New identifies a related process in *Tristram Shandy,* where the text interrupts itself with additional material to prevent itself from concluding. Implied in New's analysis is the part that the reader plays in interpreting a writer's position within patriarchy, so that, for example, our assumptions about Sterne's sexism have blinded us to an authorial fight against some of the very assumptions we take to be Sterne's. New's assertion that Sterne undermines categories of gender even as he superficially appears to present stereotypical gender portraits shares several points with Deirdre David's analysis of Wilkie Collins's *No Name.* David, in examining such scenes as Mrs. Wragge's logical undoing of the illogic of a recipe—a "male-authorized" text "written by a woman for the instruction of other women in filling male orders"—echoes both Langland's and New's interest in the possibility of plot interrupting and thereby interrogating theme. As David says, *No Name* subverts patriarchal structures of discourse as it operates on the level of plot: It offers the reader the chance to see plot coming into being, as opposed to experiencing "plot-as-product."

James Phelan also integrates formal and feminist theory in his study of William Thackeray's *Vanity Fair.* He deploys especially the category of voice as both a specific rhetorical classification and a strategy to complicate gender at the same time. Phelan's interest in the degree to which a masculine narrator can voice a feminine or feminist perspective leads him to limit strictly his definition of voice to facilitate a detailed rhetorical analysis of the narrator's shifting identifications, which culminate in his appropriating the seemingly irresistible authority of the masculine voice and perspective. Phelan's essay is rewardingly read in tandem with Margaret Higonnet's, for as Phelan invokes voice as a rhetorical category distinct from but leading toward character, Higonnet questions how effectively a well-intentioned male author can inhabit a woman's voice. The extent to which such a voice can be expressed as separate from the patriarchy that constructs it is central to her treatment of Thomas Hardy. Unlike Phelan's use of voice, Higonnet explores the concept in its phenomenological aspects, from inarticulate sounds to eloquent physiognomy and physiology, to expressive silence, to words, ideas, and social maxims.

In his reading of Lawrence Durrell's *Alexandria Quartet,* Joseph Boone (like Langland, New, David, and Phelan) also locates questions of form pressuring Western gender assumptions, especially as "issues of erotic perception, masculine subjectivity, and narrative authority" converge in the *Quartet*'s narrator. But it is also interesting how his analysis, similar to the essays of Lentricchia, Sensibar, and Oakes, considers what it means for a modern male author to experience the anxieties of "writing in and against a phallocentric discourse," an author intent upon giving "vent to possibilities 'unthinkable' within a Western construction of the masculine." Durrell presents a model of possible liberation through homoerotic impulses gratified outside the Western culture insistent upon heterosexuality. There is, of course, a model of homoerotic desire as liberation operative in Walt Whitman's texts as well. What has gone less frequently explored, however, is Whitman's attempt to voice himself out of the constrictions of patriarchy through sounding the a priori marginalized female. Karen Oakes identifies such an emphasis in the first edition of Whitman's *Leaves of Grass,* but she discovers an erosion of that affiliation in later editions, where perhaps editorial censorship encourages a more "masculine" mode. Whitman's confrontations with the limits of voicing himself through Western norms of masculinity reward us with a poet who, as he welcomes constructing himself in what he conceives as a female mode, writes his most liberated and liberating poetry. Later, however, the pressures of commercial success force him to redefine himself once more in the image patriarchy enforces as the male.

The tensions implied by these last two essays are translated by Frank Lentricchia and Judith Sensibar into a confrontation central to any inquiry such as this collection conducts: What happens when a male writer feels excluded from patriarchy because he is not patriarchal *enough;* when "manliness" is the "culturally excluded principle in a life given to poetry"; when he feels marginalized by his ill fit with the masculine paradigms of power available in the English language? Robert Frost and William Faulkner represent male authors who write out of a specific literary gender anxiety: To write is to be a woman. The fear of being "unmanned," to use Joseph Boone's term, informs Robert Frost's shaping of modernism, as the poet goes one better than Wordsworth in invoking a rugged (male) vernacular to rescue the lyric from what Frost reads as its historical effeminacy. Lentricchia's essay reminds us of Whitman's dilemma: that in addition to the Bloomian model of a father necessary for poets to write against, there is also a gender dimension always present in the anxiety toward one's forebears. Furthermore, the study of Frost engages an important question asked by U. C. Knoepflmacher of Browning and Marlon Ross of Keats: What happens when a poet rewrites his masculine forebears with an eye toward the intersection of gender and form?

Male poets, as we encounter often in this collection, frequently find it necessary to conceptualize the lyric as female, to situate it in a female space, in order to create an Ur-(mother)text against which to conceptualize *themselves* as separate, creative subjects. Judith Sensibar analyzes Faulkner's use of fictional photographs as an escape from his culture's coding of writing as feminine activity. Faulkner uses the visual images as a means of coping with the marginalization he came to expect, particularly in what he saw as a southern tradition that counted aesthetics as female occupation. Sensibar believes that Faulkner encodes in his fictional photographs lessons that "constantly undermine culturally imposed racial and gender classifications," a sensitivity long apparent to southern women writers such as Carson McCullers and Alice Walker.

William Veeder engages a concern at least tangential to those above as he asks why and how Henry James identifies himself with the "feminine." Veeder claims that a compulsory affiliation with women defends James against the threat of the "feminine" nature of his own sexuality. In a complicated psychology, James defends himself against castration and lack to the extent that he can live himself through the fictional life of a female, as created figure becomes a "compensatory fantasy." Veeder's reminder that, to Henry James, " 'Woman' as a gender construct is a social fate available to persons of either sex" shares an affinity with the attention to gender-as-structure that Langland and Oakes attribute to Forster and Whitman.

Furthermore, Veeder engages an issue important to U. C. Knoepflmacher's treatment of Robert Browning when he suggests that the appropriation of gender is inescapable to the extent that one never achieves a positive sense of one's own subjectivity, so that valuing the other-gendered person as subject is impossible. Knoepflmacher, however, argues that Browning makes his disillusioned recognition of his Romantic heroes' arrogation of the female a focus enabling formal innovation: the transformation of the subjective lyric into the dramatic monologue. The Romantics tended, according to Knoepflmacher, to appropriate the female for self-enlargement more than they genuinely voiced the female marginalized by the patriarchy against which they often positioned themselves. In contrast, Laura Claridge argues that the male British Romantics in general, and Percy Shelley in particular, situate the female in an impossible (and thereby poetically liberating) contradiction: Woman promises an authentic, new space for voice even as she underwrites the indebted genealogical grounds for the transmission of that voice. Shelley fights patriarchy in a distinctive way: He manipulates cultural assumptions about women, lack, and despair so that "woman" can end up, paradoxically, as the one who has it all, thus enabling the male poet's now gender-full literary voice.

Marlon Ross's essay on Keats also engages the issue of un-naming as a first step in writing a new language. Ross illuminates a Keats who, by fracturing an exclusively male language, negotiates the ultimate trump that patriarchy plays: How can one reject the linguistic signs of power and still be empowered? Is there a way to turn language in upon itself so that the poet can "reform discourse" toward a "wholeness beyond the limits of culture"? Donald Ault presents us with a Blake who may well be our most radical example of an author pressing the inherent elusiveness of language against the logic of traditional discourse. Ault's study of William Blake's "Little Black Boy" speaks specifically to the textual slippages of the text as the semantic field that pretends to close off the poem with teleological finality is destabilized. Ault notes that, as the poem pulls away from the mother, "the entire fiction of voices within voices, on which the patriarchal, ontotheological narrative is based, begins to stammer." As Ault's study invokes the phallic lack that Veeder and Claridge also employ as a heuristic category, the familial paradigms of absence and presence as they underwrite desire played out in language would seem constitutive elements in many artists' attempts to undo or outdo patriarchy.

When Ault—unsettling our complacent interpretation of what at first glance seems a closed text—wonders to what extent Blake self-consciously interrogated gender, we are all reminded of the complexity of intention: Who knew what he wanted, what he had achieved, for whom it was meant—and, at this moment in history, to what degree is the ascertaining of that self-consciousness necessary for our endeavor? And whom would we judge the better harbinger of the deconstruction of binary oppositions: the male artist who achieves a sophisticated position of liberation from a patriarchal straitjacket but who does so apparently innocent of the terms of gender politics; or the writer who explicitly engages the question of liberating the gender dialectic but whose textual offerings fail to go beyond the most naive models constructed throughout literary history?

Our aim has been to introduce the topic of men ill at ease with their "natural" home in patriarchy as one worthy of serious feminist inquiry. Our hope is that others will follow in our footsteps as feminism continues to broaden the scope of investigations and the depth of insight into women's and men's writing. We are ourselves indebted to critics who have focused their attention on male feminism, beginning to address the other half of the tenacious binarism of gender—the male specifics. Wayne Booth early confronted issues facing male feminist critics in his *Critical Inquiry* piece on Bakhtin, Rabelais, and feminist criticism. Stephen Heath, writing on male feminism for the *Dalhousie Review,* and J. Hillis Miller, writing on Virginia Woolf, have posed comparable questions. Elaine Showalter, as far back as the fall of 1983, brought a woman's perspective to the subject of male feminism in her *Raritan* essay, "Critical Cross-Dressing," joining her voice to those of Annette Kolodny and Gayatri Spivak in speculating about the political implications of men practicing feminist criticism. This early article was followed by intense scrutiny of the issue. Alice Jardine's and Paul Smith's *Men in Feminism* courageously presented dialogues between male and female feminist critics (although this very possibility was, of course, at issue in the collection), a volume that has resulted in fruitful controversy over fears of male coopting of feminist theory and practice. Linda Kauffman has recently completed two volumes recording conversations between male critics regarding their responses to feminism. Finally, Harry Brod has edited an interesting collection of essays called *The Making of Masculinities,* a book that tackles the questions, What is it to be male? and, post-Freud, What does man want?[11]

Other critics have turned the lens onto male writers to begin to examine the feminist bent or inclination of their works. Nina Auerbach's *Woman and the Demon: The Life of a Victorian Myth*[12] claims that Dickens, Rossetti, and Thackeray supplied "subversive paradigms of a divine and demonic female power at the cultural center of Victorian patriarchy and chivalry." J. Hillis Miller, in an essay on *The Egoist* in Heilbrun's and Higonnet's collection *The Representation of Women in Fiction,* traces the "deconstruction . . . of traditional theories of character" in Meredith's representation of Clara Middleton. He argues that "many male novelists in the Victorian period—Thackeray, Dickens, Trollope, or Meredith himself—so often project into a female protagonist the question fundamental to the novel. Can we or can we not believe that human beings, male or female, have fixed selves?" Miller points out that the "assumption that ontologically substantial characters do exist cannot be detached from the logocentrism or phallogocentrism which underlies it and of which it is a version."[13] And U. C. Knoepflmacher, in an article reprinted here as the only essay not written specifically for our collection, looked at Browning's revisions of the romantic poets as the Victorian poet struggled with the problem of voicing the feminine in himself. All of these treatments have helped to pave the way for our sustained examination here of male writers, feminism, and anti-patriarchism. Still, it has struck us how little theorizing exists on the male literary figure at war with the same patriarchy that women fight, especially since most of us teach male writers. Certainly any struggles they enact against patriarchal culture yield knowledge of the sort sure to empower everyone—women and men—in the analysis of the gender status quo.

We all, of course, are implicated in the damage that gender expectations do, and at the most sophisticated, delicate, dangerous nexus of that damage the origins and culpability become less clear than feminist theory has sometimes allowed. True, we risk here slipping into a position comfortable for all who oppress—willfully or against their wills—if we indulge in the luxurious illusion that finally no one is responsible. That is surely not our point. Rather, it is that we are all responsible, not just men, though political and economic power is still located in men-as-a-gendered-class. But we must beware of categorizing gender, even here, since this is one of the primary lessons of feminism: To say glibly that men exercise the social power is to generalize a class and to disregard the experience of individuals, many of whom could not recognize themselves in such a paradigm. Complicated gender grammars must be encouraged, with vocabularies that accommodate differences and similarities, contradictions and agreements—terms which are, by all current definitions, "out of bounds." We send forth this collection of essays in hopes that it gestures in that direction.

## Notes

1. Luce Irigaray, *This Sex Which Is Not One,* trans. Catherine Porter and Carolyn Burke (Ithaca, NY: Cornell University Press, 1985).
2. Toril Moi, *Sexual/Textual Politics: Feminist Literary Theory* (London: Methuen, 1985); Domna C. Stanton, "Difference on Trial: A Critique of the Maternal Metaphor in Cixous, Irigaray, and Kristeva," in *The Poetics of Gender,* ed. Nancy K. Miller (New York: Columbia University Press, 1986); 157–82.
3. Gerald Graff, "Response to 'The Philosophical Bases of Feminist Literary Criticisms'," *New Literary History,* Special Issue on Feminist Directions, 19, no. 1 (1987): 137.
4. Judith Fetterley, *The Resisting Reader: A Feminist Approach to American Fiction* (Bloomington: Indiana University Press, 1978).
5. Thanks to an anonymous reader who succinctly summarized the position from which we are writing.
6. Eve Kosofsky Sedgwick, *Between Men: English Literature and Male Homosocial Desire* (New York: Columbia University Press, 1985), 14.
7. Jacques Derrida, *Positions,* trans. Alan Bass (Chicago: University of Chicago Press, 1981), 3.
8. Joyce Wadler, "For the First Time, the Real-Life Models of Broadway's *M. Butterfly* Tell of Their Very Strange Romance," *People Weekly,* August 8, 1988, 91; David Henry Wang, *M. Butterfly,* in *American Theatre,* July–August 1988, special insert.
9. Stanton, "Difference on Trial," 172.
10. Juliet Mitchell and Ann Oakley, eds., *What Is Feminism?* (New York: Pantheon, 1986), 7.
11. Wayne C. Booth, "Freedom of Interpretation: Bakhtin and the Challenge of Feminist Criticism," *Critical Inquiry* 9 (1982): 45–76; Stephen Heath, "Male Feminism," *Dalhousie Review* 64 (Summer 1984): 270–301; J. Hillis Miller, "The Rhythm of Creativity in *To the Lighthouse,*" in *Modernism Reconsidered,* ed. Robert Kiely (Cambridge, MA: Harvard University Press, 1983), 189; Elaine Showalter, "Critical Cross-Dressing: Male Feminists and the Woman of the Year," *Raritan* 3 (Fall 1983): 139–43; Alice Jardine and Paul Smith, eds., *Men in Feminism* (New York: Methuen, 1987); Linda Kauffman, ed., *Feminism and Institutions: Dialogues on Feminist Theory* and *Gender and Theory: Dialogues on Feminist Criticism* (New York: Oxford and London: Basil Blackwell, 1989); Harry Brod, ed., *The Making of Masculinities: The New Men's Studies* (Winchester: Allen and Unwin, 1987).

12. Nina Auerbach, *Woman and the Demon: The Life of a Victorian Myth* (Cambridge, MA: Harvard University Press, 1982), 11.
13. J. Hillis Miller, "'Herself against Herself': The Clarification of Clara Middleton," in *The Representation of Women in Fiction*, ed. Carolyn Heilbrun and Margaret Higonnet (Baltimore: Johns Hopkins University Press, 1981), 109–10, 122.

# "John, John, I blush for thee!" Mapping Gender Discourses in *Paradise Lost*

JOSEPH WITTREICH

> . . . I to thee disclose
> What inward thence I feel, not therefore foild,
> Who meet with various objects, from the sense
> Variously representing; yet still free
> Approve the best, and follow what I approve.
>
> *Paradise Lost* 8.607–11

MODERN-DAY ACADEMICS have been well schooled, perhaps better schooled than Milton's early readership, in the lessons of patriarchy, one of those lessons being that only women fight against patriarchal attitudes, that such resistance belongs to feminist space, is occupied by its discourse, the precincts of which no man can—or should try to—enter. Whether or not today's readership approves of the Milton it sees, it typically sees but one Milton: a Milton who is ideologically fixed and fixated; a Milton who, in his "deeply masculinist assumptions," according to Mary Nyquist, is "English literature's paradigmatic patriarch" and who, in the words of John Guillory, if in *Samson Agonistes* he escapes from transhistorical misogyny, nevertheless remains confined within an ideology that "assumes the subjection of women" and to which he "gives his unequivocal endorsement."[1] That academic men and women are all too frequently speaking with one voice should not be allowed to conceal the facts that Milton himself speaks with various voices, "now one, / Now other" (4.397–98), both in *Paradise Lost* and elsewhere; that his is a poetry of multiple discourses—patriarchal, misogynous, *and* feminist—and a poetry not of single but of plural consciousness. Historically, Milton criticism was animated by the two great sexes speaking with different, often contending, voices; and even today, as a counterpoint to a feminist—and academic—rhetoric that holds that Milton is the patriarch of patriarchal poets, archly and bruisingly misogynous, we hear the voice of the female artist who, in the instance of Flannery O'Connor, counsels another woman to "throw away *The Art of Plain Talk* and keep at your Milton."[2] Milton's is a poetry not of plain talk but of double-talk, O'Connor seems to imply—a poetry whose meaning, we might infer, is to be ascertained by sliding not by but into its ambiguities and contradictions, by then unpacking its ellipses. His is a poetry that makes an art of perplexing the usual explanations.

Still, what O'Connor probably only hints at here Alicia Ostriker brings to full utterance: this "most duplicitous poet in the language" (who gives with one hand and takes with the other) illustrates the proposition that "when a poet says . . . he is doing north, look and see if he is not actually doing south. Chances are that his bent is so entirely south that he must swear total allegiance to north in order to cover the globe." Later, Ostriker points unwittingly to the passage that best illustrates such a proposition, observing, with a citation from *Paradise Lost,* that "the winning ace up any man's cheating sleeve is his assumed proximity to divinity, insisted on in all our religious traditions":

> Adam is God's image; Eve, a mere rib and sinful seductress, must in the post-Edenic world submit to her husband. St. Paul and Catholicism agree: as Christ is man's head, so man is woman's, for man was not created for woman, but she for him. Milton and Protestantism likewise agree: "He for God only, she for God in him."[3]

Milton has several cards up his sleeve apparently, which he plays against the hand held by institutionalized Christianity (and in *Paradise Lost* by Satan and then Adam)—a hand composed of the conventions and commonplaces both of misogynous and patriarchal traditions. If hearts is trump, it is a suit usually held by the Father and the Son, by Raphael and Michael (sometimes), and eventually by Eve. As an epic poet, Milton may feel obliged to cover the globe of sexual discourses; but the inflections given to those discourses—heterosexual in *Paradise Lost* but delicately homosexual in *Paradise Regained,* sometimes patriarchal and misogynous and other times feminist—are distinctly his own, hence rather different from those of C. S. Lewis, whose own remarks exhibit the same "critical prudery" they are meant to indict:

> A certain amount of critical prudery, in which I once shared, has been aroused by the account of . . . Milton's angels. . . . The trouble is . . . that since these exalted creatures are all spoken of by masculine pronouns, we tend, half consciously, to think that Milton is attributing to them a life of homosexual promiscuity. That he was poetically imprudent in raising a matter which invites such misconception I do not deny; but the real meaning is certainly not filthy. . . . An angel is, of course, always He (not She) in human language, because whether the male is, or is not, the superior sex, the masculine is certainly the superior gender.[4]

As the language of criticism has changed, so too have certain of its concerns and some of its conclusions, and the change attends the discovery that the way around misogyny and patriarchy, the way around any language or system of sexual abuse, is the way through it. To oppose misogyny, to interrogate patriarchy, is to put the dialectic of change in motion.

It is now a documented fact of Milton criticism that women historically have produced layered, crevassed interpretations through their hermeneutic of suspicion and their deconstructionist habit of double-reading.[5] They have opened as a possibility what their male counterparts quickly deny: that *Paradise Lost,* instead of codifying, conflicts with patriarchy; that, in his webbing of the conventional with the revisionary, Milton produces a poem tangled in contradictions, then uses those contradictions to formulate a critique of his own traditions. Narrative meets counternarrative in *Paradise Lost,* each separate narrative seeming to contain the seeds of its destruction, with all questions concerning characters becoming double: How do they present themselves? How are they represented by others? To pursue these questions, with special reference to Eve and Adam, is to entertain the possibility that Milton is at the forefront of an English tradition of male feminism. It is, perforce, to move against demands for "a simple answer" at the expense of poetic complexity, as well as some critics' refusals to allow Milton's poem "*any* political stance towards the equality of women *or anything else* . . . in spite of . . . any doctrinal content that Milton intended to advance."[6] Life to such critics would be death to Milton, for whom *there was* a politics to poetry and a poetry to history and whose fondest wish was to write a poem *doctrinal* (without being doctrinaire) to his nation—a poem that future generations would not willingly let die. As Stanley Fish shrewdly observes, Milton's academic critics have been promoting "a general practice" by which they hide from "the true (political) nature of . . . [their] own activities"[7]—a strategy that finds its counterpart in earlier phases of Milton criticism when the common tendency was to hide (through repeated denials) the political content of Milton's poetry and often, through deliberate distortions and mischievous misreadings, to rewrite its *sexual* politics.

There is always distortion in criticism, and the surest way of minimizing it is to complicate the critic's job, which, if it has involved ascertaining the harmonies, the continuities, in a word the *unity* of a work of art or of a tradition informing it, entails as well the discovery of dissonance, disjunction, and diversity. A criticism searching for meaning*s*, rather than *the* meaning, in *Paradise Lost* will attend above all else to conflicts and contradictions in both the poem and its traditions. For as Catherine Belsey explains in another (but still relevant) context: "In its absences, and in the collisions between its divergent meanings, the text implicitly criticizes its own ideology"[8]—or better, perhaps, criticizes the ideologies harbored within it. One pressing question for criticism involves the congruence between values *in* a text and those of the ideology, or ideologies, *in*forming it, hence whether it contains its own or is construed by another's critical consciousness. Is the ideological critique conscious or unconscious, intrinsic or extrinsic to the text? What is the attitude toward, the agenda for these ideological inscriptions? Does Milton advance this over that one; and/or does he use the concatenation to expose distorted thought and false consciousness, to elucidate the restrictive nature of any ideology, thus creating in poetry a vehicle for deliverance from all constraining systems of thought?

## Milton's Double-Talk

> But does *Milton* therefore Contradict Himself? . . . Let it be Consider'd only Who tells These Different Stories.
>
> JONATHAN RICHARDSON

Start with what Milton, through the narrator's voice in *Paradise Lost,* actually says, remembering, first, that the narrator who has been trailing Satan through Eden has by now installed himself within the mind of Satan and, more, reports the Edenic scene, with Adam and Eve now foregrounded, as it is filtered through Satan's fallen consciousness. The trailing of Satan through Eden modulates into a tracking of his mind, a tracing of its fluctuating perceptions with the narrator now seeing with the eyes, now hearing with the ears of God's and Man's chief adversary. This is the crucial passage:

> . . . *the Fiend*
> *Saw* undelighted all delight, all kind
> Of living Creatures new to sight and strange:
> Two of far nobler shape erect and tall,
> Godlike erect, with native Honour clad
> In naked Majestie seemd Lords of all,
> And worthie seemd, for in thir looks Divine
> The image of thir glorious Maker shon,
> Truth, Wisdom, Sanctitude severe and pure
> . . . . . . . . . . . . . . . . . . . . . . .
> . . . though both
> Not equal, as thir sex not equal seemd;
> For contemplation hee and valour formd,
> For softness shee and sweet attractive Grace,
> *Hee for God only, shee for God in him:*
> His fair large Front and Eye sublime declar'd
> Absolute rule: and Hyacinthin Locks
> Round from his parted forelock manly hung

> Clustring, but not beneath his shoulders broad:
> Shee as a vail down to the slender waste
> Her unadorned golden tresses wore
> Dissheveld, but in wanton ringlets wav'd
> As the Vine curls her tendrils, which impli'd
> Subjection, but requir'd gentle sway,
> And by her yeilded, by him best receiv'd,
> Yeilded with coy submission, modest pride,
> And sweet reluctant amorous delay. [4.285–311; my italics]

What needs remembering is that this is what *the Fiend saw:* He sees appearances, glosses surfaces, makes hasty inferences. What needs remarking is that here Satan's mind registers conflicting impressions: Now they *seemed Lords of all,* participating equally in and equally exhibiting divine resemblance, both enjoying "filial freedom," and as the son and daughter of God each existing under patriarchal rule (4.294); then, they *not equal seemed,* with Adam *seeming* to possess the bearing of an absolute ruler and Eve *seeming* to exist, by virtue of her *coy submission,* in *subjection* to her mate. As we will see later in *Paradise Lost,* seemings are often just that: "All seemd well pleas'd, all seem'd, but were not all" (5.617). In analogy with Satan here in Book 4, Adam, in Book 8, will register conflicting impressions of Eve: Initially she seems the "fairest" object in Creation, then in comparison with Adam, she first seems defective ("Too much of Ornament") but then "*seems* . . . in her self compleat"—"*Seems* wisest, vertuousest, discreetest, best" (see 8.484–559; my italics). If in Book 8, Raphael modifies Adam's impressions, in Book 4 Satan will check his own as shifting impressions give way to a statement of certitude:

> O Hell! *what doe mine eyes* with grief *behold*
> . . . . . . . . . . . . . . . . . . . . . . .
> Not Spirits, yet to heav'nly Spirits bright
> Little inferior; whom my thoughts pursue
> With wonder, and could love, so lively shines
> *In them* Divine resemblance. . . . [4.358–64; my italics]

Satan's soliloquy here, Adam's words there—both speeches interlock in a shared perception: "such grace . . . on thir shape hath pourd" (4.365); "Grace was in all her steps, Heav'n in her Eye, / In every gesture dignitie and love" (8.488–89).

The interpretive question posed by these parallel speeches and their fluctuating perspectives is whether Milton means to valorize the realm of appearances, thus giving parity to these various perceptions; or whether there is, instead, a still hidden order, contrary to appearances, privileging one perception over another—a hidden logic in the substructure of *Paradise*

*Lost* that cancels some of the contradictions on its surface. And I say *some,* because one of the laws governing its narrative is that in this poetry of disclosure some matters remain undisclosed, "suppresst in Night, / To none communicable in Earth or Heaven" (7.123–24); that this narrative, contrary to Adam's claim, is never "free from intricacies" or "perplexing thoughts" (8.182–83) because the mortal voice of the poet, if *less* fallen than Satan's, is still "Inspir'd with contradiction" (6.155) and "ambiguous words" (6.568) which together create interpretive dilemmas. Nevertheless, interpretive options do usually force interpretive choices in *Paradise Lost,* even if the choice is *not to choose.* Milton's poetry invites the navigation of such dilemmas for which, often, there is no resolution, encouraging hermeneutical suspicion through its conflicted surfaces and deconstructionist thinking, and through its sometimes self-canceling rhetoric. Negotiating these dilemmas often requires sorting out incongruous voices, then cataloguing as well as contextualizing their discrepant observations. This is a poem asking us to host the possibility that narrative intervention, instead of interpreting the story, is interpreted by it; that embedments of commonplace interpretation, rather than being confirmed, are challenged by the poetry. We will have to decide: Is *Paradise Lost* a bazaar of ideologies, a cafeteria of interpretations, a parade of images on which the eye merely fixes a gaze? Or is the eye meant to seize on something, approve it, and take it away? And we will have to decide each case separately.

We will have to determine, as well, the nature of the curriculum in *Paradise Lost:* What are its traditions, and is Milton traditional in his representation of them? What is the ultimate interpretive authority—the inner promptings of the poem or the traditions informing it? What is the character of this text—what is *in,* what is excluded from it? What, indeed, is the character of the Christian tradition for which the poem has seemed a conduit? As Elaine Pagels has shown, the story of Adam and Eve, one of culture's eternal paradigms, was originally and for nearly four centuries a tale of human freedom and only with St. Augustine became the story of human enslavement. The history of Genesis interpretation has but its first chapter written by St. Paul. The larger history is one of "conflicting interpretations" moving in opposite ways, with one of its most intriguing chapters (I submit) written during the seventeenth century when individual interpretations themselves become conflicted; when the politics of paradise comes to the fore in the realization that Adam and Eve, Eve and Adam, experience within themselves the first government of the world and, more, the first revolution.[9] Milton's choice of *this* myth for his epic poem has its political dimension. If something went wrong in the history covering the transmission and reception of his source-story, it is, as Mieke Bal shows, that this history is "the history of . . . the repression of the problems [in it], hence, of the heterogeneous ideology of the text, which had to be turned into a monolithic one."[10] In this regard, the reception of Genesis affords an all too exact parallel to the reception of *Paradise Lost*. What goes wrong in both instances can be represented through the shorthand, *Pauline interpretation.*[11]

It is often enough, and accurately, observed that Paul's interpretation of the Genesis creation story in 1 Corinthians allows for first Satan's and later Adam's perception of the inequality of the sexes:

> . . . he is the image and glory of God: but the woman is the glory of the man.
> For the man is not of the woman; but the woman of the man.
> Neither was the man created for the woman; but the woman for the man. . . .
> Judge in yourselves: . . .
> Doth not even nature itself teach you, that, if a man have long hair, it is a shame unto him?
> But if a woman have long hair, it is a glory to her. . . . [11:7–9, 13–15]

Ephesians 5:22–23 is relevant here as well: "Wives, submit yourselves unto your husbands. . . . For the husband is the head of the wife, even as Christ is the head of the church"; and so too is 1 Timothy 2:11–14, although this last Pauline text will achieve sharper focalization later (as an important subtext for Books 11 and 12):

> Let the woman learn in silence with all subjection.
> But I suffer not a woman to teach, nor to usurp authority over the man, but to be in silence.
> For Adam was first formed, then Eve.
> And Adam was not deceived, but the woman being deceived was in the transgression.

The momentary interlocking of passages from Milton's poem with these scriptural texts is often taken as presumptive evidence that the poet means to promulgate Pauline attitudes, not prosecute them; and this presumption would seem to be encouraged by the fact that *Paradise Lost* proper takes as its starting point the Pauline cliché that woman is in the transgression: "Th' infernal serpent, he it was, whose guile / . . . deceiv'd / The Mother of Mankind" (1.34–36)—verses which allowed Peter Bayle to conclude that Milton wrote two poems about temptation, one concerning the temptation of Jesus, the other the temptation of Eve.[12] Such clichés crop up again in Book 4 as a warning voice promises to bring Eve to Adam, "hee / Whose image thou art" (471–72), a voice that schools Eve into perceiving Adam as her "Guide / And Head" (442–43). Were it not that pitted against these common glosses is a counterstatement to subvert them, the argument would seem clinched: *Paradise Lost* redacts conventional Pauline interpretation rather than formulating its own reinterpretation of the Genesis story. Milton himself, it appears, is in the transgression—and goes into transgression most notably in Books 10–12 of *Paradise Lost.* These books, in the scrutiny they give to the Pauline cliché that woman should be silent, and in their eventual scuttling of that cliché, make it clear that, if Satan's early impressions of the new creation match with Pauline interpretation, Satan's is also an interpretation that *Paradise Lost* would refine out of existence.

Not just arguments advanced in Book 3, but Satan's own apprehensions in the "O Hell" soliloquy unsettle Pauline thinking. Against the Pauline observation that woman is in the transgression because she, not Adam, is deceived, Milton places the authority of God (and of Satan): "*Man* falls deceiv'd" (3. 130; my italics); "*Man* I deceav'd" (10.496; my italics; see also 10.577). Their authority, apparently, overrules that of the fallen Adam, hurling recriminations at Eve (10.879–80), and of Milton's sometimes Pauline narrator: Man is "not deceav'd, / but fondly overcome with Femal charm" (9.998–99, cf. 404). And the narrator of *Paradise Lost,* it bears remembering, is a man with many masks, in this instance donning a mask like that of the misogynous Joseph Swetnam: "woman doth him delude." Milton's own accomplishment, however, is to embrace the larger debate that Swetnam's brazen misogyny provoked: whether the cause of the Fall was "Deluding woman" or "Flattring and periur'd man."[13] In *Paradise Regained,* Satan reiterates his own stand on such issues, which is also God's stand: "*Adam* and his facil consort *Eve* / Lost Paradise deceiv'd by me" (1.51–52).

Moreover, to Paul's argument that what is formed first is foremost in Creation, Milton opposes God's word, as well as the example of His Son. "[N]or Man the least / Though last created" (3.277–78), says the Father to His Son who, "Second" to the Father in his begetting, is nevertheless acknowledged by God as His "Equal . . . equally enjoying / God-like fruition" (3.306–7, 408–9; cf. 5.835, 853–54). Before we ever enter upon the middle books of *Paradise Lost* and their interpretive dilemmas, before we are ever allowed to entertain the possibility that Milton continues to privilege the second over the first Genesis account of Creation, we encounter Milton's God who, here in Book 3, privileges unequivocally Genesis 1 (*man is the last created*) and who now addresses His Son as He surrenders His scepter in anticipation of the time when the Son himself will surrender that same scepter: "Then thou thy regal Scepter shalt lay by, / For regal Scepter then no more shall need" (339–40). It will not do to associate this privileging of Genesis 1, as pointed and as powerful in its ideological motivation as any other such passage in *Paradise Lost,* with modern-day feminist theologians by way of dismissing this particular privileging as "profoundly ahistorical reading"—as a product of our own time of "liberal feminism."[14] *Paradise Lost* not only contains this example of such privileging but aligns its affirmation that man is last created with an argument for equality, even among those who are second in their begetting. At least one female reader of Milton's poem, measuring things on earth by how they are in heaven, imagines the time when Adam will surrender his own scepter to Eve.[15]

In *Paradise Lost,* Adam himself undermines the Pauline logic of first-is-best by twisting it:

> Authority and Reason on her wait,
> As one intended first, not after made
> Occasionally; and to consummate all,
> Greatness of mind and nobleness thir seat
> Build in her loveliest, and create an awe
> About her. . . . [8.554–59]

If with these words Adam upsets the equality of their creation of which he has just been assured by God ("Thy wish exactly to thy hearts desire" [451]), thus prompting Raphael to contract his brow, once Raphael has set the record straight, restored the equilibrium of Creation, he himself begins to erode various Pauline dicta: Paul's appeal to nature ("Accuse not Nature" [561]) and Paul's argument for subjection (she was created for "thy love / Not thy subjection" [569–70]).[16] Doubts concerning woman's intellectual capacities, her innate wisdom, are diminished by the narrator's acknowledgment, "So spake our Sire, and by his count'nance seemd / Entring on studious thoughts abstruse, which *Eve* / Perceaving," effects her decision to retire from this scene of instruction (8.39–40), and by Raphael's reference to Eve, when admonishing Adam, she "sees when thou art seen least wise" (578). The narrator and Raphael may explain Eve's motives in withdrawing from this scene differently, but presumably it is the angel's explanation that we are to credit. Fallen and unfallen consciousness, angelic and human intelligence, perceive the world differently and differently value woman's place therein. Not only is the entire poem organized around a double consciousness but individual speeches (like Raphael's here) are often allowed to harbor twin perspectives.

If the initial books of *Paradise Lost* are a revelation of Satan, the revelation is of one whose fluctuating mind stumbles into truth. The devil speaks truth—not when he utters his apprehension of sexual inequality but when, seeing the truth first and later articulating it, his misapprehension is framed by an assertion of Adam's and Eve's equality and mutual participation in the divine resemblance: "in *thir* looks Divine / The image of thir glorious

Maker shon" (4.291–92; my italics); "so lively shines / In *them* Divine resemblance" (4.363–64; my italics). The middle books of *Paradise Lost* may keep the matter of *their* sharing the divine resemblance in question marks, but the last books of the poem allay all doubt: No one has preeminence; all dwell on even ground in the fallen world although, still addressing Adam and Eve, Michael reminds them that they were given and still possess "rule" over "All th' Earth" (11.339), that they still exhibit "the track Divine" (354), with generic Man, as Adam makes clear, "Retaining still Divine Similitude," their "Makers Image" (512, 514). Preeminence, in any event, is attributed by the narrator to Satan—"he of the first, / If not the first Arch-Angel, great in Power, / In favour and in præeminence" (5.559–61)—and by Adam to God: "tell, / Tell, if ye saw, how come I thus, how here? / Not of my self; by some great Maker then, / In goodness and in power præeminent" (8.276–79), having first been attributed to Adam by Eve in the very first words she utters in this poem (4.446–47). But then, preeminence is lodged in paradox, lost by Satan as it will be by Adam and surrendered by God as (some thought) it would eventually be by Adam. This concept is transferred, in *Paradise Lost,* from the first created to those becoming first in the ongoing process of creation. Preeminence, if thus slipping into paradox, becomes a sign of process—and progress—in a poem that is no less about the loss of paradise than about its recovery and that, if about early moments in history and within human consciousness, relates, as a part of this concern, the process by which patriarchy and misogyny enter and become entrenched in history, no less than the process by which each, in turn, is uprooted and eventually will be banished.

If patriarchy and matriarchy are mental attitudes before the Fall, both attitudes are concretized in history, actual and legendary, subsequent to the Fall: the first as woman's curse ("hee over thee shall rule" [10.196]) and the second as apparently a part of God's curse on the demons ("Mean while in Paradise the hellish pair / . . . arriv'd, *Sin* there in power . . . / . . . behind her *Death*" [10.585–88]). Male follows female in the demonic realm in contrast to earth where woman may follow man but, as we shall see, *at her bidding,* with the emphasis falling upon *their* mutuality and equality. In the concluding books to *Paradise Lost,* Milton captures wonderfully, exactly, the startling contradiction in Genesis: "thy desire *shall be* to thy husband, and he shall rule over thee" (3:16); "And unto thee *shall be* his desire, and thou shalt rule over him" (4:7).[17] Thus, even if Eve says to Adam, "now lead on" (12.614), they are, rather, "led" on, "hand in hand," by "the hastning Angel" (637–39). Milton's last imaging of Eve and Adam matches perfectly with the early representation of them "Imparadis't in one anothers arms" (4.506). Nor is there any indication that, as in conventional expulsion scenes, Eve is holding back—or still looking back. Eve is not dragged from Paradise but leaves, instead, on equal footing with Adam. Who *leads,* subsequent to Michael's departure, is for the reader to surmise. The ambiguities implanted early in the poem, then replanted in the middle books, are rooted out at last—and in such a way as to let embedded commentary be jettisoned by the environing poetry. Milton's text produces entanglements first and only later decipherments.

In *Paradise Lost,* the poetry rises up against and overrules received opinion, institutionalized interpretation, even when the Son is its mouthpiece (as in Book 10). The Son's chastisement of Adam, which finds its closest parallel in Raphael's speech of Book 8 (561–94), contains the same shifting claims concerning the sexes that we witness both in Raphael's speech and elsewhere: Now they are equals ("was shee made thy guide, / Superior, or but equal" [146–47]), and now he is her superior ("God set thee above her made of thee" [149]). But the surrounding poetry uproots the Pauline cliché as the Son is then made to observe an Eve, not an Adam, who repeating his gestures replicates his image. Adam does not want the punishment to devolve upon his head; Eve accepts it, with the verse, "Captivity led captive" (188), placing her in the line of Deborah, as well as of Mary and her son Jesus (183–84). The echo of the Book of Judges is unmistakable: "Awake, awake Deborah: awake, awake, utter a song: arise, Barak, and lead thy captivity captive" (5:12). This is, of course, the moment when (in Judges) the humble are exalted and assume dominion over the mighty and the moment, too, when the woman shares her heroism with the man.

## Milton's Transgressive Maneuvers

> . . . the Poem it self does *More than Whisper.* . . . [yet] whoever will Possess His Ideas must dig for them, and Oftentimes pretty far below the Surface.
>
> JONATHAN RICHARDSON AND SON

Books 11 and 12 move forcefully, decisively, to erase traces of patriarchy and misogyny still in evidence from earlier books. These are, of course, the conspicuously political books in Milton's poem, which have perhaps been conspicuously avoided at times because of their *sexual* politics. As criticism moved to neutralize the politics of *Paradise Lost,* it also proceeded to aestheticize, and thereby anesthetize, these books. That is, through the interpretive code of aesthetics, to which of all possible interpretive codes these books seem least responsive, the final visionary panel, indeed the whole of the poem, is emptied of all that seems disruptive both in its politics and in its theology. Books that mount an ideological critique of Milton's culture, that not only constitute an interpretation but are themselves about the act of interpretation, are faulted almost always on aesthetic grounds, probably because they have so regularly been slighted by tendentious, often trivializing, thematizations.

For a female readership, the most disturbing detail in these books has been Eve's sleeping while Adam goes atop the Mount of Vision with Michael: "How grossly do they insult us," says Mary Wollstonecraft, when they advise us that "women are formed for softness and sweet attractive grace, and docile blind obedience," thus rendering us "gentle, domestic brutes," or when, now with apparent reference to the last books of *Paradise Lost,* they represent us "as only created to see through a gross medium, and to take things on trust."[18] It might be argued that Milton is merely reaffirming the Pauline cliché—woman should be silent—by putting her to sleep, were it not that there is another overruling concatenation of biblical subtexts in Books 11 and 12. If Eve sleeps, she also dreams. Moreover, when Adam eventually comes to raise her from sleep, he finds "her wak't" (12.608) and already privy to the prophecy Michael tells Adam "at season fit" to confide in her: "Chiefly . . . / The great deliverance by her Seed to come" (12.597, 599–600). It is a prophecy she has heard before but only now understands, hence utters. God is also in sleep, and in sleep, dreams; in dreams, vision, and in vision, prophecy. Hence, it is right to say that Eve though "unseen" sees, and all has "heard."

Full of such entanglements, Books 11 and 12 are an unmasking of the strategy Milton has employed throughout his poem—his laying on the surface of his text the clichés and commonplaces the poetry itself will review and sometimes refute. The signatures of the feminine, sacred and secular, are here in full force; but the poetry also moves against them. The usual presuppositions, owing to Book 10 where Eve sheds "Tears that ceas'd not flowing" (910), lurk behind these concluding books: that woman will lose her composure while man retains his; he is stalwart, she weeps. Yet such clichés of the feminine are by Milton transferred first to he/him and then from *him* to *them:* "*Adam* . . . wept, / Though not of woman born; compassion quell'd / His best of Man, and gave him up to tears"; "*Adam* was all in tears" (11.495–97, 674). But by the end of the poem *they* weep: "Some natural tears they drop't, but wip'd them soon" (12.645). The ending of *Paradise Lost* is a moderated version of the conclusion to Book 10 where Adam and Eve, with sighs and tears, are seen "Watering the ground" (1089–90, 1101–2).

Weeping woman may be seen, she should not be heard; her role "is to be silent" (1 Tim. 2:2), the Pauline argument goes. Yet in the dialogue with

Michael, unexpectedly "*Eve,* who unseen / Yet all had heard" (11.265–66), gets both the first and the last word, whereas Adam, just as unexpectedly, falls silent. Milton invokes the Pauline text, then overturns it.[19] As if to emphasize that woman, no less than man, is empowered by language, Eve not only gets the first and last word but, in an extraordinary transgression of the Genesis text, confides that she has named the flowers: "O flowrs, / . . . which I bred up with tender hand / From the first op'ning bud, and *gave ye Names*" (11.273–77; my italics). To resist the implications of these lines on the grounds that such knowledge is dropped within parentheses is to forget that similar information concerning Adam's naming of the birds also appears unexpectedly (in parentheses) in Book 6 (73–76). Presumably, we are to credit both observations equally.[20] The point is crucial, for as Toril Moi explains, "Feminists have consistently argued that 'those who have the power to name the world are in a position to influence reality.' . . . To impose names is . . . not only an act of power, [a] 'will-to-knowledge'; it also reveals a desire to regulate and organize reality according to well-defined categories."[21] In *Paradise Lost,* Eve's naming of the flowers simply confirms what is evident earlier, in the Morning Hymn of Book 5, that like Adam she is invested with the power of language and of song, of thought and of prophecy.[22]

Milton's was a century that puzzled over—some men like Jacob Tonson were vexed by—the anomaly of man's being empowered with naming the beasts, thus being given monopoly over language and poetry; of his then sweating over Horace to learn the rules of art; and of woman's exhibiting from Sappho onward a natural gift for poetry, an innate capacity for being, or becoming, poets of creation—divine poets. Women seemed to have just as many masks as their male counterparts—and with just as much success, it was sometimes argued, could inhabit the forms of epic and tragedy, satire and prophecy; were as able as male poets to revive in their writings the spirit of Spenser, Jonson, Shakespeare and, as history shows, Milton. It seemed to some that heaven was now taking "the weakest side" and raising up women, indeed raising them to the pinnacle and allowing them "divine *Raptures,*" through which they could leave their precursors (even Elijah and Elisha) behind.[23] The idea of leading captivity captive was given a curious twist when applied to women and the arts: They were to be the conquerors and men their captives. They would sing and, through their song, silence their male competitors.

This competition of poetic voices is, apparently, coded into the last pages of *Paradise Lost;* is, indeed, part of the poem's larger encoding of both masculinist and feminist traditions. Neither Adam nor Eve is a slave to rhyme, neither's poem babbles with rhyme; but her mind-teasing "know /

goe" is altogether more artful than his tongue-twisting "blest / best / blest" (12.610, 615; cf. 553, 561, 573). His codification of platitudinous Christianity—"Henceforth I learn, that to obey is best, / And love with fear the onely God" (12.561–62)—is not so alluring as her transgression of one of the biblical subtexts for her song, "Whence thou returnest" (12.610), or so imaginative as her encapsulation of prophetic wisdom. His words require seemingly endless supplementation ("onely add . . . add / Add . . . add . . . add" [12.581–83]), hers none. Their respective poems show rebellious man, having lost Paradise, now conforming to conventional wisdom, and thinking woman, now imbued with the spirit of prophecy, imagining her way back into Paradise. Adam may lead the way out of Paradise, but Eve will point the way back into it. The mental postures of Eve and Adam, their respective capacities for reading God's visions and interpreting God's word, are remarkably different here from what they had been at the beginning of their conversation in Eden. Now *she* is the creative interpreter, as well as the mouthpiece for prophetic utterance (see n.14). Moreover, Eve's words, once their biblical subtexts are ferreted out, are encoded revelations concerning herself and her relationship to Adam. When Eve declares that "God is also in sleep" (12.611), she invokes, as was understood long ago, the biblical proclamation delivered to Miriam and Aaron: "If there be a prophet among you, *I* the Lord will make myself known unto him in a vision, *and* will speak to him in a dream" (Num. 12:6).[24] That God has spoken to Eve is evident in the fact that she already knows what Adam comes to tell her. This biblical subtext anoints Eve as a prophet and authorizes her prophetic utterance.

The biblical subtexts for Books 11 and 12, constituting a challenge to Pauline interpretation, are general and local. The one subtending both books, as Barbara Lewalski has aptly observed,[25] is Joel 2:28–29:

> And it shall come to pass afterward, *that* I will pour out my spirit upon all flesh: and your sons and your daughters shall prophesy, your old men shall dream dreams, your young men shall see visions:
>
> And also upon the servants and upon the handmaids in those days will I pour out my spirit.

It is of some importance that this passage, in the decade immediately preceding the publication of *Paradise Lost,* had been seized upon as a woman's text and as a prophecy for *this very time,* when all the Lord's people were becoming prophets and when women as prophets began to declare that, by virtue of their office, they had regained their lost equality with men.[26]

In these last days, which for so many were a harking back to the days just before Eve left Paradise, God once again was bestowing his revelation upon "the Weaker Sex" in accordance with the proclamation: "Then shall the Daughters of *Sion,* be fill'd with Praises and Songs of Deliverance: For behold the King cometh with Triumph and Victory."[27] *Paradise Lost* concludes with a triumph song, indeed is compassed round by them, with Milton balancing his song of deliverance at the beginning of the poem—of making captivity captive, of leading a new Chosen People into the Promised Land—with Eve's at the end. This is just one more of the poem's revealing symmetries. Within the story of *Paradise Lost,* of course, the triumph belongs to Eve. Its oracle, however, is the Son: "Between Thee and the Woman I will put / Enmitie, and between thee and her Seed; / Her seed shall bruise thy head; thou bruise his heel" (10.179–81). Eve thus initiates the process, hymned in the Song of Deborah, through which captivity will be led captive (10.188). The Son's words in Book 10 point to Eve's at the end of the poem, and Eve's free sonnet there reinvokes the Song of Deborah previously invoked in Book 7: "The Heav'ns and all the Constellations rung, / The Planets in thir stations list'ning stood" (562–63). The juxtaposition of these passages underscores a gentle irony, however: not earlier in the poem when she proposes a division of labor, and not now when she tells Adam to lead the way from Paradise, does she really remain fixed in her supposed station. She is not, nor by implication should she be, the fixed foot of a compass.

In contrast with Adam whose interpretations, especially in the last books, require reinterpretation, initially in these same books Eve utters words not provoking correction but prompting this supplementation: "Thy going is not lonely, with thee goes / Thy husband, him to follow thou art bound; / Where he abides, think there thy native soil" (11.290–92). In turn, Michael's supplement here forecasts the theme, affords the text, so to speak, for Eve's last words, the last *spoken* words in the poem. Those words are a song—a triumphant song—cast as a free sonnet and derived from those parts of Scripture which, as was acknowledged in the seventeenth century, "are Arguments of joy and gladness":[28]

> Whence thou returnest, and whither wentst, I know;
> For God is also in sleep, and Dreams advise,
> Which he hath sent propitious, some great good
> Presaging, since with sorrow and hearts distress
> Wearied I fell asleep: but now lead on;
> In mee is no delay; with thee to goe,
> Is to stay here; without thee here to stay,
> Is to go hence unwillingly; thou to mee
> Art all things under Heav'n, all places thou,
> Who for my wilful crime art banisht hence.
> This further consolation yet secure

> I carry hence; though all by mee is lost,
> Such favour I unworthie am voutsaft,
> By mee the Promis'd Seed shall all restore. [12.610–23]

Eve is thus given the last spoken words in *Paradise Lost,* but, what is more, unlike Adam's they require no correction—and no supplement.[29] Rather, man is silenced by them: "So spake our Mother *Eve,* and *Adam* heard / *Well pleas'd, but answer'd not*" (12.624–25; my italics). By the end of *Paradise Lost,* in books whose strategy is inversion, *subversion,* the usual order in this pairing of names is reversed: "*Eve,* and *Adam.*"

Moreover, Eve's triumph song is founded in part upon Ruth's words to her mother-in-law Naomi and, as is not usually noticed, upon Barak's similar words to Deborah. That is, Eve's words signal an ungendered "cleaving," as well as a steadfastness of mind:

> And Ruth said, Intreat me not to leave thee, *or* to return from following after thee: for wither thou goest, I will go; and where thou lodgest, I will lodge: thy people *shall be* my people, and thy God my God:
> Where thou diest, will I die, and there will I be buried. [Ruth 1:16–17]

Eve's words also echo those of Barak to Deborah:

> And Barak said unto her, If thou wilt go with me, then I will go: but if thou wilt not go with me, *then* I will not go.
> And she said, I will surely go with thee: notwithstanding the journey that thou takest shall not be for thine honour; for the Lord shall sell Sisera into the hand of a woman. And Deborah arose, and went with Barak. [Judg. 4:8–9]

The passage from Ruth, as Mieke Bal observes, comes from one of just two scriptural books named for women and paying tribute to their femininity, to their submitting to another freely, without coercion, thus asserting the efficacy of "collective heroism" over "male, individual heroism" and thereby attesting to "women's subversion . . . the legitimacy of feminine subversion."[30] On the other hand, the passage from Judges, according to Gerda Lerner, is but "one of only five instances in the [Old Testament] narrative, in which a woman is shown in a leadership position and heroic role."[31] In its anticipation of Jael's killing of Sisera, it establishes Deborah as a prophet; and in her going forth with Barak, casts her, by virtue of her moral strength, into a heroic role.

In the final moments of *Paradise Lost,* replicating Ruth's and Deborah's clinging to God as mankind's only proper guide and, simultaneously, reversing the roles of Barak and Deborah so as to privilege God's promise over Adam's presence without denying his presence, speaking now with a special prerogative from God, Eve appeals to Adam, inviting him to share in her heroism, extending an equal measure of it to him. Addressing Adam as later Barak will address Deborah, but without Barak's later perversion of the sentiment, Eve directs Adam to lead her on and, doing so, exhibits a generosity of spirit that contrasts with Barak's petulance. The blemish of character emblematized by his words contrasts with the amendment of character embodied within her utterance, with the implication that woman is now assuming the heroic posture that man surrendered, that she does so without diminishing him but in such a way as to make both copartners in the creation of a new future. Imbued with the spirit of prophecy, Eve responds to God's promise, submits to His wisdom and now, manifesting His glory, also shares it with her husband. There is *submission* here, not of Adam to Eve or of Eve to Adam, but rather a mutual submission to *their* manifest destiny, with Eve embodying in song, which itself embodies the prophecy of the Chosen Seed, the prophecy coded in her name: She forecasts not death but life, not a world destroyed but a new world creating— *a paradise restored.*

Once again in Milton's poetry it is "The meaning, not the Name," that matters: "Hail to thee, / *Eve* rightly called, Mother of all Mankind, / Mother of all things living, since by thee / Man is to live, and all things live for Man" (11.158–61; cf. 7.5). For narrative purposes obviously, Milton breaks with Genesis tradition in naming Eve before, by scriptural account, she is actually named but does so without missing the crucial point of the biblical story. "For that point," as Bal reminds us, "is, simply, creation, by differentiation—of humanity, of character"; the Book of Genesis "presents an account of the making of humanity within a progressive development of character."[32] Not until the end of this story does the myth of Eve begin—in a recollection of the naming that aligns her with God, with *all things living.* It is not the act of naming but the significance of this particular name that the final books of *Paradise Lost* record, with Eve here becoming an oracle of the truth that "to create / Is greater then created to destroy" (7.606–7). Eve, that is, becomes the prototype for a long line of females in history who epitomize the perfection of their sex, with Milton's Eve—herself a verse essay on the nature of her sex—overturning the notion that, if woman achieves intellectual parity with man, she is nevertheless shut off from the "*heroical*" intelligence achieved by some.[33]

Eve and Adam now leave Paradise hand in hand. This image neutralizes, although it may not altogether dispel, the patriarchy (along with its myth of sexual inequality) that, for some, is still all too evident in the final books of Milton's poem. The loss of paradise, so often and so readily attributed to "th'inabstinence of *Eve*" (11.476), *her* sin (519), redounds upon Adam who thinks he sees "the tenor of Mans woe / . . . from Woman to begin" (632–33) but who learns otherwise from Michael: "From Mans effeminate slackness it begins" (634). *Effeminate slackness*—in Michael's language, even at the end of the poem, there are traces of the patriarchal ideology and its interpretive distortions that Milton's poem cannot, or does not, fully erase. There is a residue of the older history that still requires canceling, that comes close to being canceled in the realization that Eve may have had her eyes "drencht" (367), but it is for a sleep like Adam's "while Shee to life was formd" (369)—a sleep, if we pursue the cross-referencing, that "op'n left the Cell / Of Fancie my internal sight, by which / Abstract . . . I saw" (8.460–62). Eve may be a silence in, an absence from much of Books 11 and 12, but both suggest not so much Milton's adherence to Pauline platitude as his advocating an attitude like Adrienne Rich's: "Silence can be a plan / rigorously executed / the blueprint to a life / It is a presence / it has a history a form / Do not confuse it / with any kind of absence."[34] Eve's silence is eventually broken in a song extraordinary both for its subtlety and its allusive power. Having taken the lead in assuring their redemption and recovery—that is, having already assumed a leadership position and heroic role in forging a new destiny, in creating a new history—Eve gives the lead back to Adam in a gesture of love. In doing so, she creates the love sonnet, thus suggesting the extent to which the modern love sonnet is a disfiguration of Eve's original, its gender bias contrasting with the gender neutrality of her song. True valor, true dignity, that song implies, reside not in the object being exalted but in the act of exalting another while maintaining an equilibrium between the two parties.

Milton's depiction of Eve, his poem's vision of woman, enabled many in the poet's early female readership to enlist him as a sponsor and to rely upon him as their ally and advocate. Yet these same women perceived, surely, that there was a zone of expectation, whatever their desires, to which Milton's poetry did not afford admittance. That, too, became strikingly evident in Eve's final words, which imply that Eve will find her paradise in Adam who, in turn, carries a paradise within himself. Milton's already substantial revision of tradition requires, from the perspective of his female readership, further revision, which thereupon provides them with an agenda for their own poetry and often fiction. For a full century and more after the publication of *Paradise Lost,* a principal theme of women's writing would be *their* attaining to a paradise within until which time there will be no paradise without, which is what it meant, apparently, for them *to know and go like Eve.*[35] By the end of the eighteenth century, when there is a withering of hope for an external paradise, there is even a tendency (in the fiction of Mary Wollstonecraft, for example) to slide by the masculine bias in the concluding lines of *Paradise Lost* where men, not women, create paradises of the mind. When Wollstonecraft's mental heroines perceive themselves as prisoners of their own bodies and walled off from the man's world, as they become quite literally prisoners of civilization, their only recourse—their one exit—is to do their own creating by building a paradise within themselves, the only one, it seems, they will ever know.

Books 11 and 12 are rife with implication. The notion that evil begins with Eve and is propagated by her daughters is counterweighted, indeed contravened, by a series of biblical subtexts, which carry the later reminder of Bathsua Makin "that Women were imployed in most of the great Transactions that happened in the World, even in reference to Religion":

> *Miriam* seems to be next to *Moses* and *Aaron,* she was a great Poet, and Philosopher. . . . The Women met *David,* singing triumphant Songs. . . . *Deborah,* the deliver of *Israel,* was without all doubt a learned Woman. . . . *Huldah* the Prophetess, dwelt in a Colledge . . . where Women were trained up in good Literature.
>
> In the New Testament we find *Anna* a Prophetess. *Philips* four daughters were Prophetesses. [*Acts* 21][36]

Eve's final words, with their encoded allusions to Miriam, Ruth, and Deborah, point to specific cases (staples in a debate during Milton's own lifetime) where woman is the copartner of man and, in the instance of Deborah, more instrumental than man in deliverance. Eve's words, and the biblical subtexts informing them, imply a contest between Adam and Eve, man and woman, his boastful superiority and blustering antagonism and her acceptance of him as "a collateral companion,"[37] and involve, too, a countering of his stridulous rhetoric with her wise counsel. In this way, she is like Miriam; but also, in her exchanging of his diatribes and complaints for songs of thanksgiving, in serving as a repository for God's grace and acting as his instrument, she is like both Ruth and Deborah.[38]

Each of the biblical subtexts informing Eve's sonnet pairs (while giving parity to) woman and man (Miriam and Aaron, Ruth and Boaz, Deborah and Barak); each of them isolates those moments in history when, because of her valor and wisdom, his venality and cowardice, her honor and his shame, woman *seems* to achieve preeminence over man. As a first edition the Eve of Book 11 may be like those wives in Milton's earlier Divorce tracts whom man is best advised to leave; but as a second edition, the Eve of Books 10–12 is like those women singled out in *Tetrachordon* who in wisdom sometimes surpass their husbands. In such isolated moments, woman is in direct contact with the divine, a fact underscored by Milton's insistence that, while Adam's visions are mediated by Michael, Eve's come directly from God. The Book of Judges affords the apt analogy here in its juxtaposition of woman's song and man's epic, implying a confrontation of gender codes and their different ideological tendencies, and through this juxtaposition invites the line of inquiry proposed by Bal: "Without wanting to deny the importance of a cultural background as a 'horizon of expectation,' we may question the legitimacy of the image of the poet 'obliged' to 'adapt' to this background. What of the poet . . . whose task was to subtly modify this horizon of expectation?"[39]

Bal asks this question of the Book of Judges; yet it is no less pertinent to *Paradise Lost,* at least in this moment of intersection between that scriptural text and Milton's poem where woman now seems more, man less, heroic than the epic genre usually dictates; where a biblical subtext focuses gender relationships explicitly between Deborah and Barak, implicitly between Jael and Sisera, while also attributing a higher tone of heroism to Deborah and Jael than to either Barak or, certainly, Sisera. In the Judges focalization no less than at the end of *Paradise Lost,* there is an inverted hierarchy, a reversal of roles. What is crucially important in *Paradise Lost,* in contradistinction to the Book of Judges, is that in Milton's poem gender codes conflict into neutrality: The coding, while altogether complimentary to woman and while asking whether this is now her world or his, argues not for female superiority but for sexual equilibrium and equality—*for a shared heroism.* What happens at the end of *Paradise Lost* is what happens in the lines Milton alludes to in Judges, then in Ruth: Man is forced to give up his assumed superiority as woman sheds her sense of inferiority in the realization that it is *she* who gives love and, with love, future life to—and through—Jesse, David, and Jesus.

If we were now to give Milton the last word, I suspect it would go something like this: Culture, which for so long has oriented itself by the commonplaces inscribed in my poem, can now reorient itself according to the revised traditions that are the creation of, and ultimately the reason for creating, this poem. The irony, of course, is that women readers, not male annotators, have, for the most part, isolated the biblical subtexts operative in Books 11 and 12 and operating in their behalf. Carla Peterson reminds us of how, in Charlotte Brontë's *Jane Eyre,* Rochester uses *Paradise Lost* to suggest ambivalent, often demeaning, attitudes toward female sexuality and of how, then, Jane refuses anymore to accept what she regards as his perverted readings of Milton's text. She prefers reinterpreting Milton in "a positive light," which involves her typifying Rochester not as Adam but as "a humbled Samson," "a chastened creature," and herself as Milton, writer and interpreter. Jane thereupon revises history so that "woman—not God and not man—is seen as the final agent in redemption," leading the way back into Eden, and as providential guide and illumined interpreter, with Peterson herself highlighting the nagging question: Is it men or women who are the distorters and defilers of *Paradise Lost,* whose appropriations damage and scar that text?[40]

## Receptions: Now and Then

... he Ever was a Dissenter.
JONATHAN RICHARDSON

One perspective on the aforementioned questions is afforded by Jane Lead, and the crucial text for our purposes is *A Fountain of Gardens* (1696), a spiritual diary recording Lead's visions from 1670 onward, and then her poem introductory to these prose meditations, "Solomon's Porch." If Milton had transposed end–time to explain origins, Lead reverses his strategy, employing the vision of Milton's last books to envision time in the moments just before the millennium. Man and woman who have "travel[ed] *hand in hand* thro' every Age" are restored to the divine resemblance they had lost, Christ now "in ev'ry Feature, ev'ry line, / Appearing": their "Senses open flye; / They see" as "The Glorious Æra *Now, Now, Now* begins." This is a time of "Illustrious" heroines, "Of Heroines Divine"—who once again "in Visionary Dreams ... See" and who in the new world are finally "unfetter'd, free."[41] Lead, echoing Milton throughout, openly appeals to her prophetic precursor:

Now, Mighty Bard sing out thy Sonnet free,
  Nor doubt, it true shall be.
    Come thou and joyn
Thy loud Prophetick Voice with mine.

At which point Milton's song becomes her own:

"Ring out ye Chrystal Sphears,
"Now bless our Humane Ears:
*For ye have* Power to touch our Senses so:
"Now *shall* your Silver Chime
"Move in Melodious time;
And the *deep* Base of Heav'ns great *Orb* shall Blow.[42]

Barak and Deborah, David and Mary, are the biblical types for Milton and Lead, who are the singers, the proclaimers of the millennium when the "True *Phinix* ... in Heav'nly Flames *Revives*"; when "Great Hero's ... must ... give way, / And learn a *Female* General to obey."[43] In Lead, *John* found *Joan* Milton, so to speak.

Only the care with which Lead traces, but in reverse, the broad outlines of the vision in the final books of *Paradise Lost* makes it seem inevitable that, like Eve's triumph song, her own will invoke "the Divine Illumined *Deborah*." If in its political aspect *Paradise Lost* could be translated into England lost, Lead insists that her own vision of paradise regained be similarly translated through the injunction of her coda: *England is now restored.* What Lead has apparently inferred from Milton is that Eve, as she explains elsewhere, whose birth had filled so many with disgust, in her life after the Fall becomes a new "Center of Vision and Revelation." Almost "immediately upon Adam's Fall," she writes, "the Eternal Word . . . did incorporate with *Eve,* whereby power and ability were given to bring forth wholly after the spirit";[44] and she could only write this way, one supposes, because she had read the last books of *Paradise Lost* as a woman who reads like the man who, in this instance, wrote as much for the woman as for the man, untrapping the senses of both and opening their doors of perception.

One way of charting shifts in discourse concerning the sexes in the seventeenth century is to recall that this century, which began with a female arraignment of Joseph Swetnam the woman hater, ends with some women embracing Milton as an ally and advocate, while their male counterparts protest (often approvingly) that Milton is actually another hater of women, outdoing Swetnam apparently and even, they will eventually argue, Euripides. Not women but men invented the dicta that Milton writes "in conformity" to traditions and in agreement with "the doctrine of the best Divines"; that reading with a note of interrogation should be suspended when it comes to Milton's representations of Eve and Adam, which, according to Thomas Newton, exhibit too many "inconsistencies" and perhaps even some false (because too complimentary) notions of the female sex.[45] But these are simply the terms by which, under Newton's aegis, *Paradise Lost* became institutionalized in the eighteenth century when more often than not the work of the editor or commentator involved eradicating ambiguities from Milton's poem, thereby restricting the range of interpretive possibilities, and then manipulating the poem into orthodoxies in such a way that *Paradise Lost* now becomes an answer to the very questions it was designed to pose.

Neither Newton nor, for that matter, the Jonathan Richardsons would countenance the implications of earlier editors, like Patrick Hume or Richard Bentley, who regarded Milton, albeit in different degrees, as a poet writing *with,* not against, women. Hume is exceedingly delicate in his annotation for *Paradise Lost* 4.299: "Hee for God only, shee for God in him." He concedes that "[t]his Asseveration of our Author seems maintainable from St. *Paul*'s Doctrine," even that Milton's initial representations of Eve and Adam may *seem* "an Argument and Indication of . . . Subjection"; but Milton "sweetens" his portrayal of Eve, pouring into it *his* version of tenderness and love. "Some think," says Hume, that Adam gave Eve "this Name by way of *Ironie* and cruelest Reproach. . . . But our *Poet* better applies it to the early Promise of the Victory over *Satan* . . . as do the most Judicious and Authentic Commentators."[46] Still, in his annotations, Hume is altogether more guarded, certainly more conservative, than Bentley, whose constant argument is that, "through his whole Poem," Milton "had certainly that in his View, to make the Female Sex favour it." For Bentley, the power of Milton's poetry forces a recasting of that crucial line, "Hee for God only, shee for God in him"—"A shameful Error to have pas'd through all the Editions"—so that it now should be read as "He for God only, She for God AND Him."[47] And that is how, in numerous adaptations and translations belonging to the eighteenth century, the line was read: *She for God And Him.* It does not matter whether we think this emendation accentuates or attenuates the supposed sexism in Milton's line; at least Bentley's intention is clear. Today's readers may have submitted too easily and unquestioningly to what by Newton came to be established as the orthodox premises of Milton criticism or to what currently seems to be a working premise of feminist literary history: that, as Mary Poovey argues, the seventeenth-century idea of woman as deceiver and seducer, going into a dizzying spin in the eighteenth century, emerges, now emended, in the Victorian notion that " 'The hope of the age is in woman' ":[48] *She* will set all matters right. This *supposedly* Victorian idea of woman, already there in Jane Austen's *Persuasion* and a hidden inscription in the last books of *Paradise Lost,* is brought out of concealment and achieves focalization in the song that, by Lead's fiction, she and Milton sing together.

One of the many ironies of the current critical moment—and it is in so many ways (and so richly) the moment of feminist criticism—is that feminism is busy denying Milton a space in the discourse he helped to spawn. Witness the feminism of Gerda Lerner:

> A literary canon, which defined itself by the Bible, the Greek classics, and Milton, would necessarily bury the significance and the meaning of women's literary work, as historians buried the activities of women. The effort to resurrect this meaning and to re-evaluate women's literary and artistic work is recent. Feminist literary criticism and poetics have introduced us to a reading of women's literature, which finds a hidden, deliberately "slant," yet powerful world-view.[49]

Milton's place in the literary canon was created for him by others—at a cost and *at a loss* that may be calculated by pronouncements such as Lerner's. On the other hand, Milton's place in the history of what, today, we call feminist discourse is legitimated in Milton's own century by a female writer like Jane Lead.

This conspicuous discrepancy needs sharp focusing: The place accorded Milton by some feminist discourse in its seventeenth-century phase is precisely the place being denied to Milton by much feminist discourse today. From the now prevailing perspective, the foregoing pages are likely to appear as an effort to recuperate an already (and justly) discredited cultural authority; but from the perspective of Milton's own century "the take" on these pages would probably be different, thus engendering an altogether different set of questions: What cultural forces conspired against Milton and eventually silenced the feminist sentiment in *Paradise Lost?* Is a sexist Milton the deterministic product of inescapable cultural forces firmly holding this poet within their grasp or, rather, the invention of a later history that has hidden Milton's motives and distorted his commitments? The pressing questions for criticism are not whether Milton would now be a lesser poet, as he was once a greater poet, because of his supposed sexism—or whether sexism would be less objectionable if Milton had not opposed it—but instead: *What sort of poet was Milton anyway?* And what sort of gender discourses, what sexual attitudes, does his poetry portray and promulgate? The risk in deploying the critical approach afforded by feminism is that it may seem to eventuate in the wrapping of Milton's poetry in anachronistic concerns and interpretations. The marvel is that the questions with which feminism floods Milton's poetry, and the ensuing critical debate, however anachronistic they may *seem,* are, in fact, among the very first interpretive questions and the instigators of early critical debate concerning Milton's poetry. We have tended to define the first concerns of Milton criticism in terms of the rhyme controversy and biblical hermeneutics without owning up to the facts that (1) there is a politics, indeed a sexual politics, to rhymed and unrhymed verse and (2) there is also a politics to biblical hermeneutics and poetics, which here would bridle and there would free interpretive activity, with Milton achieving by 1683[50] the status of sponsor for revisionistic interpretation even when it involves interpolations or supplementations to the scriptural text. If from the vantage point of some, this essay is caught in a hopeless contradiction and, worse, a blistering irony (dissident feminism effects the further entrenchment of canonical Milton, further crediting an already discredited cultural authority), from the viewpoint of others, perhaps, the essay negotiates its way around contradiction, and out of such irony, by delving into an anterior question: What is the nature of the culture and the disposition of the society that Milton's poetry would authorize?

*Paradise Lost* is *in part* a woman's text and in that capacity outdoes the Bible—is to be distinguished from the Bible—in the history it attributes to woman through Milton's depiction of Eve. Not only does *Paradise Lost* elaborate woman's history, it gives to woman a prominent place in a history that, after the Fall, she more than Adam determines. If *his* fall instigates and perpetuates the cycles of history, *her* resurrection ensures that those cycles will be broken, that a redemptive pattern and providential design will overtake those cycles and finally prevail. It may be, as Lerner remarks, that

"Women had no history—so they were told; so they believed"; but Milton announces otherwise. In the aftermath, *in the immediate aftermath,* of *Paradise Lost,* they begin to believe otherwise. If woman's history is a way of creating, raising, transforming female consciousness, of building "a world free of dominance and hierarchy, a world that is truly human," *Paradise Lost* is a central document in such a history, an example of "compensatory history,"[51] and a principal agent in the formation of a female consciousness—and a female literature. As women writers began to aspire increasingly to re-create the language of Eve before the Fall, they discovered that Milton had preceded them in this effort.

In Book 4, in the story of Eve's awakening, Milton shows how women participate in the process of their own subordination, internalizing the sense of inferiority, the learned disparagements of their sex, that patriarchal voices teach them. But as his poem proceeds, it becomes clear that certain forms of patriarchy before the Fall, modulating into misogyny afterward, are Satan's devices (and Adam's), misrepresenting the situation of the sexes for which God, the Son, and the angels provide fitter representation, although even their representations do not at every point agree. Woman's history is in the eye of the beholder, Milton seems to be saying, and different characters perceive that history differently. Within the expanded consciousness of *Paradise Lost,* within the expanding consciousness of certain of its characters (the privileged witnesses) woman is both actor and agent in history; she is central, not marginal, to the building of civilization and to the progress and eventual transformation of history. What may be a distorted, because censored, record of her history is straightened, clarified, in a poem that reports the history of what *she* experienced and of what *she* has done—and will do: She may be the first to lose Paradise, but she is also the principal agent in its recovery. In the prelapsarian books of *Paradise Lost,* Milton restores a history to women; in the last books of the poem, he restores women to history.

Let us not, though, exaggerate our claims for Milton: he did not provide a complete history—or a history completely undistorted. On the other hand, let us not silence legitimate claims either; he has contributed important chapters to such a history, giving woman a place and prominent role in history, returning to her a voice, and redeeming her as a witness. *Paradise Lost,* by unsettling traditionalist explanations, institutionalized interpretations, begins to redress the balance and, doing so, should be credited just where it has been discredited: with conceptualizing woman's role in history and thus with contributing to the formation of a consciousness, male and female, that would emancipate both sexes from the diminishing, demeaning consequences of all systems of domination.

The question has been asked: "Could it be that it was the 1660s and not the 1960s that was the era in which feminism was born?"[52] And it is an especially intriguing question when we remember that, for all its reticence about sexuality, the seventeenth century—and Milton's poem—translated sexuality into discourse, made of such proliferating discourses a mosaic, riddling in its conception and problematizing in its intention. If the seventeenth century was, as Michel Foucault contends, "an age of repression," full of "instances of muteness which, by dint of saying nothing, imposed silence," or "Censorship,"[53] *Paradise Lost* averts repression and censorship, breaks silence, by saying *something* but saying it deviously—through coded allusions, through contradictions. *But it says it nonetheless,* in more than whispers. To answer the aforementioned question in the affirmative, as its author seems to wish, is to move for a revaluation of *Paradise Lost* in its historical moment, is to engage in a review of its contributions to, its manifestations of, another kind of history—*woman*'s history. And it is, after all, a woman, projecting herself into the figure of a male monster, who distinguishes *Paradise Lost* from other "patriarchal" histories (by Plutarch, by Goethe), Milton's poem exciting "different and far deeper emotions. I read it . . . as a true history."[54] In behalf of this much maligned monster, perceptive as he/she is, it needs to be said that, if the kind of reading sketched in the foregoing pages is ever to be mainstreamed, it will be owing to his/her early sponsorship.

Woman's history *is* inextricably a part of man's history and, as Mary Shelley implies, can best be written in terms of it even if, sometimes, that entails writing against it. Because woman's history has been isolated does not mean that in its telling it *should* be isolated from man's history, or from the inscriptions of patriarchy and misogyny so deeply etched within it. What *Paradise Lost,* as an ideological index, reveals is that such inscriptions need not be promotional. If Milton's poem is a product of these masculinist discourses, as a product it exhibits such discourses, their traditions, in a moment of dawning consciousness—in *the* moment when patriarchy, becoming aware of, admits to its own divisions; in *the* moment when feminism invades male-sponsored, until then male-biased discourses and, instead of militating against, nurtures egalitarian concerns and humanistic values. To be male, as Donald Pease smartly argues, is not necessarily to be patriarchal; but neither is it to be other. It may necessitate doing from the inside of one's traditions—its languages, its habits of mind, its modes of discourse—what others will do from the outside. It may involve putting explosives within the foundation of such discourse so that, when they detonate, it too will be demolished, freeing not just others but also the tyrannized self. The tactic may be subversive, but the objective (in Pease's fine formulation) is "the emancipation of both slaves and slaveholders"[55]—the liberation not just of women but perhaps of Milton himself.

No thinking person of Milton's day—or of Milton's party after the failed Revolution—could avoid observing complicity between patriarchy and monarchy, the one upholding the other. The moment the Revolution failed is *the* moment when patriarchy backfired on Milton and his cohorts, the moment when Milton was free to mount his critique as a critique was once mounted against him by Robert Filmer.[56] Is there any more striking evidence of how complicated Milton's relations with patriarchy were becoming than a book of the poet's own time, insisting upon the patriarchal underpinnings of monarchy—a line extending from Adam to Charles—and then gently denouncing Milton for his subversion of both patriarchy and monarchy? It does well to see, with William Myers, two Miltons: one of whom "indulges in an 'hysterical revenge fantasy' . . . in the anti-prelatical pamphlets, and advocates military dictatorship during the Civil War," and the other of whom challenges "the engrossment of patriarchal authority by royalist ideologues before and after the Civil War."[57] And it does equally well to see in *Paradise Lost,* as does Richard Corum, two texts, one of "obedient submission" and another of "subversive mutiny."[58] But it still needs to be remembered that the times, as well as Milton's personal circumstances, prevent his challenge from being an open attack, instead ensuring that it will take the form of an ambush. But therein lies a risk: poetry with such dazzling footwork and slick maneuvering, if meant to ambush, may itself be ambushed. *Paradise Lost* has thus been caught repeatedly in a curious predicament. No matter how many cards Milton has up his sleeve, and no matter how he plays them, he seems to have been unable to win even for losing: "still thou may'st complain / That yet too much *Patriarch* does remain."[59] However, even when losing, Milton's mind turned to regaining what was lost. He kept faith in time of trouble, and his faith was very much Virginia Woolf's: that a republic (Milton would say a new paradise) might still be brought into being by a poem.

## Notes

The title for this essay derives from the following report in Leigh Hunt's *Examiner,* August 22, 1808, 508: where in "The History of Britain . . . MILTON describes Earl GODWIN's daughter as 'commended much for beauty, modesty and *beyond what is requisite in a woman—learning,*' the late Mr. GILBERT WAKEFIELD made this apostrophe [marginally] with his pencil:—JOHN, JOHN I blush for thee!" Much of the research for this essay was conducted, and the essay itself was written, with the assistance provided by a PSC-CUNY Research Award. Quotations of Milton's poetry are from *The Complete Poetry of John Milton,* rev. ed., ed. John T. Shawcross (Garden City, NY: Doubleday, 1971). I am grateful to Mary Ann Radzinowicz and her colleagues for the opportunity of presenting an early version of this essay as a lecture to the English Department of Cornell University (November 1988).

1. See Mary Nyquist, "The Genesis of Gendered Subjectivity in the Divorce Tracts and in *Paradise Lost*," in *Re-membering Milton: Essays on the Texts and Traditions*, ed. Mary Nyquist and Margaret W. Ferguson (London: Methuen, 1987), 101, 106; and John Guillory, "Dalila's House: *Samson Agonistes* and the Sexual Division of Labor," in *Rewriting the Renaissance: The Discourses of Sexual Difference in Early Modern Europe*, ed. Margaret W. Ferguson, Maureen Quilligan, and Nancy J. Vickers (Chicago: University of Chicago Press, 1986), 106.
2. See O'Connor's letter to Janet McKane (July 26, 1964), in *Letters of Flannery O'Connor: The Habit of Being*, ed. Sally Fitzgerald (1979; rpt. New York: Random House, Vintage Books, 1980), 595.
3. Alicia Ostriker, *Stealing the Language: The Emergence of Women's Poetry in America* (Boston: Beacon, 1986), 41 (the proposition is attributed to Donald Hall), 137. Such duplicity, Ostriker explains, is characteristic of *Blake*'s Milton and "arises when an idea must be simultaneously denied and affirmed—when, in other words, the poet is driven by something forbidden to express but impossible to repress" (41). The best discussion of "duplicity" in *Paradise Lost* is provided by John R. Mulder, " 'Ambiguous Words and Jealousies': A Secular Reading of *Paradise Lost*," *Milton Studies* 13 (1979): esp. 146, 147, 164.
4. I am grateful to Ben Scott for drawing my attention to this fascinating example of what the language of criticism once was; see C. S. Lewis, *A Preface to "Paradise Lost"* (London: Oxford University Press, 1942), 109. Forthcoming work by Gregory Bredbeck and Claude J. Summers on the (homo)sexual temptation in *Paradise Regained* is ample, indeed impressive, evidence of a new sensibility and sophistication in critical discourse.
5. See, e.g., Joseph Wittreich, *Feminist Milton* (Ithaca, NY: Cornell University Press, 1987), as well as the following essay supplementary to the one printed here: "Mapping Sexual Discourses: The Example of *Paradise Lost*," forthcoming in *"Grateful Vicissitudes": Essays on Milton in Honor of J. Max Patrick*, ed. Harrison T. Meserole and Michael A. Miklajczak.
6. See, e.g., Lawrence W. Hyman, "Must We Pin Milton's Shoulders to The Mat?" *Milton Quarterly* 21 (1987): 122. Hyman's *Paradise Lost* wreathes various discourses, masculinist and feminist, but withholds (indeed, withdraws) from rendering any valuations, hence from approving the best. Cf. Leslie Brisman who, in *Milton's Poetry of Choice and Its Romantic Heirs* (Ithaca, NY: Cornell University Press, 1973), explores the way in which options are expressed, alternatives experienced, in *Paradise Lost* while insisting that "Milton is everywhere concerned with the act of choosing" (1).
7. Stanley Fish, "No Bias, No Merit: The Case against Blind Submission," *PMLA* 103 (1988): 744.
8. Catherine Belsey, "Constructing the Subject: Deconstructing the Text," in *Feminist Criticism and Social Change: Sex, Class and Race in Literature and Culture*, ed. Judith Newton and Deborah Rosenfelt (London: Methuen, 1985), 57.
9. Elaine Pagels, "The Politics of Paradise," *New York Review of Books* 35 (May 12, 1988): 29. And, also by Pagels, see *Adam, Eve, and the Serpent* (New York: Random House, 1988), esp. 98–126.
10. Mieke Bal, *Lethal Love: Feminist Literary Readings of Biblical Love Stories* (Bloomington: Indiana University Press, 1987), 131.
11. The extent to which *Paradise Lost* is written in sympathy with Pauline interpretation is explored in Edward LeComte, *Milton and Sex* (New York: Columbia University Press, 1978), esp. 53, and in Anne Ferry, "Milton's Creation of Eve," *Studies in English Literature, 1500–1900* 28 (1988): 113–32. LeComte and Ferry come to decidedly different conclusions.

12. Peter Bayle, *Milton: The Critical Heritage,* ed. John T. Shawcross (London: Routledge and Kegan Paul, 1970), 116.
13. Adam's words here recall Swetnam's declaration that "Moses describeth a woman thus: . . . they were made of the ribbe of man . . . a ribbe is a crooked thing good for nothing else, and women are crooked by nature"; and his words also recall Swetnam's observation of the discrepancy between what women are "outwardly" and what they are "within," as well as his insistence that they are "from the Deuill"—in appearance "sweet intisements" but in actuality "Serpents." See Joseph Swetnam, *The Araignment of Lewde, idle, froward, and vnconstant Women* (London, 1615), sigs. A4, B; pp. 3, 15, 41, but also sig. A4 and p. 4. See, too, *Swetnam the Woman-hater: The Controversy and the Play,* ed. Coryl Crandall (Lafayette, IN: Purdue University Studies, 1969), 3.3.97, 196–97; see also 5.2.275.
14. Such is Nyquist's argument; see "Genesis of Gendered Subjectivity," 101–2. Philip J. Gallagher argues differently, and quite compellingly, that Milton privileges Genesis 1; see "Creation in Genesis and in *Paradise Lost,*" *Milton Studies* 20 (1984): 169, 183, 185. If we use *Paradise Lost* to reconstruct the first conversation in Paradise, we should notice that Adam reads what will become the Genesis account of Creation backwards, moving from the conclusion to Genesis 2 (4.481–88) to the conclusion for Genesis 1 (4.411–39). He then moves backwards through Genesis 1, from "*it was very* good" to "let them have dominion," while interpolating into the Genesis 1 account the story of the interdiction: "well thou knowst / God hath pronounc't it death to taste that Tree" (4.426–27). Following upon the heels of Adam's revisionary reading of Genesis is Eve's platitudinous redaction of Pauline interpretation of the Genesis account (4.440–43; cf. Ephesians 5:22–23). Within *Paradise Lost,* as Eve sloughs off clichéd interpretation Adam becomes more and more its mouthpiece.
15. Jane Adams, *Miscellany Poems* (Glasgow, 1734), 155.
16. I do not at all wish to hide the enigmatic character of this speech, which slides, in a very few lines, from *her* superiority, to *their* implied equality, to *her* subjection. These few lines are framed by others, which gender wisdom female and which then draw attention to an earlier episode and to Eve's superior wisdom: "[she] sees when thou art seen least wise" (8.578). If we take into account how, historically, these lines were read, they illustrate, perhaps better than any others in the poem, the dictum of Richard Helgerson: "An absolutist message can be extracted from *Paradise Lost.* But so can its republican antagonist. Milton was capable of both, but he was incapable of transcending either" ("Recent Studies in the English Renaissance," *Studies in English Literature* 26 [1986]: 192). If I can use these lines to advance a feminist reading on the authority of Lucy Hutton (see *Feminist Milton,* 67), John Leonard can use them, alternatively, to insist upon a masculinist and patriarchal reading (see "Milton and Women," *Essays in Criticism* 39 [1989]: 73). Given his insistence upon the directness and plainness of Milton's statements (78, 83), Leonard could do no better than to take Samuel Slater's "translation" of these lines as his authority; see Slater, "A Discourse Concerning The *Creation, Fall* and *Recovery* of Man," *Poems in Two Parts* (London, 1679), esp. 9. My point is, very simply, that distortion works both ways and becomes especially evident when masculinist and feminist readings are set side-by-side; both readings erase subtleties, nuances, and ambiguities from Milton's texts, but since it is the feminist readings that have, historically, been repressed it is also these readings that provide quickest access to the masculinist distortions.
17. On these lines as they are involved in possibly deliberate editorial displacement, see Bal, *Lethal Love,* 126–27.
18. Mary Wollstonecraft, *A Vindication of the Rights of Woman* (1792), ed. Carol H. Poston, 2d ed. (1975; New York: W. W. Norton, 1988), 19–20, 53. Wollstonecraft's latter comment would seem to have more bearing on the last books of *Paradise Lost* than on Book 8 (which in a footnote she cites). In the former instance, Wollstonecraft's valuation of Milton and Milton's Eve is soon complicated as she proceeds to distinguish between

God's intention in creating Eve, together with Adam's initial conception of what Eve should be, and Eve's self-demeaning perception of herself in Book 4. Here Wollstonecraft is a discerner of *inconsistencies* in *Paradise Lost* and in a poet who seems to be in conflict with himself. Moreover, Wollstonecraft's use of Milton in her polemic should be contrasted with her reference to him in her fiction where *Paradise Lost* figures not only as a woman's text but as a text for *thinking* women. See both *Mary: A Fiction* (1788), ed. Gina Luria (New York: Garland, 1974), where, depicted as a prelapsarian Eve (28, 30), Mary reads *Paradise Lost* (3, 25) in contrast to her mother who reads only sentimental novels, "and, had she thought while she read, her mind would have been contaminated" (8) and *Maria or The Wrongs of Woman* (1798; New York: W. W. Norton, 1975), where the heroine is both a recipient of a parcel of books, "a mine of treasure" which includes *Paradise Lost* (34), and a reader obviously of other of Milton's poems (51; the phrase quoted on this page is from *A Mask*). Sentimental novels, not Milton's poems, are the corrupting texts in these novels, where *Paradise Lost,* in contrast, is a liberating text (or can be so) and where this poem plays an important role in the formation of female consciousness, even when women must sometimes enter into an antithetical relationship with it.

19. See the (I believe mistaken) argument by Christine Froula, "When Eve Reads Milton: Undoing the Canonical Economy," *Critical Inquiry* 10 (1983): 321–47; and also by Froula, "Pechter's Specter: Milton's Bogey Writ Small; or, Why Is He Afraid of Virginia Woolf?" *Critical Inquiry* 11 (1984): 171–78.
20. Nyquist argues otherwise; see "Genesis of Gendered Subjectivity," 100. Cf. Diane McColley, "Eve and the Arts of Eden," in *Milton and the Idea of Woman,* ed. Julia Walker (Urbana: University of Illinois Press, 1988), 104–5: "Even though Adam and Eve were joined and enjoined by God to dress as well as keep the Garden, it was unheard of before Milton to show them gardening, and especially to make Eve a gardener even more committed and original than Adam, and so a figura of the poet's own work; and equally unheard of to join her in naming the creatures by having her name the flowers . . . : *naming,* until then, had been Adam's prerogative" (see also 108, 118, n. 17). With regard to the first part of McColley's comment, and in view of what actually occurs in Milton's poem, it is worth remembering Rachel Speght's argument that, because woman is a helper, there should be no division of labor, though, if in fact man is "the stronger vessel," he should do more of it (*A Mouzell for Melastomus,* in *The Women's Sharp Revenge: Five Women's Pamphlets from the Renaissance,* ed. Simon Shepherd [London: Fourth Estate, 1985], 70). In *Paradise Lost,* Adam does less, taking no part in Eve's domestic duties and letting her tend the garden while he remains, and is eventually rebuked for the impropriety of certain questions he addresses to Raphael. Moreover, if the division of labor originates in patriarchal thinking, by having Eve propose it Milton also exhibits the extent to which she has been schooled into and is made to submit to such thinking.
21. Toril Moi, *Sexual/Textual Politics: Feminist Literary Theory* (London: Methuen, 1985), 158, 160.
22. Adam and Eve's Morning Hymn is "Thir" spontaneous orison, reflective of "thir thoughts"; it comes from both "thir lips" (5.145, 150, 209). Otherwise so sensitive to gender questions in *Paradise Lost,* Richard Bentley misses the point here, wanting to alter their hymn so that "I" becomes *we* (5.202) and "my Song," *our* song (5.204), but also imagining (thus printing) their hymn as alternating voices. By Bentley, some lines are assigned to Adam, others to Eve. What Bentley forgets is that this is a spontaneous, glorious song of praise coming to both equally, each inspired and each singing the song separately as if *they* were one. The unity and harmony of the song image their own equality and oneness, their joint capacity for receiving and processing vision and revelation. See Bentley, *Milton's "Paradise Lost"* (London, 1732), 153: "the whole Hymn . . . actually divides it self into Parts Interlocutory; and I have presum'd to put it so, though not warranted by any Edition. It cannot displease, that I have given the Mother of Mankind

her Share in this fine Piece, and not let her stand mute, a Hearer only." It is noteworthy (as Diane McColley remarks) that "In their unfallen conversations, she has almost an equal voice—217 lines to Adam's 230" (see "Eve and the Arts of Eden," 108) and noteworthy, too, that Eve is named before, not after, the Fall. By whom, we are not told. We know only that Adam, by his own account, named her "Woman" (8.496), though he addresses her, by Eve's account, as "Eve" (4.481). These facts do not accord with the Genesis account, allowing for the inference that whoever names Adam also names Eve. Was Eve named by God or one of the angels as in some of the earlier literary analogues for *Paradise Lost?* Milton allows for the question but provides no answer to it.

23. See the first three and the fifth dedicatory poems to Jane Barker's *Poetical Recreations* (London, 1688); the quotation is from the second of these poems. Barker's debt to Milton is discussed by Leslie Moore in *The Creation of Milton* (Stanford, CA: Stanford University Press, forthcoming). That women did, *and do,* "wear the Bayes" is illustrated by Bathsua Makin's catalogue of female poet-prophets from classical up to her own time; see *An Essay to Revive the Antient Education of Gentlewomen, in Religion, Manners, Arts and Tongues* (London, 1673), 16–20, 24, 29.

24. See Christian Cann, *A Scriptural and Allegorical Glossary to Milton's "Paradise Lost"* (London, 1828), 281.

25. See Barbara Lewalski, *"Paradise Lost" and the Rhetoric of Literary Forms* (Princeton, NJ: Princeton University Press, 1985), 259.

26. The principal example is Mary Cary, *A New and More Exact Mappe or, Description of the New Jerusalems Glory* (London, 1651), 236–28. For discussion of Cary in relation to Books 11 and 12, see Wittreich, *Feminist Milton,* 108–9.

27. J. W. Petersen, *A Letter to Some Divines* (London, 1695), 117–18, 129. Petersen here contends that biblical sanction for the female prophets derives not only from Eve but from "*Hannah, Mary,* the daughters of Philip, and many others" with Joel then prophesying "the Particular Gifts of the Spirit to the *Handmaidens,* and to the *Daughters;* which Prophesie has not hitherto in its full extent been Accomplish'd."

28. See Thomas Ager, *A Paraphrase on the Canticles; or, Song of Solomon* (London, 1680), 6.

29. Eve's words here unfold the same sorts of ironies deployed by Katherine Philips in her poem, "To Antenor, on a Paper of Mine Which J. J. Threatens to Publish to Prejudice Him." Better the wife assume the burden of guilt, for in placing it on her husband she may well reinforce the notion of her own inferiority. See the discussion by Elizabeth Hageman, "The Matchless Orinda: Katherine Philips," in *Women Writers of the Renaissance and Reformation,* ed. Katharina M. Wilson (Athens: University of Georgia Press, 1987), 579, 583.

30. Bal, *Lethal Love,* 69, 85. Lewalski hears Ruth's words in Eve's; see *"Paradise Lost" and Literary Forms,* 277.

31. Gerda Lerner, *The Creation of Patriarchy* (New York: Oxford University Press, 1986), 165. On biblical women prophesying, see Wittreich, *Feminist Milton,* 105–9; and on Eve as a prophet, see John Goodwin, *The Returne of Mercies; or, The Saints Advantage by Losses* (London, 1641), 28: "*Eve,* upon the birth of *Seth,* . . . speaks with a kind of Propheticall spirit." Goodwin, on the other hand, is often much harsher than Milton in his judgments of Eve; see, e.g., *The Butchers Blessing, or the Bloody Intentions of Romish Cavaliers* (London, 1642), 3.

32. Bal, *Lethal Love,* 112, 130; see also 129.

33. Anna Maria von Schurman, *The Learned Maid; or, Whether a Maid May Be a Scholar: A Logick Exercise* (London, 1659), 26, but see also 38. In the second of these citations Schurman is referring to Beverovicus, *The Excellency of the Female Sex* (London, 1639). Cf. Makin, *Antient Education of Gentlewomen,* 29: "My intention is not to equalize Women to Men, much less to make them superior. They are the weaker Sex, yet capable of impressions of great things." Other women of Milton's time think differently, and more generously, about their intellectual capacities. See, e.g., Philo-Philippa, "To the Excellent

*Orinda,*" in *Kissing the Rod: An Anthology of Seventeenth-Century Women's Verse,* ed. Germaine Greer et al. (New York: Noonday Press, 1988), 204–9; see also 186 and passim.

34. Adrienne Rich, "Cartographie of Silence," in *The Dream of a Common Language* (New York: Norton, 1978), 17. It has been remarked that *vision* (the organizing scheme for Book 11) is the "organizing metaphor of patriarchal history; or men's relationship to technology, weapons, and war"; see Alice Jardine, "Men in Feminism: Odor di Uomo Or Compagnons de Route?" in *Men in Feminism,* ed. Alice Jardine and Paul Smith (London: Methuen, 1987), 61. However, when such a perception is applied to Book 11, with it tumbles forth the irony of Milton's encapsulating in *vision* the misery, fever, and fret of human history. Milton uses this sequence of visions from biblical history to expose *man*'s failings—what it is that devalues *him* and why *she* must redeem him from the history he creates and restore history in the process.
35. Hannah More is one woman who seems to have heard this rhyme in *Paradise Lost;* see Wittreich, *Feminist Milton,* 105.
36. Makin, *Antient Education of Gentlewomen,* 8; cf. 24.
37. Speght, *A Mouzell for Melastomus,* 69.
38. For the use of these biblical women in seventeenth-century polemic, see ibid., 69, 75; but also in the same volume (Shepherd, *Woman's Sharp Revenge*), Esther Sowername, *Ester hath hang'd Haman,* 96–98.
39. Mieke Bal, *Murder and Difference: Gender, Genre, and Scholarship on Sisera's Death,* trans. Matthew Gumpart (Bloomington: Indiana University Press, 1988), 19; see also 30, 116, 118, 121.
40. Carla Peterson, *The Determined Reader: Gender and Culture in the Novel from Napoleon to Victoria* (New Brunswick, NJ: Rutgers University Press, 1986), 103–4, 107.
41. Jane Lead, *A Fountain of Gardens,* 3 vols. (London, 1696–1701), 1, sigs. $E^{v}$ (my italics; cf. F2), E2, $E2^{v}$, E3 (see also G2), F2, $F3^{v}$, G. Volume 1 is dated 1696 (although, in a second copy owned by the British Library, volume 1 is dated 1697), volume 2 is dated 1697, and volume 3 is in two parts (the first dated 1700 and the second 1701). Though quite rare, this collection was reprinted four times.
42. Ibid., sig. $F4^{v}$.
43. Ibid., sig. G2-$G2^{v}$.
44. Ibid., 2:138, 172–73; and see also *The Signs of the Times* (London, 1699), 1.
45. *Paradise Lost,* ed. Thomas Newton, 9th ed., 2 vols. (London, 1790), 1, sig. h (the phrase is Joseph Addison's) and 377; 2:135 (this variorum commentary was first published in 1749). To be completely fair to Newton, it should be noted that he (1) gives Bentley's reading for 4.299; and (2) says Dr. Pearce approves of such a reading and the emendation it forces, the proof of which is supplied by 10.150, "made of thee, / And for thee": "we cannot but wish it was admitted to the text" (1.280). Editor Newton, however, does not admit this emendation to *his* text.
46. Patrick Hume, *Annotations on Milton's "Paradise Lost"* (London, 1695), 144, 146, 294–95; but cf. 239–40, 269, 285–86. From Newton's perspective, Milton's tact and delicacy serve other ends: Milton describes "with the greatest art and decency the subordination and inferiority of the female character in strength of reason and understanding" in Book 9 where, finally, the hesitancies of earlier and awkward formulations give way to a position that is certain and right. Here, any suspicion of Milton's courting women's favor is dispelled. Newton's earlier inclination to emphasize Adam and Eve's "mutual subordination" gives way to an emphasis in the annotations accompanying Books 9–12 on *her* subordination–an emphasis observed throughout the notes to *Paradise Lost* by Richardson and his son, where Adam is represented as Eve's God and Lord with Eve under "the Power of her Husband," as Eve herself is said to acknowledge (see *Paradise Lost,* ed. Newton, 1:292; 2:189; and the Richardsons, *Explanatory Notes and Remarks on Milton's "Paradise Lost"* [London, 1734], 153, 155, 345, but also 219–21.

47. Bentley, *Milton's "Paradise Lost,"* 117, 129–30 (my italics); see also 153. Less steady in his commitment to such a reading, Hume expresses his conservatism in his annotations to *Paradise Lost* 8.543 and 10.196, where he argues, first, that Adam is "chiefly" in God's image and, then, that "The subjection of *Eve* to *Adam* was natural, even in Innocency," and, later, when he intellectualizes Adam's misogyny by way of excusing it (see *Annotations on "Paradise Lost,"* 239, 269, 286). Moreover, though Zachary Pearce credits Bentley's emendation for 4.299—"Dr. B. is right in reading *God* AND *Him;* and to the proof which be brings add X.150"—he also nullifies the spirit of that emendation in his pointed insistence upon the inequality of the sexes even to the point of suggesting that the "Interlocutory Parts" assigned by Bentley to Adam and Eve in their Morning Hymn should be revised so that what is masculine is articulated by man and what is feminine is spoken by woman—and not vice versa as Bentley would have it (*A Review of the Text of Milton's "Paradise Lost"* [London, 1732], 121, 162).
48. Mary Poovey, *The Proper Lady and the Woman Writer: Ideology as Style in the Works of Mary Wollstonecraft, Mary Shelley, and Jane Austen* (1984; rpt. Chicago: University of Chicago Press, 1985), ix. Poovey is quoting Edwin Hood.
49. Lerner, *Creation of Patriarchy,* 225.
50. See Matthew Poole, *Annotations upon the Holy Bible,* 2 vols. (London, 1683–96), 1, annotation to Genesis 3:1: "A late ingenious and learned Writer represents the matter thus, in which there is nothing absurd or incredible," even if that "Writer" (presumably Milton) produces a discourse that "is not in the Text," his words are to be credited. The prefatory note makes clear that these annotations "do not pretend . . . to translate Mr. Pooles Synopsis *Criticorum* [printed in 4 volumes between 1669 and 1676 and reprinted in 1678]" (1, sig. A3); and, in fact, nothing in *Synopsis critoricum,* 1:31–33, really corresponds with the apparent Miltonic citation in this annotation. The authors should be taken at their word: their annotations are supplementary to Poole's and represent "a new Version of the Scripture" (1, sig. A3), obviously influenced by Milton here and possibly in the annotation for Genesis 1:26.
51. Lerner, *Creation of Patriarchy,* 219, 13, 229.
52. Joan K. Kinnaird, "Mary Astell: Inspired by Ideas," in *Feminist Theorists: Three Centuries of Key Women Thinkers,* ed. Dale Spender (New York: Pantheon, 1983), 29.
53. Michel Foucault, *The History of Sexuality: Volume I. An Introduction,* trans. Robert Hurley (1978; rpt. New York: Random House, Vintage Books, 1980), 17.
54. Mary Shelley, *Frankenstein,* ed. Maurice Hindle (London: Penguin, 1985), 171.
55. See Donald Pease, "Patriarchy, Lentricchia, and Male Feminization," *Critical Inquiry* 14 (1988): 385. Pease's essay is a response to another by Frank Lentricchia who, in turn, responds in agreement with Pease: "Male is not equivalent to patriarchy" ("Andiamo," ibid., 412).
56. Written early (with Milton's First Defense in mind) but published late, Robert Filmer's *Patriarcha: Or The Natural Power of Kings* (London, 1680), is a telling document.
57. William Myers, *Milton and Free Will: An Essay in Criticism and Philosophy* (London: Croom Helm, 1987), 13. The embedded quotation is from John Carey, *Milton* (London: Evans, 1969), 71.
58. Richard Corum, "In White Ink: *Paradise Lost* and Milton's Idea of Women," in Walker, *Milton and the Idea of Woman,* 142.
59. *A Paradox against Life . . . An Heroick Poem* (London, 1681), 5.

# Job's Wife and Sterne's Other Women

MELVYN NEW

> Those who hold the pen—write. Moses was a man. That's why he wrote that a man could have ten wives, but if a woman looked at another man she had to be stoned. If a woman had held the pen she would have written the exact opposite.
>
> I. B. SINGER, *The Magician of Lublin*

IN A RECENT ARTICLE on Sterne's handling of sexual relations in *Tristram Shandy,* Ruth Perry suggests one way in which some "French feminists—Luce Irigaray, Julia Kristeva, and Helene Cixous preeminently—" would have discounted Singer's wry, seemingly evenhanded comment: Convinced by Lacan, they would argue "that the entire symbolic, verbal order is male, no matter who holds the pen. This is how the culture maintains and upholds male privilege at the profoundest level of thought, and disenfranchises female reality." With this conviction in mind, Perry goes on to find *Tristram Shandy* to be "a man's book if ever there was one," which is not too surprising given the fact that Sterne's culture and language ("the very laws of grammar, syntax, and semantics reproduce the patriarchal order") are the same as our own and hence phallocentric.[1]

I would like to disagree with this reading but have difficulty locating a language that is not "phallocentric" and hence not guilty of reproducing those patriarchal (or colonizing) tendencies that Perry so deplores. What I will suggest in this essay, therefore, is simply that when such a new language does come about, Sterne's writings will, I suspect, seem closer to it than will Perry's—or Irigaray's, or Kristeva's. I am not at all certain what literary criticism will sound like in its new language, but here is a typical passage in the old that might serve as a touchstone: "We recognize that Walter is a hopeless intellectualizer, and that he takes refuge from life in endless theorizing, but it is a loved, familiar foible, and we do not read it as callousness about her pain and danger" (Perry, "Words for Sex," 35). What I most respond to in this passage is the voice of authority, telling me what "we recognize," what we "love," and what "we do not read"; it is, in that important sense, a patriarchal reading despite its content.

But Sterne, I suggest, teaches us to read differently. For example, since there is no disputing tastes, and since everything has two handles, a less patriarchal writing of Perry's observations might read: "I think that Walter is a hopeless intellectualizer and resent his taking refuge from life in endless theorizing; nonetheless, I love this familiar foible (though other readers do not and find him both ludicrous and culpable), and I do not think he is callous about her pain and danger (although other readers have taken many pains to demonstrate just how callous he is)." That is to say, I do not so much want to oppose Perry as to suggest a criticism perhaps closer to Sterne's own insights, a criticism that hovers among the alternative readings that books and life and love (the particular subject of the discourse) seem always to offer. More particularly, I would like to read Sterne with two quotations firmly in mind from a book I begin to suspect was as close to his heart as any other, Pierre Charron's *Of Wisdome*.[2] The first sets out the problem: Wisdom consists, Charron writes, of being "free from presumption and obstinacy in opinion; vices very familiar with those that have any extraordinary force and vigor of spirit; and rather to continue in doubt and suspense, especially in things that are doubtfull, and capable of oppositions and reasons on both parts, not easily digested and determined. It is an excellent thing, and the securest way, well to know how to doubt, and to be ignorant" (453). And the second offers a solution, which I take to be the beginning of a nonphallocentric discourse: "Peremptorie affirmation and obstinacie in opinion, are ordinary signes of senslesnesse and ignorance. . . . It were good to learne to use such words as may sweeten and moderate the temeritie of our propositions, as, It may be, It is said, I thinke, It seemeth, and the like" (335).

Sterne was, of course, an astute observer of "obstinacie in opinion," which he often labels "hobby-horsical" behavior; he was also, I would like to suggest, an ardent explorer of alternatives to it, ever resistant to the temptations of absolutism, ever aware as well of the human proclivity to both dominate and succumb. Moreover, as numerous readers have noted, Sterne's exploration most often followed the byways of human sexuality, particularly, as is readily apparent in *Tristram Shandy* and *A Sentimental Journey,* within the institutions of marriage and courtship. In reversing the common sequence of the two (that is, courtship *followed* by marriage), I follow the clue of Sterne's own fictions, which begin in the Shandys' marital bed but end, despite his clerical robes, his enervated condition, and, I suspect, even his own deepest inclinations, with the grotesque *Journal to Eliza* and, at the very last, his hand stretched across the space between two beds, reaching for the end that remains out of sight. I cannot here follow all the stations of Sterne's exploration but will make four separate excursions, each marked by a single exchange of dialogue between a male and female. My aim is not so much to rescue Sterne from Perry's charge of phallocentrism as to suggest he already understood its dangers and was, in his life and writings, exploring ways to rescue himself.

The first exchange, significantly, is one Sterne borrowed from Scripture; it appears in his sermon "Job's Expostulation with His Wife" (2.15) and is taken from Job 2:9–10: "Then said his wife unto him, Dost thou still retain thine integrity? curse God, and die. But he said unto her, Thou speakest as one of the foolish women speaketh. What? Shall we receive good at the hand of God, and shall we not receive evil? In all this did not Job sin with his lips." Insofar as there is any significance to the ordering of Sterne's sermons, "Job's Expostulation" may have an influential place—the final sermon of his first collection, published in two volumes in 1760, just after the overwhelming success of the first two volumes of *Tristram Shandy.* Sterne's thesis is a commonplace one in eighteenth-century Christian apologetics: The Stoic (classical) philosophy fails to answer human needs; only Christianity, in its acceptance of human weakness and in its consolations, is capable of doing so. But what interests me particularly in the exchange between Job and his wife is Sterne's interest in the meanings and motivations behind the exchange—the manner in which meaning eludes the commentator, in which the text, far from imposing an authoritative interpretation, becomes a field for potentialities: "Though it is not very evident, what was particularly meant and implied in the words" of Job's wife, he writes, we can ascertain something from Job's reply to them.[3] The strategy of interpretation is significant, placing the sentence into a dialogue, judging its meaning from the response it elicits. It is, for Sterne, a key to understanding human communication, for always in his fiction meaning is shown to inhere in the space between speaker(s) and auditor(s), a mutual and balanced exchange between two or more voices.

Moreover, the key word in her sentence is thrown into the deepest possible doubt: "On the other hand, some interpreters tell us,—that the word *curse,* in the original, is equivocal, and does more literally signify here, to bless, than to blaspheme" (215). This is not, to be sure, Sterne's own quibble but a commonplace in Scripture commentary, as for example in Matthew Poole's *Annotations upon the Holy Bible:* "But although this word sometimes signifies *cursing* . . . yet most properly and generally it signifies *blessing*, and so it may very well be understood here as a Sarcastical or Ironical Expression."[4] Sterne had read Poole or a similar commentator, for he too talks of considering the sentence "a sarcastical scoff at Job's piety" (216). And once the possibility of interpretation is opened, new alternatives suggest themselves; Sterne, "without disputing the merits of these two interpretations," offers a third, "still different from what is expressed in either of them": "instead of supposing them as an incitement to blaspheme God,——which was madness,——or that they were intended as an insult,——which was unnatural;—that her advice to curse God and die, was meant here, that he should resolve upon a voluntary death himself [that is, suicide]" (216–17). Behind this suggestion, Sterne argues, is the wife's "concern and affection" for Job, her knowledge that "he was a virtuous and an upright man, and deserved a better fate"; indeed, "her heart bled the more for him" (217–18). In short, without forcing one view over another (although his rhetoric cannot help but be swayed by his *new* interpretation), Sterne shifts the moment of scriptural dialogue into a domestic scene, binding husband and wife together in mutual affection and desperation and finding the meaning of their words in the interplay of their feelings. Most particularly, Sterne avoids the temptation to view the wife as a fool ("foolish woman," that is, "The fool hath said in his heart, There is no God" [Ps. 14:1]) or a shrew (the standard, long-standing interpretations),[5] opting instead for an idealized marital context where "concern and affection" dominate.

I would also call attention to the aggressive nature of the wife's advice, as paraphrased by Sterne: "since thou hast met with no justice in this world,—leave it,—die—and force thy passage into a better country" (219). No character in Scripture (excepting Adam and Christ) can be seen as more the innocent victim of brute paternalistic power than Job, whose God allows him to be used as an object in a duel of strength with Satan. Indeed, Job's response to his wife's advice is precisely that of the victim, "receiving" good, "receiving" evil. But in the exchange wrought by "concern and affection" she rejects receptivity for penetration, her "force thy passage" suggesting an active resistance to omnipotence. Job rejects her advice; and, indeed, earlier commentators had linked such advice to the devil, suggesting in no uncertain terms that Eve and Job's wife be read as analogous figures.[6] It is of particular interest, therefore, that Sterne seeks a sympathetic reading of the sentence, understanding the relationship between Job and his wife in the context of domestic regard and the exchange of traditionally assigned roles; it is a pattern we shall see repeated in the fictions.

We cannot date Sermon 15, but without doubt it was written before *Tristram Shandy,* possibly a decade or more earlier. The story of Job is never too far from Sterne's mind, however, when he portrays the Shandy family,[7] and insofar as Walter Shandy is thwarted and tormented in every plan of his life, we might recognize in Elizabeth Shandy a counterpart to Job's wife. The dialogue between the two is one of Sterne's most consistently brilliant feats in the work. For our purposes, we might as well begin with the first exchange as with any other: "*Pray, my dear,* quoth my mother, *have you not forgot to wind up the clock?——Good G—!* cried my father, making an exclamation, but taking care to moderate his voice at the same time,——*Did ever woman, since the creation of the world, interrupt a man with such a silly question?*" (1.1).[8] Critics have often been harsh with Mrs. Shandy, seeing in her portrayal by Sterne a marginalized, dull, and insignificant woman in a fiction about male relations.[9] She is considered, much as Walter considers her, colorless, passive, stupid, long-suffering, and the like. But to consider anyone through Walter's eyes is to consider the world through the eyes of a foolish person, and that itself should alert us to the richer possibilities of Sterne's portrayal. Surely, we need not sympathize with Walter, for example, in his exasperation with Mrs. Shandy's question. Consider, again, the situation: Locked in a marital embrace, Walter brings to bear what is left of his sciatica-weakened loins to the task at hand, while Mrs. Shandy, physically beneath him, has—as in that wonderful scene in Woody Allen's *Annie Hall*—mentally relocated herself to sit by the side of the bed, observing the scene and thinking of other things to be done on Sunday nights. This is not perhaps her failure of sexual appetite but his of performance, and Sterne is shrewd enough to see the relationship between the two often—if not always—in that light.[10] From the many clues of Tristram's illegitimacy that hover over the text, abetted by Mrs. Shandy's own unrelenting hints in that direction,[11] her views of midwives versus Walter's, and her role in child rearing versus the never-to-be-ready *Tristrapaedia,* Sterne seems again and again to give the edge to Mrs. Shandy in wit, perception, intelligence—and *mastery* of the situation. In Sterne's satire of the Shandy household, Mrs. Shandy represents, as much as Yorick, many of the values Sterne holds most dear.

The exchange tells us something more. Behind Mr. Shandy's concern with the interruption is his theory of the Homunculus, a "phallocentric" theory of generation if ever there was one, namely, that the entire child in miniature is in the sperm.[12] Several of Walter's theories can be dismissed as distinctly ludicrous or purposefully anachronistic, as, for example, his embrace of the long-discredited patriarchal politics of Robert Filmer.[13] The animalculist theory, however, was still credible in the 1760s, although under pressure from an opposing school, the ovulists. What is important, therefore, is Sterne's own (nonscientific) skepticism about a theory that, like the legal judgment in the case of the Duchess of Suffolk (4.29.391) that "the mother was not of kin to her child," appears to him patently absurd. What Sterne rejects, I would suggest, is a point of view that argues against his own sense of mutuality in the domestic (procreative but, more significantly, marital) relationship. Walter Shandy's procreating by himself, the image manifest in the opening exchange with Mrs. Shandy, finds analogues throughout the fiction, where separation, isolation, impotence, and finally death everywhere threaten the Shandy males; that the work is comic and, finally, affirmative in its belief that communion and love can be found thriving in this world is, I would suggest, the result of the triumph of a feminist view over the phallocentrism of a goodly portion of the world. No person is more important than Elizabeth Shandy in her embodiment of Sterne's argument against the "singleness" (and "singlemindedness") of the Shandy males.

Still, Mrs. Shandy does not seem to share the affection and care that Sterne sought to find in Job's wife—unless we consider her interest in her children as its manifestation. The marriage itself is, at best, an estranged one, modeled, one is tempted to suggest, upon Sterne's own failed marriage to Elizabeth Lumley.[14] The causes of that failure are captured in this first exchange, which is not an exchange at all; Mrs. Shandy is not responding to Mr. Shandy, and his retort clearly does not answer her question. More important, his effort to bring the moment to its necessary (for him) conclusion, his desire to impregnate his wife in a powerful and possessive gesture, is defeated on two counts. First, Mrs. Shandy's interruption scatters and disperses the animal spirits; and, second, we have at least the suspicion planted that his seed falls not on barren but on occupied ground and hence falls sterile. If Tristram's eight-month birth is in reason as much as any husband can expect (1.5.8), we nevertheless must leave some room for a nine-month gestation; if Mrs. Shandy is already pregnant, Mr. Shandy's efforts are obviously as untimely as his later work on the *Tristrapaedia*—and as futile.

I have elsewhere argued that the energy of *Tristram Shandy* lies in its capacity to interrupt itself with additional material, to prevent itself from concluding.[15] Mrs. Shandy might be said to embody that spirit of interruption, digression, incompleteness—of suspense, in Charron's sense of the word. Her body in one place, her mind in another, she captures the true Shandy spirit that refuses to reduce oneself or one's world to a single hypothesis. Further, as Sterne sought his digressive energy in the work of others—and found as well an anxiety of emulation in his desire to keep up with the digressive likes of Rabelais and Burton, Cervantes and Montaigne—so Mrs. Shandy has possibly been preinscribed, though more to Mr. Shandy's anxiety than her own. Indeed, she may be said to embody in two distinct ways the digressive spirit of *Tristram Shandy;* and insofar as she does give birth to a son named Tristram in the course of the fiction, she must be said to have generated the work. Or, put another way, Walter's urge to drive toward his conclusion, Tristram's straight line at the end of volume 6 ("The *best line!* say cabbage-planters" [6.40.572]),[16] and Toby's inclination to show Mrs. Wadman the very place—on the map—are all projections of male failure in the Shandy household; Mrs. Shandy's interruption is the fertile moment out of which Sterne's entire fiction will emerge.

This reading of the opening scene of *Tristram Shandy* is constructed on a fiction I would like to call momentarily into question, namely, that a text trying to close itself is "male," where a text striving to remain open is "female." There is a question of appropriation here that perhaps underlies this entire collection of essays, for one should be wary of a thesis that turns Rabelais, Cervantes, Montaigne, Burton, and Sterne, that is, the entire satiric or Menippean tradition, into "feminist" writing. What seems to have happened is that we discovered *first* that certain forms of nonnovelistic fiction also had literary interest, indeed, as much interest perhaps as the so-called realistic novel, which modern critics inherited as the *type* against which to measure all long narratives; and, *then,* in a shrewd political gesture, the heretofore marginalized forms were appropriated by the heretofore marginalized readers (women, blacks, postmodernists, lovers of Sterne as opposed to lovers of Fielding) as the genres of their own voices. Such a scheme is bound to be questioned by a rectifying fiction in the near future. In the meantime, however, one clue remains in the opening dialogue of *Tristram* that might enable us to accept our present paradigm for the nonce with only a few additional qualms. *Tristram Shandy* is a book about human truths, and perhaps the single most evident truth of its world is that male and female have different shapes; surely no other work readily comes to mind with more slits, cracks, crevices, buttonholes and keyholes, on the one hand, or more sticks, fingers, noses, and artillery on the other. This, in turn, establishes one clear dichotomy, even in a world that resists the simplicities of dichotomous thinking: The act of penetration differs from the act of reception. But if we return to Job's wife for a moment, recall my suggestion that her advice was to penetrate (to force a passage), Job's response to remain receptive to "good" and "evil." In *Tristram* also, the physical structures seem to be deceptive. Mr. Shandy, "penetrating" his Mrs. Shandy, cannot overpower her mind or possess her body; she remains unpossessed, un-"penetrated," by his desires. Conversely, she is clearly not receptive, despite the fact that he is "in" her. His drive toward completion is met with digression, his theory scattered and dispersed upon the shoals of Mrs. Shandy's otherness. What I would like to suggest, most tentatively, is that in this incompatibility might be found the seeds for two of the fictions by which we image forth the world—the one, Walter's fiction, phallocentrism, which overpowers the world with ideas, the other, Elizabeth's fiction, which undercuts ideas with the world. Insofar as *Tristram Shandy* is a work of the second order, Mrs. Shandy, a true skeptic (satirist?), is its creator.

But of course Sterne wrote the work, and somewhere in the course of his writing he seems to have become fascinated with the idea that the fundamental incompatibility examined in the Shandy household had to be resolved into a better union of male and female, one that would, after the last volume of *Tristram* appeared, address Sterne's own pressing anxieties: his bad health, his domestic unhappiness, his dubious salvation. His first excursion during the final year of his life was a desperate flirtation with a married woman thirty years younger than he. We know about Eliza Draper primarily through Sterne's letters to her and the portion of his "Journal to Eliza" that he did not send to her.[17] His second, and far more successful excursion is the aptly named last fiction of his life, *A Sentimental Journey;* in that work, Sterne captures, if only intermittently, a sexual dialogue at one and the same time genderless and procreative and, above all, acceptable to Grace.

The "Journal to Eliza" is in the shape of a dialogue with one voice: "wrote the last farewel to Eliza by M^r^ Wats who sails this day for Bombay—inclosed her likewise the Journal kept from the day we parted, to this—so from hence continue it till the time we meet again—Eliza does the same, so we shall have mutual testimonies to deliver hereafter to each other" (135). The motif of mutual journal keeping is depressingly obsessional as the journal continues; for example:

> *April 16:* I shall read the same affecting Account of many a sad Dinner which Eliza has had no power to taste of. [137]

> *May 13:* Surely 'tis not impossible, but [I] may be made happy as my Eliza, by so[me] transcript from her . . . we taste not of it *now,* my dear Bramine[18]—but we will make full meals upon it hereafter. [152]

> *June 2:* By this time, I trust You have doubled the Cape of good hope—and sat down to your writing Drawer, and look'd in Yoricks face, as you took out your Journal; to tell him so. [157]

> *June 15:* Mark!—you will dream of me this night—and if it is not recorded in your Journal—Ill say, you could not recollect it the day following. [165]

> *June 21:* I long to see [your journal]—I shall read it a thousand times over If I get it before your Arrival—What would I now give for it—tho' I know there are *circumstances* in it, That will make my heart bleed. [168]

And, finally,

> *July 7:* I can see and hear nothing but my Eliza. remember this, when You think my Journal too short, and compare it not with thine, which tho' it will exceed it in length, can do no more than equal it in Love. [179]

We have here a dialogue with an imaginary correspondent, wished into being by the author's own desire. Far more accurate a perception of the relationship is perhaps supplied by Sterne's depressing assessment of June 30:

> I have wrote [a mutual friend] a whole Sheet of paper about us—it ought to have been copied into this Journal—but the uncertainty of your ever reading it, makes me omit that . . . which when we meet, shall beguile us of many a long winters night.—*those precious Nights!*—my Eliza!—You rate them as high as I do. . . . They are all that remains to us—except the *Expectation* of their return—the Space between is a dismal Void—full of doubts, and suspence. [173]

The desire for correspondence is double-edged in Sterne's journal. On the one hand, he wants to bridge the empty space between himself and Eliza, between male and female, with a language that nourishes and heals—and we must remember that Sterne's entries are replete with accounts of his decrepitude at this time.[19] On the other hand, the correspondence he seeks has at least as much to do with reflecting himself as with reaching another (or, indeed, being reached by another)—as he writes his journal, he must see Eliza at her desk writing hers. Indeed, the many references to sensibility and sentiment, sympathy and pathos in the "Journal" all appear to come from this single urge, to find in another human being one's own self:

> I want You to be on the other side of my little table, to hear how sweetly your Voice will be in Unison to all this—I want to hear what You have to say to Your Yorick upon this Text. . . . how pathetically you would enforce your Truth and Love upon my heart to free it from every Aching doubt—Doubt! did I say—but I have none—and as soon would I doubt the Scripture I have preach'd on.

The burden of the "correspondence" then, is enormous: "for if thou art false, my Bramine—the whole world—and Nature itself are lyars" (175). Sterne has, it seems to me, trapped himself in the very toils he had set for Walter Shandy. Driven by sickness, by a painful estrangement from his wife and daughter, by what he almost certainly feared, his impending death and judgment, the "Journal to Eliza" is a fabric of lies designed to keep reality at a comfortable distance. And the cornerstone of the fabric is the lie of possession, of knowing—the core of the Shandy males' failure and of Sterne's sad failure here: "leave [my expressions of doubt] as a part of the picture of a heart that *again* Languishes for Possession—and is disturbed at every Idea of its Uncertainty" (175). Behind the sentimentalism of the "Journal," behind its language of feeling and sympathy and suffering,[20] behind even its empowering of Eliza as both his God ("all powerful Eliza" [179]) and his alter ego ("I resemble no Being in the world so nearly as I do You" [161]), is a desperate push for power, the need to triumph over, to gain control of, his own sickness and death. The cost—his familial relations, his accurate perception of reality, his inevitable disappointment—is inconsequential in the face of his need to dominate, and the journal plunges blindly forward in its self-deceptions for four months. As the "space" between them widens, in time and in distance, the idea of possession becomes more and more obsessional: "and in proportion as I am thus torn from your embraces—*I cling the closer to the Idea of you,*" he writes on July 7 (178). It is, I would suggest, Sterne's lowest point.

As with many forms of obsessional behavior, one cure appears to be the granting of what the patient most believes he desires. On July 27 Eliza's "dear Packets" arrive from over the seas, and Sterne spends the evening and the next day, until dinner, reading "over and over again the most interesting Account—and the most endearing one, that ever tried the tenderness of man" (185). Five entries later, Sterne ended the "Journal to Eliza."[21] Eliza's "Journal," we must suspect, could not sustain the fiction he had created; whatever else Eliza Draper was, she was not "up to the ears" in love with Sterne as he had forced himself to believe, was not anguishing over her loss as he had convinced himself he was anguishing (as in a mirror) over his, was not, in short, penetrated by his own desires or possessed by his own imaginings. The silence into which Sterne wrote from April through July was a sustaining space; Eliza's interruption of that silence scatters and disperses Sterne's animal spirits, and he wisely withdraws to a far more fertile field, his own art, in order to complete *A Sentimental Journey.*

One would tend to think rather badly of Sterne for his "Journal to Eliza" (though not, I hope, for the "moral" reasons of Thackeray),[22] did we not know he was writing it simultaneously with the *Journey,* a work that seems in important points to reverse the course of his "dialogue" with Eliza, returning Sterne to the sustainable insights of his view of Job's wife and of Mrs. Shandy. The final exchange I will discuss occurs in a chapter appropriately entitled "The Translation." Though it is apparent from the chapter and the one following that the title refers to the "translating" of nonverbal gestures into verbal statements, I would suggest, as well, that Sterne is interested here in "translating" a discourse of opposition and cross-purpose into one that promises, through correspondence, the creative harmony of a peace that accepts difference. Beyond that, Sterne is also "translating" sentimental expressions of that harmony (the eighteenth-century gambit he was simultaneously using unsuccessfully in the "Journal to Eliza") into a language more appropriate to human beings in whom "nature has so wove her web of kindness, that some threads of love and desire are entangled with the piece."[23]

"Upon my word, Madame, said I when I had handed her in [to her carriage], I made six different efforts to let you go out—And I made six efforts, replied she, to let you enter" (173). The scene is the doorway to a concert in Milan, where Yorick encounters the Marquesina di F***,[24] as she attempts to exit. The situation is one we have all experienced: "she was almost upon me before I saw her; so I gave a spring to one side to let her pass—She had done the same, and on the same side too; so we ran our heads together: she instantly got to the other side to get out: I was just as unfortunate as she had been; for I had sprung to that side, and opposed her passage again—We both flew together to the other side, and then back—and so on—it was ridiculous" (172). The beautifully matched dance stops when Yorick stands still and allows the Marquesina to pass, after which he follows her to her carriage to apologize in the exchange quoted above. The dialogue continues: "I wish to heaven you would make a seventh, said I—With all my heart, said she, making room." The chapter then concludes with Yorick's assertion that "the connection which arose out of that translation" afforded him more pleasure than any other he made in Italy.

In a work replete with unrealized flirtations, the "connection" is a moment of fulfillment unique in the *Journey* in its implicit actualization. It is noteworthy, therefore, that it takes place in a portion of Yorick's journey that remained "unwritten," namely, the journey to Italy. Perhaps it is a projection of the fulfillment to be achieved at journey's end, after all has been learned and experienced; or perhaps, more subtly, it suggests that "connection" must always be that portion of our journey that remains unverbalized, unwritten. What is most apparent is that Sterne finds a moment of absolute harmony in the stasis he portrays as a silent dance which brings about the exchange of gender-oriented responses. Yorick, forgoing his attempts to control the exchange, does "the thing I should have done at first—I stood stock still" (172). The Marquesina, seizing the opportunity, penetrates the space between the two and passes through. Only then does Yorick resume the aggressor role, pursuing her down the passageway, but his pursuit ends in the stasis of the dialogue under discussion, mirroring the earlier static dance in its neatly balanced arrangement of "six different efforts," and the highly charged play on "letting in" and "letting out." I would like to suggest that in this wonderful dialogue Sterne has found an analogy for Charron's wisdom: "It were good to learne to use such words as may sweeten and moderate the temeritie of our propositions, as, It may be, It is said, I thinke, It seemeth, and the like" (335).

In the chapter just prior to this one, entitled "The Gloves," we have a very similar exchange—so similar, indeed, that the juxtaposition of the two chapters, otherwise unrelated, appears to my mind quite purposeful. The scene is one in which Sterne's insistence upon human sexuality undercuts his age's attempt to mask desire with the language of sentiment. In the *grisset*'s shop, Yorick is fitted for a pair of gloves, a scene of the utmost delicacy, the feeling of the *grisset*'s pulse, and of the utmost sexuality, insofar as the fitting of a glove is yet one more trope for sexual union. But this time, Sterne gives us a hint of completion, one that significantly sets language aside:

> There are certain combined looks of simple subtlety—where whim, and sense, and seriousness, and nonsense, are so blended, that all the languages of Babel set loose together could not express them—they are communicated and caught so instantaneously, that you can scarce say which party is the infecter.
>
> . . . she had a quick black eye, and shot through two such long and silken eye-lashes with such penetration, that she look'd into my very heart and reins. [168–69]

The nonverbal gesture, which Sterne uses so successfully in *Tristram Shandy* to allow Walter and Toby to bridge some of their mental and emotional gaps, is here made a viable path between the baffling conflicts of the self and the elusive intentions of the other. Most significantly, this movement from self to other is imaged first as a silent sexual balance, much like the stasis before the concert door ("which party is the infecter?"),[25] followed by the male surrender of aggression (pursuit) to the female who "penetrates" his reins. Perhaps Sterne's major insight into the nature of human desire is the idea that the most satisfying human harmony is achieved when the female penetrates and the male receives. I would prefer to believe that, with the model of Christian love constantly before him in his clerical role, Sterne could perceive the genderless potentiality of this exchange: Christ the incarnate God could enter us, male and female both; and male and female both could receive Christ; and I particularly lean toward this view because the strong sexuality of the passage is so much more in tune with traditional Christian belief (including the belief that man is born into a body) than with the secular sentimentality that was replacing it.[26] But even if we cannot accept the idea that Christianity provided Sterne's answer to male–female relationships, it does seem evident that sometime during the course of his own married and "unmarried" life—and perhaps most poignantly in his encounter with Eliza—Sterne came to value both the moments of "stasis" when male and female "correspond" fully with one another and the subsequent moments of "exchange," in which self and other become a creative (procreative) whole.

The problem of entering into, penetrating the other, the problem of knowledge, holds Sterne's attention throughout the middle of *A Sentimental Journey.* Of particular significance for unraveling Sterne's commentary on the Age of Sentimentality are the chapters concerned with a caged starling, a bird the Sterne family used on its coat of arms, identifying its dialectical rendition *starn* with Sterne.[27] Yorick "translates" the bird's song as "I can't get out," but for Sterne the exercise of translation, no matter how energetically pursued, is often nothing more than words, "sentiment . . . sans amour." Significantly, Yorick replays the encounter with the Marquesina; the bird cannot "get out," and Yorick, try as he might imaginatively to enter into the bird's captivity, cannot "get in": "I could not sustain the picture of confinement which my fancy had drawn" (203). The bird is passed from hand to hand but is never freed, for the roles remain always the same: "all these [the owners] wanted to *get in*—and my bird wanted to get out" (205). This failure is more than a failure of imagination; insofar as Yorick's efforts to identify with the starling are conscious and aggressive (filled as they are with English Francophobia), they are diametrically opposed to the exchange of roles that Sterne finds necessary for true penetration and connection. Until the bird is allowed to leave the cage and Yorick can enter it, Sterne sees no communication taking place, despite the emphasis his contemporaries placed on moral sensibility and empathic understanding. There are actions missing here—the freeing of the bird, the entering into captivity—that no intensity of sentiment, no virtuosity of language can replace. Sterne's interest is focused on the nature of that action, the paradoxical passivity that seems its necessary concomitant, and the transfer of (sexual) identity that is achieved at the moment of fulfillment.

A more successful encounter occurs in the closing pages of *A Sentimental Journey,* in Yorick's penultimate encounter with a woman, the lovesick Maria. The scene revisits an earlier portrayal in *Tristram Shandy,* and the gesture of reinvention is an important one. Here, at the end of his life, with his wife and daughter permanently separated from him, with Eliza an ocean apart from him, literally and figuratively, Sterne rewrites male–female relations in a manner at once self-justifying and self-condemning; he writes, in short, as a man about to be held accountable for his conduct before a higher tribunal than this world can offer. Nowhere in his previous writing does Sterne come closer to portraying a workable union of desire and language than in this second encounter with Maria. As he weeps with her in mirrored, balanced actions ("Maria let me wipe them [her tears] away . . . with my handkerchief.—I then steep'd it in my own—and then in hers—and then in mine—and then I wip'd hers again"), he discovers in a convincing manner the strongest sense of identity, not with Maria but with himself: He discovers the existence of his soul.

> I felt such undescribable emotions within me, as I am sure could not be accounted for from any combination of matter and motion.
>
> I am positive I have a soul; nor can all the books with which materialists have pester'd the world ever convince me of the contrary. [271]

The feeling, significantly, is not free from sexual desire.[28] Yorick's description of Maria is really the first time he "sees" the woman he is with as a physical being rather than a sentimental construct:

> Maria, tho' not tall, was nevertheless of the first order of fine forms—affliction had touch'd her looks with something that was scarce earthly—still she was feminine—and so much was there about her of all that the heart wishes, or the eye looks for in woman, that could the traces be ever worn out of her brain . . . she should *not only eat of my bread and drink of my own cup,* but Maria should lay in my bosom, and be unto me as a daughter. [275][29]

The last part of the passage paraphrases Nathan's parable of the poor man's ewe lamb (2 Sam. 12:3), which is cared for as Yorick vows to care for Maria; the source alerts us to the fact that not only should we not burden "as a daughter" with complex interpretation but also that it is a moment of legitimate insight on Yorick's part. Nathan uses the parable to recall to David his sin of taking Bathsheba from Uriah, David being Sterne's favorite example of the stern moralist who is severe to other sinners but blind to his own transgressions. As such, the biblical allusion reminds us again of the question of identity; as David is forced to acknowledge his desire (and his sinfulness), so Yorick, finally, comes to an honest acceptance of his own desires—free from sentiment, from deception, from innuendo, from repression.

It is within this context of a hard-won embrace of the complex nature of man, a compounded creature, that Yorick's famous apostrophe to sensibility in the next chapter might best be understood. It has often marked Sterne as the foremost sentimentalist of a sentimental age, often been used to suggest Sterne's celebration of the "heart" over all else. But coming late as it does in the *Journey,* its context is the exploration that has preceded it of sensibility's relation to desire, and in this context we understand "sensibility" as that particular capacity which makes love possible: the awareness of the wholeness of the human experience, including both the exchange of sexual roles, aggressor and recipient, active and passive, and the knowledge that sensibility is not limited to those stirrings we can accept with clean hands and uplifted hearts:

> —Dear sensibility! source inexhausted of all that's precious in our joys, or costly in our sorrows! thou chainest thy martyr down upon his bed of straw—and 'tis thou who lifts him up to HEAVEN—eternal fountain of our feelings! . . . all comes from thee, great—great SENSORIUM of the world! which vibrates, if a hair of our heads but falls upon the ground, in the remotest desert of thy creation. [277–78]

Yorick's prayer is an assertion of providence (Matt. 10:29–31), God's continuing hand in human affairs despite the Fall, despite the intricate web of good and evil that human life has become, despite even, perhaps, the phallocentric nature of postlapsarian language and society. Yorick's prayer is a *humble* assertion of faith.[30]

And faith is answered by "Grace," the penultimate chapter of everything Sterne ever wrote. Tristram had found a similar moment of communion in the peasant dance at the end of his tour through France, although the moment is tainted by repressed desire, Nannette's "cursed slit" in her petticoat (7.43.649–51). Nothing interferes, however, with Yorick's appreciation of this moment. In harmony at last with himself, he is able to be in harmony with others. The beautiful assertion that he beholds "*Religion* mixing in the dance" (284) is an insight gained through travel and loneliness and, perhaps we should add, glancing at Sterne's biography again, the impending threat of death, which renders the need for human connection all the more intense and necessary. Importantly, the "grace" is not spoken but acted out; but equally important, Yorick is able to find the words to express the joy of the dance without equivocation or innuendo. The distance between Tristram and Yorick at this point is the measure of the spiritual peace Sterne found in *A Sentimental Journey;* and the distance between the Sterne of the *Journey* and of the "Journal to Eliza" is his awareness and acceptance that the moment of "Grace," of insight, of possession, of knowing something, anything, for certain, is ultimately no more than a moment in the rush of life. Tristram flees from insight, Walter Shandy chokes it to death; Yorick is simply unable to sustain it, which, in a fallen world, is man's natural relationship to grace.[31] And so the "Case of Delicacy" is the final chapter, reminding us that the quest is as long as life itself, that however else we may recall Yorick, recall any human life, including our own, it is also the portrait of a person forever reaching across the void for the person (the knowledge) on the other side.[32] Insight, love, wholeness, grace, all are possible for the human being in this model, but none permanently. What is permanent is the difficulty of living with impermanence, the intense desire to possess completely and forever that which we hope will afford a moment's insight or a moment's pleasure; and insofar as that difficulty and that desire encourage our surrender to the twin aggressions of absolutism and order in the face of life's complexity (and joy), Sterne would seem to be urging us (and himself) to seek a better solution.

It is in this manner that I think Sterne initiates a feminist discourse, if that is what stands in opposition to the phallocentric one. But even in this last moment, Sterne might teach us something more, for both "feminist" and "phallocentric" are already words so loaded with human passions that they recall nothing so much as Walter's faith in names and Tristram's insistence that "noses" mean only "noses." One of Sterne's richest insights, I believe, is that only by eschewing naming and the expectations of order and domination that naming entails do we ever achieve—however tenuously—the creative unions and correspondences, the communications and intercourses, which at fortuitous moments arrest us in a lifetime of otherwise vain pursuits. One age might label his attitude antirationalistic, another might call it fideistic skepticism, a third might simply point to the New Testament (see, e.g., 1 Cor. 13), and a fourth might retreat further, perhaps to Job: "For we are but of yesterday, and know nothing, because our days upon earth are a shadow" (8:9). In the last fifteen years, this Socratic (Nietzschean) assault on authority and certainty has become the privileged discourse of "feminist" thinking. While one must admire the political (and, I hope, moral) astuteness that seizes so defensible a high ground as its own, it seems rather dubious that the label will long stick to the stance, if only because the individual human mind seems unable to rest in uncertainties and drives always to empower itself—to speak in phallocentric terms even while condemning them, indeed, in order to condemn them. Sterne seems able to point us toward another language, but our difficulty in ever learning to speak it is suggested by our inability to escape Walter's "logic": Were a young boy to be named Judas, he would be forever ruined. When we can argue ourselves out of an "obstinacie in opinion" such as that, a new discourse will have begun.

## Notes

1. Ruth Perry, "Words for Sex: The Verbal-Sexual Continuum in *Tristram Shandy*," *Studies in the Novel* 20 (1988): 29.
2. Charron wrote in French, *De la sagesse*, translated as *Of Wisdome* by Samson Lennard in ?1612. Sterne definitely quotes from the work at the very end of *Tristram Shandy*, as first pointed out in Françoise Pellan, "Laurence Sterne's Indebtedness to Charron," *MLR* 67 (1972): 752–55. The editors of the *Notes* to *Tristram Shandy* (3 of the Florida Edition, ed. Melvyn New, with Richard A. Davies and W. G. Day [Gainesville: University Presses of Florida, 1984]), point as well to Charron's possible influence in the opening pages (3:39–40). Charron is basically a compiler and organizer of Montaigne's thoughts; *Of Wisdome* is a rich compendium of the ideas of Renaissance Christian skepticism, one vital strand of which is woven into the quotations offered. It is as well, I suspect, a more important book for Sterne than we have yet fully realized.
3. Laurence Sterne, *The Sermons of Mr. Yorick* (London, 1760), 2:213–14; hereafter cited in text.
4. Matthew Poole, *Annotations upon the Holy Bible* (London, 1688), s.v. Job 2:9–10.
5. Here, for example, is William Warburton's commentary in *The Divine Legation of Moses*, 6:2: "Let us take her, as she is presented to us, on the common footing. She acts a short part indeed, but a very spirited one. [Quotes Job 2:9.] Tender and pious! He might see, by this prelude of his Spouse, what he was to expect from his Friends. The Devil indeed assaulted Job, but he seems to have got possession of his Wife. Happiness was so little to be expected with such a Woman, that one almost wonders, that the sacred Writer, when he aims to give us the highest idea of Job's succeeding felicity, did not tell us, in express words, that he lived to bury his Wife." Several pages later he calls her Satan's agent. (*The Works* [London, 1788; rpt. ed., Georg Olms, 1978], 3:277, 279). For an account of the

complex relationship between Warburton and Sterne, see Melvyn New, "Sterne, Warburton, and the Burden of Exuberant Wit," *ECS* 15 (1982): 245–74.

6. In addition to the passage from Warburton quoted in n. 5, see, e.g., John Mayer, *A Commentary upon the Holy Writings of Job, David, and Solomon* . . . (London, 1653), s.v. Job 2:9: "It may seem strang[e], that when all his Children perished, that his Wife was preserved still alive. . . . the most common received opinion was, that Satan spared her, that by her he might be yet further tempted to curse God. . . . And this seemeth most probable." Sterne's distance from this sort of thinking is well worth complimenting.
7. See Everett Zimmerman, "*Tristram Shandy* and Narrative Representation," *Eighteenth Century: Theory and Interpretation* 28 (1987): 131–33.
8. Quoted from *The Life and Opinions of Tristram Shandy, Gentleman,* ed. Melvyn New and Joan New (Gainesville: University Presses of Florida, 1978), 1:2; hereafter cited in text.
9. James A. Work shaped a generation's attitude toward Mrs. Shandy with his comments in his introduction to his popular textbook edition of *Tristram:* "My mother indeed, though she appears rarely, says little, and has 'no character at all,' is one of the most delightful of Sterne's creations. . . . she is chiefly notable for her inability—or lack of desire—to say anything for herself. And in her placid, vegetal existence, which is itself a bathetic commentary on the practical value of his [Mr. Shandy's] fine theorizing, she . . . acts as a foil to my father" ([New York: Odyssey Press, 1940], lvi–lvii). Work was perhaps thinking to praise Mrs. Shandy, but "placid" and "vegetal" are not useful words for that purpose.

   A useful corrective to this view is an essay by Leigh A. Ehlers, "Mrs. Shandy's 'Lint and Basilicon': The Importance of Women in *Tristram Shandy,*" *SAR* 46 (1981): 61–75. See also the interesting comments on Mrs. Shandy in James Swearingen, *Reflexivity in "Tristram Shandy": An Essay in Phenomenological Criticism* (New Haven: Yale University Press, 1977), 221–26. Perry appreciates Ehlers's essay but dismisses it as a "humanistic interpretation" (Perry, "Words for Sex," 30); she does not mention Swearingen.

   A spirited and convincing defense of Mrs. Shandy is in Helen Ostovich, "Reader as Hobby-horse in *Tristram Shandy,*" *PQ* 68 (1989): 325–42. I served as a referee for this essay and when rereading it in print became aware of its influence on my present comments, although I had not retained a copy.
10. Cf. Ian Watt's comment on the scene in the introduction to his edition: "if Pavlov's dog could have talked, it would, under similar circumstances, no doubt have echoed Mrs. Shandy's words" ([Boston: Houghton Mifflin, 1965], xiii). The remark seems to me unfair, as does Watt's equation of Mr. Shandy's "complete intellectual and emotional impasse with his wife" with Sterne's own difficulties with Mrs. Sterne (xii). What interests me most particularly, in fact, is that Sterne seems to associate Walter Shandy with Elizabeth Sterne's failings, his own position with that of Mrs. Shandy; see below, n. 14.
11. See New, *Notes,* 3:51–52, n. to 8.1–3. My own favorite hint is that given in an exchange between husband and wife in one of their beds of justice:

    > But indeed he is growing a very tall lad,—rejoined my father.
    > ——He is very tall for his age, indeed,—said my mother.——
    > ——I can not (making two syllables of it) imagine, quoth my father, who the duce he takes after.——
    > I cannot conceive, for my life,—said my mother.———
    > Humph!——said my father. [6.18.526–27].

    Mrs. Shandy's triumph seems to me splendidly obvious.
12. New, *Notes,* 3:44, n. to 2.19 ff. For a full discussion, see Louis A. Landa, "The Shandean Homunculus: The Background of Sterne's 'Little Gentleman,'" in *Restoration and Eighteenth-Century Literature: Essays in Honor of A. D. McKillop* (Chicago: University of Chicago Press, 1963), 49–68.
13. New, *Notes,* 3:378, n. to 466.1 ff. Of particular interest to us here is the debate between

Filmer and Locke perhaps being alluded to in Trim's recitation of his catechism. Filmer had based his argument in favor of patriarchy in part on the fifth commandment's injunction to honor one's father; Locke chided him in *Two Treatises of Government* with the reminder that the text reads, Honor thy father *and* mother.

14. See Arthur H. Cash, *Laurence Sterne: The Early and Middle Years* (London: Methuen, 1975), 78–86 and passim. Cash records the evidence of Elizabeth Montagu, the famous bluestocking who was Mrs. Sterne's cousin: "She was always taking frump at somebody & forever in quarrels & frabbles." And again: "M[rs] Sterne is a Woman of great integrity & has many virtues, but they stand like quills upon the fretfull porcupine, ready to go forth in sharp arrows on y[e] least supposed offense; . . . the only way to avoid a quarrel with her is to keep a due distance" (84). How very much more like *Walter* than *Elizabeth* Shandy does she sound!
15. In New, "Sterne, Warburton."
16. See New, *Notes,* 3:442, n. to 572.6, for the possible sexual overtones of "planting cabbages."
17. The most readily available edition of the "Journal to Eliza" is that by Ian Jack (with *A Sentimental Journey*), for the Oxford English Novels series (London: Oxford University Press, 1968), and I have quoted it in my text. However, Lewis Perry Curtis's reprinting of the "Journal" in *Letters* (Oxford: Oxford University Press, 1935) should also be consulted. The full details of the relationship are sensitively dealt with by Arthur Cash in chapter 7 of *Laurence Sterne: The Later Years* (London: Methuen, 1986), 268–304. An earlier portion of the journal that Sterne actually sent to Eliza has been lost; and none of her writings to him has survived.
18. Apparently, Eliza called Sterne Bramin and he responded, typically enough, with a feminized version, Bramine.
19. Cash, *Later Years,* 288–91 and passim.
20. I can agree with Eve Kosofsky Sedgwick's analysis of sentimentalism ("this warm space of pathos and the personal") as a "complicated male strategy for . . . empowerment," though I believe the description is far more apropos of the "Journal to Eliza" than of *A Sentimental Journey,* which she analyzes without much regard for Sterne's humor, irony, or self-correcting, self-reflective language; see *Between Men: English Literature and Male Homosocial Desire* (New York: Columbia University Press, 1985), 67–82. Sedgwick seems to believe that, if she does not proceed in a "churlish, literal-minded" manner, the work proves too seductive; that it is Sterne's good sense that seduces her is an idea she does not readily entertain. Interestingly, she does not seem to have read the "Journal" or anything else by or about Sterne, which may be the reason her reading of the *Journey* strikes me as so thesis-dominated, so self-assured, and so possessive of the text. In short, her criticism is "imperialism with a baby face," as she rather accurately labels sentimentalism; a phallocentric discourse, in Perry's vocabulary.
21. Cf. Cash, *Later Years,* 302: "Eliza had done as Sterne had urged: she had written unstintingly about her illnesses—'rhumatism,' 'fever,' 'fits,' 'Delirium.' He copied some of her description for Anne James [Curtis, *Letters,* 388]. Certainly he felt much sympathy. But he had not found in her letters what he longed to see, a declaration of her love for him." Cash convincingly demonstrates that only three of the last five entries were written immediately after July 27; of the remaining two, the one dated August 4 was probably written at the end of September and then predated; and the final entry, November 1, is Sterne's closure to the "Journal." It laments: "—And now Eliza! Let me talk to thee—But What can I say, What can I write" (188).
22. See Cash, *Later Years,* 284, n. 68.
23. Laurence Sterne, *A Sentimental Journey,* ed. Gardner D. Stout (Berkeley: University of California Press, 1967), 237; hereafter cited in text.
24. Some attempt was made to identify the Marquesina with a real person, one Marchesa Fagnani, but as Cash notes, "the identification is doubtful" (*Later Years,* 235); see also

Stout's discussion of the episode (*Journey*, 343–44). Any encounter in the pages of Sterne with a woman whose name is indicated by an *F* followed by three asterisks ought to raise a healthy suspicion.

25. In this chapter, as in "The Translation," the emphasis is everywhere on the balanced, mirroring, dancelike actions of the couple; e.g., "She begg'd I would try a single pair, which seemed to be the least—She held it open—my hand slipp'd into it at once—It will not do, said I, shaking my head a little—No, said she, doing the same thing"; and again: "The beautiful Grisset look'd sometimes at the gloves, then side-ways to the window, then at the gloves—and then at me. I was not disposed to break silence—I follow'd her example: so I look'd at the gloves, then to the window, then at the gloves, and then at her—and so on alternately" (168). As we shall see, the same alternation is created in the description of the meeting with Maria.
26. A fine recent essay making this point is Donald R. Wehrs, "Sterne, Cervantes, Montaigne: Fideistic Skepticism and the Rhetoric of Desire," *CLS* 25 (1988): 127–51. Wehrs anticipates the conclusion of my own reading when he writes: "Like Lacan, [Sterne] views desire as inherently unfulfillable; it projects a narrative course that is necessarily open-ended. However, Sterne suggests that the narrative of desire need not simply substitute, digressively, one metaphoric deferral of fulfillment for another. . . . Instead, his work is 'digressive, and it is progressive too,—and at the same time' [*TS*, 81] because the narrative of desire leads to a skeptical suspense that opens the way for a faith through which the partiality of every earthly fulfillment becomes tolerable" (141). And again: "Sterne discerns the trace of divine benevolence behind the perpetual suspension of certainty and the open-ended narratives of desire such suspensions establish" (131). Wehrs's essay appeared simultaneously with my essay, "Proust's Influence on Sterne: Remembrance of Things to Come," *MLN* 103 (1988): 1032–55, which coincides with his on many points.
27. See Stout, *Journey*, 205–6.
28. Cf. Joseph Chadwick, "Infinite Jest: Interpretation in Sterne's *A Sentimental Journey*," *ECS* 12 (1978–79): 194: "Yorick's rhetoric here mixes sentimental with sexual admiration. . . . we cannot define Yorick's interest in Maria as purely sentimental or purely sexual." See also Arnold E. Davidson and Cathy N. Davidson, "Yorick contra Hobbes: Comic Synthesis in Sterne's *A Sentimental Journey*," *Centennial Review* 21 (1977): 282–93, esp. the discussion of Maria, 288–90.
29. Cf. "Journal to Eliza," 184, where Sterne talks of reposing "all his Cares" and melting "them *along with hers* in her sympathetic bosom." The transfer of the nurturing function from Eliza in the "Journal" to Yorick in the *Journey* is noteworthy.
30. This present reading of *A Sentimental Journey* is derived from my essay, "Proust's Influence on Sterne." To that essay I added a "Post Postscript" in defense of my Christian troping, applicable, I suspect, for this essay as well. That I introduce a Christian vocabulary, just at that point where I should be introducing the radical new language that eschews phallocentrism, will surely puzzle and disappoint. That is, however, the lesson of the exercise, for the reading I am trying to achieve in both essays is one that does not drive forward to inevitable conclusions; does not read Sterne within our own institutional biases (we cannot escape ideology, but we might make some small efforts to discomfort monolithic academic bandwagons); and, in short, a reading that does not make Sterne "one of us." To my mind, any truly new mode of discourse (i.e., one not phallocentric) would have to free us all from "presumption and obstinacy in opinion," leaving us happily and gratefully in "doubt and suspense"—a *gracious* state of inquiry, if not a state of Grace. The disruptive appearance of this Christian vocabulary strives to do just that.
31. Cf. Charron, *Of Wisdome*, 62: "there is no desire more naturall than to know the truth: we assay all the meanes we can to attaine unto it, but in the end all our endeavours come short; for truth is not an ordinary booty, or thing that will suffer it selfe to be gotten and handled, much lesse to be possessed by any humane Spirit. It lodgeth within the bosome of God. . . . Man knoweth not, understandeth not any thing aright, in purity and in truth as

he ought." Cf. Wehrs, "Sterne, Cervantes, Montaigne," 131–32: "From a Christian perspective, the desire for certitude is potentially heretical, an attempt to assume the attributes of God by abrogating a divinely ordained disjunction between this life, where we see only through a glass darkly, and the life to come, where we shall see face to face."

32. Cf. Davidson and Davidson, "Yorick contra Hobbes," 290: "Sterne . . . knows that such sexual-religious rapture [as experienced with Maria] must be temporary and transient. Not surprisingly, Yorick's new meeting with a woman . . . devolves into an unconditional refutation of the hyperbolic sentiments elicited during his encounter with the mad Maria." I would suggest, instead, that, rather than refutation, we have ratification of both the truth and the fugacity of moments of Grace.

# Where's Poppa? or, The Defeminization of Blake's "Little Black Boy"

DONALD AULT

Thou readst black where I read white.

WILLIAM BLAKE,
"The Everlasting Gospel"

*The Little Black Boy.*

My mother bore me in the southern wild,
And I am black, but O! my soul is white;
White as an angel is the English child:
But I am black as if bereav'd of light.

My mother taught me underneath a tree
And sitting down before the heat of day,
She took me on her lap and kissed me,
And pointing to the east began to say.

Look on the rising sun: there God does live
And gives his light, and gives his heat away.
And flowers and trees and beasts and men recieve
Comfort in morning joy in the noon day.

And we are put on earth a little space,
That we may learn to bear the beams of love,
And these black bodies and this sun-burnt face
Is but a cloud, and like a shady grove.

For when our souls have learn'd the heat to bear
The cloud will vanish we shall hear his voice.
Saying: come out from the grove my love & care,
And round my golden tent like lambs rejoice.

Thus did my mother say and kissed me,
And thus I say to little English boy.
When I from black and he from white cloud free,
And round the tent of God like lambs we joy:

Ill shade him from the heat till he can bear,
To lean in joy upon our fathers knee.
And then I'll stand and stroke his silver hair,
And be like him and he will then love me. [Blake, *Songs of Innocence*]

CAN IT BE AN ACCIDENT that anomalous textual details, especially in punctuation and syntax, begin to pervade Blake's "Little Black Boy" immediately following the mother's unacknowledged disappearance from the poem?[1] That such a question has not usually been asked about this poem is a symptom of the way the surface plot of racial difference and theological rationalization obscures both the issue of gender and its relation to the text's grammatical destabilization. Furthermore, the fact that the poem is narrated through a fiction of voices within voices conceals the extent to which gender and grammatical uncertainties depend on the text's being printed and not literally spoken.

By emphasizing the way racial, geographical, and cultural differences are transformed into ontotheological differences, the poem diverts attention from its most fundamental movement—a turning away from a (bodily, present, "real") mother toward a (utopian, absent, "imaginary") father.[2] This movement most specifically entails a shift from an emphasis on what the father cannot do ("bear," give birth) to what the mother cannot do ("be like him," be male).[3] The narrative gesture of voices within voices allows this movement to be performed by the agency of the mother's speaking; her voice serves as the initiation into the (linguistic, "symbolic") authorizing power of the father.[4] The mother's speaking voice thus becomes a medium of exchange between males (black boy, English boy, father).

The printedness of the text facilitates the connection between the mother's disappearance and grammatical disruption. Prior to the mother's disappearance, reading problems arise primarily when focus is directed toward microscopic semantic details; immediately after the mother (textually) vanishes, unreadable syntax, punctuation, (de)capitalization, and indeterminate pronoun references suddenly erupt into the visible surface of the poem's printed text. It is as if the absent (repressed) mother returns to the poem (exerts her denied presence) through the fabric of the text's visible degrammaticization of itself in unreadable syntax, punctuation, and pronoun references, opening up a radical otherness that opposes the (male? white?) reader's desire to stabilize the poem's close.

From this perspective the poem structurally provides a convenient phallocratic hierarchy. Racial otherness is subordinated to ontotheological narrative; gender difference (both social and grammatical) is subordinated to racial difference; and sexual difference (the biological/psychological dynamics of sexual desire) is subordinated to gender difference. In the process of this narrative displacement, the poem encourages a reading that subordinates or disregards (makes disappear) numerous, seemingly peripheral, impertinences—semantic wordplay, logical inconsistencies, and syntactic ellipses—in favor of its dominant racial, social, religious, and ideological features. This disappearance of anomalous features structurally parallels the mother's metonymic departure from the poem. The mother vanishes more surely than does the metaphorical "cloud" of racial difference, whose promised absence is the constitutive precondition for admission into the utopian world authorized by "his voice."

Since it is the process by which the mother disappears from/into the poem that exposes the potentially violent (mother/father) subplot of the ostensibly benevolent (theological/racial) narrative, it is appropriate to move through the poem metonymically, piece by piece (a strategic trope sometimes associated with the feminine over against masculine metaphorics),[5] beginning with the title.

"The Little Black Boy.": What does this have to do with the mother/father subplot? As the poem unfolds, white/light is associated with the father, and black is associated with the mother (and consequently with natural childbearing—the southern wild of Africa being metonymically aligned with the mother's genital area, later to be called by Freud the "dark continent" of femininity); consequently, the issue of maternity and paternity is already embedded in the initial identification of the "boy" with blackness, that is, with the mother. It is only in the title that the "speaker's" gender is specified; without the title, the speaker could be a female who wants to be a male ("like him").[6]

Probably the most seemingly innocuous word in the title ("The") acquires its primary significance retroactively, in the future of reading the poem, for it is missing in line 22, where "the English child" of line 3 becomes "little English boy." In the title "Little" serves to make the emergent word "Black" benign, diminished in authority and sexual power, since, according to the *OED,* "little" specifically refers to prepubescence, suggesting a nonthreatening male sexual member. Consider the alternative: "The Big Black Boy."

One other point bears mentioning here: The word "blake," the familial (i.e., patriarchal) name literally handed down by the father of the author of "The Little Black Boy," has its etymological roots in whiteness, meaning "pale" and "shining white" (*OED*); yet the word "blake" looks and sounds so similar to "black" that "blake" was often confused with "black": "the words are distinguishable only by context and often not by that" (*OED*). In this sense Blake's name, which precedes and authorizes the poem but is invisible within it, already subverts the initial binary opposition between black and white by participating in both at once. This covert subversion of the white/black (father/mother) opposition carries over into the fictionality of the poem's speaker (who is supposedly identified, given identity, by this title). The "Black Boy" is both *utterly distinct from* the "Blake" who is technically a member of the white, adult, English, imperialist culture and *identical with* the "Blake" who is simultaneously "male" and "other" (excluded as "mad," etc.) and thus a revolutionary outcast from dominant English culture. Thus "blake," a (substantive) noun associated with the name transmitted by Blake's father plays off against "Black," a (subordinate) adjective the poem will associate with mother: The name "Blake" is missing from the poem just as the father is literally missing except in the utopian hope of the speaker.

At the beginning of the poem, being born (inevitably from the mother) and being black are syntactically and ontologically parallel for the black boy: "My mother bore me . . . *And* I am black" versus "*But* I am black" two lines later. In between, the syntax effects a split between the speaking subject's ontological identity and (his) soul—between "I" and "soul," not between "body" or "skin" or "face" and soul. (The "I" will return only after a detour through those features we might have expected in the place of "I" in lines 2 and 4, "bodies" and "face" and their substitutes "cloud" and "grove.")

"I am black [blake?], but O! my soul is white [blake?]": Being black is parallel to being born, but punctuation that visually suggests gender difference (the vaginal "O" and the phallic "!") interrupts that continuity and implies that (at this point) white (blake) is not what he wishes he were but rather is an intrusion into his identity, a contamination of his pure "black" (blake) identity (his "I," associated with his mother). Only with the mediation of "White as an angel *is* the English child [Blake?]" does "black" begin to take on negative characteristics. The initially ungendered English child is white [blake] through and through, with no contaminating alienation from his/her soul. In the fourth line "but" no longer attaches to the intrusive, contaminating "white" as it did in line 2 but attaches to his identity itself: "But I am black." Now black is seen no longer as an identity syntactically parallel to being born but as a negative deprivation, as a residue of something taken away that nevertheless constitutes his identity. This residual blackness, associated with the defining characteristic of the mother, further aligns the black boy with the feminine and implies an absence of the father (and masculinity). The fundamental shift here is from "white" (which participates in the prebinary subversion "blake") to "light," a new term that utterly enforces binarity and calls forth the need for explanation from the (black) mother. In this semantic shift, it is now as if "light" were the origin not only of the white soul but of his entire being, which has been diminished ("bereav'd") by a nameless agent. "Bereav'd," visually bearing the mark of its lost vowel, is paralleled by the only other such bereavement of a vowel in the text, in "learn'd" (line 17), which should mark not a loss but a gain, but which subversively participates in the speaker's bereavement via the mother's teaching "underneath a tree" (which cuts them off from the light, the syntax suggesting that "underneath a tree" is not only where the teaching occurs but what is being taught). Thus, while the black boy can make a positive comparison of the English child's whiteness to religious purity ("White as an angel"), he slips into the syntax of grammatical subordination and ellipsis (paralleling the emerging subordination of the mother) when attempting to characterize his blackness: "I am black as if [I were or have been] bereav'd of light"). What is grammatically elided here is his (subjunctive or present perfect) assertion of identity, precisely that of which he is bereav'd. To the extent that black is associated with his mother, his syntax asserts (by means of the deleted agent of bereavement) that mother, undergoing grammatical subordination, is responsible for his dispossession that increasingly becomes an ontotheological analogue to a castration he yearns to undo.

Yet the poem discourages this possibility, for in the prepubescent context of "The Little Black Boy" the female does not seem at all threatening or castrating; her story seems well intentioned. It is also clear that she is not what in psychoanalytic shorthand is called the phallic mother, the totalizing (yet veiled) lost object of desire for which the child yearns, since the poem embodies such a decisive turning from the mother toward the father, revealing a desire to be like him and not like her, culminating in the emergence of a homo-sexual ("like him") brotherhood of father, black boy, and English boy. Because females are not explicitly included in the concluding utopian vision, the mother's vision must be perceived by the black boy as insufficient because her narrative persists in identifying the male child with his mother, the "we" of her tale, whereas he changes that reference unequivocally to males in his extrapolation of her story. The black boy's later need to retell her tale indicates how it has aroused his own desire, and the substance of his retelling reveals what that desire is.

The mother's indoctrination speech seems to be either the cause of or an attempt to explain why the black boy perceives a split between identity and soul and why he perceives his blackness as privation, that is, why there is a difference between black "I" and the white "English child." Instead of developing the possibility that the English child has no blackness (i.e., has no mother or, more realistically, has the same [white] father but a different [white] mother), her tale diverts attention from the mother function to the association between light and the father that was omitted ("bereav'd") from the end of stanza 1. In the third stanza, "God" enters as a surrogate for the absent father—though initially unacknowledged as such—who lives "there," not here with us but "there" on the "sun." Is it her own sense of (learned?) insufficiency that leads her to tell the story justifying the distance of the source of white/light? Is she explaining what she does not have (the phallus) when she says, "Look on the rising sun," an occulocentric gesture which, at one level at least, contains an image strongly suggestive of a tumescent phallus?

This association of light with the phallus is facilitated by the mother's use of the (uncapitalized)[7] masculine possessive pronoun "his" twice in line 10, which could refer either to "sun" (conventionally masculine and homophonic with "son") or to "God" (conventionally the father). In the former reading God is giving the *sun's* light away (just as the black boy suspects that his own light has been taken away, establishing a covert parallel between himself and the sun/son). This ambiguity of pronoun reference, which is barely noticeable here, will become urgent by the end of the poem.

As the poem unfolds, the terms that would allow these binary oppositions between mother/black and father/light to stay in place begin shifting so quickly and so subtly that it takes convoluted logic to trace their transformations.[8] For instance, the syntactic and semantic dimensions of stanzas 3 through 5 incorporate a series of substitutions that progressively problematize "we," the bonded mother and child. First this "we" is separated from the "flowers and trees and beasts and men" who receive comfort and joy without, apparently, having to learn to "bear" (a word associated with the mother, but which is progressively undergoing semantic transformation). Then this "we" participates in a shift in which the initial split between identity and soul ("I am black, but O! my soul is white") becomes the more conventional distinction between body and soul and ends with "we" being identified with the souls of mother and child, assimilating the previous "we" to a peremptory phallic sameness.[9]

This second shift involves the body/face being equated metaphorically with a cloud, which disappears by association with female procreation (souls learning to "bear"), and analogized to a grove, whose shade is to be transcended by means of male authority ("his voice"). This shift is quite complex and calls attention to itself by apparently involving a grammatical error (a singular verb with a plural subject) at precisely the moment (in lines 15–16) the "we" (mother/child) is separated both from "men" and from "these . . . bodies and this . . . face," paving the way for the absorption of "we" into the previously alienated (white) "soul" that has learned to "bear." This apparent breakdown of syntax can be remedied, however, if "bear" retains a trace of its original function of giving birth. Read: "That we may learn to bear the beams of love / And these black bodies," a compound direct object that allows the clause "and this sun-burnt face / Is but a cloud, and like a shady grove" to be grammatically correct. This remediable grammatical transgression appears at exactly the point where the fundamental terms of the mother/child bonding are being strained: After the mother disappears from the poem, grammatical anomalies are no longer correctable without mentally rewriting the visible surface of the poem.

Before the mother drops out (is turned away from by the black boy), she quotes "his [future] voice," doubly subordinating her role. The vanishing of the cloud is now seen to be insufficient to release the bonded "we" from bondage to the "grove," which is the place of the mother's tale; this act of liberation, of coming out from underneath the tree where the mother is teaching, must be authorized by "his voice."[10] Yet, as noted before, the mother's voice does not seem castrating, and "his voice" seems not to prohibit but rather to enable, to call forth. These voices (which terminate at precisely the same point in the poem)[11] may well exhibit the hallucinatorily benevolent side of patriarchal sexual politics in prepubescent form, the desire to be accepted and loved by the father, even (or especially) when the mother's gestures express love and tenderness toward the male child, emphasized here by the fact that the word "kissed" brackets her story.

The mother's tale fails to acknowledge any sexual difference within the "we" for, according to her, "his voice" will authorize the mother and child to rejoice together, undifferentiated, around "his" tent,[12] in a state of sexual innocence, "like lambs," even though the mother and child are clearly at different stages of sexual development as the tale is told. This vanishing of the cloud and this calling forth from the grove, which continue to identify the speaker with the mother, make visible the alienating difference between the black boy and the authority issuing from an undetermined masculine source—"his voice." In order to "rejoice," mother and child must keep their place, "round [his] golden tent." The black boy unequivocally identifies these closing words as his *mother's,* even though these words were equally "his"—an utterance of the unspecified male voice that authorizes emergence from the grove.

In immediately turning toward "little English boy" (no longer the ungendered "child" of line 3), and consequently away from his mother, the black boy attempts to assert his affiliation with maleness. The lines in which this turning is recorded—"Thus did my mother say and kissed me, / And thus I say to little English boy."—mark the emergence of the first unresolvable grammatical anomaly in the poem. Although the general sense of these lines leads the reader to expect that the words to follow will be a direct address to "little English boy," the period at the end of line 22 invites the reader to revise this assumption: Now it seems as if the speaker repeats (as if offstage) the exact story his mother told him and then generalizes the consequences of telling this story (and this assumption is confirmed to the extent that the rest of the poem is not a direct address but is in the third person). It is precisely at this point, where the black boy turns away from his mother and "child" becomes "boy," that the definite article is cut off (reinforcing the grammatical castration motif), just as the absence of "the" makes it possible for "little" to serve as a verb in line 22—"thus I say to [be]little [or make little] English boy"—an ambiguity that would itself be cut off by the inclusion of the definite article either before or after "little."[13]

The next line, "When I from black and he from white cloud free," exhibits even more urgent grammatical incompleteness, which could be "corrected" in at least two different ways, through active or passive voice (mirroring the simultaneous distinction between and superimposition of "his [active] voice" and the mother's [passive] voice). Here are two alternative ways of filling in the gap in this line: "When I from black and he from white cloud [are] free," and "When I from black and he from white cloud free [ourselves]." The absence of a word in the text that would decide between these very different completions tends to be subordinated (in reading) to what seems to be a more important semantic and logical anomaly: Where does the "white cloud" come from? This semantic move involves a filling in of a previously unacknowledged gap in the mother's story (which omitted reference to "English boy" altogether) by analogical replacement. The speaker's desire to affiliate himself with English/male requires that he and English boy be similar, so English boy must have a cloud, too; but filling in this semantic gap occupies the space in the line where the syntactically completing word could materialize. Thus it is precisely at the point he turns from (and tries to advance beyond) his mother that the poem suddenly becomes readable only by filling syntactic holes and/or revising the grammatical categories of the words being uttered/read.

The syntactic incompleteness that emerges when the mother drops out of the poem is accompanied by an additional reading problem: The third-person narration and the male gender of the English boy provide the syntactic environment in the text for a mystifying intersection of all the males (excluding the little black boy)—a conflation, by means of indeterminable masculine pronoun references, that invokes an entirely patriarchal utopia (God/father/sun [son]/English boy) and yet antipatriarchally destabilizes the semantic field that pretends to close off the poem with teleological finality.

This final movement of "The Little Black Boy" begins with double analogical substitutions in line 24: "And round the tent of God like lambs we joy," which mimics but does not duplicate line 20 of "his"/mother's voice. The first substitution is "the tent of God" for "my tent." In the mother's story it was a male but unspecified voice ("his [uncapitalized] voice") that referred to "my tent," even though there was nothing in the rhyme or meter of line 18 to prevent her from saying, "we shall hear *God's* voice." But the black boy has to reach back to line 9 (the first and only other time "God" was mentioned in the poem) to specify by a proper name (indeed, *the* proper name) what before was only an (indeterminate) masculine possessive. The second substitution involves exactly the same word but now with different referents—"we"—which before referred to the black boy and the mother but now refers to the black boy and little English boy.

The first two lines of the last stanza introduce yet more visible grammatical and/or semantic destabilization, this time through (the absence of) punctuation, as well as a further (syntactic) reminder of the black boy's estrangement from his mother. If we let "Ill shade him from the heat" stand as it is—without immediately succumbing to the temptation to "correct" the line by inserting a mental apostrophe in the word "Ill" so that it becomes "I'll," parallel to the clearly marked "I'll" in line 27—the line is still readable in a way that line 23 is not. If "Ill" is a noun, read, "Ill [evil, wrongdoing, distress, misfortune, sickness, error (*OED*)] shade him from the heat," which so radically calls into question the benevolent tone of the mother's story that it seems unlikely that the black boy could be aware of what he is saying, *if* this is what he is saying. If "Ill" is an adverb, read a command, "[You] ill [with aversion, displeasure, offense; defectively, imperfectly, poorly (*OED*)] shade him from the heat," which would imply a hostility equally foreign to the black boy's conscious tone, *if* this is what he is saying. But these literally readable versions of this part of the line call into question the entire poem as a speech act rather than a reading act: At this point we could know whether the absent apostrophe is a "mistake" *only* if we could hear the word spoken audibly. Thus, as the poem pulls away from the black boy's relation with the mother toward his relation with "him," the entire fiction of voices within voices, on which the patriarchal, onto-theological narrative is based, begins to stammer.[14]

The second half of line 25, "till he can bear," closed by a comma, at first seems to bring "him" closer to the function of the mother, but the next line undermines this assumption, first, by cutting off an object for "bear" (which has always appeared transitively with a clear direct object up to this point in the poem) and, second, by turning directly toward the "father," who is explicitly mentioned for the first time in the poem: "till he can bear, / To lean in joy upon our fathers knee." The eruption of the father into the poem is accompanied by the unreadable absence of a necessary apostrophe: "fathers" must be possessive, and, since there is only one "knee," there must be only one father; so it should read "father's," but it does not. The semantic impossibility of "fathers" being plural possessive suddenly calls attention to the black boy's desire that he and little English boy have the same father—or does it? The word "fathers" sits there in its potential plurality, raising the specter of questionable paternity even as the next (singular) word attempts to thwart it. Is it an accidental offshoot of Blake's tendency to omit apostrophes in possessives that it *just so happens* that the only point in the poem where an apostrophe must be unequivocally inserted for readability (since there is no difference in sound here as with "Ill" and I'll) occurs just as the father is (for the one and only time) mentioned? The "fathers" appearance is marked by an absence which acts as if it were the return of the repressed mother's (now destabilizing) presence.

With God, English boy, father, and (by implication) son (sun)[15] in the immediate context, the main focus of unreadability in the last two lines derives from indeterminable masculine pronoun references. Any attempt to stabilize these masculine pronoun references runs into serious trouble. But this is true only if all possible referents are male. Since either the English boy or the father could have silver hair, the first appearance of an ambiguous pronoun reference occurs in line 27.[16] Although this reference is ambiguous, it seems to pose no real problem, but it lays the foundation for the problem to come; this ambiguity simply enacts the sameness (interchangeability) of English boy and father. After this point, however, this interchangeability does not work, nor does the attempt to make the pronouns always refer to the English boy or to the father. If we destabilize the last line by selectively breaking up pronoun referents, there seems to be no problem: "[I'll] be like him [father/God] and he [English boy] will then love me." But how do we know this is what we are supposed to do in reading the line? The reading problem would be solved for us if the line read, "And be like *H*im and *h*e will then love me"—only if earlier possible pronoun references to God (and the word "Father" itself) were capitalized throughout the poem. It is the innocence of the line (with its train of monosyllables) and its not so innocent invocation of simultaneous interchangeability and difference between males that problematizes, makes unreadable, the end of the poem. It just so happens that the speaker's relationships to these figures (who are the same by virtue of their gender) are not interchangeable.

"[I'll] be like him": This pronoun should refer to the father, especially if "father" is (conventionally) collapsed with "God" (and further back with the unspecified male voice of the mother's story), as the poem's narrative encourages. To "be like him" indicates the boy's aspiration to identify with the phallus/father (since color difference has supposedly vanished/been transcended along with the clouds). It is important that he does not say, "we'll be the same," for this would simultaneously stabilize the line by removing the problem of reference and ambiguate the gender identification that is now the only stable thing in his statement as it stands. It is also important that he does not say, "he'll be like me," which would again remove gender specification (which, as we have seen, could be related to castration anxiety—"[I'll] be like him" in that I will have the phallus; I'll be like him and not like my mother) and further would logically make the masculine pronoun refer only to English boy, thereby stabilizing not only this pronoun reference but, more importantly, the next (final) one as well, which, as the poem stands, is the most problematic of all.

"[A]nd he will then love me." This should refer to English boy, since it seems unthinkable that the masculine (father/God) voice that called to the mother and child as his "love & care" could all along not have loved the black boy. Indeed, the entire moral of the mother's story depends on their burden/bearing being transformations of or associations with "beams of love." The possibility that "he" refers to the father calls into question, at the very last moment of the poem, the identity between father and God and the benevolent male voice of the mother's story, and it further calls into question the unspoken assumption that being "like him," having the phallus, will guarantee his being loved by "him." If this narrative were not about "little" boys but about adolescent sexuality, the desire to possess the phallus could engender fear and hostility (rather than love) on the part of the father.

The father never does materialize in this poem except in the black boy's utopian vision. The father's real absence and the mother's narrative to rationalize it, at one level, serve to prevent the black boy from preparing for mature adult sexual relations. He cannot envision a future when he is not "little," yearning to be incorporated into the phallocratic order of sameness that he believes will guarantee love from the (absent) father. The mother, who is by definition sexually mature and (symbolically if not literally) abandoned by the father/lover (especially if we keep in mind the conflation of and difference between father [sun/son] and God that inhabits the end of the poem), may herself desire a (fantasized) relationship to paternal/masculine authority that escapes the burdens of mature sexuality. There is no evidence of the joy of adult sexuality in the mother in this poem: Her love is totally directed toward the male child who acts, in psychoanalytic terms, as a substitute phallus for her, which helps explain why she wants to keep him bonded to her by telling him her story of their future union with an absent masculine authority. Instead, he turns from her, indoctrinated into a submissive role in the masculine order from which she is excluded.

Because the tortured dynamics of the sexual impasse in this poem so manifestly parallel those of the racial exploitation to which Blake was unequivocally opposed, it seems plausible that Blake was demonstrating how the emphasis on one form of oppression (racial) by the violence inherent in benevolent patriarchy implicates (and obscures) another, more universal, form (the subordination of the feminine). The degree to which Blake could have consciously manipulated the peculiarities of his text in a way that could invite readers to participate directly (through decisions made in the act of reading) in a scenario of dominance and subordination and at the same time make it possible for readers to break free of those entrenched forms of patriarchal power perhaps belongs to the realm of the genuinely undecidable.

## Postscript

When Elizabeth Langland suggested that I write a piece on "feminist voices" in Blake's poetry, it seemed an easy task. Having just completed a study of what I called "anti-Newtonian" strategies in Blake's *Four Zoas,* I was certain that the disruptive, subversive, interventional, discrepant, and incommensurable features of Blake's text (such as anarchistic punctuation, decapitalization and subversive spacing of words, visible syntactic surfaces, indeterminable pronoun reference, etc.) were unquestionably "antipatriarchal," and that I could marshal innumerable examples to demonstrate how Blake's verbal style appropriated something like feminist discourse (paralleling Luce Irigaray's call to jam the theoretical/systematic machinery of phallocentric thinking),[17] even though strong feminist critics have argued that, in terms of Blake's "myth," females, the feminine, and women come off rather badly.[18] Part of my confidence derived from the fact that in my notes on *The Four Zoas* as visual text I had already begun to draw conclusions that sounded vaguely "feminist." For example, I noted in relation to the text blocks that cut into the image portions of Blake's designs for Edward Young's *Night Thoughts,* which Blake used for writing much of the text of the *Zoas* manuscript:

> The[se] designs . . . arouse the anxiety that accompanies viewing . . . cut-away bodily images. Imagining the drawings complete behind the text by connecting the lines that have been cut off by the sharp borders of the word-space requires a bodily dis-memberment and re-memberment. In ruthlessly cutting off the drive toward closure and completeness that informs the ordinary, ego-affirming visual imagination, this incisive, dis-membering tabula rasa opens up a space to be filled in by language. By denying access to the (imaginary) unified body of another, this interposition of the (symbolic) cutting edge that opens up a space for words threatens the unity of the viewer's own ego-body—an enactment of the textual castration explored by Jacques Lacan and others. But Blake undoes this cut by making the visible words of his text resist absorption into phallocentric grammar.[19]

I decided to perform this experiment on "The Little Black Boy" because it seemed a likely candidate for exploring biological/political issues of feminism, and yet it seemed more challenging in that it appeared to be less likely to offer itself up to analysis of the discursive textual effects sometimes associated with (especially French) feminism because it so dramatically contrasted to Blake's later (often mystifying and intimidating) prophecies where technical subversion abounds in both verbal and pictorial dimensions. Even the illuminations to "The Little Black Boy" seemed not to exhibit features like the radical cutting of verbal text into the visual images I had noted in *The Four Zoas* pages. In fact, the illuminations seemed symmetrically placed in a noninterruptive way beyond the borders of the poem and, in addition, seemed (at least relative to *The Four Zoas* pages) to be involved in "representation" of the verbal dimensions of the text. Though in this essay I have not gone into an analysis of the visual problems that parallel the verbal, I quickly saw how my initial assumptions about both the words and the illuminations were wrong.

A further problem arose: As soon as I started considering Blake's poetry from the perspective of sexual or gender difference, it became clear that situating Blake's "feminist" voice exclusively at the level of disruptive visual and verbal discourse was an exceedingly abstract move, divorcing the question from the political and social issues on which feminism, at some level, ultimately turns. In addition, I realized that attempting to label these discursive peculiarities of Blake's work as somehow "feminist" really added little, if any, explanatory power to what I had already said about Blake's text. Not only did such a critical act seem unexplanatory, it seemed totally inauthentic for me to engage in a discourse that suppressed my own biology and cultural programming by assuming such an easy (phallocentric?) equation between "antipatriarchal" and "feminist" discourse. So I decided not to attempt to demonstrate that I could appropriate the feminine or even to reveal how a male writer I admire might have achieved such an appropriation. In short, I decided that in this experimental essay I would simply approach Blake with the same questions I usually ask, but with special sensitivity to those aspects of his poetry that betray significance for gender or sexual difference. I have no doubt that the argument I have produced is deeply implicated in phallocentric discourse. In fact, it is probably unthinkable outside of the operations authorized by so-called phallic categories.

As the essay developed I found it necessary to confine myself to statements about the effects the poem was producing rather than, as I had hoped, reaching some conclusion about Blake's intentional (or even unconscious) attempt to appropriate something I could identify as "the feminine." I think I succeeded pretty well in evading the question whose answer would, perhaps, have been the most important result of my attempt to confront Blake's "feminism": To what extent are the specific textual features of Blake's poetry that could be called antipatriarchal intentional, and to what extent are they simply occurrences in language—that is, the way language happens in Blake's poetry—independent of Blake's will, or at least in undecidable relation to his conscious intention? Could the endless textual anomalies that have recently been shown to have astonishingly significant functions in Blake's poetry really be "accidental" products of mysterious processes of language and of the peculiar conditions under which Blake produced his works? Nelson Hilton, whose work stands at the frontier of discovering the startling wordplay in Blake, at times acts as if it were undecidable whether these processes are simply the product of his own canny interpretation or are traces of genuine, remarkable genius on Blake's part.[20] Thus I am constrained to end this essay asking essentially the same question with which I began: Could all this be accidental, or are these effects of a master strategist attempting to stake out something like a feminine space for his textual production? But must not this question and even its phrasing immediately recoil on me? Have I not simply invoked another pair of binary oppositions—intention and accident, mastery and occurrence—that always seem to turn up as if in an inevitable and endless chain? Should not authentic feminist writing take us a step farther away from such binary thinking? But does it help to play with a radical other, the middle voice, androcentric discourse, or the androgyne (as Barthes, Derrida, and many others have done)? Or could this be just another utopian hope, a desire to return to a mythical prefallen state prior to (or in addition to) the splitting up of the world into active and passive, male and female, dominance and submission? Must we, as Blake said, "repeat the same dull round" of the Romantic ideology all over again?

*Note:* In a dream I showed this manuscript to Blake, who told me that he was "not uncomfortable" with my reading of "The Little Black Boy."

## Notes

1. In "Un-reading 'London,'" in *Approaches to Teaching Blake's "Songs of Innocence and of Experience,"* ed. Robert F. Gleckner and Mark L. Greenberg (New York: MLA, 1989), 133–37, I examine the way anomalous details of punctuation (such as missing apostrophes in possessives) serve to destabilize grammatical categories and make revisionary rewriting of the poem necessary if it is to be readable. Though I mentioned the parallel between the poem's ostensible objects of attack—the male-dominated church, state, and marriage—and the poem's undermining of the patriarchal linguistic categories through which reading becomes possible, the scope of that essay prohibited me from drawing more far-reaching "feminist" or psychoanalytic conclusions; but it is not hard to see how

central the role of lost father and mother is to that poem, which begins with the speaker wandering (as if) in search of something in every face he(?) meets (the absent, lost father?) but finding only the institutional traces of the oppressive patriarchy, ultimately leading him to what obsesses him "most," that harlot's cry in relation to childbirth and marriage. Inhabiting the mental space of the child of a harlot mother (since no other trace of the female/mother/feminine shows up in the poem [excluding the blood running down palace walls, a war image that doubles for menstruation, deflowering, rape, and childbirth]), the speaker is irrevocably cut off from knowledge of his paternal origin. Of some interest for this present essay on "The Little Black Boy" is a point that got edited out of "Un-reading 'London'": The first and last words in "London" that fail to use apostrophes to mark their role as possessives are the two appearances of "Infants"; these words cannot be plural and must be possessive (given their syntactic environment), and "Infants" is the first and last word in a series in the poem where the addition or subtraction of the apostrophe does not change pronunciation (as it might in "thro'" "charter'd," or "mind-forg'd"). Is it an accident that this bracketing of the series of words that can be singular or plural, possessive or nonpossessive, by the addition or subtraction of such a punctuation mark ("of weakness"?) should mean "unable to speak," since the difference is literally unable to be spoken and can only be read? In "Un-reading 'London'" I tended to treat such effects as conscious strategies on Blake's part. I am now beginning to call such an easy solution into question.

2. My use of "real" and "imaginary" here, as well as "symbolic" (below) in relation to the law of the father, signals my awareness of a kinship between my interpretation and Lacanian psychoanalysis. I use these terms somewhat loosely (nontechnically) so that I do not believe my account of Blake depends on Lacan's categories of explanation. My assumption is that Blake can shed light on Lacan in much the same way Lacan can shed light on Blake.
3. The phrase "be like him" has usually been taken to refer to the black boy's color, but here I am suggesting that the phrase points to the condition of "being male," possessing the phallus, etc. This reading seems all the more plausible in light of the entangled masculine pronoun references at the end of the poem and the supposed transcendence of color difference the narrative promises.
4. The use of Lacan's term "symbolic" at this juncture seems particularly apt since, although it does not directly address language as prohibition, what is at stake here is the ontotheological authority of language voiced specifically by a utopian absent male who transmutes into God and the father.
5. See Domna C. Stanton, "Difference on Trial: A Critique of the Maternal Metaphor in Cixous, Irigaray, and Kristeva," in *The Poetics of Gender*, ed. Nancy K. Miller (New York: Columbia University Press, 1986), 157–82.
6. The *OED* indicates that "boy" can be a verb meaning to act like or be like a boy, a possibility which is not thwarted but encouraged by the otherwise anomalous period at the end of the title. This use would, of course, be ungrammatical—it should be "The Little Black [noun] Boys [singular verb]"—but we find a similar "mistake" (a plural subject with a singular verb) in the body of the poem itself (lines 15–16).
7. It is easy to make too much of decapita[liza]tion and its relation to castration and the subversion of capitalism, but in this particular poem the problem seems particularly acute. Many of the reading problems (especially toward the end of the poem) derive from the uniform uncapitalization of masculine-gendered pronouns, especially as they get embroiled with the absorption of capitalistic/religious images like "golden tent" and "silver hair" into the primary goal of the speaker's desire.
8. For example, as God gives light and heat *away* (disperses, not gives *to*), "flowers and trees and beasts and men *recieve [sic]*" "Comfort" and "joy"—yet here the absence of punctuation in line 12 problematizes even this reception. Similarly, at first, "men" seem to include all humans (including, one might suppose, black women and children), but the next line

begins to confute this: "we are put" threatens to cut off the "we" (mother and speaker) from the previous list of recipients. Yet at first it is a gentle exclusion, for the syntax suggests that perhaps all humans must learn to "bear the beams of love" (a term that involves a fairly radical shift from "light"). By line 15, however, it has become clear that "these black bodies" and "this sun-burnt face" bind the mother and speaker together over against the "men" who receive comfort and joy without, apparently, having to "learn to bear" (originally the mother's function, now beginning to shift its meaning from "giving birth" to "enduring" or "withstanding," which meanings begin retroactively to contaminate the verb's first appearance in line 1).

9. The inverted syntax of "For when our souls have learn'd the heat to bear" draws attention away from two drastic substitutions in these lines: It is no longer "we" but "souls" that are doing the "bearing," and it is no longer "beams of love" but "heat" that is being borne/born. It is not the "souls" that survive the vanishing of the "cloud," however; it is "we." The mother's narrative seems to claim that their bodies will disappear (vanish), which should leave souls; instead, however, "we" are left, as if the condition of their (previously alienating, white, father-associated) souls has now completely taken over their identities. Stated otherwise, as "we" is separated off, blackness detaches itself from being constitutive of identity and bonding with the mother and becomes characteristic only of their bodies/faces, images which are then to be discarded as the speaker and mother become assimilated to the functions of the previously alienated soul.

10. Although initially the relation between the cloud and grove seems to be one of similarity ("Is but a cloud, and like a shady grove"), in stanza 5 it is the difference between them that is important: The metaphoric cloud becomes associated with the mother by virtue of its relation to "bearing" and disappears, while the simile of the grove becomes reified as a place associated with the authorizing male voice of the mother's speech.

11. Although the speaker says, "Thus did my mother say," the words he has just quoted are the words of "his voice," which has taken over the mother's story. Although the last words the mother speaks are the words "his voice" will speak in the promised future, the speaker of the poem refers to these words as only those of his mother—i.e., he emphasizes that he did not literally hear "his voice" but only heard the mother quoting its desired future utterance; the mother's voice is only the simulacrum of "his voice." Blake intensifies this effect by failing to use any quotation marks to set one voice off against (or inside) another. In "William Blake Illuminates the Truth," *Critical Studies* 1 (1989): 43–60, Jerome McGann demonstrates how Blake uses a similar strategy of nonpunctuation in *Jerusalem*.

12. "Tent" is a curiously female image that problematizes the entire narrative the mother is telling: Tents shield from the light and heat, so where is "he" in relation to the lamblike rejoicers? Inside or outside the tent? Consequently, what is "his" relation to the light and heat the mother and speaker have to learn to bear?

13. The absence of the definite article opens up a syntactic indeterminacy that is aided by an alternative meaning of "say": to try or attempt to do something. The line could then bear this reading: "And thus I *try* to belittle or make little [the] English boy." In this one act of omission, the speaker makes the English "child" into a "boy" and tries to make him "little." In either case—whether "little" is an adjective or a verb—there is a definite article missing, which, as noted above, suggests castration or the desire to undo castration. A similar meaning of "say" in line 8—"And pointing to the east began to say."—allows the otherwise anomalous period there to be more grammatically feasible.

14. The capital "I" enters the last stanza contaminated by a double "l," making "Ill," not "I'll," as in the next to the last line of the poem: Note "till" (future, utopian hope) contains "ill" but not "I'll." Further, the placement of "Ill" at the beginning of line 25 ambiguates the function of the capital "I" itself. Is it capitalized because it denotes the speaking subject or because the first letter of a line of poetry (in Blake's day) was conventionally capitalized? The relation of this issue to "I" of capitalism, the interconstitution of the competitive ego and colonial exploitation, is too dense for exploration here, but it is

crucial to the issue of confused pronoun references at the end of the poem, which could be disentangled by resorting to capitalizing one or more of the masculine pronouns in the last two lines. Perhaps it is sufficient to note here that uncapitalized "ill" is not only part of the utopian future ("till") but also of one of Blake's favorite ways of signing his first name ("Will"), which shows up twice in the poem as a verb (lines 18 and 28) in relation to that same utopian hope.

15. It is important not to overlook the fact that in the illumination to the second page of the text of this poem, the figure who visually occupies the place of the father looks like Jesus (the son), sometimes with a sunlike halo around his head, spatially analogous to the image of the sun on the first page of the text. Other anomalies abound in the illuminations, especially if we take variant copies into account.
16. The *OED* indicates that "silver" can mean both lustrous as a general color or specifically the color of hair of an aged man, and, of course, it is a standard of economic exchange.
17. For example, in Luce Irigaray, *This Sex which Is Not One,* trans. Catherine Porter and Carolyn Burke (Ithaca, NY: Cornell University Press, 1985).
18. See, for example, the various discussions of Blake's relation to feminism and sexual discourse in *Blake: An Illustrated Quarterly* 16 (1982–83): 148–83. Anne K. Mellor in "Blake's Portrayal of Woman" (148–55) and Alicia Ostriker in "Desire Gratified and Ungratified: William Blake and Sexuality" (156–65) argue in very different ways for Blake's complicit underwriting of patriarchal discourse and the subordination of the feminine. Two male writers in this issue of *Blake* make a case for Blake's more radical relation to the feminine and patriarchy; see Nelson Hilton, "Some Sexual Connotations" (166–71) and Michael Ackland, "The Embattled Sexes: Blake's Debt to Wollstonecraft in *The Four Zoas*" (172–83). See also Susan Fox, "The Female as Metaphor in William Blake's Poetry," *Critical Inquiry* 3 (1977): 507–19; Diana Hume George's persuasive "Blake and the Feminine," in her *Blake and Freud* (Ithaca, NY: Cornell University Press, 1980); and Brenda Webster, *Blake's Prophetic Psychology* (London: Macmillan, 1983), and her more recent article based on that book, "Blake, Women, and Sexuality" in *Critical Paths: Blake and the Argument of Method* (Durham, NC: Duke University Press, 1987), 204–24.
19. Donald Ault, *Narrative Unbound: Re-visioning William Blake's "The Four Zoas"* (Barrytown, NY: Station Hill, 1987), 470.
20. See Nelson Hilton, *Literal Imagination: Blake's Vision of Words* (Berkeley and Los Angeles: University of California Press, 1985). Hilton's lead in the analysis of semantic and aural playfulness in Blake has had a significant influence on this essay.

# The Bifurcated Female Space of Desire: Shelley's Confrontation with Language and Silence

LAURA CLARIDGE

IN *The Rape of the Lock*, Alexander Pope sets out to rape Belinda/Arabella of her threatening excess of meaning—the artifice out of which she creates herself—and to make her into a virgin, a blank page. Paradoxically, that is, accession to eighteenth-century male society will "virginalize" her, the female equivalent in this poem to the castration that Pope fears to be the potential of the art-full female. Such a dangerous creature explodes beyond the law, beyond the word, and she embodies a *jouissance* capable of taking its pleasures in a lapdog or a husband—the differences notwithstanding. Popean, or conservative, fear suggests the male Augustan writer's tendency to bring the woman back within the law, to achieve comedic endings.[1] The canonized British Romantic poets, however, attempt by and large to use this mythical unbridled female power as a space that engenders authentic poetic voice, a method that allowed for the enabling literary illusion that the male poet could pass over his father, over the Law of language that bound him to a tradition unable to speak his infinite (and therefore inevitably fragmentary) desire. There are two obvious dangers to such an experiment: (1) The poet can mystify "woman" so that the female as goddess becomes the hidden theme; and (2) he can appropriate the female in his quest for a male self-definition that incorporates what he sees as his opposite.[2]

Certainly, Wordsworth might seem to approach a "closet" deification of the female. Though it did not produce a feminist poet, however, the complexity of his attraction to the female, coupled with his Romantic revolutionary impulse, produced a sexually sensitive one who would take the possibility of the virgin, of the blank page, as a potent form in which to envision the language of desire, a language of original and—the penultimate oxymoron—procreative virginal capacities. The whiteness of Emily in *The White Doe of Rylstone* and the transparency of Idonea in *The Borderers*, both women loyal to fathers who though clearly loving are obviously their moral or intellectual inferiors (with the narrative deliberately creating this imbalance), prefigure Shelley's Beatrice and Byron's suggestion of the-woman-in-Juan in *Don Juan.* These figures all function as a transparent medium through which corrupt meaning enacts itself even as the medium begins to point to an uncorrupt moment of silence beyond all fathers and beyond all lawful desire; they approach, that is, a Romantic jouissance, exceeding what language can accomplish, even as it is important that a fidelity to the law help actualize this new silent language. I would hold that, as a rule, the Romantic poets neither mystify nor appropriate the female (though Wordsworth comes fairly close); they usefully invoke her potential as function of meaning, as signifier of cultural contradiction instead. Exciting feminist critique of just this tendency is currently under way, with Anne Mellor's already well-established volume on feminism and Romanticism having provided crucial paths to explore.[3] I therefore want to situate my own discourse as deliberately swerving from such significant and even redefinitive analyses, much of which would maintain the dependence upon appropriation of the female for production of the male Romantic ego or consciousness. There is yet another way to conceive of the textual play of gender in Shelley's poetry, for example, a negotiation of voice that might be present in the other male literary lions of the period as well—though a matter to be pursued outside the confines of this essay. I wish to posit that Shelley explores ways to escape "maleness" through trying to articulate that part of "femaleness" which remains (he mythologizes) outside the "benefits" of the patriarchal language that he would disavow.

Percy Shelley may well be the Romantic poet who takes fullest advantage of the opportunities open to male writers who can hypostatize the female as a bisexuality that seeks "the (w)hole phallic thing" while dependent upon difference and distinction, a kind of impossible desire that has it both ways. In a reciprocal sexual economy, Shelley speaks the female—in hopes that she will voice him—as functional conduit of meaning, as a marker of the inevitable slippage of meaning that inheres in language, even as we assure ourselves of having fixed the terms of our match between mental intention and graphic or oral representation. In the remainder of this essay, I shall follow Paul Fry's suggestive observation that "In the *Defence,* and everywhere in the poetry too, there is much that could be called a Lacanian psycholinguistics in embryo."[4] We can conceptualize, for instance, Shelley's use of the female in terms of Lacan's paradigm of the phallus: Both posit that their chosen representational mark is not distinctly gender-bound but functional instead, intersecting with the gender it appears to replicate only insomuch as resonances of that gender strengthen our understanding of its bisexual inscription. The phallus, insists Lacan, is not the same as penis, but as representation of that which everyone wants and no one has, its suggestions of male sexuality remind us of (1) the pressure of the Father's Law in patriarchal cultures, and (2) the repetitive nature of desire as tumescence versus detumescence: the metonymic condition of being. Woman, as Shelley uses the figure in much of his poetry, represents the limits of exerting pressure against an irretrievably inflected, unoriginal language: Woman as function enacts a desire whose possession of the absent phallus seems more plausible than that of a man's chance, and whose incongruity—the woman as phallus, or with phallus—threatens (the poet ecstatically hopes) to penetrate as other-than-the-father the very limits of patriarchal language. Thus Shelley uses this representation of woman to get himself to another place—the closest to a space anterior to language that he can achieve and still remain a poet.

I now wish to suggest the ways in which the females help to engender poetic voice in three texts by Shelley: the early *Alastor* and the more mature works, *The Cenci* and *Epipsychidion,* all of which record the poet's near obsession with achieving self-expression through language that is inevitably inauthentic and anterior, at the same moment that it is self-constitutive. Most recent attempts (brilliantly in such cases as Susan Brisman, Jerrold Hogle, Daniel Hughes, William Keach, and Stuart Peterfreund) to deal with these linguistic concerns have concentrated upon Shelley's belief in the metaphoricity of language and origin. I instead want to locate moments where Shelley applies women to the task of helping him to escape the patriarchy of language, as he explores the production of meaning through a double rendering of the female, who will function as both saturated and empty signifiers;[5] and I wish thereby to imply, incidentally, the danger of feminist criticism that would take as its major operative term the guilt of male authors who "use" the idea of woman as enabling them to write. Without relying upon the obvious possibilities of androgyny or homosexuality as good fights, at least, against patriarchy, Shelley shores his battle for poetic freedom upon a refusal to thematize consistently the female as a maternal space of preoedipal bliss, in a position prior to the eruption of the Law.

*Alastor* is the quintessential Romantic poem of death and desire. It is also the text that puts most clearly into relief the dilemma of the poet abdicating his claim to a social, phallic voice in order to remain true to himself—and not, as some recent critics might suggest, merely to relocate himself on the side of the mother, in a preoedipal world which, Shelley knows better than such readers, is itself already implicated in the genealogies of language. In *Alastor,* Shelley alerts us as early as 1815 that he is willing to embrace Hegel's Pyrrhic victory of mastery over the slave by killing that slave—language. Yet the death the poet seeks is not that entanglement of treachery and despair which some psychologies of the text have suggested but a final location of jouissance.[6]

Citing the omission of fire in Shelley's cataloguing of the elements as the narrator invokes Mother Nature, Harold Bloom concludes that Shelley as narrator-poet was assuming the identity of the fire; he is brother to the other elements.[7] Fire becomes for *Alastor*'s narrator-poet an emblem of maleness, a phallic giver of life—an equivalent of the fictional poet's real-life creator. Thus there is mutual illumination of both character and creation through the conspicuous absence of fire in the invocation. The conflation of fire and phallus is an easy one, with the waxing and waning of both objects, with their penetration of darkness. Since the Mother does not possess the phallus, it is the poet's potential gift to her. But there is always the suggestion of indebtedness that clings to fire and phallus; the Promethean son stole it from the gods. The Law continues to step in and thwart the "lover's" offering, so that finally neither nature nor the male poet can arrogate this originating metaphor without acknowledging its belated possession, its diminished authority. Shelley is different from Wordsworth in accepting that a male poet lacks the phallus as does the mother; it is Wordsworth's *covert* awareness of this dilemma that provokes the greatest tension in his corpus, but in Shelley the knowledge underwrites the poetry's dominant structure versus its status as Wordsworthian subtext.

*Alastor*'s living poet (the narrator left behind to record the vision of the true, solitary poet) will use as the necessary fiction to engender his pen the belief that he is a poet-son who achieves the big bang of death, who gives his mother the fiery phallus and therefore antedates the father:

> Mother of this unfathomable world!
> Favor my solemn song, for I have loved
> Thee ever, and thee only; I have watched
> Thy shadow, and the darkness of thy steps,
> And my heart ever gazes on the depth
> Of thy deep mysteries. [18–23][8]

The narrator tells of strange encounters with the vagaries of death, all calculated to give answers to primal questions "of what we are" (29). His search for knowledge has been mixed "With my most innocent love, until strange tears / Uniting with those breathless kisses, made / Such magic as compels the charmed night / To render up thy charge" (34–37). The erotic language points to the typical Shelleyan linkage of sex and death. In death, one transcends the Father as mediator and achieves instant union of subject and object. Thus sexual union (the collapse of ego boundaries in the orgasm of love) assumes its metaphorical function for outsmarting language and creating original meaning.

Shelley offers in *Alastor* two alternatives: the dead poet's quest for reunion with an earlier and unalienated self that in its refusal to be overruled by the father will conflagrate in death; or the narrator's borrowed existence as a poet, framing another's story in a language inherited—but at least alive. The initial *engendering* of the narrator's voice is his attempt to give the phallus to the mother (Mother Earth at the poem's beginning), to develop a rationale for needing to write: a space that would seem to call for the presence of his pen. Thus the potency of the female-outside-the-Law (what much French-inspired feminism might talk of as the semiotic or fluid maternal space) at first appears necessary for Shelley to enact his appropriation of language, of what we typically term the patriarchal space of writing or, even, the tradition. I will suggest that Shelley instead recognizes quickly that his writing depends upon a more complex myth of a female both *already* full and simultaneously empty: lacking the phallus, yet constituted by it (in language).

In opposition to the authorial tradition of writing the woman, inscribing her, much of British Romantic poetry acknowledges the urgency to write for her, to her, not to gain access to a magical, maternal moment but quite the reverse: *to gain access to the order of language.* It is as if Shelley entertains the one momentous possibility that recent feminist criticism and psychoanalytic theory rarely consider: Woman—as well as man—may "be" language and Law, precisely because she (as he) lacks the phallus, is in a constant state of desire. The very collusion of procreative biological powers with social powers of language (powers of the pen[is]) might well be too much for either women or men to entertain given the apparently intractable preference to construct theories based on binary oppositions of separate powers. What *if* woman *does* have it all—and thus the virulent discrimination against her throughout culture? But then again, what if man has it all too? In both cases, I'm suggesting, however oddly, that we translate the psychoanalytic truth that neither male nor female has the phallus into the possibility that both genders can pretend to having it.

The preface to *Alastor* emphasizes a dialectic of desire that moves from the child stage of object relations to the human desire born when the infant enters the symbolic world of the cultural father:

> So long as it is possible for his desires to point towards objects thus infinite and unmeasured, he is joyous, and tranquil, and self-possessed. But the period arrives when these objects cease to suffice. His mind is at length suddenly awakened and thirsts for intercourse with an intelligence similar to itself. He images to himself the Being whom he loves. . . . He seeks in vain for a prototype of his conception. Blasted by his disappointment, he descends to an untimely grave.

Nonetheless, of greater importance to the possibility of poetic vocation that Shelley was working out than the solitary poet is the poet-left-behind, the inauthentic poet. Enslaved by language, he notes (with words, of course) the sleep that the authentic poet images even in death (701)—and if we connect this sleep with that which prevented annihilation with the veiled maid, we have a conflation of identities and subjects that manages to contain it all: a dead "real" poet who never writes, who knows the consummation of death, but who is survived by a mirrored poet in language who keeps the real poet's desire alive—by repeating the dead poet's desire even as he strives to record it.

Shelley's Augustinian epigraph to *Alastor*—"Not yet did I love, and I loved to love. I sought what I should love, loving to love"—expresses the drama of desire that becomes, after the text turns from the Mother, the narrative motor of this poem. "Loving to love" or desiring desire ensures that desire infinite life. Complete consummation kills it. When Shelley translates consummation of desire into consummating his desire of the Other, the Law, he reaches the silence of death that is the end of *Alastor.* Articulating one's own desire fully is proof of authenticity in *Alastor.* The narrator-poet may be a scribe for another, but the vision that attends the solitary poet in his sleep is an extraordinary expression of one's encountering one's own desire, a therapeutic session that would have been a triumph for Lacan himself; and for Shelley, a complicating of the earlier myth of desire for the Mother. When the poet questor's "strong heart" sinks and "sicken[s] with excess of love" (181), as he gazes upon the visionary maid of the "ineffable tale" (168), we can do far better than to note the classic description of narcissism. What is more important as this passage constitutes a poet or enables a voice—perhaps even an entire poetics—is the extent to which the epipsychidion union becomes an ascesis even as it becomes a saturation; it becomes a blanking out of the word, of meaning, even at the moment of one's apparent achieving of selfhood. And the agent of this poetic enabling, the creation of the blank page, is a woman. The blank page that we often lament as the mark of woman's blotting out by literary history rebounds as the very source of poetic strength in Shelley, and not, I hasten to add, as the back over which he must climb to write as a freed man. Regardless of Shelley's failures in his real life as a feminist, he liberates gender in his poetic use of it.

This poet must encounter his own desire in a female form because the mythic female both escapes the phallus and retains it; she gives birth to the word as a procreative agent even as she can refuse to name the father of that word; she escapes the phallus precisely because she admits her castration more dramatically than does the equally castrated male. Furthermore, the "veiled maiden" teaches the narrator two conflicting truths about desire: that there is only lack behind the veil, a lack which is the very form *and* content of language itself, the vehicle and tenor; but that at the same time, if language is desire, that desire can, at the unconscious or dream-world level, know itself as its own and cease talking. Thus the need for the two poets of this story: One keeps talking at the end (similar to the Julian in that other frame tale, *Julian and Maddalo*), and the other is silenced (as is Julian's madman, entombed with his female half). Negotiating his desire in his own way at a level that escapes language, the mute poet of *Alastor* yet achieves articulation. The Arab maid who visits the solitary poet (ten lines before his vision of the veiled maid) was merely Real—carrying food from her father's tent and made of the very flesh and blood Shelley would later disavow as bearing upon *Epipsychidion,* a poem he nonetheless acknowledged as autobiographical. The Real is never enough, for it is only a part of the equation of desire; the Real is acted out in the Imaginary and Symbolic orders, those orders which constitute desire even as the Real passes through their defiles. Still, if the Real is necessary to constitute desire, desire is necessary to stutter at—to repeat—the act of articulating the Real. So it is that Shelley the poet seeks for his poetic persona a figure that collapses the Imaginary and Symbolic modes of coming to one's identity: This female figure is not a sentimentalized other half, completing an organic whole, but the Lacanian Other where mother and father intersect, the Law encompassing both, even as each depends upon a mirrored ego to become a subject.

The Imaginary by itself represents a regression, a return to Mother Earth; the Symbolic, a too easy accession to tradition and the chains of language. Combining the two, we have the sexualized veiled woman of *Alastor,* who will urge the poet to his conflagratory end—the consummation of silence—but who will pull back beneath the cover of the veil just in time, so that her yielding becomes illusory as her substantiality "dissolves": The poet will still be left yearning.

> He reared his shuddering limbs and quelled
> His gasping breath, and spread his arms to meet
> Her panting bosom: . . . she drew back a while,
> Then, yielding to the irresistable joy,
> With frantic gesture and short breathless cry
> Folded his frame in her dissolving arms.
> Now blackness veiled his dizzy eyes, and night
> Involved and swallowed up the vision; sleep,
> Like a dark flood suspended in its course,
> Rolled back its impulse on his vacant brain. [182–91]

It is precisely this tease of near consummation that impels the solitary poet forward "eagerly" to pursue "Beyond the realms of dream that fleeting shade" (205). Shelley foregrounds the literary association of "dying" and sexual orgasm in the question immediately subsequent to his "Does . . . death / Conduct to thy mysterious paradise, / O Sleep?" (211–13). That is, the dream maiden is the visionary's desire, his excess of self-love, that, once consummated and dying in its own way, will not have to repeat itself (to enter language) again. But Shelley would never have it quite this simple, so that even the sexual "dying" is withheld, in order to leave room for the conclusion, imbricated with both poetic authenticity and indebtedness: The "true" poet in his death-in-sleep will be outlived by the poet framer, the poet in language at the end.

What is exciting about the way Shelley situates the female is precisely his lack of gender thematizing. It is the epipsyche who helps him get beyond language, and since he assumes a heterosexual perspective, for him that epipsyche will be female. From this perspective, a woman, presumably, would have access to a space that would liberate her too—to the heterosexual woman, this space would be male. In this manner, Shelley complicates the current critical implication that male equals patriarchy and female an innocence of it. Such an equation has led to the notion that to undo the bonds of language and patriarchy one need only "write as a woman" (whatever that is) or "write in the place of woman" (wherever that is). Shelley plots his escape by writing from a projection of the fantasized self outside the ego, the displacement of excess self-love that Freud insists underlies any love of another and that Shelley locates in the epipsyche.

If the visionary maid in *Alastor* allows Shelley to experiment with a "pure" achievement of self, Beatrice in *The Cenci* is a philosophical compromise who presents the paradox of desire and the moral poet's dilemma. In the *Defence,* Shelley clearly states the extraordinary power he accords the imagination as the great instrument of moral good: "Imagination is as the immortal God which should assume flesh for the redemption of mortal passion." But where Beatrice's imagination fails (if we can even admit failure in the face of what she suffers) is in allowing itself to be robbed of its singularity through the insistence of a Jupiter-like patriarchal language, a language of curse that in *Prometheus Unbound* must be unsaid. Trapped in language that becomes more and more ominously metaphoric for the patriarchy that controls the world of this play, Beatrice is part of a master–slave dialectic that makes escape from contamination impossible for anyone. "And what a tyrant thou art, / And what slaves these; and what a world we make, / The oppressor and the oppressed" (5.3.73–75). Yet, to the extent that the woman gives up her femaleness (the blank page that lacks the phallus and, in Shelley's poetics, thereby has a greater chance at authentic voice than the male) and assumes the phallus, she loses.

It is not the literal rape, however, the penis, that undoes Beatrice; Shelley's drama depends upon this point: She is pure until she accedes to the phallus instead, a patriarchal language of revenge.[9] Shelley believes that Beatrice has a chance to be neither oppressor nor oppressed and that she gets caught up in the cycle anyway. Still, different from her oppressors, Beatrice encounters a particular end: She will become the virgin that Pope thought he wanted Belinda to become, that he hoped would castrate her of the threatening excess artifice. A blank page on which no one else can write except as on a palimpsest, Beatrice is another Romantic transparent signifier, through which all things pass but which never results in the final meaning that tormentors such as Count Cenci would locate in her. Beatrice (like Emily in Wordsworth's *White Doe*), betrayed by the men all around her and by a political system that betrays them as well, becomes silent. It seems an odd value system that privileges silence, but certainly it is one familiar to twentieth-century artists—to Samuel Beckett, to the musician John Cage, even to James Joyce, whose violent forcing and contorting of language finally share a real affinity with Shelley's pushing of language to its limits in order to experience the saturation of silence, the first moment subsequent to jouissance. It is in the violated woman of *The Cenci* that Shelley locates this purity.

Shelley's task in *The Cenci* is to unname the father, just as it was in *Prometheus Unbound,* a play he left after act 3 in order to write *The Cenci,* before concluding his cosmic epic of unsaying the chains of language. Naming, of course, carries extraordinary weight to Shelley; it is the secular equivalent of divinity, as his *Defence,* if nothing else, makes clear. By refusing to name the rape, both author and Beatrice escape a certain slippage of self that always occurs in the castration of language. Unspeaking the word represents to Shelley an individual's truest integration with an unstained world. To name is to acknowledge, and if Shelley at once identifies the poet as true legislator of the universe in Plato's sense in the *Cratylus*—that is, legislator as namer—he at the same time affects a provocative textual speed and accretion of wrenched images[10] aimed at foregrounding the metaphoricity of language. Such a style so effectively at the same time defamiliarizes language that he gives the illusion, at least, of an *unnaming* of the old and a creation of a blank page that enables, not enervates.

Shelley appears to be saying, we must become as woman, not gender but function, which term he defines only as possible when one can unname the language that would seem to pin down, rather than uplift. And the first step in that unnaming involves emasculating language of its pretense at full signification. "What are the words which you would have me speak," Beatrice asks Lucretia:

> I, whose thought
> Is like a ghost shrouded and folded up
> In its own formless horror. Of all words,
> That minister to mortal intercourse,
> Which wouldst thou hear? For there is none to tell
> My misery . . . [3.109–14]

Even as Beatrice is penetrated, she remains transparent, no mere vessel to contain the phallus but structured somewhere else—the Lacanian equivalent of "in another place"—in a desire that effectively, fantastically—if only temporarily—escapes the phallus. She situates her desire in a singular way; and if it seems violent that she must be raped incestuously to be free, potentially, of patriarchy, remember that it is his own father, mythologically, who tortures Prometheus and whose penetration Prometheus must encounter and reject by becoming transparent to it, by allowing paternity to pass through him without fertilizing patriarchal procreation.

But in one important way this stain of patriarchy is necessary, for it allows Beatrice to assume her castration along with all subjects who would become part of the generation of language, of stories that have a reason to remain extant, of lives that still need to be lived. Until the organism achieves desire in its own way, total satisfaction is deferred and desire remains alive, to be told and retold, in a repetition that seeks satisfaction even as it knows that consummation will prove it no longer necessary. Beatrice is the newly translated veiled/unveiled maid from *Alastor,* who here takes up with the narrator-poet, rather than the poet questor, so that her murder of the father makes of her an erotic text still in need of writing. Similar to the poet left to tell the story of the dead one in *Alastor,* she becomes a signifier not yet so saturated that its independence can be total. In this drama of desire Shelley implicates us the audience even if against our will, so that the real function of the text is to determine not Beatrice's guilt or innocence but our own as readers and interpreters.[11] "It is in the restless and anatomizing casuistry with which men seek the justification of Beatrice, yet feel that she has done what needs justification; it is in the superstitious horror with which they contemplate alike her wrongs and their revenge, that the dramatic character of what she did and suffered consists," he says in his preface. Beatrice is dramatic because we contemplate her actions, because we interpret; we give meaning. Her saturation into silence in effect demands it. We become again that poet framer of *Alastor,* whose desire has not yet been recognized but who can at least stick around to tell the story of one whose desire, in this case, approaches knowing itself as authentically its own. As with Byron's *Cain,* for example, and actually as is true of so much Romantic poetry, renovation through interpretation seeks to displace the *killing* act of interpretation that merely repeats without understanding. The need constantly to interpret anew promises to keep poetry alive, as language becomes a new language if we choose to read with imagination—with desire—that escapes the patrilineage of old formulas.

If the female characters in *Alastor* primarily act out the voicing of a poet through silence, while Beatrice achieves through her suffering and subsequent parricide a kind of saturation that gestures toward undoing patriarchal speech, the slippage of such basically discrete functions which are often, though not always, programmatic in these poems becomes the economy driving one of Shelley's most complex invocations of the female, Emilia Viviani in *Epipsychidion.* Emily clearly embodies the two positions of language and silence in one person; but then, as I've deduced from *Alastor* and *The Cenci,* the two positions from which Shelley's poetic persona would write *are* one: They are both the poet who is writing this poem and the one who desires his desire to be recognized and fulfilled. Against language as guarantee of desire, then, and woman as the desire that binds the poet to the word or the real, we juxtapose again the silent female, the saturation of the Arab maid, or of Emily outside her prison. In fact, Emily is the veiled maiden whose total possession was denied the poet questor years before in *Alastor,* but who is now accessible because they both have doubled their identities in the expanded Shelleyan negotiation with silence and speech:

> I stood, and felt the dawn of my long night
> Was penetrating me with living light:
> I knew it was the Vision veiled from me
> So many years—that it was Emily. [341–44]

No words effect this vision; it is the satiation of the perfectly heard ineffable; but equally significant, it is *penetration of the male* through female fullness—the light; and through absence—the lack of patriarchal linguistic signifiers. This full-but-empty female merely figures the poet himself—with the benefit that a silent, spent poet cannot record his vision, and hence the sated, silent female stands in as his double, inscribing his vision through her silence, even as he inscribes *her* silence through *his* pen. This epipsyche becomes the medium of saturation, the recognition of desire and death, but with all the accretions of meaning that culture has bestowed upon "dying," not least of which is the sexual suggestion of postorgasmic spentness. One of Lacan's favorite images, St. Thérèse in ecstasy, would function well as a Shelleyan epipsyche, either as her desire is recognized, in jouissance, or in the next moment, in which we envision the martyr's death. That a woman frequently refurbishes and recodes that spent desire, thus enabling poetic voice and vocation, testifies more to Shelley's sense of the bisexuality implicit in identity or desire than to any particular attention to gender. Gender and even sex work as helpful metaphors to en-gender the linguistic repetition of himself, of his desire, with Shelley becoming a poet as he writes. In some ways, Shelley may well be one of our least phallic writers, if we understand Lacan's rendering of phallus to mean all-knowing, all-powerful, promising closure. Lacan's belief that no one has the phallus—that both men and women are castrated—is a tenet, perhaps the major psychological premise, upon which Shelley's writing depends.

Thus Emilia, "Thou mirror" as the speaker addresses her, is the position to which Shelley aspires in *Epipsychidion* as the escape from the bondage of language. Yet those chains are necessary to leave behind the trace of the Real poet who has spoken. Shelley accepts the being-in-patriarchy necessary to engender voice as a condition for all poet-prophets, as Emily as epipsyche *also* equals *poetry* or *language.* There is Shelley himself—the authentic visionary—and his epipsyche, poetry, which records his vision. No preoedipal silence here: the woman, Emilia Viviani as occasion for this poem, forces what would be poetic silence instead to be recorded in the genealogy of language.

But how to make of language an instrument of great moral good? *Epipsychidion* is not a poem about flesh and blood; it is a poem about language and love and how the two are related. As Shelley writes John Gisborne, it is not his "own"—because it aims at knowledge of the Other where he comes into being. Listen to how the narrator addresses Emilia, or the "Sweet Spirit" of the poem's opening line: "too gentle to be human, / Veiling beneath that radiant form of Woman / All that is insupportable in thee / Of light, and love, and immortality!" (21–24). Already we encounter the oddest of forms—irradiant, yet veiling something as well as radiating it; woman is merely the form. The speaker continues:

> Thou mirror,
> In whom, as in the splendour of the Sun
> All shapes look glorious which thou gazest on!
> Aye, even the dim words which obscure thee now
> Flash, lightning-like, with unaccustomed glow. [30–34]

Appearing to be contingent upon thought as prior to language, his dim words (which obscure the true poetry that the mirror's association with the sun suggests) are illuminated by the very radiance of the form that veils. What is flashing, lightninglike, however, is not a language that is renewed now that it is in touch with an essence or thought preceding words but because it cohabitates with the generative nature of desire. Here is the lack bred precisely at the juncture where words become inadequate for expressing "true" self, even as that untrue self constituted through the inadequacy is all there really is, imagining itself in the mirror to be whole now, and fractured before. If it were not for this illusion of the mirror, convincing us that we can be unified, coherent, and self-imaged, there would be no quest, no repetition, which is the psychic drive in the human, to have his or her desire recognized. The lack that both ensures the inauthenticity of self-identity and constitutes desire is the very stuff of which poetry, at least Romantic poetry, consists.

Language, or poetry, speaks of the repetition that Lacan redacts from Freud as the true aim of desire—to be recognized, not to be fulfilled. If consummation of desire were the true aim, there would be "a more efficient path than repeated insistence"; similarly, "if the goal of the death instinct were simply the reduction of all tension, it could surely find a quick path to death."[12] For Lacan, desire must be conserved until it is recognized as such; and to be recognized, it must pursue its aim "only in its own fashion." The particular achievement of *Epipsychidion* is its ability to have it both ways: for Emilia Viviani to represent desire confronted and desire deferred infinitely through the chains of language. In this paradox, Emily functions as antilanguage, the opposite of those chains of lead that would drag the lover/narrator and his ideal back to earth; yet the poem maintains at the same time the equation that Emily equals poetry. She either blanks out the word or assumes the rhythms of desire that would repeat themselves until recognized. But we must acknowledge that (outside of psychoanalytic status as a psychotic) there is no objective confirmation of one's desire going improperly recognized; it is the subject who makes that (inevitable) call. So we are led to inquire: Do those who desire have a stake in maintaining their desire as unrecognized? Is this the life principle—the only means of staving off death; is desire both eros and end?

Emily as metonymic desire itself, more than a metaphor of it, helps the speaker to write and to repeat and to interpret; the confusion and conflation of reference to past and present women significant to the narrator are the signifying chain that Emily puts into place, that her mythical position as enabler of voice allows to progress as poetic production of meaning. Lacan's perception about the intersection of deferral and desire in linguistic structures is suggestive: "the signifier, by its very nature, always anticipates meaning by unfolding its dimension before it. As is seen at the level of the sentence when it is interrupted before the significant term: 'I shall never. . . .' " Such partial signification (all signification) still makes sense to us, "and all the more oppressively in that the meaning is content to make us wait for it."[13]

Shelley brilliantly deploys Emily as the virgin pointing to the absence that makes us wait for full-fillment, even as he also uses her as an originating metaphor to signify yet the next female who will link with her as an endless conduit of meaning. The lover/narrator does not appropriate her in the silence of inscription that imprints the Cenci phallic act and, at times, a Wordsworthian defense: "I am not thine: I am a part of *thee*" (52), he claims instead. She lures him "Towards sweet Death" because she threatens to satisfy him, to allow him a recognition of his desire that ends the need for repetition, just as the visionary maid enacts in *Alastor,* where the poet who sees himself potentially unveiled loses the justification ever to speak. Hence it is the paradox of poets whose desire would be recognized that in such consummation is their death, the end of the need to repeat. Emily—or rather the feminist Ideal of Intellectual Beauty[14] for which Emily becomes the signifier—produces a synaesthesis, a saturation of meaning:

Warm fragrance seems to fall from her light dress
And her loose hair; and where some heavy tress
The air of her own speed has disentwined,
The sweetness seems to satiate the faint wind;
And in the soul a wild odour is felt,
Beyond the sense [. . .] a mortal shape indued
With love and life and light and deity,
And motion which may change but cannot die; . . .
  A Metaphor of Spring and Youth and Morning;
A Vision like incarnate April, warning,
With smiles and tears, Frost the Anatomy
Into his summer grave. [105–14; 120–23]

Significantly, the speaker follows this conceit with "What have I dared? where am I lifted? how / shall I descend, and perish not?" (124–25). This last line implies what is at stake: to descend from the regions of the skylark (where Emilia can transport him) places him back in language while it bars his "true" song; and, through coding the anxiety in a question, it implies the truth about the nature of survival as a poetic voice: language the enabler, as it leaves the poet a story to tell. For, once again, the narrator of this poem pursues not meaning but a conveyor of meaning. Rather, he seeks both, but he knows that to rest in achieved meaning is to stop writing; one need not deliver the whole truth more than once.[15]

In fact, in this poem the *radiancy* of the Intellectual Ideal Beauty protects against achieved, saturated meaning as well as potentially effecting it: She is too bright to penetrate. "She met me, robed in such exceeding glory, / That I beheld her not" (199–200); her voice comes to him from "the fountains, and the odours deep / Of flowers"; from breezes, rain, bird song, from "all sounds, all silence" (206–9), "in form, / Sound, colour–in whatever checks that Storm / Which with the shattered present chokes the past" (210–12): all conveyors of meaning, bearers of the word, though still Barers of the word, and barrers of the word that would claim to have penetrated to the bottom of things. Emily may be locked in a prison, but true Love can never be barred, and woman as linguistic signifier simultaneously, impossibly, functions here as metaphor for that which cannot be barred even as she cannot be penetrated meaning-fully against her will:

> The walls are high, the gates are strong, . . .
> . . . but true Love never yet
> Was thus constrained: It overleaps all fence:
> Like lightning, with invisible violence
> Piercing its continents; like Heaven's free breath,
> Which he who grasps can hold not. . . . [396–401]

The tension created by Shelley's valuing of opposites and explosion of Western logic is perhaps the primary energy informing his work. Certainly, the ferocity with which a union of souls can bypass the ordinary productions of meaning attracts the visionary narrator, as he can approach infinity through it:

> We shall become the same, we shall be one
> Spirit within two frames, oh! wherefore two?
> One passion in twin-hearts, which grows and grew,
> Till like two meteors of expanding flame,
> Those spheres instinct with it become the same,
> Touch, mingle, are transfigured; ever still
> Burning, yet ever inconsumable:
> In one another's substance finding food. [573–80]

When, however, this union threatens to achieve precisely what the one who desires thinks he wants, consummation—"One Heaven, one Hell, one immortality, / And one annihilation" (586–87)—the narrator exclaims, "Woe is me!"—and invokes the oppressiveness of language as his defence, even as he appears to be lamenting its oppression: "The winged words on which my soul would pierce / Into the height of love's rare Universe, / Are chains of lead around its flight of fire" (588–90). But that fire is the radiance we have heard throughout in Shelley's poetic woman, the radiance that both promises and threatens to allow the poet to see himself face to face, to know his desire as his own, to locate the lack in his subjectivity which institutes that desire. Such a moment, the "flight of fire," is, it turns out, always implicated in the metaphors of those chains of lead, at least if there is to remain any psychological mandate to repeat oneself. The "winged words" must fail to articulate an epipsychidion union, or he will face, as he proclaims, annihilation. Emily is the medium of that failure, as well as the myth of a potential success: Emily—"Thou Mirror"—as silent reflection, luring him to death; it is the inadequacy of (poetic) language, an Emily imprisoned in the patriarchal convent walls, that also pulls him *back* from death. Emily can be the virgin, the blank page of seductive silence, but she is also the occasion of this poem, its language holding to earth the poet who would soar with her beyond its prisonhouse. Without her "chaining" his "flight of fire" there would be no *Epipsychidion*. Thus she is the word even as he would have her enact its annihilation.

Shelley's poetry is, of course, traditionally perceived as being unusually difficult: abstract, abstruse, perhaps unnecessarily complicated. A major cause of this effect upon the reader is the severe work he urges upon language in order for it to fulfill his opposite ends: Shelleyan language collapses and embodies both form and content as it seeks *repeatedly* to inscribe a path for itself leading outside itself, to the possibility of authentic presentation as opposed to re-presentation. Shelley writes of and in the repetition of desire seeking its own path.

This refusal to fix through gender a theme meant for woman—or man—to play out marks a subtlety to the strategies enabling what has long been noted as Shelley's brilliant versification. Our recognition of the ways in which he invokes cultural myths of the female as both too empty (in need of the phallus) and too full (consummation complete), in order to convert into an enabling paradox the crippling contradiction of authentic silence that would speak through indebted voice, suggests that we would do well to re-open to scrutiny other writers who specifically grappled with questions of language, indebtedness, and freedom. Perhaps we have too readily imposed easy schemes of gender positions, oppositions, oppressions, and appropriations on writers of the past, without affording them the chance to help us define patriarchy as a complicated third term, one far more complex than the simplistic premises of male accountability and female innocence would allow.

## Notes

1. For an extended analysis of this issue too long to repeat here, see my "Pope's Rape of Excess," in Gary Day, ed., *Sexuality in Literature and Film* (London: Macmillan, 1988), 129–43.
2. Clearly, to some extent I disagree with U. C. Knoepflmacher's position in his essay herein that the Romantics frequently used the female in precisely this way. His larger point, however—that *Browning* read the Romantics this way and converted the lyric subject into the ironic dramatic monologue—has proven extremely stimulating to my own thought on how formal innovation can occur through disillusionment with patriarchal models.
3. Anne K. Mellor, ed., *Romanticism and Feminism* (Bloomington: Indiana University Press, 1988).

4. Paul H. Fry, "Made Men: A Review Article on Recent Shelley and Keats Studies," *Texas Studies in Literature and Language* 21 (1979): 451.
5. As we confront the contradiction in Shelley's bifurcation of female-as-linguistic-function or enabler, we would do well to consider what William Keach, *Shelley's Style* (New York: Methuen, 1984), says about Shelley's apparent confusion regarding language: that "some forms of contradiction and even obscurity may be necessary to the reflections of a volatile verbal sensibility" (3). For instance, the slippage in language that is cause for both celebration and despair in Shelley's *Defence* also underwrites the very attempt to write a poetry. It is no wonder that deconstruction found in Shelley an auspicious host, for an enabling premise of his canon is a fluidity *not* essential, as in a French feminist version of the semiotic, but structurally inevitable for any verbal articulation.

   For other recent provocative readings of Shelleyan encounters with the conventions of language, see Susan Hawk Brisman, "'Unsaying His High Language': The Problem of Voice in *Prometheus Unbound*," *Studies in Romanticism* 16 (1977): 51–86; D. J. Hughes, "Coherence and Collapse in Shelley, with Particular Reference to *Epipsychidion*," *ELH* 28 (1961): 260–83, and "Kindling and Dwindling: The Poetic Process in Shelley," *Keats–Shelley Journal* 13 (1964): 13–28; Jerrold E. Hogle, "Metaphor and Metamorphosis in Shelley's 'The Witch of Atlas,'" *Studies in Romanticism* 19 (1980): 329–32, and "Shelley's Poetics: The Power as Metaphor," *Keats–Shelley Journal* 31 (1982): 159–97; and Stuart Peterfreund, "Shelley, Monboddo, Vico, and the Language of Poetry," *Style* 15 (1981): 382–400.
6. See, for instance, Barbara Schapiro's interpretation of *Alastor* as gloomily nihilistic in *The Romantic Mother: Narcissistic Patterns in Romantic Poetry* (Baltimore: Johns Hopkins University Press, 1983), xiii.
7. Harold Bloom, *Poetry and Repression: Revisionism from Blake to Stevens* (New Haven: Yale University Press, 1976), 105.
8. Textual citations are taken from Donald H. Reiman and Sharon B. Powers, eds., *Shelley's Poetry and Prose* (New York: Norton, 1977).
9. John Donovan glosses Shelley's heuristic interest in the "ethical purity" potential in incest as a "freedom from fear which precedes right action and which results from the mind's clear gaze at the contrarities of nature, without and within" (90) in "Incest in *Laon and Cythna:* Nature, Custom, Desire," *Keats–Shelley Review,* Autumn 1987, 49–90. For Shelley, incest, if freely chosen, can function sexually as a potent imaginative union of the identical-yet-different, a union where, in a sense, one experiences collapse that still insists upon a return to separation and distinctness. This model is hardly recognizable, of course, in Western familial arrangements, where incest imitates instead Cenci-like possession. And, of course, since the mode of sexual intercourse in *The Cenci* is rape versus consent, the sexual act there is the antithesis of "ethical purity." That the transgression is rape by the father allows for the sexual construction to serve violently as a metaphor for patriarchal ravage.
10. See esp. chap. 5 in Keach, *Shelley's Style.*
11. Julia Kristeva, "Within the Microcosm of 'The Talking Cure'" in *Interpreting Lacan,* ed. Joseph H. Smith and William Kerrigan (New Haven: Yale University Press, 1983), claims as Freud's legacy the proposition that "interpretation necessarily represents appropriation, and thus an act of desire and murder" (33).
12. Jane Gallop, *Reading Lacan* (Ithaca, NY: Cornell University Press, 1985), 104.
13. Jacques Lacan, *Ecrits: A Selection,* trans. Alan Sheridan (New York: Norton, 1977), 153.
14. Nathaniel Brown, "The 'Brightest Colours of Intellectual Beauty': Feminism in Peacock's Novels," *Keats–Shelley Review,* Autumn 1987, 91–104, reminds us that for the Shelley circle, his vaunted phrase "intellectual beauty" carried feminist connotations, particularly in its support of Mary Wollstonecraft's premise, in *A Vindication of the Rights of Woman,* that "intellectual beauty" in women is too often met with indifference, versus the almost universal appreciation attending a woman's physical beauty (91–92). It is very important,

then, to position the feminist connotation of this key phrase in Shelley's "Hymn" within the other and primary philosophical context in which he uses it—a "Humerian scepticism, though with affinities to both Berkeleian idealism and Plato's philosophy of Ideas" (91). Such a program insisted upon the immaterial nature of reality—finally, if implicitly, the role of interpretation in naming reality. In other words, Shelley deliberately casts this already philosophically awkward amalgam into the form of the female, that which represents also a more complicated cultural engagement with the phallus, with the law, and with language than does the son. It is this very excess of meaning that Shelley locates in woman which motivates him to have her mark the place of the infamous "fading coal," his mythic space of previously unapprehended vision and the linguistically indebted interpretive acts its conception en-genders.

15. Thus Shelley comes very close to creating an *écriture féminine,* a plural, fluid movement that, to use Catherine Clement's phrase, is a "coming" to writing, though Shelley always is careful to defer the climax, to tease language to its near breaking point instead.

# Beyond the Fragmented Word: Keats at the Limits of Patrilineal Language

MARLON B. ROSS

IN HER STUDY *The Romantic Fragment Poem* (1986) Marjorie Levinson asserts the intentionality of fragmentation in the poetry of the romantics. Asking why Keats's *Hyperion* "break[s] off before its appointed end," she appeals to what I call an evolutionary parable, a story of progression that asserts the capacity to gain, if not increasingly greater control over experience itself, at least greater control over a language that orders and expresses experience. Fragmentation becomes, for Levinson, a sign of Keats's successful maturation, his mastery over his past and his precursors as well as over himself.[1] *The Fall* "surpasses" *Hyperion* even as it depends on the previous poem to mark the mastery of its progression, and, Levinson says, it "demonstrates on every level Keats's autonomy. We see at once by this work that Keats has escaped the influence of his great precursors and that he has surpassed himself—surpassed 'Hyperion'!"[2] Paradoxically, Keats's "autonomy" is achieved through "dependent" forms, his own developmental narrative mastered through undeveloped fragments; his discourse supposedly succeeds by fracturing itself.

I wonder, however, whether this evolutionary parable—both the one that Keats writes and the one that Levinson rewrites and celebrates—is not fractured in a more fundamental sense. As Levinson herself recognizes, *Hyperion* serves to assert Keats's gaining of adulthood through language that is "causal, univocal, linear." I would go further than this and suggest that the poem desires to assert not just Keats's coming into *manhood* but also his coming into discursive power—and that, in fact, the latter is considered a sign of the former. The poem aims to prove the poet's capacity to perform forcefully the discursive rituals of his culture, rituals which define poetic maturity in terms of patrilineal performance. That is, Keats recognizes that to make himself into, to be accepted as, a great poet he must seek to renew and re-form all previous poetic discourse by engendering a lasting line of descendants who will be bound to use language according to his re-formation of it. The "great" poet's capacity to re-form his linguistic tradition is, however, an illusory kind of reform, in that his renewal of language merely affects the forms in which discourse is uttered without effecting a change in the structure of discourse itself. Re-formed discourse does not inevitably give us new ways of structuring discourse, does not give us new rituals that can change the ways in which we interact verbally, in which we inhabit our culture through the use of language. Instead, re-formed discourse gives us new ways of carrying out already established verbal interactions, new costumes for old customs. We can see, then, that re-form prevents real reform by deluding the poet into thinking that his grand performance in establishing a lasting line of followers who will mimic his discourse is a kind of progression, when actually it is nothing more than a validation of his culture's power over him and over language use. Ironically, then, if Keats manages to re-form the specific discursive rituals of his precursors, seeming to circumvent the discipline of his poetic fathers, his success will only bind him more tightly to the greater rituals of his unreformed culture. In fact, because it is patriarchal culture that has defined discursive power as the capacity to re-form the fathers' discourse, by seeking to avoid the discipline of the fathers Keats subjects himself to the discipline, subjects himself to the rituals of his fathers' culture. Culture's rule over discursive rituals assures its power over poetic discourse.

By the same logic, however, in order for patriarchal culture to be sustained, its rituals must be practiced, not necessarily in all modes of discourse but in those modes that predominate or in enough modes to maintain its predominance. Patriarchal culture cannot fully abrogate the intrinsic malleability of language, since it is this malleability that enables discourse to occur in the first place. Because discursive rituals are based on the malleability of language, a poet cannot re-form language without also dallying with genuine discursive reform. If a poet attempting to re-form tradition is automatically a potential reformer of cultural discourse, how does culture discourage reform while encouraging re-form? As we shall see, Keats, desiring a life beyond the prisonhouse of cultural discourse, most certainly experiments with the nonpatrilineal potential of language, as he hesitates to perform the rituals demanded within patriarchal culture. When he tries to explore nonpatrilineal uses of language, however, he is immediately perceived, and perceives himself, as impotent. To hesitate patrilineal performance is to refuse patriarchal power; to refuse patriarchal power means to give up power as it is practiced within culture; to have no power within culture makes it all the more difficult to have power over culture, to have power to change culture. How can one reject the signs of power and still be empowered? How can one reject the strictures of patrilineal discourse without also being disciplined by that discourse? How can one progress as a poetic soul without performing the rituals that determine progression? How can a poet take (progress) his culture beyond discourse as it is practiced toward revolutionary discourse if the only notion of progress is the one predetermined by the old culture, if the notion of "progress" is itself the premise on which the rituals of the old cultural discourse is based? This is the quadruple bind that Keats finds himself in, and that fractures each poem in which he aspires to reform discourse by giving words new forms of power, by giving them a wholeness beyond the limits of culture as it is learned, known, perpetrated, and perpetuated through language.

"The phenomenology of the fragment is the phenomenology of human awareness," Thomas McFarland says in *Romanticism and the Forms of Ruin*.[3] Levinson and McFarland both see the romantic fragment as an *intentional* form of human achievement—the former as mastery over time itself by "chronicling" a progression in awareness, however futile, and the latter as mastery over the "forms of fragmentation," over both the consciousness of fragmentation and the poetic expression of that consciousness. Edward Bostetter, on the other hand, takes romantic fragmentation as a thoroughly unintentional loss of control over the very poetic intentions that promise control. The "abandonment" of *Hyperion*, Bostetter suggests, "at the point of revelation was a sign of doubt and imaginative failure" on Keats's part.[4] Wholeness of poetic form becomes the sacrificial victim of a vision that fragments itself unintentionally, a vision internally fragmented by its own inherent limits. In order to understand Keats's self-fragmenting vision, we need to consider how an evolutionary parable functions within the culture that Keats desires both to master and to revolutionize, for his writing of that parable is not so much a natural progression toward "adulthood" as it is a culturally determined will to power, which conflicts with the urge toward a revolutionary reordering of discourse. Once we resituate Keats's discourse within the culture that authorizes it, the question of intentionality must resurface. If the poems reveal a fundamental split within Keats's desire, a fracture marked by cultural politics, then how intentional can their fragmentation be? Also, could it be possible that these fragments expose a fissure within the culture itself, a fissure that culture seeks to hide because, while signaling the limits of an individual's power over his own discourse within culture, that fissure also unintentionally exposes the potential limits of culture's power over language, a faultline of potential weakness within the cultural economy?

My interrogation of Keats's tendency toward fragmented discourse is grounded in two major premises. The first is that we can make a valid distinction between the way language operates systemically and the way it operates in historicized discourse. I am not interested in describing the structural foundations of a system here; rather, I want to examine how one specific kind of language usage—romantic poetic discourse—operates as culturally bound exchanges between a poet and the demands of his readers, between a poet and the demands of his own desire, between a poet and the demands of cultural tradition. The second premise is that poetic discourse operates no differently in relation to intention than cultural discourse in general. I tend to question writers like Julia Kristeva who suggest that poetic discourse *by its very nature* tends to suspend or break the normative functions of language in patriarchal culture.[5] The way a poem, even the most avant-garde poem, communicates (is written and read) depends on the cultural practices available to poet and reader alike. Poetic discourse, like all discourse, is bound by the history of its practices within a particular culture. This does not mean, of course, that poetic discourse cannot rebel against the historicized rituals that inform and re-form it. The question is whether, or to what degree, such discourse, whether poetic or not, can revolutionize culture itself. The question is whether, or to what extent, "revolutionary" language tends to subvert anything other than itself, anything other than its own attempt at cultural communication. This second premise means that poetic discourse has no special privilege in relation to the culture that authorizes it. In fact, the very idea that poetic language *is* privileged is one of the cultural premises that rules poetic performance in the English literary tradition that Keats finds himself enamored of and frustrated by. Merely because we can write and read *as though* poetic language transcends the culture that authorizes it does not mean that such poetic language actually does transcend the rituals that conventionally enable its communication and efficacy within culture. Perhaps Keats is writing, then, not only at the limits of his historical situation, as Levinson might claim, or at the limits of the "human situation," as McFarland might claim, or at the limits of his own desire, as Bostetter might claim, but also and more importantly at the limits of his particular culture's discursive knowledge, at the outmost periphery of a culture's articulation of itself.

Twice Keats sets out to narrate the fall of Hyperion, and both times he stops writing before completing the narration. We know it is not because Keats could not complete a narrative poem. He completes several long ones with no evident difficulty or discomfort. On the other hand, there are other instances of Keats's stopping before finishing. If we do not take these fragments as either universally inevitable (assuming that every poem is a fragmented form) or purely accidental (assuming that all poetic motives and ends must be reduced to the happenstance of self-unmotivating language), then we can claim that there are significant reasons for the incompletion of these narratives and that their state of fragmentation may have at least a common denominator. If we consider the narrative poems that are completed (if not artistically "finished"), we find that they all come under the general rubric of romance: *Endymion, Isabella, The Eve of St. Agnes, Lamia.* Except for *The Eve of St. Mark,* which is so much a fragment that it is impossible to define its genre, all of the completed narratives are concerned with the quest for innocent love, albeit a quest perverted or subverted in some way in almost all of the poems. On the other hand, the narrative fragments are all poems that are concerned with the quest for power: *Calidore* and the *Hyperion* poems. This distinction between love and power, though it may at first appear both simplistic and arbitrary, helps us to understand (1) the way in which Keats's own desire is fractured, (2) the way in which his desire conflicts with the demands of his culture, and (3) the way in which patriarchal culture always attempts to heal a fissure that it necessarily inflicts within itself.

In *Endymion,* Keats explores the bower of innocent love; it is a bower that enables him to escape, however temporarily, the doubts and uncertainties that later become definitive of poetic power for him.

> A thing of beauty is a joy for ever:
> Its loveliness increases; it will never
> Pass into nothingness; but still will keep
> A bower quiet for us, and a sleep
> Full of sweet dreams, and health, and quiet breathing.
> Therefore, on every morrow, are we wreathing
> A flowery band to bind us to the earth,
> Spite of despondence, of the inhuman dearth
> Of noble natures, of the gloomy days,
> Of all the unhealthy and o'er-darkened ways
> Made for our searching: yes, in spite of all,
> Some shape of beauty moves away the pall
> From our dark spirits.[6]

This notion of poetic language as an infinite bower of beauty forgets temporarily the schematized performance demanded in patrilineal discourse. Bower poetry is a kind of nonperformance or, as Keats terms it, "negative capability," which is based on aestheticized identification rather than self-empowering mastery. Frances Ferguson has explained one such kind of "love language" as evidenced in Shelley's intercourse with Mont Blanc. "In *Mont Blanc,*" Ferguson writes, "Shelley falls in love with a ravine, a river, and a mountain not because of the nature of those objects but because of his own, his human, mind, which cannot imagine itself as a genuinely independent, isolated existence." And as Ferguson points out, "Mont Blanc" is Shelley's attempt to align "epistemology with love."[7] I think, however, that the definition of love which Ferguson quotes from Shelley applies even more to Keats's bower poetry than to Shelley's own metaphysically oriented poetic discourse. He defines love as "that powerful attraction towards all that we conceive, or fear, or hope beyond ourselves, when we find within our own thoughts the chasm of an insufficient void and seek to awaken in all things that are a community with what we experience within ourselves."[8] As Ferguson suggests, Shelley's "love language" results not so much from the "nature of those objects" that he seeks to commune with as from the nature of his own mind. Keats's bower language, on the other hand, seems more radical to me, exactly because it results from an intense desire to annihilate the identity of self, as he says, for the sake of other natures.[9] The poet subjects himself willingly to other natures, which then become subjects in themselves rather than merely denatured objects. They become indiscriminately subjects of the poet's nature while remaining subjects within themselves.

Within the bower, poets and readers can revel in the ecstatic experience of otherness redefining the limits of self. The other's inclusion within the self becomes a form of participation itself, rather than invasion and impregnation for the end of establishing a lasting line. It is like "An endless fountain of immortal drink, / Pouring unto us from the heaven's brink" (1.23–24). Generating endless discriminations in an attempt to experience all of experience, encouraging a democracy of identifications in an attempt to include all inclusions, this dream of love is also an articulation of ceaseless excitement without disturbance, peace without banality, mortality without the finality of death:

> Nor do we merely feel these essences
> For one short hour; no, even as the trees
> That whisper round a temple become soon
> Dear as the temple's self, so does the moon,
> The passion poesy, glories infinite,
> Haunt us till they become a cheering light
> Unto our souls, and bound to us so fast,
> That, whether there be shine, or gloom o'ercast,
> They always must be with us, or we die. [1.25–33]

The bower grows within our souls and binds us—not the normative kind of binding, as we shall see, practiced within Keats's culture, but binding for the sake of fertile differentiation. What Keats attempts to write in and into *Endymion* is a kind of *objectless* desire that fulfills itself by yearning for itself, a desire that has no objects because every object is itself a desiring subject, a desire that has no objectives except to increase the pleasure of desire. This bower discourse embraces the infinite "essences" within each thing, binding and referring each to each, endlessly reproducing a love for such endless referential binding. Such a poem does not describe or reflect or moralize on the world; it escapes the world by re-creating its own world in itself, ironically while insistently referring innocently to the world it seeks to evade. The bower is a place so easeful that it can include the diseased world (in fact, according to its rule of infinite inclusions, it must) without its own ease being disrupted, for the bower composes (makes and eases) a discourse whose communicative rituals are defined by a participatory love for aestheticized experience. Since infinite wonder is a type of wholeness, the bower brings wholeness by making beautiful (worthy of wonder) that which appears to be ugly in the world, transforming the pall of death into "some shape of beauty." The limitless capacity of words (their malleability) helps to create a fountain of delight ever renewing itself. And as these words seem to refer to external things (the world with its attendant gloom), they magically remain true to the logic of their own internal beauty, making sense (communicating) by remaking the external world into the internalized image of ever-changing words.

How would this participatory discourse work as poetry? It would work something like *Endymion,* though, as Keats was aware, this romance falls far short of his ideal. The most important rhetorical attributes of such discourse for our purposes include: (1) the wandering series, (2) profuse but lucid imagery, and (3) tropes of imitative identification. We can see all of these at work in the third verse paragraph of *Endymion.* The design of the paragraph is characteristically simple, for how can every reader be invited in if some are turned away by obscurity? The paragraph is simply an additive series that moves from the "full happiness" of Keats's prospective tracing in the first two lines to the uncertain path, dressed in green, a color that encourages us to "speed / Easily Onward, thorough flowers and weed." The uncertainty of the path is not an impediment except insofar as it is a pleasing deferral of our "onward" motion, causing us to linger and idle, to wander aimlessly from flower to flower. And our aimless wandering claims for itself the naturalness of erring exactly because it makes erring impossible, because it makes erring a wonderfully pure pleasure rather than a sin. Wandering that precludes all possibility of erring is very dissimilar from Wordsworth's teleological wandering at the beginning of the *Prelude.* Whereas Wordsworth cannot lose his way because his journey is predestined by nature, Keats and his readers must lose both the way and themselves in the way. They must forget themselves as they take pleasure *in* endless wandering, rather than *through* wandering to some predetermined end. *Endymion* reads as though Keats is unsure of his way because he is, like Spenser, unsure of his way. Each new turn of the story, whether predictable or not, is a pleasure, for it is the constant turning that is the aim of the story's aimless movement. The plot is progression without progress, where incident and accident are always pleasurable openings for a new path, where each new path promises a bowery maze.

This prospective paragraph itself, for instance, is a series of the most natural kind. It ambles through the seasons, each season itself being transformed into an infinite maze, each transferring its beauty and joy to the next. We begin in spring: "Now while the early budders are just new, / And run in mazes of the youngest hue" (1.41–42). We move through and within summer and autumn:

> And, as the year
> Grows lush in juicy stalks, I'll smoothly steer
> My little boat, for many quiet hours,
> With streams that deepen freshly into bowers.
> Many and many a verse I hope to write,
> Before the daisies, vermeil rimm'd and white,
> Hide in deep herbage; and ere yet the bees
> Hum about globes of clover and sweet peas,
> I must be near the middle of my story.
> O may no wintry season, bare and hoary,
> See it half finished: but let autumn bold,
> With universal tinge of sober gold,
> Be all about me when I make an end. [1.45–58]

It would be a mistake to think that Keats desires a mere year to write this story; he desires a lifetime, and one without terminus, in which each season becomes an age within itself, an infinite bower to be explored. The wandering series would, of course, be familiar to Keats's readers due to poets like Spenser and Thomson. This device, however, can easily be used performatively to reaffirm patrilineal discourse rather than for the ends of bowery love. In other words, it could be used as a way of proving a poet's mastery over so many mazes, as a way of asserting a poet's capacity to amaze others, who become lost in his ways never to enjoy their own, who become imitators of his discourse never to discover their own. If Keats had used the wandering series in *Endymion*, for instance, to demonstrate how easy it is to err from the proper path, rather than how pleasurable it is to forsake the notion of the proper path, he would have been using it to sustain patrilineal discourse. Instead, the tale enjoins us to participate not in order to disown ourselves but rather in order to chart our own wanderings among the poet's serial mazes, not in order to perform correctly a predetermined ritual but rather in order to share mutually in the spontaneous ritualization of remaking discourse as a shared activity. In effect, it becomes the ritual of constantly remaking the rituals of discourse. Keats invites his readers to fall, like Endymion, in love with objects, taking them as subjects, while being led by desire to some arbitrarily happy conclusion, instead of, as in patrilineal narrative, forever claiming the need to lead and shape every object into a predetermined objective.

In addition to the wandering series, Keats uses a more novel trope, imitative identification, a kind of metonymy in which each essence participates in the other by dissolving itself into the other while retaining its own essence. There are many instances of it in this single paragraph. Keats says about Endymion's name: "The very music of the name has gone / Into my being, and each pleasant scene / Is growing fresh before me as the green / Of our own vallies" (1.36–39). The name is turned (in)to music, which composes (again in both senses) Keats's "being." The name is not simply metaphorically musical; it *is* music. To speak it or hear it remakes the self in the idiom of music. Keats's existence is now constituted by that naming music (EndymionEndymionEndymion), the repetition of redolent sound that transforms itself magically into purely aestheticized melody. The magical music of the name represents, of course, the magical bower of poesy. The name is to music what "the green / Of our own vallies" is to "each pleasant scene" that grows within the poet's mind; the name is the word that grows magically within the poetic imagination. Just as music usurps the name (giving it feature, form, and function), so the fanciful scenes of the poem usurp the actual green valleys. The pleasant scenes "growing fresh" (growing always anew) before him both are and are not the green valleys of the real world before him. As Keats sends his "herald thought into a wilderness," his mind becomes a wilderness of wonder, where everything is itself and yet everything else at once, where we can always move forward and never move toward an end. This process of indiscriminate naming transfers the attributes of one "essence" to those of another, introjects subjectivity into every object, making it a space to be inhabited and enjoyed rather than an objective to be gained, and labels everything as though it must partake of everything else even as it retains its own uniqueness. Such a process, as we shall see, is opposed to the act of naming in the discourse authorized by culture. It is also different from the metonymy of Freudian displacement, for it is not a mechanism that enables the unconscious to operate as an engine of repression. Keats's metonymic transferrals are fully conscious, without becoming *self*-conscious, for the pleasure of indiscriminate naming lies in recognizing how boundaries become bridges, how subjectivity can become contagious without also becoming the fatal illness of self-propagation.

"They alway must be with us, or we die," Keats says. The profuse lucidity of the diction, the endless meandering around, in, and through serial mazes, the universalization of metonymic relations—all of these hope to forestall the "wintry season, bare and hoary." The only apparent threat to this dream of participatory love within the bower is the barrenness of death. The paradox of this kind of democratic discourse is that it must, if it is true to itself, discriminate among forms of barrenness, that it must indiscriminately include its most apparent threat, death itself. And like life itself, the poem must come to an end, must annihilate itself—a reality that everywhere haunts its feverish profuseness, its infinite multiplication of "many and many a verse." As Richard Macksey points out, *Endymion* ends so awkwardly because "Mortal man is not Apollo; the earth is not heaven."

> The situation of the poet, like that of his language, is one of continual "usury" in the erosive and fragmenting as well as the additive sense. The radical—and ineradicable—fact in Keats's mind is the mutual incompatibility of the human and the ideal climates, of "life" and the "legend," of experience and the language that would comprehend it.[10]

In addition to this ultimate incompatibility between heaven (the bower) and earth (patriarchal culture), there is a conflict between endlessly discriminating inclusiveness and the reality of exclusions, the reality that excluding is what enables the pursuit of inclusivity. Keats wants the happiest synthesis: both the infinite inclusiveness of never ending and the aesthetic wholeness of formal closure. Obviously, he cannot have both, but he can have an ending, however awkwardly forced, which makes the poem appear to be a whole that contains infinity in itself, that contains infinity in its endless a-mazing naming of itself.

However awkwardly *Endymion* ends, it does end. Ironically, the ease of the bower diminishes the threat of ending. We can always have the pleasure of beginning again; enter a new bower, write a new poem, or because each bower is loaded with ore, reenter the same bower and retrace its infinite series of mazes yet again. Bower poetry invites the luxury of idle rereading. The alternative is to do what Keats does in his other romances: pervert the dream of love, subvert the bower by bitterly bringing attention either to the potential evil that must always be entertained when innocence reigns inclusively (as in *Lamia*) or to the deadly finality of even the most innocent act of aesthetic concluding (as in the closure of *The Eve of St. Agnes*). Perhaps we could say that the world's disease contaminates the quest for participatory, innocent love in these romances. The dream of love must always be infected by the disease of reality and harbored under the shadow of death.

The biggest problem with the bower is not so much its apparent unreality, however, as its implicit powerlessness to affect reality. The bower is merely a lapse, an escape. "[S]o I will begin / Now while I cannot hear the city's din" (1.39–40), Keats says, entering the bower. The din of the city is the noise of civilization, of culture and its "despondence." Discourse in the city, as opposed to language in the bower, is a tower of Babel, where self-individuating selves clamor and vie for attention and power, where playful discrimination and participation fall into division and strife, where the luxury of idleness is reprimanded as undisciplined laziness and loitering, and where progress (the movement of culture toward some realizable end) is real even though it is perverted toward selfish ends. Although bower poetry uses language in a way that allows us temporarily to forget patrilineal rituals, it does so unfortunately by giving ultimate value and power to the dominant reality that it seeks to escape. As we have seen, in the bower progress is temporarily annihilated in favor of a kind of progressless progression. It is the timelessness of the dreamspace, the untimely idleness of escape. Can the "work" of revolution be sustained by dreamplay that refuses to progress even beyond itself? Can discourse be revolutionary if it forsakes the right of timely intervention and timed progression toward a shared goal? Could it be that bower discourse ignores that language must work for revolution before it plays within the ideal? Because bower language is the nostalgic discourse of a remembered or imagined Eden, rather than the working discourse that charts a path toward a new Eden, it cannot be revolutionary. It defines poetic language always as a dreamy and harmless cousin of a powerful tyrant. The bower derives its pleasure from its status as an illusive, protective, self-containing, self-restraining space of pure beauty within a larger world of real woe. Such poetic discourse—no matter how seductive—effects (and affects) only itself. Because bower poetry merely holds at bay the patrilineal uses of discourse, it cannot alter the cultural rituals that perpetuate the patrilinearity of discourse. Ironically, by refusing the notion of progress offered by patriarchal culture, bower poetry refuses a notion of progress beyond culture as it is known. In effect, in worshiping the bower, Keats gives up his chance to rename his culture, to revise how his culture names itself.

At first, this may appear to be simply a conflict between the proverbial "man of action" and "man of contemplation." It is not. The choice is not between writing poetry and leaving poetry behind in order to do something else. Rather, the choice is between writing poetry of one kind or another. Furthermore, it is not merely a conflict between Keats's desire and the world he inhabits, between heaven and earth; it is also a conflict within Keats which splits his desire and turns it against itself. One way of thinking about this is to say that Keats has internalized (as he must) the cultural rituals that enable language to have meanings, that enable poets to write and be read. I would rather, however, conceptualize this conflict within Keats's desire as a battle between dissonant urges, each belonging to his culture as well as to him, but one dominant, the other recessant. It is this conflict between the demand for patrilineal performance of language and the desire for a liberated use of language that frustrates Keats in his *Hyperion* poems and ultimately causes their fragmentation.

To love infinite deferral of identity, rather than to plunge headlong into a self-empowering progression, is to err in the eyes of Keats's culture. The poet's guilt for erring, for loitering, reveals itself in the preface to *Endymion* both as a kind of self-castigation or inward lashing, a desire to claim the loitering as a mere phase that the poet will ultimately purge from his discourse, and as a kind of lashing out, a desire to punish the patriarchs who he knows will judge his loitering as poetic impotence. In this self-castigation and lashing out, Keats not only preempts the loitering of the poem to do penance for his erring; he also succumbs to the guilt that culture infuses within him to assure the victory of patrilineal (self)discipline. "The imagination of a boy is healthy, and the mature imagination of a man is healthy," Keats says in the preface to *Endymion,* as he appeals to the making of his own evolutionary parable. "[B]ut there is a space of life between, in which the soul is in a ferment, the character undecided, the way of life uncertain, the ambition thick-sighted: thence proceeds mawkishness, and all the thousand bitters which those men I speak of must necessarily taste in going over the following pages" (103). In this parable, it is Keats who resides in the unhealthy state of undecidedness and who will proceed, presumably through confusion, to a healthy state of maturity. *Endymion*'s "love language" is temporalized by the poet's desire to father and further his discourse as a powerful language within the cultural hierarchy. This need to create a stage for bower desire signals how patrilineal discourse everywhere haunts *Endymion.* In effect, Keats creates an evolutionary parable in order to stem the tide of his insecurity, in order to drown out the smug security of his critics. The stages of his parable necessarily become status positions within an implicit hierarchy. By placing himself in the second stage, he hopes to preempt the discipline of his critics by disciplining himself, and at the same time he hopes to promote a sense that he is not really idly wandering or being led somewhere he cannot know but that he is shaping his own destiny, as he passes from the innocence of youth through temporary weakness and confusion to the wholesomeness of manly maturity.

The preface to *Endymion,* then, discriminates in a way altogether different from the discriminations within the poem, for the preface names in order to objectify and discipline (both Keats and his potential critics). The difference between the critics and himself becomes a threat to him, a threat and yet a promise. It tells him that he may never claim their conviction in his powers as a poet, and therefore he must either castigate himself or convince himself of their real impotence, or both. The will to power, the desire to overcome his foes and win their allegiance, the desire to become his foes by being accepted by them, overwhelms the dream of love espoused within and by the poem.

> This may be speaking too presumptuously, and may deserve a punishment: but no feeling man will be forward to inflict it: he will leave me alone, with the conviction that there is not a fiercer hell than the failure in a great object. This is not written with the least atom of purpose to forestall criticisms of course, but from the desire I have to conciliate men who are competent to look, and who do look with a zealous eye, to the honour of English literature. [102]

If the rhetoric of the poem invites all who can read to dwell within the bower of poesy, the preface prefigures the dilemma that Keats feels in making so generous a gesture to all. This passage contains all of the attributes that characterize patrilineal discourse: schematizing compromise; performance, purposiveness, and spectatorship; and, perhaps most important, the establishment of territorial claims for the sake of engendering a lasting line of powerful discourse within culture. Keats feels compelled to point out his "inexperience, immaturity, and every error denoting a feverish attempt" while saying that even "a year's castigation" would not improve the poem he has written (102). By attempting to "conciliate" these men, however, Keats also necessarily conciliates his own desire. He invests the "zealous eye" within himself, an eye that is always beforehand vested within the self, for it is this eye that teaches us how to look, how to keep a zealous eye on the honor of tradition and its properties, how to grow up properly in a culture that rules through the rituals of its self-disciplining discourse.

John Gibson Lockhart, the most infamous of Keats's reviewers, represents the extreme of patrilineal discourse. He names only in order to discipline: to separate the powerless from the powerful, to advance his own claim to cultural power by asserting his authority to name, to punish those who would presume a claim to cultural power without having followed the prescribed rituals of empowerment. Lockhart establishes a bastard line of descent, naming it the "Cockney School," in order to claim zealously his own power within the legitimate line of descent. Lockhart's aim is not to get Keats to write better poetry but rather to stop him from writing all poetry: "if Mr Keats should happen, at some interval of reason, to cast his eye upon our pages, he may perhaps be convinced of the existence of his malady."[11] Discrimination is conceptualized always as exclusiveness, error as the failure of having taken the proper route to an appropriate end. "Destined" for the "career of medicine," Keats errs so far as to determine his own "career" as a poet. Thus Keats, desiring to paint himself as the healthy young poet, is disciplined by Lockhart, who classes him among "uneducated and flimsy striplings" incapable of understanding the "merits" of "*men of power.*"[12] Keats's preface fails, as it must, to serve its purpose. His self-castigation encourages the patrilineal discourse of others, encourages others who desire power over him to castigate him, to see his poem as a failed performance rather than as an experiment in participatory discourse, to see it as a potential line of descent naming its objects as territorialized objectives rather than as a bower of indiscriminate naming. Just in the way that culture perpetuates its own rituals of hierarchized power through the patrilinearity of its discourse, so Keats unwittingly sets in motion a spiral of contestation in which each writer attempts to outperform his adversaries.

When Keats moves from the Endymion to the Hyperion myth, he attempts to progress from a dream of love to the will to power. It is not by coincidence that the Hyperion fragments attempt to narrate how the ruling gods must fall in order to make way for new ones, how the fathers must give way to the sons. Anxious to assert his own claim to manhood, Keats, against the current of his own desire, attempts to teach himself how to perform the rituals of patrilineal poetry. As Keats writes to Haydon:

> [T]he nature of *Hyperion* will lead me to treat it in a more marked and grecian Manner—and the march of passion and endeavour will be undeviating—and one great contrast between them will be—that the Hero of the written tale being mortal is led on, like Buonaparte, by circumstance; whereas the Apollo in *Hyperion* being a foreseeing God will shape his actions like one.[13]

Bringing his bower poem into the world of realpolitik, he makes an analogy between his earlier hero and Napoleon, an ironic analogy considering Napoleon's real power in the world but appropriate considering Napoleon's inevitable "fall" and Keats's impending realization of Apollo's own limits. Unlike Endymion, Apollo "will shape his actions," will lay claim to his legitimate reign by fathering his discourse in his own image.

This apparent acceptance of patrilineal rituals translates into the following stylistic practices in the poem: (1) high, hard, disciplined diction; (2) an unrelenting pace toward momentous climax and closure, almost to the extent that the poem becomes pure "action"; (3) constant images of measure, whether of increase or diminishment, rising or falling, violent invasion or projection. Stripping his language to a "manly" terseness, Keats steps willingly into the barrenness that he has attempted to keep at bay in *Endymion.* His lean and hardened language serves to gauge his renewed engagement with the world of power and its demands. His description of the doomed god Hyperion serves well to represent the newly acquired discipline and momentum of his language:

> He enter'd, but enter'd full of wrath;
> His flaming robes stream'd out beyond his heels,
> And gave a roar, as if of earthly fire,
> That scar'd away the meek ethereal Hours
> And made their dove-wings tremble. On he flared,
> From stately nave to nave, from vault to vault,
> Through bowers of fragrant and enwreathed light,
> And diamond-paved lustrous long arcades,
> Until he reach'd the great main cupola;
> There standing fierce beneath, he stampt his foot,
> And from the basements deep to the high towers
> Jarr'd his own golden region; and before
> The quavering thunder thereupon had ceas'd,
> His voice leapt out, despite of godlike curb,
> To this result: [1.213–27]

Narrating the determined progress of "aching time" and "moments big as years" (1.64), the language is as driven as the gods, desperate to act, irritated by delay, threatened by the possibility of erring. Because what is at stake is the rule of the world itself—a "ripe progress" (1.125) "[t]oo huge for mortal tongue or pen of scribe" (1.160)—we can afford neither to linger nor to make uncalculated moves in the wrong direction. The grandness and hardness of the style, as opposed to the delicate and intricate detail of *Endymion*'s bower, are supposed to signify not only a matured manly vision but also a toughened stance in relation to the reality he once sought merely to escape. Like Hyperion himself, Keats is now willing to stand his ground and claim his rightful place in the world.

Unlike the serial wandering of *Endymion,* this poem moves in phrases catapulted by the sheer force of active, almost manic verbs. It is Hyperion who shapes and drives the action, but he too is driven by it. Activity is being forced upon him (the flaming robes that give a roar and scare away the hours, the voice that leaps out) as the crisis is being forced to its moment. Hyperion, Keats's alter ego, embodies the poet's own split desire, driving toward a disciplined manhood in order to be allied with power but also driven by the very rituals of the discourse he would control. The irony of this passage is that Hyperion inhabits and represents the bower that must be left behind once the crisis is forced, once he must fight to gain or retain power. In such passages, it is as if Keats is literally disciplining his "former" self, purging the bower that he cannot totally surrender. Hyperion's movement "From stately nave to nave, from vault to vault" is a fierce parody of *Endymion*'s objectless wandering, turning that wandering into the frenzied determination of a god shaping his own future, even though that future be his doom. The "bowers of fragrant and enwreathed light" that we explore idly in the previous poem now become the direct object of Hyperion's wrath. The "golden region" that is "jarr'd" represents the false security of the bower, which must be transformed into a space of active contestation. "Am I to leave this haven of my rest, / This cradle of my glory, this soft clime, / This calm luxuriance of blissful light," Hyperion asks.

This is the question that each god must ask, even though the answer is clear and unavoidable. The kind of imitative identification celebrated in *Endymion* is replaced here with "transitive" predication. Activity is always bound by discrete motives and objects, enacted by discrete subjects toward determinate objects and established ends. In fact, imitative identification becomes the very threat that the father god Saturn names as the condition of his fall:

> —I am gone
> Away from my own bosom: I have left
> My strong identity, my real self,
> Somewhere between the throne, and where I sit
> Here on this spot of earth. [1.112–16]

Saturn's loss of his "strong identity, [his] real self," represents his fall from power because it figures the incapacity to name, at will, the objects of his power. Feverishly, with the hyperactivity of one who knows that he is soon to be merely an object in someone else's discourse, Saturn commands Thea to search out and identify his only remaining hope, Hyperion. But his capacity to name objects and objectives at will is lost.

> A little time, and then again he snatch'd
> Utterance thus.—"But cannot I create?
> Cannot I form? Cannot I fashion forth
> Another world, another universe,
> To overbear and crumble this to nought?
> Where is another Chaos? Where?" [1.140–45]

Accustomed to a world where his own patrilineal discourse is unthreatened, Saturn finds himself snatching utterance, fashioning words that refuse to father forth a world of objects to his calling. Instead of the raw material of chaos, he has only the form of his own outmoded discourse to mold, and soon that too will be snatched by mightier gods projecting their own claims to father their own world from the power of their words.

Like Hyperion, his double/foil Apollo must be forced from the bower and into the world of manly strife. As opposed to the participatory discourse of the bower, the patrilineal discourse of power demands that even the most similarly identified "essences" be divided and compete against each other. Thus Hyperion and Apollo, each the spitting image of the other, must refuse metonymic transference. Ironically, as the narrative moves relentlessly from old to new, from Hyperion to Apollo, in an attempt to reach its climax and claim its god-making objective, the progress falters dramatically. What Keats realizes is that the discourse of the new gods mimics that of the old, that power mimics itself and forces would-be gods to name objects with the same tireless rituals practiced by the dethroned patriarchs. How can Apollo empower a new order without falling in one of three directions: (1) merely mimicking the old order by replicating its rituals with different words; (2) becoming an unintentional parody of the old order by mimicking its powerful discourse but without its actual power in the world; (3) rejecting the old order and its discourse entirely but in doing so falling into an ineffectual private realm of fanatically obscure language?

The conflict between the bower and the will to power resurfaces as a conflict between the new gods and the old, between the culture that is already fathered and the one that the new god desires to father. Though this conflict expresses itself as inadequacy on Keats's part to express the "dire" moment of climax, the climactic shift from one kind of power to another kind, it is as much a failure of discourse itself:

> Thus in alternate uproar and sad peace,
> Amazed were those Titans utterly.
> O leave them, Muse! O leave them to their woes;
> For thou art weak to sing such tumults dire:
> A solitary sorrow bests befits
> Thy lips, and antheming a lonely grief.
> Leave them, O Muse! for thou anon wilt find
> Many a fallen old Divinity
> Wandering in vain about bewildered shores. [3.1–9]

This conventional appeal to the Muse is more than merely conventional here. It represents the "impotence" of one individual's speech to father forth a new language/knowledge freed from the established rituals of patrilineal discourse. How can he create a new world when his discourse itself is fashioned by the old, when even his attempt to "father" is a ritual determined by the discourse he seeks to disclaim? Keats singly as an "individual" poet can only will a discourse bewildering to his readers, whose discourse is already determined by the knowledge Keats would transform, unless he becomes more than merely an "individual" poet, unless he becomes "great." But literary greatness itself is a concept constructed and determined by patrilineal rituals.

In the fragmented final book of *Hyperion,* Keats intuitively realizes that his poem has become a parody (unself-consciously?) of patrilineal discourse. Anxious to make his new words powerful, he imitates the old discourse all too well, subverting his own attempt to move beyond that discourse. Therefore, the final book, brought to grief and despair by this realization, falls into a private language that obscures itself and thus weakens its power to establish a new public discourse for culture's use. Rather than moving relentlessly to a newly ordered discourse, the poem instead transits toward a private realm of grief, a realm in which even the Muse herself is too "weak to sing such" tumultuous desire. And thus Keats, the would-be great poet, his Muse, who represents his potential for greatness, and his readers all are stranded within an elegiac dreamspace, in which "A solitary sorrow best befits [our] lips, and antheming a lonely grief," a dreamspace as ineffectual as *Endymion*'s bower but lacking *Endymion*'s innocently optimistic playfulness.

Paradoxically, this fragmented book must elegize the birth of a new god, who is doomed to be a deadly replica of the old. The Muse will find, Keats says, numberless fallen divinities "Wandering in vain about bewildered shores," and yet the "tumults dire" of a world enmeshed in "alternate uproar and sad peace" continue unabated. This fragmented book, then, is both an elegy for the innocent bower that is "stampt" on fiercely by Hyperion, the ruling patriarch, and an elegy for the dream of a new order that forever dies into an unarticulated, ineffectual private language. Thus Keats's other alter ego, Apollo, is also split. He does not desire to leave the bower for a world of strife, and yet he desires to "father" a new language beyond patrilineal discourse. His doom is foreshadowed, however, in his likeness to the old gods of power, a likeness that he desires to repress as a sign of his potential for renewal. Apollo must "die into life" (3.130) because his very birth is an aborted death. Just as Saturn cries out for "another universe" (a "covert," Thea calls it [1.152]), just as Hyperion mourns "to leave this haven of [his] rest," so Apollo mourns with the foresight of a god:

Throughout all the isle
There was no covert, no retired cave
Unhaunted by the murmurous noise of waves,
Though scarcely heard in many a green recess.
He listen'd, and he wept, and his bright tears
Went trickling down the golden bow he held. [3.38–43]

The "golden bow," the promise of his new rule, becomes the bearer of his tears. "Where is power?" Apollo asks, but before the answer can be articulated in words that we can understand, the poem breaks off. We as readers become like Apollo himself, waiting the revelation of Mnemosyne: "While I here idle listen on the shores / In fearless yet in aching ignorance" (3.106–

7). The wish-fulfilling dream of a new order cannot realize itself without a language to name its being:

> Knowledge enormous makes a God of me.
> Names, deeds, gray legends, dire events, rebellions,
> Majesties, sovran voices, agonies,
> Creations and destroyings, all at once
> Pour into the wide hollows of my brain,
> And deify me. [3.113–18]

The poem breaks off because the knowledge that would enable us to deify ourselves lies always on the other side of the only discourse we know how to use. If Mnemosyne were to speak, could we understand her tongue? If Keats were to write the words, would our old-fashioned rituals of communication serve to hold the newly fashioned knowledge, or would we have to become, like Apollo, widely hollowed out? The narrative aborts itself because it has nowhere else to go. It has reached the limits of discourse as we have "fathered" it, and as it reaches for that new knowledge just beyond the old, it trails off into muteness. "Mute thou remainest—mute! yet I can read / A wondrous lesson in thy silent face," Apollo says wistfully to Mnemosyne as he "raves" in his "aching ignorance" (3.111–12).

There is noticeable "regression" (or nostalgia) in Keats's language in the unfinished third book of the first *Hyperion*. His discourse returns to the dream of the bower, a space in which the manly strife for power is disrupted by the private desire for peace:

> Let the rose glow intense and warm the air,
> And let the clouds of even and of morn
> Float in voluptuous fleeces o'er the hills;
> Let the red wine within the goblet boil,
> Cold as a bubbling well; let faint-lipp'd shells,
> On sands, or in great deeps, vermilion turn
> Through all their labyrinths; and let the maid
> Blush keenly, as with some warm kiss surpris'd. [3.15–22]

We could easily be in *Endymion*'s easeful world of love again, but we are not. Sensing his own regression to the bower and no doubt feeling distress at its return, not desiring to linger between the momentous climax that has refused to come and the bower that invites his lingering, Keats "abandons" the poem. Before, to wander was a joy forever. Now, he fears "Wandering in vain about bewildered shores."

Leaving the first *Hyperion* to mute itself, Keats proceeds to the second *Hyperion*. Rather than resting in muteness, he attempts again to rescue poetry, believing that it can create a discourse that is powerful without merely rehearsing the patrilineal rituals of power. But instead of retreating into the sharable (communicable) peacefulness of the innocent bower or the sharable experience of elegiac disappointment as at the end of the previous fragment, in *The Fall,* appropriately named, Keats falls, from the very first word, into the obtuseness of private language. *The Fall of Hyperion* is subtitled "A Dream" as much because it is a retreat into the private self as because it promises a visionary view of the new discourse. "Fanatics have their dreams, wherewith they weave / A paradise for a sect," he says in the first line. The poet, like the religious fanatic, is blessed with unarticulated knowledge, but whereas the fanatic only has to share his "dream" with a sect of faithful believers, only has to communicate his paradise to those for whom the vision is already communicated, the poet is cursed with attempting to communicate his vision of paradise to culture as a whole, to the worldly masses who must be "hollowed out." Whereas the fanatic can afford to forgo the use of language, since his divine dream cannot be embodied in language in any case and since those who will believe do not need language to convince them, the poet must use language, however unsuitable, because his goal is to embody the dream and because it is only language that can acculturate the dream, making it powerful within culture. Desiring to trace the "shadows of melodious utterance" (1.6), Keats wants to hold firmly to his belief in poetry's power to fashion communicable words for a new world:

> For Poesy alone can tell her dreams,
> With the fine spell of words alone can save
> Imagination from the sable charm
> And dumb enchantment. [1.8–11]

"Whether the dream now purposed to rehearse / Be poet's or fanatic's" (1.16) is yet unknown, for the dream remains unarticulated. Perhaps Keats finds himself, like the fanatic, weaving a "paradise for a sect," writing an obscure, private code for the already saved. Perhaps he finds that he is unable to do what Moneta claims she will:

> "Mortal, that thou may'st understand aright,
> I humanize my sayings to thine ear,
> Making comparisons of earthly things;
> Or thou might'st better listen to the wind,
> Whose language is to thee a barren noise,
> Though it blows legend-laden through the trees." [2.1–6]

Once again the word is fragmented, for in whatever way Keats attempts to humanize his sayings, his visionary language becomes a "barren noise," laden with the "earthly things" he seeks to transform, trapped at the limits of a discourse he desires to transcend.

By its very nature, genuine discourse cannot be private, although language as a system can be. Once it becomes a private language, it is no longer discourse, which is always communicable beyond the world of self. By the same token, language that is obscured by the dreamy privacy of its desire cannot be revolutionary, for it "falls" always into disuse and abuse, rebelling against itself, leaving intact the ordinary uses of language. Although *The Fall* is not an escape into the bower, it is virtually as powerless to effect discursive change. And so we find Keats fragmented by a double bind. In order to revolutionize discourse, he must make it communicate beyond the obscurity of a private dream, but in order to communicate it, he must either resort to the very rituals of discourse that he seeks to countermand or retreat into a bower discourse of happy escape, where language, although it is shared, is powerless to progress beyond its own discursive idleness and marginality and thus is incapable of effecting discursive reform. As the second *Hyperion* earnestly seeks to avoid the fall into private grief and then the regression to the bower that fragment the first *Hyperion,* and as it seeks to substitute a visionary or liberating use of language for mimicry of patrilineal discourse, it turns against discourse as it is known and thus unwillingly obscures, disempowers, fragments, and mutes itself. Realizing the dream requires us to avoid both fantasy and fanaticism, requires us to leap across the fractured word into a world that we have yet to articulate, though we, with Keats, have imagined it—waiting—just beyond the limits of our words.

## Notes

1. Marjorie Levinson, *The Romantic Fragment Poem: A Critique of Form* (Chapel Hill: University of North Carolina Press, 1986); see esp. 181.
2. Ibid., 181.
3. Thomas McFarland, *Romanticism and the Forms of Ruin: Wordsworth, Coleridge, and Modalities of Fragmentation* (Princeton, NJ: Princeton University Press, 1981), 3.
4. Edward E. Bostetter, *The Romantic Ventriloquists* (Seattle: University of Washington Press, 1975), 8.
5. See, for instance, Julia Kristeva, *Revolution in Poetic Language,* trans. Margaret Walker (New York: Columbia University Press, 1984), 50–57, 61, 79.
6. John Keats, *The Poems of John Keats,* ed. Jack Stillinger (Cambridge, MA: Harvard University Press, 1978), 1.1–13. Subsequent references are from this edition and are cited in the text.
7. Frances Ferguson, "Shelley's *Mont Blanc:* What the Mountain Said," in *Romanticism and Language,* ed. Arden Reed (Ithaca, NY: Cornell University Press, 1984), 207.
8. Percy Bysshe Shelley, *Shelley's Prose; or, The Trumpet of a Prophecy,* ed. David Lee Clark (Albuquerque: University of New Mexico Press, 1954), 170.
9. *The Letters of John Keats,* ed. Hyder Edward Rollins, 2 vols. (Cambridge, MA: Harvard University Press, 1958), 1:387.

10. Richard Macksey, "'To Autumn' and the Music of Mortality: 'Pure Rhetoric of a Language without Words,'" in Reed, *Romanticism and Language,* 278.
11. John Gibson Lockhart, "Cockney School of Poetry," rpt. in *The Romantics Reviewed: Contemporary Reviews of British Romantic Writers,* prt. C, ed. Donald H. Reiman (New York: Garland, 1972), 90.
12. Ibid., 91.
13. *Letters,* 1:297.

## *Vanity Fair*: Listening as a Rhetorician—and a Feminist

JAMES PHELAN

THACKERAY'S *Vanity Fair* almost demands inspection by anyone interested in contemplating the issues surrounding the topic of "male feminist voices." His decision to survey the booths of Vanity Fair by charting the progress of two very different women through it leads him into numerous representations of and reflections on women in patriarchy, while his own virtuoso performance as the showman of Vanity Fair leads him to adopt many poses and many voices. Furthermore, although Thackeray's focus is on women in a society that we clearly recognize as patriarchal, his primary purpose is not to offer a feminist critique of that society but to expose the multifarious workings of vanity within it. The vision of women in society that emerges is, I think, sometimes compatible with and sometimes antithetical to the view offered from a consistently feminist perspective. Consequently, to assess the nature and significance of the showman's "male (sometime) feminist voices," we need tools of both rhetorical analysis and feminist criticism. The rhetorical perspective will allow us to develop (1) some conceptual model for defining and investigating voice in written discourse and (2) some conception of the novel as a total communication from Thackeray to an intended audience.[1] The feminist perspective will allow us (1) to foreground those elements of the total communication most pertinent to the text's revelation of the relations between the sexes and of societally constrained male and female behavior and (2) to evaluate both the voices of the showman and the total communication from Thackeray.

It is of course somewhat misleading to speak of *the* rhetorical perspective and *the* feminist perspective; many different kinds of critical views travel under each banner. The rhetorical perspective I shall employ here is concerned with texts as communications from authors to readers through multiple stylistic, generic, and cultural codes. The feminist perspective I shall employ here is concerned with the way these codes reveal the text's overt or covert concern with gender and gender roles. I shall treat the rhetorical and the feminist perspectives as largely compatible, especially in exploring the workings of voice in the novel. Thus the feminist perspective will help to foreground certain features of the text that must be accounted for in the rhetorical analysis. Furthermore, as the two perspectives work together, I will be concerned with how Thackeray's text implicates the implied reader in its views of gender and the workings of Victorian culture. When I move from analyzing the role of voice to evaluating that role and what it accomplishes, the perspectives will diverge somewhat because they place a premium on different values, and each one seems incomplete in the eyes of the other. The feminist perspective will privilege the book's position on gender and the kind of reading experiences entailed in the text's treatment of gender issues; the rhetorical perspective will privilege (its understanding of) Thackeray's overall purpose and will try to relate the treatment of the gender issues to that larger purpose. If the results of the evaluation from each perspective do not coincide, then we shall have to think harder about the relation between the two perspectives.[2]

## The Concept of Voice: Some Rhetorical Principles

Voice is one of those critical terms (genre, theme, irony, pluralism are others) that are frequently used but rarely defined with any precision. The result is that we now have no commonly accepted meaning for the term, no clear understanding of what constitutes voice, let alone what makes one kind of voice more effective than another.[3] My understanding of voice is influenced by the rhetorical perspective I bring to it: I want to specify the role of voice in the communication offered by a narrative. My understanding, indebted to Bakhtin's work, is composed of three interrelated principles about language in use and three consequences of those principles.

1. *Voice is as much a social phenomenon as it is an individual one.* This principle follows from the observation that wherever there is discourse there is voice. Just as there can be no utterance without style, there can be no utterance without voice—although, of course, just as some styles are more distinctive than others, so too are some voices. In the case of, say, a memo from the university registrar to the faculty stipulating that grades must be in by a certain date, one might be tempted to say that there is no voice in the discourse, that what speaks is some bureaucratic machine. In one sense, this might be true; the discourse may not be at all expressive of the registrar himself or herself. But that is just the point: The letter signals not the absence of voice but rather the presence of one voice rather than another. We recognize that voice not because we recognize the author of the letter but because as social beings we have heard that voice speak to us on other occasions.[4] Or to put the point another way, we identify a voice as

distinctive because we recognize how it plays off other voices. If the registrar wrote the memo in heroic couplets, we'd hear his voice through the juxtaposition of the bureaucratic voice with the poetic one.

In discussing the written memo, I am also postulating that, although voice is a term that seems to privilege speech over writing, it is a concept for identifying a feature of both oral and written language.

2. *Voice is the fusion of style, tone, and values.* Though mediated through style, voice is more than style and in a sense is finally transstylistic. There are markers of voice in diction and syntax, but the perception of voice also depends upon inferences that we make about a speaker's attitude toward subject matter and audience (tone) and about the speaker's values. Style will reveal the register of a voice, and sometimes its location in space and in time relative to the things it describes and to its audience. But for inferences about personality and ideological values, style is a necessary but not a sufficient condition: By itself style will not allow us to distinguish among possibilities. Similar diction and syntax may carry different tones and ideologies—and therefore different personalities—while the same personality and ideology may be revealed through diverse syntactic and semantic structures. For example, in the first chapter of *Pride and Prejudice,* Mrs. Bennet echoes the diction of the narrator's famous opening remark that a "single man in possession of a good fortune must be in want of a wife" by referring to Mr. Bingley as "a single man of large fortune." The similar style is spoken with different tones—the narrator's voice is playfully ironic, Mrs. Bennet's serious and admiring—and communicates different values—the narrator mocks the acquisitiveness behind Mrs. Bennet's speech. Austen uses the similar style to emphasize their different voices, their different values and personality. Later, in describing Mrs. Bennet at the end of the chapter, Austen changes the tone of the narrator's voice. "The business of her life was to get her daughters married; its solace was visiting and news." Although the change in tone indicates a difference in the voice, the consistency of the values expressed enables us to regard the difference as a modulation in the voice rather than the adoption of a whole new one.

A corollary of this principle is that speech acts and voice are related in the same way that voice and style are. If a speaker typically gives commands rather than makes requests, this speech behavior will influence our perception of her voice. Nevertheless, a request and a command can be spoken in the same voice, as Browning shows us in the Duke of Ferrara's monologue: "Will't please you rise?" "Notice Neptune taming a sea-horse / Which Claus of Innsbruck cast in bronze for me!" The same attitudes and values of (falsely) polite imperiousness are communicated through both speech acts. And two commands can be spoken in two different voices, as Shakespeare shows us through Lady Macbeth: "Come, you spirits . . . unsex me here," and "Out, damned spot!" In sum, both locutionary and illocutionary acts contribute to but do not determine our sense of voice.

3. As Booth and Bakhtin (among numerous others) have amply demonstrated, the voice of a narrator can be contained within the voice of an author, creating what Bakhtin calls the situation of "double-voiced" discourse. Significantly, *the presence of the author's voice need not be signaled by any direct statements on his or her part but through some device in the narrator's language—or indeed through such nonlinguistic clues as the structure of the action—for conveying a discrepancy in values or judgments between author and narrator.* (In fact, one of the defining features of homodiegetic narration is that all such discrepancies must be communicated indirectly.) In the first sentence of *Pride and Prejudice,* Austen's style and tone allow her to communicate the way she is undermining a literal reading. In homodiegetic narration, our perception of the authorial voice may have less to do with style and tone than with the social values at work in the discrepancy between the voices. When Huck Finn declares, "All right, then, I'll go to hell," there is nothing in his sincerely resolute utterance of this phrase of civilized Christianity to signal that Twain is double-voicing his speech. We hear Twain's voice behind Huck's because we have heard and seen Twain's values earlier in the narrative; we thus place Huck's acquiescence to social Christianity within a wider system of values that condemns the values of its voice and endorses Huck's decision.

Double-voicing can of course also occur within the explicit syntax or semantics of an utterance. When Samuel Butler has a speaker say, "As luck would have it, Providence was on my side," he is using the style to bring two different social voices into conflict. In cases such as this one, the author's voice functions as a crucial third member of the chorus that may debunk both voices, approve both, or privilege one.

Three main consequences follow from the interaction of these principles with some other assumptions I make about narrative.[5]

1. *Voice exists in the space between style and character.* As we attribute social values and a personality to voice, we are moving voice away from the realm of style toward the realm of character. But voice, especially a narrating voice or a "silent" author's voice, can exist apart from character-as-actor. Voice has what I have elsewhere called a mimetic dimension, but it need not have a mimetic function.[6] That is, voice exists as a trait of a speaker, but it need not be the basis for some full portrait of that speaker. In many narratives, especially ones with heterodiegetic narrators, the voice of the narrator will be his or her only trait, though modulations within a voice will of course suggest other traits. In homodiegetic narratives, the narrator's

voice is more likely to be one trait among many. And the same, of course, holds true for the voices of characters in dialogue.

2. Voice is an element of narrative that is subject to frequent change as a speaker shifts styles, alters tones, or expresses different values, or as an author double-voices a narrator's or character's speech. The corollary of this point is that, even as voice moves toward character, it maintains an important difference in its function. Whereas many narratives require consistency of character for their effectiveness, *consistency of voice is no necessary requirement for its effective use.*

3. Voice is typically a part of narrative manner, part of the how of narrative rather than the what. That is, like style, it is typically a mechanism (sometimes a crucial one) for influencing its audience's responses to and understanding of the characters and events that are the main focus of narrative.[7] Like any other element, voice could itself become the focus of a specific narrative (arguably this situation obtains in *Tristram Shandy*), but more commonly it will be a means for achieving particular effects. Thus *we cannot expect an analysis of voice to yield a comprehensive reading of most narratives,* though we should expect that such an analysis will enrich significantly the way any narrative achieves its effects.

Just as the three principles in my account of voice move the concept away from style and toward character, the last two consequences of the principles move the concept back toward style. The point again is that voice exists in the space between style and character.

## Some Functions of the Showman's Multiple Voices

In order to understand the functions of the showman's voices, we need a fuller explanation of the context in which they are heard. Broadly defined, Thackeray's purpose in the narrative is to expose the condition of universal vanity he describes in the final paragraph: "Ah! *Vanitas Vanitatem!* Which of us is happy in this world? Which of us has his desire? or, having it, is satisfied?"[8] To achieve this purpose, Thackeray invents his dramatized male narrator and has him tell the story of the progress of two very different women through a society that consistently reflects and reveals the ineradicable but multifarious vanity of its inhabitants. This story is frequently (though not ubiquitously) linked with gender issues: Not only does the male narrator comment on the careers of the women, but those careers themselves expose the patriarchal structures as well as the vanity of society. Again speaking schematically, we can see that Thackeray takes his two female characters, places them in the same setting but in different circumstances in the opening chapters, then sends them off in different directions so that he might conduct a relatively comprehensive survey of nineteenth-century society; he then brings them back together at the end of the narrative as a way to achieve closure.

He uses Amelia to explore the workings of vanity in the private sphere—the realm of the home and the heart—and he uses Becky to explore those workings in the public sphere—the realm of social climbing and social status. In keeping with his overriding thematic purpose, Thackeray uses Amelia and Becky, first, as a means to expose the vanity of others and, second, as exemplars of certain vain behaviors. In the case of Becky, the procedure works effectively and straightforwardly. He gives her a temporary license to succeed in her vain pursuits by playing upon the greater vanity of others, and then, once she has exposed that vanity in creatures ranging from Miss Pinkerton to Lord Steyne, he takes the license away and emphasizes what has never been far from the foreground of the narrative: Becky's own vanity-driven life. In the case of Amelia, however, the situation is more complex. He uses her constancy, love, and dependence on George first as a way to expose the vanity of George and those like him; later, Thackeray tries to expose the negative side of these very same qualities as he shows how they ultimately destroy Dobbin's love for her—and thus the chance for happiness for them both.

Although the stories of Becky and Amelia have clear beginnings, middles, and ends, although the characters move from an initial situation to a final one, the principle controlling the linking of episodes is, for the most part, an additive rather than an integrative one. That is, unlike a novel by Jane Austen in which the significance of each episode derives from its consequences for and interaction with later episodes, *Vanity Fair* is built upon episodes that typically derive their significance from their contribution to the overriding theme of ubiquitous vanity.[9] One consequence of this broad design is that it allows Thackeray to vary the way in which he treats his characters. Sometimes they appear to be autonomous beings for whom he wants us to feel deeply, sometimes obvious artificial devices for making his thematic points, and sometimes largely incidental to the showman's disquisitions about the workings of society.

One consequence of this fluctuation is that it allows the showman great freedom in his use and selection of voice. He can move from intimacy to distance, from formality to informality, from treating the characters as puppets to treating them as people, provided that the movement remains in the service of the thematic end. Indeed, because of the additive structure and the length of the whole narrative it is almost incumbent upon Thackeray to take full advantage of that freedom and make the narrator's performance one source of our sustained interest in the narrative.[10] The performances I will focus on here are, though not fully representative, illustrative of many other transactions that go on between Thackeray and his audience. As this way of talking about the narrative performances indicates, I see the showman as Thackeray's mouthpiece; the only distance between author and narrator is created by the author's knowledge that the narrator is created. On this reading, the showman is the knowing source of the numerous ironies of the narrative discourse. Thackeray, in other words, does not communicate to his audience behind the showman's back but rather uses the protean showman as the orchestrator of virtually all the narrative's effects. It is of course impossible to do justice in a single essay to the range of effects Thackeray achieves through his use of voice; I focus here on two passages that represent the extremes of his attitude toward the patriarchal elements of Vanity Fair.[11]

In chapter 3 the showman comments upon Becky's interest in Jos Sedley:

> If Miss Rebecca Sharp had determined in her heart upon making the conquest of this big beau, I don't think, ladies, we have any right to blame her; for though the task of husband-hunting is generally, and with becoming modesty, entrusted by young persons to their mammas, recollect that Miss Sharp had no kind parent to arrange these delicate matters for her, and that if she did not get a husband for herself, there was no one else in the wide world who would take the trouble off her hands. What causes young people to "come out," but the noble ambition of matrimony? What sends them trooping to watering-places? What keeps them dancing till five o'clock in the morning through a whole mortal season? What causes them to labour at piano-forte sonatas, and to learn four songs from a fashionable master at a guinea a lesson, and to play the harp if they have handsome arms and neat elbows, and to wear Lincoln Green toxophilite hats and feathers, but that they may bring down some "desirable" young man with those killing bows and arrow of theirs? What causes respectable parents to take up their carpets, set their houses topsy-turvy, and spend a fifth of their year's income in ball suppers and iced champagne? Is it sheer love of their species, and an unadulterated wish to see young people happy and dancing? Psha! they want to marry their daughters; and, as honest Mrs. Sedley has, in the depths of her kind heart, already arranged a score of little schemes for the settlement of her Amelia, so also had our beloved but unprotected Rebecca determined to do her very best to secure the husband, who was even more necessary for her than for her friend. [28]

The showman speaks here—for the most part—in the sociolect of the genteel upper middle class. He is someone who knows and feels comfortable in the social circuit of that class: the well-informed gentleman speaking politely but firmly—and with a certain air of superiority—to a group of women from the class. His diction is generally formal, but he will occasionally drop the register to something more familiar—"mammas" or "take the trouble off her hands." Furthermore, the genteel and formal qualities of the voice are reinforced by the parallel structure of the rhetorical questions and their well-chosen concreteness—"four songs from a fashionable master at a guinea a lesson." In adopting his air of knowing gentility, the showman also positions himself at a considerable distance from Becky. He calls her "Miss Rebecca Sharp" at the outset, and even later when he speaks of her as "our beloved but unprotected Rebecca," his sympathy does not overpower the distance. As a result of the genteel stance and the cool distance from Becky, the voice appears to be considering her as a "case," one that he is finally sympathetic to but one that he is interested in as much for what it generally illustrates.

Within this general sociolect, there are significant modulations—so significant, in fact, that even as we read we come to see the dominant voice as a pretense, one that the showman puts on to expose the limitations of the values associated with it. The showman's strategy is twofold: He occasionally lets a certain aggressive element enter the genteel voice; and, more dramatically, he temporarily shifts to a voice that is critical of the dominant one and then lets this voice invade and subvert the dominant. One major consequence of this strategy is that while making his apologia for Becky the showman offers a powerful indictment of courtship behavior in this male-controlled society.

The showman adopts the genteel voice right away, but in the second half of the first sentence the voice momentarily drops into a different, franker register as the showman mentions "the task of husband-hunting." The phrase not only calls to mind the image of the social circuit as a jungle where women are the predators, men the prey, but also insists on the hunt as work rather than sport. Although the showman quickly readopts his genteel voice, everything he says in the rest of the sentence is now double-voiced, undermined by the candid, antigenteel voice of the earlier phrase.

When the genteel voice calls the business of the hunt "delicate matters," we register not only the discrepancy between this description and "the task of husband-hunting" and the corresponding conflict between the values associated with each but also the showman's privileging of the antigenteel voice: His reference to "the task of husband-hunting" makes the phrase "delicate matters" an ironic euphemism. When the showman modulates his voice in a different way by moving from the formal tone of the genteel voice to an informal and affectionate one with his reference to "mammas," the earlier presence of the frank, antigenteel voice strongly ironizes the new modulation—and, indeed, the whole clause in which it appears. When the showman tells us that "the task of husband-hunting is generally, and with becoming modesty, entrusted by young persons to their mammas," we recognize the disparity between the image of the hunt and the alleged modesty of those in the hunting party. Moreover, we infer that the "young persons" have no choice about "entrusting" the hunt to their "mammas": The mammas manage, whether the daughters entrust them to or not, as we learn more directly later when we are told that "Mrs. Sedley has . . . arranged a score of little schemes for the settlement of her Amelia." We see, in short, that the real predators are those that by another name we call "mammas." This realization in turn adds another layer of irony to the phrase, a "kind parent to arrange these delicate matters."

The initial reference to husband hunting as a "task" is echoed in the aggressive note that repeatedly creeps into the showman's use of the genteel voice: "What *sends them trooping* to watering-places?" "What *keeps* them dancing . . . ?" "What *causes them to labour* . . . ?" (It is worth noting here, if only in passing, that the grammar of the passage suggests that "them" refers to "young people" but "young people" actually means "young women.") "What *causes respectable parents to take up their carpets, set their houses topsy-turvy, and spend a fifth of their year's income . . . ?*" (Italics mine.) The aggressive note is given more emphasis toward the end of this series of questions, when the showman slides very smoothly from the genteel voice to the franker, antigenteel one of the first sentence. His reference to the young people wearing "Lincoln Green toxophilite hats and feathers" is parallel to the previous phrases about their learning musical instruments. But once the topic of archery is introduced through this description of their clothes, the showman quickly appropriates the earlier hunting metaphor: What keeps them doing all these things "but that they may bring down some 'desirable' young man with those killing bows and arrows of theirs?" The result is that the showman strongly reinforces the subversion of the social values implied in the dominant voice: These genteel "young persons" and their "mammas" are no better than prisoners of their patriarchally imposed task, the purpose of which no one has even mentioned yet—nor has anyone apparently given any thought to what happens once the hunter has bagged her game. In other words, as the passage proceeds, it implies that the mammas and their daughters are no less prey than the young men: They are driven to their "task" by the values of the patriarchal society that insist that a woman must be married and married as "well" as she can.

The critique of "courtship" in the Fair reaches its high point in the final sentences of this passage as the showman turns to answer his own questions about the motives for the behavior he describes. His interjection, "Psha!," followed by the direct assertion, "they want to marry their daughters," marks the entrance into the passage of a third voice—a more honest, more direct voice than the genteel one that has been speaking so far. With this third voice, the showman is overtly setting himself above his genteel audience to reject their pretense and speak a truth that they also know but don't usually admit. This shift then sets up the final statement as an apologia for Becky's behavior, one that is convincing according to the values associated both with the genteel language he once again adopts—"so also had our beloved but unprotected Rebecca determined to do her very best to secure the husband"—and, significantly, with the new superior voice—"who was even more necessary for her than for her friend."

Because the new voice is clearly superior to the dominant one and because it is not ironized the way that the genteel one is (note all the undercutting in the description of "honest Mrs. Sedley" and her "schemes"), the apologia has real force. Yes, what Becky is doing is no different from what every other woman in this jungle does; yes, precisely because she has "no kind parents," a husband is more necessary for her than for Amelia. Yet the presence of the earlier subversion of the dominant voice and its values complicates this apologia. The case for Becky works only in terms of the values that we have been made to question by the earlier interaction between the voices; the case does not recognize how the very role that Becky "justifiably" adopts (i.e., mamma's role) has been exposed as itself constrained by patriarchy, as itself something to be lamented rather than celebrated. Consequently, by the light of the values associated with the frankest voice of the passage, the apologia is unconvincing. In this sense, then, the superior voice of the last few sentences of the passage is itself undercut; though it drops the pretenses of the genteel voice, it does not question the basic assumptions and values of the upper-middle-class social circuit, assumptions and values that reinforce the power of the patriarchy even as they have negative consequences for both women and men.

## Evaluating the Showman's Voices

The interaction between this superior voice and the earlier, antigenteel one highlights an important effect of the passage that is characteristic of Thackeray's position throughout the novel. By insisting on both the limitations of and the constraints on Becky's behavior, the showman offers a critique without offering an alternative. The power of the Fair is such that virtually no one can get outside it. The corollary of this point has been well illustrated by the rhetorical analysis of the passage: The power of the patriarchy is also often such that no one can get outside it. It seems fair to conclude—at least tentatively—that Thackeray's analysis of Vanity Fair is in part a critique of the patriarchy, and a critique which comes through a voice that is clearly identified as male. Let me now probe that tentativeness, by looking first at some other elements of the chosen passage and then at the novel more generally.

The very positioning of the male voice in relation to the "ladies" addressed in the passage raises a question about the thoroughness of the critique, about whether the rhetorical setup of the passage works against the message conveyed through the modulation of the voices. Note, first, that the address to "ladies" is made in the showman's genteel voice, the one that is most undercut in the whole passage. As that voice takes on and reflects the values of the genteel society, it takes on the assumption that the man can tell the "ladies" the truth about their behavior. When we see that this voice doesn't have the truth, this assumption is itself called into question. In that respect, the narrator–audience relationship reinforces rather than undercuts the message conveyed through the voices.

The passage, to be sure, does not suggest that the "ladies" see the full critique; instead, it presupposes that they will agree with the superior voice of the final sentences. But that presupposition does not make the rhetorical setup one in which we participate in an easy putdown of the ladies. Instead, it suggests that the "ladies" of genteel society, like Becky, the mammas, and the superior male voice, are caught in the trap of patriarchy. The rhetorical setup would offer the reader an uncomfortable position if it presupposed some assumption by Thackeray, as orchestrator of the play of voices, that men could see the full critique but women couldn't. The passage offers no evidence of such an assumption. Thus Thackeray's critique of courtship has strong affinities with one we might make from a feminist perspective.

Nevertheless, I think that the analysis so far indicates not only Thackeray's considerable virtuosity in the manipulation of voice but also a potentially negative—or at least rhetorically risky—side to that virtuosity. The complex interplay of voices and their effects leads us back to their source, to what we might call the metavoice of the showman. In addition to the qualities of wit, intelligence, learning, and a willingness to criticize, the showman's virtuosity here leaves him and us outside the fray, complimenting him and ourselves on our superior knowledge as we look down upon the Fair and those caught in it. Although there are places in the narrative when the showman indicates that he too can't escape the traps of vanity, his frequently displayed penchant for one-upmanship at the expense of his characters and his addressed audiences sometimes makes us uncomfortable. We feel that we're asked to participate in the metavoice's smugness or snideness or superciliousness.[12] This feature of the metavoice obviously has consequences for any evaluation of it, but this feature has an especially noteworthy role in a feminist evaluation.

When we look at the novel more broadly than we have so far, we soon see that the showman is hardly Jane Eyre's brother under the skin. His most obvious limitations are that he does not follow consistently through on his insights into patriarchy's shaping of women's behavior and that he sometimes reveals his own complicity with the patriarchy, thus inviting the reader to join in that complicity. Many instances could be cited to make these points, especially his ambivalent treatment of Amelia, but perhaps the clearest evidence is in the famous passage in chapter 64 describing Becky as "syren."

> I defy any one to say that our Becky, who has certainly some vices, has not been presented to the public in a perfectly genteel and inoffensive manner. In describing this syren, singing and smiling, coaxing and cajoling, the author, with modest pride, asks his readers all round, has he once forgotten the laws of politeness, and showed the monster's hideous tail above water? No! Those who like may peep down under waves that are pretty transparent, and see it writhing and twirling, diabolically hideous and slimy, flapping amongst bones, or curling round corpses; but above the water line, I ask, has not everything been proper, agreeable, and decorous, and has any the most squeamish immoralist in Vanity Fair a right to cry fie? When, however, the syren disappears and dives below, down among the dead men, the water of course grows turbid over her, and it is labour lost to look into it ever so curiously. They look pretty enough when they sit upon a rock, twanging their harps and combing their hair, and sing, and beckon to you to come and hold the looking-glass; but when they sink into their native element, depend on it those mermaids are about no good, and we had best not examine the fiendish marine cannibals, revelling and feasting on their wretched pickled victims. And so, when Becky is out of the way, be sure that she is not particularly well employed, and that the less that is said about her doings is in fact the better. [617]

The interplay among voices is characteristically complex here, as the showman gives the very picture he is praising himself for having suppressed. He uses a refined, almost prissy voice to praise himself for his decorum, and then, when talking about what he has not done, he adopts a melodramatic one that likes to dwell on the seamier side of things. The alternation between these voices is clear and striking throughout but perhaps nowhere more so than when it occurs within the same sentence: "has he once forgotten the laws of politeness, and showed the monster's hideous tail above water?" The hierarchy established between the voices brings the snideness of the showman's metavoice into play. The melodramatic voice is privileged here: The chief effect of the passage is to convey the showman's clear condemnation of Becky as a hideous female creature.[13] The refined voice acts as a cover under which the showman asserts that Becky is ugly, fiendish, and murderous. Thackeray's early understanding of how Becky's behavior can be seen as shaped and constrained by the patriarchy seems to have vanished. Instead, the showman enjoys himself at Becky's expense and asks us to do the same as he links her with a whole group of creatures whose evil derives in part from their femaleness and especially from their female sexuality.

In linking Becky this way, the showman is not only performing an all too familiar sexist maneuver but asking his readers to enjoy the cleverness of his performance. We are left in the position of either joining him in his perpetuation of the values of the patriarchy or repudiating the performance, clever and skillful though it is. From the feminist perspective, the choice is simple, and our evaluation of Thackeray and the book as a whole must be very mixed indeed.

At the same time, Thackeray's sliding away from a feminist perspective on his female characters can be approached from a different direction, one that privileges the rhetorical perspective. If Thackeray has the perspective sometime, why doesn't he have it all the time? Or, to put the question another way, are there good—or at least plausible—reasons, within the working of the narrative itself, why he would turn away from the insights yielded by that perspective?

If we consider the narrative as a whole once again, then the lack of consistency in the critique of the patriarchy can be seen in a different light. Thackeray is a moralist as well as a social analyst, and he insists on locating some instances of vanity and its related sins—as well as its opposite virtues—in individuals themselves: Consider his treatment of Jos Sedley on the one side and of Dobbin (for most of the narrative) on the other. Since his aim is to show the multifarious and ubiquitous operations of vanity, then sometimes he uses Becky and Amelia as instruments for exposing vanity in others or in the structures governing the society, and at other times as exemplars of certain manifestations of the problem. If Thackeray used his female protagonists only as instruments of exposure, then his critique of patriarchy would be stronger and more consistent, but his demonstration of the omnipresent workings of vanity would be weakened.

In other words, our evaluation is complicated here by our awareness of Thackeray's purpose. It is one thing to fault him for failing to be consistent in his exposure of patriarchy if such exposure is his purpose, quite another to fault him for that when the accomplishment of a different purpose makes the inconsistency almost necessary. In the first case, we would be meeting him on ground that he has staked out for himself; in the second, we are insisting that he occupy our ground. The first case is unproblematic, the second more intriguing. We can, I think, still fault him: From the feminist perspective, his very purpose is questionable, because his attempt to locate vanity in Becky and Amelia is tantamount to blaming the victim. But our awareness that we are making him occupy our ground should also, I think, give him a chance to talk back. Why are you so convinced that these women are only victims? Is not your concern with the patriarchy as a social institution itself too limited, one that does not sufficiently consider—as my book does—the ways in which certain women manipulate it for their own vain or otherwise unworthy ends?

These questions from a hypothetical Thackeray yielded by our rhetorical understanding of the book can of course be answered from the feminist perspective; for example, the manipulation can itself be seen as the only possible alternative they have. Indeed, one might project Becky herself into a twentieth-century feminist perspective and listen to her voice evaluate Thackeray's treatment of her and Amelia. These answers in turn would create further response from our hypothetical Thackeray, who in the presence of Becky could employ his skill at modulating voices to make his case. Exactly where such a dialogue would end will no doubt vary from reader to reader, according to how strongly each believes in certain key matters such as the influence of social organization on individual behavior. The larger point for my purposes here is that the rhetorical and feminist perspectives usefully complicate our responses to Thackeray's achievement with voice and with the narrative as a whole. Despite the limitations I have pointed to—indeed, to some extent because of them—*Vanity Fair* offers a rich encounter to any rhetorician who tries to listen to it as a feminist.

## Notes

1. Since I assume that my readers' patience is not infinite, I will not demonstrate the *how* and the *why* of my characterization of the novel here, but let me state a few principles. Thackeray's novel can be seen as a rhetorical act, a communication that he is offering to an implied audience that real readers are asked to join. Our understanding of that communication depends on our apprehension of the sequence of choices the novelist has made from beginning to end, an apprehension according to how those choices affect our participation in and understanding of the issues, characters, events, and narrative discourse of the whole. For a much fuller model of fiction as rhetoric, one that includes the how and why of such analysis, see my *Reading People, Reading Plots: Character, Progression, and the Interpretation of Narrative* (Chicago: University of Chicago Press, 1989).
2. A further word about the setup—and the follow-through—of the essay. I am acutely aware that in an essay of this length I cannot do justice to the complexity of the showman's voice—especially when some of the essay is spent on matters other than analyzing the voice itself. I offer what I have developed here as a place to start on that much larger project, a place that offers some foundation in its general discussions of voice and of evaluation but that needs a lot more construction arising from extended analyses of the showman's discourse.
3. In part 2 of *The Rhetoric of Fiction* 2d ed. (Chicago: University of Chicago Press, 1983), "The Author's Voice in Fiction," still probably the most widely read discussion of voice in the Anglo-American critical tradition, Wayne C. Booth never seeks to identify the distinctive features of voice but instead uses the term loosely to refer to the author's *presence* and its overt manifestations through the commentary of a reliable narrator or its covert

incorporation through the manipulation of an unreliable narrator. Booth's imprecision with the term does not impede his argument, which is really about authors' uses of different kinds of rhetoric for different ends, but the imprecision is, I think, symptomatic of the way Anglo-American critics have thought about the term.

Mikhail Bakhtin's work on "double-voiced" discourse does, I think, provide the richest source for anyone who wants to delve into the concept of voice more fully, and in what follows I acknowledge an enormous debt to his discussion in the chapter "Discourse in the Novel," in *The Dialogic Imagination* (Austin: University of Texas Press, 1981). Nevertheless, to adopt Bakhtin's work entirely means to view the novel only as a site of multiple voices. That principle has its uses, but here I want to retain the notion that voice exists alongside character, style, event, setting, and so on.

4. Here my interest in voice diverges from that of Peter Elbow, who wants to investigate what makes a voice distinctive and personal. His interest follows naturally from his purpose of teaching students of writing to develop distinctive voices, and I do not think our difference amounts to a serious disagreement. I would just point out that when a writer develops a distinctive personal voice or idiolect he simultaneously develops a relationship to one or more sociolects as well. Elbow's voice is distinctive—but distinctive within a broader sociolect of academic critical discourse. See Elbow, "The Pleasures of Voices in the Literary Essay: Explorations in the Prose of Gretel Ehrlich and Richard Selzer," in *Literary Nonfiction: Theory, Criticism, Pedagogy,* ed. Chris Anderson (Carbondale: Southern Illinois University Press, 1989).
5. These assumptions—that narratives are themselves translinguistic, that the effects of narratives derive from the shaping of character, action, diction, and voice into a complex synthesis designed to produce an emotional and cognitive effect—are developed more fully in Phelan, *Reading People, Reading Plots.* I mention them here to mark my difference from Bakhtin, who wants to make the essence of the novel its heteroglossia, its interaction among the values contained in its voices.
6. See Phelan, *Reading People, Reading Plots,* esp. the introduction, for a fuller discussion of this difference.
7. For a discussion of how style functions relative to other elements of narrative, see my *Worlds from Words: A Theory of Language in Fiction* (Chicago: University of Chicago Press, 1981).
8. William Makepeace Thackeray, *Vanity Fair: A Novel without a Hero* (Boston: Houghton Mifflin, 1963), 666; hereafter cited in text by page number. The novel was first published serially in 1847–48 and in book form in 1848.
9. There are exceptions of course. Sometimes episodes cluster together into larger incidents that make the thematic point—most noteworthy here is the mininarrative surrounding the end of Becky's intrigue with Lord Steyne. And, given the device of following the same cast of characters, Thackeray can, as the narrative progresses, return to material that he has used earlier and give it some new uses. He does this recycling most obviously at the end of the narrative when Becky shows Amelia the letter George wrote her before Waterloo and when Becky reattaches herself to Jos. For a somewhat different account of the pattern of the whole, see Mark H. Burch, " 'The world is a looking-glass': *Vanity Fair* as Satire," *Genre* 15 (1982): 265–79.
10. This point in a sense builds upon the case that Juliet McMaster has made for the importance of the showman's commentary in her thoughtful study, *Thackeray: The Major Novels* (Toronto: University of Toronto Press, 1971).
11. For some worthwhile studies of Thackeray's technique along lines different from the ones I am developing here, see Geoffrey Tillotson, *Thackeray the Novelist* (Cambridge: Cambridge University Press, 1954); John Loofburrow, *Thackeray and the Form of Fiction* (Princeton, NJ: Princeton University Press, 1964); James Wheatley, *Patterns in Thackeray's Fiction* (Middletown, CT: Wesleyan University Press, 1967); Ina Ferris, *William Makepeace Thackeray* (New York: Twayne, 1983); S. K. Sinha, *Thackeray: A Study in*

*Technique,* Salzburg Studies in English Literature 86 (Salzburg: Institut für Anglistik and Amerikanistik, 1979); and Elaine Scarry, "Enemy and Father: Comic Equilibrium in No. 14 of *Vanity Fair,*" *Journal of Narrative Technique* 10 (1980): 145–55.

12. In *A Rhetoric of Irony* (Chicago: University of Chicago Press, 1974), Wayne Booth has persuasively argued that all irony involves victims—or at least potential victims: those people who don't get it. The difference between Thackeray's ironic one-upmanship and, say, Austen's ironic treatment of Mrs. Bennet is that Austen's narrator, unlike the showman, never gives us ironic commentary about Mrs. Bennet that also announces her own superiority. Indeed, although Austen's narrator frequently speaks ironically, she rarely gives direct ironic commentary in her own voice about any character but instead uses the irony to establish norms that can themselves ironically undercut a character's speech (quoted or reported) or behavior. She is not showing off at the character's expense the way Thackeray sometimes appears to do.

13. G. Armour Craig, "On the Style of *Vanity Fair,*" in *Style in Prose Fiction,* ed. Harold Martin (New York: Columbia University Press, 1959), 87–113, argues that in many cases the narrator's coyness about Becky's guilt, e.g., in her relationship with Lord Steyne, adds to the complexity of the issue. McMaster, *Thackeray,* makes a similar point. As will become clear, I do not think the coyness works that way in this passage.

# Projection and the Female Other: Romanticism, Browning, and the Victorian Dramatic Monologue

U. C. KNOEPFLMACHER

We shall become the same, we shall be one
Spirit within two frames, oh! wherefore two?
SHELLEY, *Epipsychidion*

What I see is that I have become Total-Image, which is to say, Death in person; others—the Other—do not dispossess me of myself, they turn me, ferociously, into an object, they put me at their mercy, at their disposal, classified in a file, ready for the subtlest deceptions. BARTHES, *Camera Lucida*

BROWNING'S 1864 monodrama "James Lee's Wife" contains a remarkable passage in its ninth and last section, "On Deck." The "ill-favored" female speaker, ready to annul herself by migrating "Over the sea," has "conceded" the failure of her union with James Lee, the object of her desire. The speaker accepts her self-exile from the apathetic "mind" of the man she continues to worship: "Nothing I was" will, she has now come to realize, ever find a "place" in that masculine mind. And yet, boldly and unexpectedly, she imagines a future moment in which a depleted James Lee "might" fade into

a thing like me,
And your hair grow these coarse hanks of hair,
Your skin, this bark of a gnarled tree,—
You might turn myself! [368–71][1]

The metamorphosis the speaker envisions is neither the natural outcome of aging nor a wishful act of supernatural witchery. Her visionary casting into the future is a projection (from *pro-jacere:* to throw ahead). But what is involved is not the kind of "projection" that led a Paracelsus or an Agrippa, those alchemist-transformers with whom Percy Shelley and Browning identified, to cast powders into a crucible. It is, instead, a purely mental act.

What James Lee's Wife, the woman without a name of her own, envisions, then, is nothing less than a mental restoration of the identity she has lost. Though physically alive, she has become obliterated in James Lee's mind and hence has become more radically excluded than the extinguished Porphyria and Last Duchess, whose outward forms are at least remembered by the male minds who drained their vitality. Like still another martyred female, Pompilia, James Lee's Wife requires an acknowledgment of kinship to take place in the mind of her denier. She can be animated only through such a rebirth of consciousness. She thus assigns herself a role somewhat like that played by the mute Dorothy whose "wild eyes" allow her brother to behold "in thee what once I was." But James Lee is not an eager Wordsworth. To conquer his obdurate resistance, his Dorothy does not merely wax silent but also resolves to place herself out of the reach of any "word" or "look" from him. She understands that only by evading him can she ever hope to force him to grasp her true import. Her removal may cause James Lee to reimagine—and reimage—his own selfhood; only then will he be able to take the next step and recognize his wife's image as a specular analogue or epipsyche of himself:

> Strange, if a face, when you thought of me,
>   Rose like your own face present now,
> With eyes as dear in their due degree,
>   Much such a mouth, and as bright a brow,
> Till you saw yourself, while you cried "'Tis She!" [353–57]

The young Browning who more than thirty years earlier had addressed the figure of Pauline as the equivalent of Wordsworth's Dorothy or of Shelley's Emilia Viviani had also tried to see himself in a female mirror:

> And then I was a young witch whose blue eyes,
> As she stood naked by the river springs,
> Drew down a god: I watched his radiant form
> Growing less radiant, and it gladdened me. [112–15]

Still, the female impersonations of the *Pauline* poet who repeatedly likens himself to a "girl" were but a spasmodic expression of his "wild dreams of beauty," those yearnings after a complementary otherness which, like Shelley's search for an inconstant "Intellectual Beauty," must remain unfulfilled. Although James Lee's Wife despairs of fusion as much as the *Pauline* poet, her self-removal frees her from the impotence that marks his mental agitations. She thus is actually closer to the figure of Pauline herself, the Frenchwoman who distances herself from the romantic effusions of "*mon pauvre ami*" in a footnoted prose gloss to the poem (Browning's first experimentation with a female voice). She hence is even closer to Browning's own distancing intelligence, especially as it had begun to operate, significantly enough, in "Porphyria's Lover" (1836) and "My Last Duchess" (1842), where Browning returned to the motifs of *Pauline* by ironically exposing a male speaker's inadequate attempts mentally to possess a Female Other.

When Browning renamed as "James Lee's Wife" the poem he had four years earlier titled "James Lee," he signified his full understanding of the reversal he had produced through the creation of still another layer in a multilayered sequence. That sequence went back from poems in *Men and Women* (1855), in the previous decade, to earlier dramatic monologues such as "Porphyria's Lover" and "My Last Duchess," and from these to his youthful *Pauline*, and beyond, to the romantic conversation poem and to those lyrics and narratives by Shelley and "by a Mr. John Keats, which were recommended to [Browning's mother] as being very much in the spirit of Mr. Shelley."[2] To understand the genesis of the dramatic monologue and to appreciate also the impact that Browning's development of the monologue had on latter-day romantic seekers of a female Muse—Rossetti, Morris, and Swinburne—the critic must carefully unravel each of these strands and assess their full interrelation.

## 1

It is no coincidence that "James Lee's Wife" should have been conceived after the death of Browning's own wife, that female "moon of poets," only one of whose "two soul-sides" her worshipful, Endymion-like mate had been able to extol "out of my own self" in "One Word More," at the end of *Men and Women*. In her poetry as well as in her own person, Elizabeth Barrett had tried to maintain that Keatsian "central self" she has Aurora Leigh adopt. Barrett thus furnished Browning with a further link to the romantic idealization of a female complement who might restore an incomplete male self. She was his Mary Godwin, his Emilia Viviani. As I have briefly shown elsewhere, his elopement with Elizabeth was a self-conscious reenactment on the part of both lovers of Percy Shelley's own flight abroad, thirty-two years before, with another daughter shackled by a father.[3] Yet long before the famous letter of January 10, 1845, in which he offered his worship to the unseen "dear Miss Barrett," Browning had been what, around the same time, George Henry Lewes called Shelley, "*par excellence*, the 'poet of women.'"[4] The elopement, after all, merely confirmed him in the role of liberator of an imprisoned Muse he had all along assumed in his verses. It was a fantasy come true. He could become the Perseus who was destined to "save" the alluring Andromeda-figure coveted by the impotent *Pauline* poet ("But change can touch her not—so beautiful / With her fixed eyes, earnest and still" [658–59]). He could be the manly Count Gismond, a St. George figure, who rescues from opprobry and defamation the damsel he will marry. Pauline's successors had proliferated in the 1842 *Dramatic Lyrics.* In the same volume in which he reprinted "Porphyria's Lover" and for the first time published "My Last Duchess," "queen-worship" vies with the depiction of thwarted lovers, Cristina, the Lady of Tripoli, Artemis, Siora, Gertrude. With the publication in 1845 of the *Dramatic Romances and Lyrics,* their number had greatly multiplied.

Yet Browning's lifelong urge to represent the imaginative possession of a female epipsyche was punctured, in true romantic fashion, by severe doubts. And these doubts were exacerbated by dissatisfactions with the lyric and narrative forms he had also inherited from his precursors. In his own lyrics and romances, severance and betrayal abound. Incompleteness is far more prominent than the fusion of complementary selves. But only in the form of the dramatic monologue first developed in "Porphyria's Lover" was Browning able to scrutinize that incompleteness without the melodramatic overtones that made "In a Gondola" so inadequate a revision of Keats's "Isabella" and without the sentimentality that marred an otherwise unimpeachable lyric such as "The Lost Mistress." His early female speakers still remained two-dimensional (one would never think of "Count Gismond" as "Count Gismond's Wife," despite its female voice). Yet in those monologues in which Browning parodied his own male desire to flatten women into the "fixed" and immovable Andromedas of graphic art—in poems such as "Porphyria's Lover" and "My Last Duchess," once again, but also in "Andrea del Sarto," "The Bishop Orders His Tomb," and even "Fra Lippo Lippi"—his own art suddenly became powerfully and magically three-dimensional.

"Porphyria's Lover" and "My Last Duchess"—more closely analyzed in section 2—feed on the very incompletion they depict. They still render the appropriation of a Female Other who is portrayed as elusive and silent; at the same time, however, they introduce a critical distance that was absent in the lyrics and the dramatic romances. Removed as either lyricist or narrator, Browning now ironizes the act of projection by which a devouring male ego reduces that Female Other into nothingness. Animations of a process of deanimation, these monologues thus self-consciously mock the poet's very own enterprise. Though an ironist, the poet also acts as abettor and accomplice, for he too flattens a female anima into a mere image, a representation, an object of art.

Still, if the Browning who animates the pathological windings of the Lover's and the Duke's minds ostensibly partakes of their suppression of the Female Other, he actually maneuvers the reader into becoming that suppressed Other's chief ally. Even more than Andrea's Lucrezia or the dying Bishop's long-deceased, yet still jealously hoarded mistress, Porphyria and the Duchess have become deformed into static images. They thus assume the inertness of those frozen and "fixed" photographic stills that Roland Barthes reads as emblems of a cruel art (of nineteenth-century origins) of depersonalization.[5]

But Porphyria and the Duchess have lost more than a freedom of motion. Imprisoned as they are within a male's rhetoric of justification, they have also become bereft of a voice of their own. It is their very voicelessness, however, that stirs in us the process of identification that James Lee's Wife hopes to produce, through her absence and silence, in her husband's mind. It is because they are mute that the reader is prompted to adopt the same role of liberator that Browning delegated to chivalric surrogates such as Count Gismond. Unless rescued by the reader, Porphyria and the Duchess remain the perennial captives of masculine speech.

Thus, just as Barthes the reader of fading photographs is provoked into restoring to the photographer's subjects the motions and identities that they have lost, so is the reader of "Porphyria's Lover" and "My Last Duchess" stimulated into reanimating what Browning's speakers have deanimated. We are drawn into a process of restitution and reconstitution. Whether consciously or not, Browning thus cleverly delegates to his readers a task that neither he nor his romantic predecessors had been able to represent to their full satisfaction.

It was a brilliant solution to a plaguing problem that went back before *Pauline,* to the beginnings of the century. For, as a lyric poet manqué, Browning was able to profit from the experimentations of those romantic subjectivists who had sadly discovered that their desire for fusion with another could all too easily convert that other into a mere projection of the lyricist's male self. Hence, before we can assess the full achievement of "Porphyria's Lover" and "My Last Duchess," we must wind back to those earlier beginnings and try to unravel some further layers in this complicated genealogy.

Robert Langbaum was surely correct when, in *The Poetry of Experience,* he stressed the "movement toward objectivity" inherent in the productions of romantic poets for whom "subjectivity was . . . the inescapable condition."[6] Yet, whereas in 1957 Langbaum still felt compelled to rescue romanticism from the "charges" made by modernists overeager to signal their "independence" from their nineteenth-century roots, we no longer need to mount such a defense. Indeed, in the intervening quarter of a century, the emphasis has shifted in exactly the opposite direction. The influence of critics such as Harold Bloom has made us too disposed to read the poetry from Blake to Stevens as a smooth, uninterrupted continuum. If, as Bloom repeatedly would have it, Browning is a latter-day Shelley,[7] there are nonetheless highly important formal differences that sharply separate Browning's from preceding efforts to overcome the "inescapable condition" that Langbaum so well describes: the plight of an individual ego "isolated within himself," bereft of an "objective counterpart" for his subjective will and feelings (*Poetry of Experience*, 28). These differences become most notable when we specifically look at the romantic search for a "counterpart" of the opposite gender, a topic that strangely seems to interest neither Langbaum nor Bloom, for all its centrality to their respective concerns.

"Be thou me!" an "impetuous" Shelley urged the "Maenad"-like West Wind. The famous apostrophe could just as well have been uttered by all those equally impetuous romantic seekers who coveted an Eve in order to replenish the vacancies experienced by a solitary Adamic self. Whether factual or mythified, alive or dead, human or immortal, the romantic epipsyche became an increasingly problematic emblem that allegorized the male's unsatiated desire for fusion. In his very first conversation poem, "The Aeolian Harp," Coleridge could ask "pensive Sara" to act as a counterweight for his flights of fancy by having her recline her cheek against him in their "Cot" (a posture that Browning was to reverse carefully in his macabre parody of this idyllic cottage scene in "Porphyria's Lover"). Soon, however, the silent helpmeet on whose "more serious eye" Coleridge's speaker projected his own misgivings about the unbridled use of the imagination (in Miltonic double negatives better suited for admonishing archangels than for Sara Fricker) fades out altogether. She is so much "at rest" in "Frost at Midnight" that her restless mate can appropriate her maternal role by bestowing a new Edenic birth on their infant son; she becomes replaced as a "woman beyond utterance dear" by her namesake in "To Asra"; both she and that namesake lose their individuality in "Dejection: an Ode." There, as in Browning's "Childe Roland," the subjective capacity for projection becomes a curse. The speaker now parades the isolation produced by this dubious gift before the "Dear Lady" to whom, in earlier drafts of his great poem, Coleridge had given the names of William and Edward.

This pattern of denying to the female the position to which she had first been exalted was to become a romantic paradigm. If in Wordsworth's earlier poems, as Margaret Homans has perceptively suggested, "the quietude," not just of Dorothy the living sister but also of dead sister-spirits such as Lucy Gray or the Margaret of the Ruined Cottage, "verifies the power of the poet's performative words,"[8] the feminine pagan sources of that power become dissipated in the later poetry when the Female Other once again turns into a male Christian deity. In "She Was a Phantom of Delight," the gleaming "Apparition" that glides, Porphyria-like, into the poet's field of vision soon dissolves into a mundane woman engaged in "household motion," who is acknowledged to retain at best "something" of the "Angelic light" formerly conferred on her by the poet's recoiling imagination. Masculine history and masculine religion take over in the later books of *The Excursion* and in the "Victorian" revisions of the 1805 *Prelude*.

In Byron's poetry, too, whether in the obsessive lyrics of parting such as "Fare Thee Well" and "To Augusta" or in dramas like *Manfred* (where the male protagonist can receive nothing more than an echo of his own name from Astarte's shade) and, most persistently, in *Don Juan*, where all romantic liaisons come to naught, the desired Female Other can never be embraced. Haidée, whom Juan still worships as his lodestar before he is forced to enter the harem in woman's clothing but whom he quickly forgets thereafter, can neither live nor expire in his arms. The only fusion possible is between Haidée and another male, the piratical father who causes her death:

I said that they were alike, their features and
  Their stature, differing but in sex and years;
Even to the delicacy of their hand
  There was resemblance. [*Don Juan*, 4.45]

Female victim and male victimizer can blend in death, equally forgotten by memory, resting in unvisited tombs. In Byron's masculine world, the Female Other must necessarily be sacrificed. Not until "James Lee's Wife" and its pendant piece "Dis aliter visum," significantly subtitled "Le Byron de nos Jours," and, most significantly, "Pompilia" would Browning counter this dispiriting vision by restoring to Byron's silent Haidée a genuine voice of her own.

It was the immediate precedent of the younger romantics, however, as Harold Bloom rightly insists, that was most forcefully engraved in the mind who moved from *Pauline* (modeled after confessional romances such as *Alastor, Epipsychidion,* and *The Fall of Hyperion*) to the dramatic monologue spoken by Porphyria's deranged lover. Bloom perceptively recovers some of the Shelleyan "subtexts" that lurk in Browning's poetry. But his oedipal emphasis on masculine rivalry leads him to miss one of the chief attractions which Shelley, that "poet of women," held for the young Browning and leads him also to underestimate the significance of a Keats he casts as Tennyson's, but not Browning's, poetic "father" (*Poetry and Repression,* 177, 143–74, passim).

Let us consider first the case of Keats. "Porphyria's Lover" can be seen as a deliberate revision of "The Eve of St. Agnes"—or, to indulge in Browning's macabre joke, what might be called an "Eve of St. Agnes" with a "twist." The ironies and ambiguities embedded in Keats's semiallegorical treatment of projection are sharpened by the psychological realism of a poem in which the active Porphyro turns into Porphyria and the illusions of the hoodwinked Madeline turn into the delusions of a mad male fantasist. But it is not just Keats's single poem that provides a Bloomian subtext for "Porphyria's Lover." The Boccaccian Porphyro who penetrates Madeline's bower is merely one of many Lovers whose recurrence throughout Keats's entire canon Browning also rescrutinized.

Whether it is the Endymion with whose search for Cynthia the early Keats had already identified in "I Stood Tip-Toe" ("He was a Poet, sure a lover too, / Who stood on Latmus' top" [193–94]) or the "bold Lover" on the Urn who must remain content with a "She" who cannot fade (17, 19) or the ever-smitten Hermes who can blend with the nymph who, "like a moon in wane, / Faded before him" (*Lamia,* 136–37) or the acolyte who wrests Psyche away from Cupid's embrace in order to place her into "some untrodden region of my mind"(51), the figure of the Lover persistently acts as the chief agent of Keats's desire to blend sexual consummation with the stasis of immortality. That stasis is associated either with godhead (as it also will be in the closure of "Porphyria's Lover") or with the permanence of art (as it will be in "My Last Duchess"). Yet the lyrical reconciliation of the mutable and the permanent can only be expressed as a subjective wish fulfillment. Only wishfulness can combine, in Keats's last great sonnet, a simultaneous enjoyment of the "steadfast" "unchangeable" qualities of the distanced "Bright Star" and of the breathing motions of a living woman's warm, white "breast" against which the reposing lover can lie "pillow'd" (the original version read "*cheek*-pillow'd").

Browning must have recalled some of these Keatsian touchstones in "Porphyria's Lover" (where Porphyria makes the Lover recline his "cheek" against her bared "white" shoulder). But he invokes them more directly in the sixteenth section of "One Word More," where he questions the fulfillment of the wish that Cynthia might "turn a new side" to her mortal gazers. "Unseen" by herdsman, huntsman, steersman, the other face of that female moon remains

> Blank to Zoroaster on his terrace,
> Blind to Galileo on his turret,
> Dumb to Homer, dumb to Keats—him, even! [6162–65]

Browning's doubts, however, were fully anticipated by Keats himself. His skepticism is evident in the ironic treatment of a Porphyro who violates the "chamber of maiden thought" or of a Lycius incapable of sustaining the vision that is Lamia.[9] Keats was as aware as Browning of the dangers of subjectivity. If that subjectivity could happily result in Endymion's transfiguration or in the internalization of Psyche, it could also deanimate and kill. The "pale knight" who fails to read the "language strange" of a Belle Dame sans Merci, the entranced Lycius who must die depleted, or the weak "dreaming thing" apostrophized by Moneta are all exemplars of the self-destructiveness inherent in a desire based on projection. In "Porphyria's Lover," Browning simply reverses the process by having the Lover kill the very object of his desire.

Although in "Porphyria's Lover" Browning was able to accentuate ironies already inherent in Keats's narratives, his infatuation with Shelley's own cult of the woman was not easily shaken. Not until after the 1852 "Essay on Shelley" did he discover the full record of the infidelities of the Sun-Treader whose idealizations of the Female Other he had earlier emulated. Browning's reluctant dissociation from *Alastor* and *Epipsychidion* in *Pauline* had been artistic, not emotional. Yet, in the 1855 " 'Childe Roland to the Dark Tower Came,' " that hallucinatory and "de-idealizing" monologue (Bloom, *Poetry and Repression,* 175), the dissociation had become more profound. It is significant that there should be no females in that poem of pure projection. The knight who journeys to the Dark Tower is not charged with the mission of rescuing an immured female. He is no St. George about to free a chained maiden, no Perseus rescuing Andromeda, no chivalric Count Gismond or Gareth or Lancelot (as in Tennyson's or in Morris's poems). Yet it is precisely the *absence* of a female object that makes the quest so gripping as an exercise in pure projection.[10] Absence *is* Presence, as Browning would have James Lee's Wife discover.

By the time Browning came to write "James Lee's Wife," a poem which by his own account, interestingly enough, was to dwell on "people newly-married," trying futilely "to realize a dream of being sufficient to each other, in a *foreign land* (where you can try such an *experiment*) and finding it break up,—the man being *tired* first, and tired precisely of the love,"[11] the repudiation had become complete. He could at last see Shelley plain. Browning was now wholly disenchanted with the experimental love-ethic of a poet who had tried to share Harriet Westbrook and Mary Godwin or, later, Mary and Emilia Viviani or, later still, Mary and Jane Williams. It was an affront to the widowed Browning's Victorian respectability. But it was more. Despite its negative emphasis, "James Lee's Wife" reinstates that Female Other, which Browning now felt Shelley had tarnished. Browning had already fashioned critiques of a male's denial of the feminine in "Porphyria's Lover" and "My Last Duchess." But whereas Lover and Duke had at least tried to possess the Female Other, the "tired" James Lee rejects fusion altogether. As Browning now knew, Shelley too had wearied in his quest for an ideal he despaired of finding in any living woman.[12]

Like James Lee, and unlike the Browning who clung to a remembered happiness with Elizabeth Barrett, Shelley had never been satiated in his search for Intellectual Beauty. The *Alastor* poet who impales himself on the thresholds of consciousness could at best encounter a reflection of his own eyes. The speaker of *Epipsychidion,* who also dies in the course of his quest, similarly despairs of a female projection of his own self: "I measure / The world of fancies, seeking one like thee, / And find—alas! mine own infirmity" (69–71). Neither Emilia the Sun nor Mary the blotted Moon, "whose pale and waning lips" shrink "as in the sickness of eclipse" (309–10), nor even Clare Clairmont, that other astral body so abruptly introduced as a Comet "beautiful and fierce" (368), could satisfy an ever-hungry Astrophel.

But if Keats questioned that hunger, Shelley relished it as a means of propulsion until, wearied, he turned away from the Female Other with something of the same disgust with which Victor Frankenstein destroys the half-completed Monsteress he had tried to fashion. In one of the last letters he was to write before he immolated himself like the poets of *Alastor* and *Epipsychidion,* he provided a fitting epitaph for his culmination of the romantic quest for an epipsyche:

> The "Epipsychidion" I cannot look at; the person whom it celebrates was a cloud instead of a Juno; and poor Ixion starts from the centaur that was the offspring of his own embrace. If you are anxious, however, to hear what I am and have been, it will tell you something thereof. It is an idealized history of my life and feelings. I think one is always in love with something or other; the error, and I confess it is not easy for spirits cased in flesh and blood to avoid it, consists in seeking in a mortal image the likeness of what is perhaps eternal.[13]

In "James Lee's Wife," Browning gave a voice to the "something or other" Shelley treats as an abstraction. In part 8 of the poem, he added a stanza in which the Wife adopts Shelley's bitterness as well as some of his phrasing:

> I have my lesson, understand
>    The worth of flesh and blood at last.
> Nothing but beauty in a Hand?
>    Because he could not change the hue,
>    Mend the lines and make them true
> To this which met his soul's demand,—
> Would Da Vinci turn from you? [294–300]

Leonardo the artist, she conjectures, would not dismiss a spirit cased in "flesh and blood" for an unrealizable ideal. But James Lee has dismissed her. And so, as Browning reluctantly came to admit, would have Percy Bysshe Shelley.

## 2

In "Porphyria's Lover" ("PL"), as in Keats's "Eve of St. Agnes" ("EA"), we are presented with a contrast between a cold outside world and a warm interior. Yet, in each poem, it is the passionate outsider penetrating that interior who brings warmth to the immobile dreamer within: Just as Porphyria immediately kneels to make "the cheerless grate / Blaze up, and all the cottage warm" ("PL," 8–9), so does her namesake, "burning Porphyro," with "heart on fire," try to melt the "chilly nest" he has invaded ("EA," 159, 75, 235). Their efforts, however, are half-successful at best. If Porphyria cannot thaw her unresponsive lover by placing his "arm about her waist" and by pillowing his cold cheek on her "smooth white shoulder bare" ("PL," 16–17), Porphyro cannot rouse the sleeping Madeline by sinking his "warm, unnerved arm" on her "pillow" ("EA," 280, 281).

The coldness of the outside world and its instability somehow cling to each of these intruders. Death's pallor envelops them, for all their warmth and vigorous movement. Kneeling before Madeline, Porphyro sinks "pale as smooth-sculptured stone"; when, on waking, she sees him as "pallid, chill, and drear!" he becomes associated with the "pallid moonshine" in which her taper "died" (297, 311, 200). Even when, "flush'd," he springs back into motion, Madeline's fears seem borne out by ominous details wedged into the narrative: the blowing frost-wind, iced gusts, and setting moon undermine Porphyro's "impassion'd" professions of eternal devotion. Yet Porphyria's Lover is warier than Madeline. Though Porphyria assures him that the "thought of one so pale / For love of her" has caused her to brave the elements and try to free her "struggling passion," the Lover finds insufficient comfort in the knowledge that "passion *sometimes* would prevail" ("PL," 28–29, 23, 26; italics added). Instead, he stares guardedly at Porphyria's damp clothes and "soiled gloves" before deciding to convert that "sometimes" into a "forever," a moment of eternity. He will not risk the fate of his romantic predecessor.

Hence, whereas Madeline resorts to trustfulness, Porphyria's Lover remains suspicious. Madeline accepts Porphyro's assurance that what he calls an "elfin-storm from faery land" ("EA," 343) sanctions their joint removal from the "bloated wassaillers" at the feast (346). She thus submits to her abductor and vanishes in the chilly exterior: "And they are gone: aye, ages long ago / These lovers fled away into the storm" (370–71). Porphyria's Lover, on the other hand, will not venture beyond his mental cell. He fears that he will be no more able to "restrain" Porphyria than did "to-night's," momentarily deserted, "gay feast" ("PL," 27). If Madeline comes to disregard the blowing "frost-wind," Porphyria's Lover considers the "sullen wind" to which he has listened "with heart fit to break" as an emblem of the instability that might again engulf this brief "moment" of communion (2, 5, 36). The woman who found it so difficult to "dissever" herself from the stormy world without may prove to be as unreliable as Porphyro; while alive, she can at best momentarily "shut the cold out and the storm" (24, 7). Thus, only by freezing her into a stony permanence can this pale Lover preserve her temporary fire. Though he will tell us that the "cheek" of the woman he has strangled still blushes "bright beneath [his] burning kiss," he has conferred on her his own deathly pallor (47, 48). The Lover who resembled Madeline has transformed himself into Madeline's possessor.

Browning's poem thus inverts Keats's narrative: The external coldness into which Porphyro ominously transports "so pure a thing" ("EA," 225) becomes internalized by the Lover who wants to preserve Porphyria's purity by making her permanently "mine, mine, fair, / Perfectly pure and good" ("PL," 36–37). Yet Browning also has the Lover internalize the skepticism that in Keats's poem is presented through a "negative capability" that relies on imagery and multiple points of view. Porphyro's name (as well as Porphyria's) is derived from the Greek word for purple (as Keats knows when he alludes to the "purple riot" in Porphyro's heart); as such, the name suggests a warm hue, as well as a high station.[14] But the vermilion dye of porphyry is obtained by pulverizing ("porphyrizing") a hard red shell or equally hard red slab or rock (as Keats again suggests when he describes Porphyro as a "smooth-sculptured stone," a "throbbing star," a "vermeil dyed" shield for Madeline's beauty ["EA," 297, 318, 336]). Madeline's warm lover, regarded by Angela as "liege-lord of all Elves and Fays" (121), may thus well be a cold-blooded immortal like Lamia or Merlin's "Demon" (171).

What Porphyria's Lover fears, however, is not the draining of his lifeblood by a vampiric immortal but rather the mutability of the mortal woman he identifies with the raging wind. Stony and still, unresponsive to her overtures, he awaits the moment in which he can rob Porphyria of her animated movements. Porphyro devises a quick stratagem to bypass the revelers at the feast and enter the "maiden's chamber": "Sudden a thought came like a full-blown rose" ("EA," 139, 187, 136). Similarly, a "sudden thought" has prompted Porphyria, according to the Lover's account, to leave the gay feast and venture into his chamber ("PL," 28). But her "thought" was a mere impulse, destined to be—or so he fears—short-lived. It is his own mind that searches for a stratagem as he, outwardly still passive and virginal, debates "what to do"until he lights upon the "thing" that might allow him to preserve her (35, 38). By draining Porphyria of her life, he can assume the mental control of a Porphyro. The "Bold Lover" forever frozen on Keats's stony Urn can never kiss his unfading "She": "though thou hast not thy bliss, / For ever wilt thou love, and she be fair!" (19–20). In the stony tableau devised by Porphyria's Lover, however, that "bliss" becomes attainable. The necrophilic Lover kisses the dead woman; but, what is more, he can now impose his own mental processes on the mind whose inconstancy he had earlier feared:

> I propped her head up as before,
> Only, this time my shoulder bore
> Her head, which droops upon it still:
> The smiling rosy little head,
> So glad it has its utmost will,
> That all it scorned at once is fled,
> And I, its love, am gained instead! ["PL," 49–55]

Converted into an "it," Porphyria's head no longer has the power of volition; instead, "its will" is that of her subjective interpreter. She has become an object for the Lover's projection, for he can now impute to her his own wishes without any fear of contradiction.

The mechanism of projection was also at work in "The Eve of St. Agnes," where Porphyro played on Madeline's wishful and childish trust in the "visions of delight" promised to virgins on St. Agnes's Eve. Yet Madeline had come to sense a disparity between subject and object, wish and reality. Moreover, her misgivings were reinforced by a narrator who cast doubts upon her "shaded" dream by his frequent interventions and by juxtaposing her fantasies to those of the Beadsman and Angela. There are no such narrator and no such subsidiary characters in "Porphyria's Lover." As in the companion piece to this poem, "Johannes Agricola in Meditation," we are from start to finish within the "madhouse cell" of the Lover's screened-off mind.

As an exercise in the subjectivism of projection, "Porphyria's Lover" thus raises certain questions that validate my earlier contention that Browning devised a parody of the romantic quest for a Female Other. Whom is the Lover addressing? Where is he located? Given the absence of a verifiable interlocutor and a verifiable setting such as Browning was to provide six years later in the poem usually considered to be his first bona fide dramatic monologue, "My Last Duchess," how trustworthy, ultimately, is the Lover's account? We have the authority of Keats's narrator that Porphyro entered Madeline's chamber and exploited her dream. We cannot at all be sure that a Porphyria actually sought out the egocentric speaker who, at the very outset of his monologue, projects his internal turmoil on the "vexing" storm outside.[15] Has this speaker, whose very identity depends on his act of projection (the poem was originally called, quite simply, "Madhouse Cell, No. II"), truly killed Porphyria? Indeed, does a "Porphyria" really exist in a shape other than in his mind?

The similarity in the names of "Porphyro" and "Porphyria" may, after all, involve more than the reversal traced above. It may well suggest that not only Browning but also the deranged speaker whom Browning animates is a latter-day romantic who knows his Keats. The "story" of "Porphyria's Lover" could thus be read as a pure fantasy told by a reader of "The Eve of St. Agnes" who, after identifying with Madeline's desire for the phantasm of a lover, does not want to share her disenchantment. That male reader thus feels free not only to reverse the gender of Keats's protagonists but also to devise a different outcome to gratify his crazed need for "pure" possession. In this sense, the Lover's confident assertion, "No pain felt she; / I am quite sure she felt no pain" ("PL," 41–42), actually would be true. The strangling of a purely imaginary object of desire can cause no pain to an actual human being "cased in flesh and blood."

By the untrustworthiness of his speaker, Browning teases the readers of "Porphyria's Lover" into trying to provide a "story" of their own. But the scenarios we may concoct are just as untrustworthy. We may want to visualize a murderer who, surprised by the guard, still hovers gleefully over the body of an actual victim; or, if we accept the murder as imaginary, we may prefer to glimpse a madman in a cell. We may also be tantalized into furnishing some antecedent narrative of star-crossed lovers or one in which a passive visionary who has seen a nameless high born lady from afar (one "born in purple," a "porphyrogenite") dreams that this "She" will visit and worship him. The possibilities are multiple, but all such conjectures are destined to remain futile. Our need to entertain them, despite that futility, only helps to sharpen Browning's ironic emphasis. Our mental narratives delude us into thinking that we can confer permanence and objectivity on what remains erratic and subjective. By inventing alternative "stories," we hope to distance ourselves from the grotesque Lover. Instead, however, we partake of the very same craving. To master a problematic instability we, too, yearn for some spurious form of permanence.

It is precisely such an assumption of a spurious godlike immutability that links "Porphyria's Lover" both to its 1836 pendant poem "Johannes Agricola" and to the 1842 "My Last Duchess," with its own dramatization of the displacement of a Female Other by a male figure playing the role of

God. The last two lines of "Porphyria's Lover" jar the reader almost as much as the strangling acknowledged in line 41: "And all night long we have not stirred, / And yet God has not said a word!" (59–60). God's voicelessness recalls the Lover's own deliberate silence when "called" by Porphyria. He and God and now she remain unstirred, at one. If Johannes Agricola the Antinomian professes, "Night by night," to be able to reach the abode of a deity who has exempted him from damnation, so does the Lover exult in newly gained invulnerability. In the seventeenth century, the theologian Ralph Cudworth had inveighed against those "Porphyrianists" (the followers of Arius and Porphyrius) who made "their Trinity a foundation for creature-worship and idolatry."[16] Though not a follower of Porphyrius, the third-century neo-Platonist, the Lover is nonetheless a "Porphyrianist" in his own way. His "creature-worship" of a woman of "flesh and blood" has resulted in her deanimation into a cold idol. By appropriating her mentally, he has become, he thinks, immune and immovable, like God. In the "night" of his own mind, he has shaped a new triune Identity. Whether Porphyria is his dead victim or merely a figment of his imagination thus does not matter. She remains in either case an eidolon whose possession he regards, in true romantic fashion, as licensing his elevation to godhead. Like the artist figures in the later monologues, who can confer life as well as arrest it, Porphyria's Lover professes to be actuated by his desire for another. Yet his love stands exposed as a monomaniacal self-love.

A similar self-love obviously operates in "My Last Duchess," a poem discussed by Browning critics, and ably so, far more often than "Porphyria's Lover," yet seldom seen in its own pendant relationship to the earlier poem. The similarities between the two works are significant; but so are the differences. The Lover who must dominate the "stooping" Porphyria by freezing here into a posture of submissive dependence resembles the Duke of Ferrara who chooses "Never to stoop" (43). The Duke, too, deanimates a Female Other who threatens his need to remain in absolute control of his rigid mental world. But this calculating aesthete, though every bit as monstrous (and possibly more so), is not a crazed, improvising, pale Lover whose words are subject to doubt. Unlike that dehistoricized speaker's voice, his own carries the authority of specific time and place, the staples of Browning's future monologues.

We do not know whom the Lover addresses and why, or whether he addresses anyone at all. We do know the identity of the Duke's interlocutor and know, moreover, that other viewers have previously been shown the portrait he ritually unveils "by design" (6). Indeed, it is the Duke's compulsive need for repetition that belies his efforts at composure and control. A new Duchess may be his current "object" (53), but his previous effort to objectify a living woman into a frozen painting still seems to unsettle him. The "curtain" he removes for the Count's emissary thus gradually unveils a mind that is more disturbed than it would admit. If the reader of "Porphyria's Lover" becomes a voyeur at Bedlam who ultimately can no more "dissever" truth from fantasy than the subjective Lover himself, the reader of "My Last Duchess" becomes a detective who wrests away the control the Duke desires by seizing on the "objective" clues that have been provided. These clues permit us to judge the Duke far more unequivocally than we could ever judge the Lover.

The chief clue is provided by the Duchess herself. Like Porphyria, she exists solely within the speaker's words. Yet Browning permits the reader to free the Duchess from the Duke's possessive "My" in ways that Porphyria could never be disengaged from her Lover's strident "she was mine, mine." There is a further difference. It is his yearning for an Ideal that prompts the Lover to drain a woman's "flesh and blood." The Duke, however, has failed to grasp that such a feminine Ideal had actually animated his own world. If the blush on Porphyria's dead countenance was purely imaginary, the "spot of joy" preserved in Pandolf's painting still confounds the Duke's literalism (21). He will never understand how "such a glance came there" (12). Yet the details he furnishes carry symbolic meanings that continue to defy him. The "white mule" on which "my lady" was wont to ride, the offering of a "bough of cherries" brought to her by a worshiper, are iconographic details traditionally associated with the Virgin Mary. A democratic mediatrix, an earthly Madonna, has gone unnoticed by a mind determined not to stoop. The "approving speech" with which this kindly Madonna received all who greeted her has been extinguished, like her original "blush" (31). Empowered by Browning's art of inference, however, the reader can reactivate her receptivity, adopt the mediating role that she has lost, and thus restore to her what the Duke continues to deny.

Unlike the Duchess and Porphyria, Browning's later women are allowed to speak. Of these, Pompilia, a full-blown version of the earthly Madonna, modeled after Barrett's Marian Earle (and Barrett herself), certainly remains the most notable. Even when dead or silenced, however, Browning's later incarnations of the Female Other continue to confound the male's attempts at mental possession. The fair "she" appropriated by that other art collector, the Bishop of St. Praxed's (a church named, significantly enough, after a female martyr), will find avengers in her sons. In "Andrea del Sarto" Lucrezia enacts the inconstancy that Porphyria's Lover had feared. But her behavior defiles her would-be possessor more than herself. She is an unchaste Cynthia whom he must share with others: "My face, my moon, my everybody's moon" (29). Her mobility sets in relief the impotence of this "half-man." Although Andrea would, like Porphyria's Lover, dearly want to restrain the woman's movements, he can only paralyze himself. His self-loathing strangles his very dream of artistic immortality in a New Jerusalem where he, as the elect decorator of a fourth great wall, might join Leonardo, Raphael, and Michelangelo, "the three first without a wife" (264). Sadly, he realizes that he remains walled in by the mental prison that Lucrezia can flee. If she acts as Andrea's foil, so does Fra Lippo Lippi, who also breaks out of the confinement of mental and physical cells, for Lippo knows that Ideal and flesh cannot be "dissevered." Accordingly, at the end of his monologue, he suddenly defers to the voice of "the sweet angelic slip of a thing" whom he casts in the role of rescuer, a female version of Perseus or St. George. She embodies the paradox he cannot resolve. She is an image, a St. Lucy, a type in a painting; yet she is also the Prior's niece, a married woman, very much alive, and, as such, one who arouses Lippo's desire.

## 3

In *Jocoseria* (1883), one of his last volumes of poetry, Browning movingly recalls his dead mate in the fine lyric "Never the Time and the Place." The writer of dramatic monologues once more assays the romantic lyrical mode he had been forced to relinquish. Whether consciously or not, however, he resorts to the same imagery he had used in "Porphyria's Lover" almost half a century before. And he does so now without the defensive ironies that had marked his earlier, seminal incursion into timelessness and placelessness. "Where is the loved one's face?" the speaker asks plaintively and then proceeds to answer his own question:

> In a dream that loved one's face meets mine,
> But the house is narrow, the place is bleak
> Where, outside, rain and wind combine
> With a furtive ear, if I strive to speak,
> . . . . . . . . . . . . . . . . . . . . . . .
> Outside are the storms and strangers: we—
> Oh, close, safe, warm sleep I and she,
> —I and she! [5–9, 20–22]

James Lee had yet to mature before he could glimpse a female face like his own. But the seventy-year-old Browning was more than ready to exclaim, "'Tis she!" No "half-man" like Andrea, he had given expression to a feminine self. And in *Jocoseria* he once more strove to speak in the female voice. In his poem "Mary Wollstonecraft and Fuseli," Mary Shelley's mother utters an artistic credo that is unmistakably Browning's own. Fuseli can sublimate emotions into his controlled compositions, but she toils "at a language" that in its very roughness retains her "strong fierce" passionate core. Elsewhere in *Jocoseria,* in the Talmudic tales of Balkis and Solomon, and Lilith and Eve, Browning blends his feminism with his growing philo-Semitism, the product of a similar identification with the victims of a cultural oppression that relied on mental projection as much as prejudice.

It is significant that *Jocoseria* was originally supposed to include "Gerousios Oinos," Browning's attack on the later Tennyson, Morris, Rossetti, and Swinburne. What prompted Browning to cast his contemporaries as "mere servingmen" unrestrainedly quaffing the diluted "true wine" of the elder English poets, thinking it "bettered and bittered" by mixing it with beer? He had become defensive about his own stature after Alfred Austin's attack; yet Tennyson had been just as shabbily treated by Austin, and, moreover, younger poets like Swinburne had indignantly rallied to Browning's side. As his letters to Isa Blagden show, Browning genuinely disliked the supposed dilutions of meaning in the later *Idylls of the King,* the later poems of Morris, and the verses of Swinburne and Rossetti, all marred by "the *minimum* of thought and idea in the *maximum* words and phraseology."[17] Yet even this artistic difference seems insufficient to account for the excessive vehemence of Browning's attack in "Gerousios Oinos"—an excessiveness he seemed to acknowledge when he suppressed publication of the poem.

It was not mere difference that so disturbed Browning but a shocked recognition of kinship. Tennyson's "Lucretius," his most Browning-like dramatic monologue, had appeared in 1868. The trio of younger poets had also adopted Browning's central theme of the Female Other—from Morris's 1856 "Defence of Guenevere" to Rossetti's 1870 "Jenny" and "A Last Confession." To be sure, his impact on these younger poets was far from exclusive. Their female portraits were also indebted to a Tennyson who had, after all, published "Mariana" and "The Lady of Shalott" even before Browning printed—and withdrew—his *Pauline* (which Rossetti was to rediscover) and who had written "Tithon," the original version of "Tithonus," around the very same time that Browning composed "Porphyria's Lover." Yet the Female Other whom the pre-Raphaelites represented on canvas and in verse, like Swinburne's Proserpines and Sapphos, owed as much, or more, to Browning.

"One face looks out from all his canvasses," Christina Rossetti wrote in an implicit criticism of her brother's work ("In an Artist's Studio"). Whether queen or "nameless girl" or angel or saint, the Female Other now allowed a younger generation of artists to "feed" upon "her face by day or night." Browning agreed: "Yes,—I have read Rossetti's poems," he wrote Isa Blagden, "you know I hate the effeminacy of his school,—the men that dress up like women,—that use obsolete forms, too, and archaic accentuations to seem soft" (*Dearest Isa,* 336). Were not these lovers of the Female Other like his own Porphyria's Lover? Rossetti had even indulged in necrophilia by wresting his poems from Lizzie Siddal's corpse. Looking at the face that glanced at his from their paintings in pen and pencil, a shocked Browning saw not the flush of joy of a Last Duchess, as if she were alive, but the grimaces of ladies of pain, adulteresses, femmes fatales, prostitutes, and vampires. The younger nympholepts were not just "feeding" off the representations of England's elder poets; these hungry "servingmen" were also consuming the very substance of the elderly Browning's own poetry.

In "John Jones's Wife," a Swinburne who had become disenchanted with Browning did, in effect, just that. By writing a parody of "James Lee's Wife," the younger poet could openly appropriate Browning's mode and subject matter and go one better. In his attack on Browning in "The Chaotic School," the essay he left in manuscript, Swinburne denies Browning the skill of impersonating a true woman: "How does it fare with his Colombes, Constances, Mildreds, Phenes, who are visibly fleshless and senseless? Analyze the doings and sayings of the wife of Jules or the mistress of Norbert; the utter mechanical absurdity of the monstrous parts they have to play is equalled by the tight, hoarse, intermittent, hard, febrile manner of their utterances: as far from emotion as from reason."[18] Swinburne thus transforms the voice of James Lee's Wife into the voice of a Female Other wronged by Browning's art; his speaker's quarrel is not just with "John Jones" but with her original creator:

My skin might change to a pitiful crone's,
  My lips to a lizard's, my hair to weed,
My features, in fact, to a series of loans;
  Thus much is conceded; now, you concede
You would hardly salute me by choice, John Jones?"[19]

Like the speaker in Keats's ode who wrests Psyche away from Cupid, Swinburne the parodist has become a rival lover. But his rivalry stems from an acknowledgment of the very kinship the older poet so eagerly tried to suppress.

Browning had come to see himself as the jealous preserver of both the memory and the voice of his female "moon of poets." He could not accept this "effeminate" competitor, whose "florid impotence" he denounced (*Dearest Isa,* 333). And yet Swinburne's criticism was an act of generosity. "I do *not* count Browning a lyric poet proper," he wrote, "nor properly a dramatic, as he breaks down in dialogue; but his greatness as an *artist* I think (now more than ever) established to all time by his *monodramas*. I say *artist,* or poet, as well as thinker."[20] It is significant that this tribute should have come shortly after Swinburne's close reading of the monodrama "James Lee's Wife." It was a tribute he was to extend in his elegiac "Sequence of Sonnets on the Death of Robert Browning" in 1889. There, he celebrated Browning for his capacity to "see / The heart within the heart that seems to strive" (*Complete Works,* 6:148). And that innermost heart remained, for both poets, always essentially female.

This attempt at a chapter in literary history would not be complete without my calling attention to the centrality, in all Victorian poetry, of the patterns of projection I have described. In "The Voice" (1912), Thomas Hardy, that relic from the Victorian Age, still tried to animate a dead Female Other: "Woman much missed, how you call to me, call to me, / Saying that now you are not as you were." Browning's contribution to English poetry was both his attempt to give voice to a Female Other and his persistent skepticism about the process of projection that such a voicing involved. Like Keats, who might have become the greatest of Victorian poets, Browning knew that poetry, like all art, can distort the Other into what she is not. It was that skepticism which gave rise to the dramatic monologue and which led to a mode simultaneously ironic and idealistic that Browning came to perfect and to bequeath to later poets.

## Notes

An earlier version of this essay appeared in *Victorian Poetry* 22 (1984): 139–59.

1. All citations from Browning's poetry are taken from *Robert Browning: The Poems,* ed. John Pettigrew and Thomas J. Collins, 2 vols. (New Haven: Yale University Press, 1981); the quotations from romantic poetry in section 1 are taken from *English Romantic Writers,* ed. David Perkins (New York: Harcourt Brace Jovanovich, 1967).
2. Edmund Gosse, *Personalia,* quoted in George Willis Cooke, *A Guide-Book to the Poetic and Dramatic Works of Robert Browning* (Boston and New York, 1896), 204.
3. U. C. Knoepflmacher, "On Exile and Fiction: The Leweses and the Shelleys," in *Mothering the Mind,* ed. Ruth Perry and Martine Brownley (New York: Holmes and Meiers, 1984).
4. *Westminster Review* 35 (1841): 330.
5. Roland Barthes, *Camera Lucida: Reflections on Photography,* trans. Richard Howard (New York: Hill and Wang, 1981), 14–15.
6. Robert Langbaum, *The Poetry of Experience: The Dramatic Monologue in Modern Literary Tradition* (New York: Norton, 1963), 28.
7. Harold Bloom, "Browning: Good Moments and Ruined Quests," *Poetry and Repression: Revisionism from Blake to Stevens* (New Haven: Yale University Press, 1976), 175–204.
8. Margaret Homans, "Eliot, Wordsworth, and the Scenes of the Sisters' Instruction," *CritI* 8 (1981): 224.
9. That skepticism is already in evidence as early as "Sleep and Poetry" in the deliberate infantilizing of the speaker who relies on "fancy" in order to catch the nymphs, to play with their fingers, and to touch merely "their shoulders white / Into a pretty shrinking with a bite / As hard as lips can make" (104–8).

10. Bloom holds that the all-masculine " 'Childe Roland' exposes the Romantic imagination" by the speaker's induction in a "visionary company of loss" (*Poetry and Repression,* 199, 200); his insight might have been borne out by a closer look at the identity of the speaker's two precursors in "the Band," Giles and Cuthbert.
11. Quoted in Richard Curle, ed., *Robert Browning and Julia Wedgewood: A Broken Friendship as Revealed in Their Letters* (New York, 1937), 109. Only the last italics are Browning's.
12. By adopting a female point of view, Browning attacked the weariness of a male romantic egotist, much as Mary Shelley had done in *Frankenstein,* the novel which, significantly enough, always remained one of Elizabeth Barrett's favorites.
13. *The Letters of Percy Bysshe Shelley,* ed. Frederick C. Jones (Oxford: Oxford University Press, 1964), 2:434.
14. For these and subsequent connotations, see *The Compact Edition of the OED* (1971).
15. Like Keats, Browning seems acutely aware of Coleridgean antecedents: If the storm tends to "vex" the Lover by its unruliness, it is the opposite state of "calm," unhelped by "any wind," that "vexes meditation" for another cottage dweller in "Frost at Midnight" (8, 9). Coleridge's speaker moves from inward paralysis to a dynamic animation of the landscape he devises for his child; Browning's Lover draws Porphyria into the frosty stillness of his mental cell. "Dejection: An Ode," Coleridge's other "midnight" poem, is also recalled in "Porphyria's Lover." Unable to find fuel in "that inanimate cold world" his imagination projects, Coleridge's agonized speaker seeks vainly to remove the "viper thoughts, that coil around my mind," by listening "to the wind" (51, 94); Porphyria's Lover, beset by similar anxieties, prefers to relieve his agony by coiling his thoughts around Porphyria's "little throat."
16. The citation is from Cudworth's *True Intellectual System* (1678), quoted in the *Compact OED,* 2:2242. It is noteworthy that in the so-called Porphyrian scale or tree (also reproduced in the *OED*) the "Animate" should be identified not with an "Incorporeal" substance such as the Christian soul but with a "Corporeal" substance as much prized as its "Sensible" and "Rational" analogues. Long ago, C. R. Tracy ("Browning's Heresies," *SP* 33 [1936]: 618) pointed to the theological slant of the *Monthly Repository,* where "Johannes Agricola" and "Porphyria's Lover" originally appeared, in order to account for the religious satire of the former poem. The same case should be made for its companion piece, not usually recognized as a similar incursion into a heretical theology.
17. March 22, 1870, in *Dearest Isa: Robert Browning's Letters to Isabella Blagden,* ed. Edward C. McAleer (Austin: University of Texas Press, 1951), 333.
18. *New Writings by Swinburne,* ed. Cecil Y. Lang (Syracuse, NY: Syracuse University Press, 1964), 53.
19. *The Complete Works of Algernon Charles Swinburne,* ed. Edmund Gosse and T. J. Wise (London, 1925), 5:268. The lines quoted are the conclusion of the poem.
20. To William Michael Rossetti, October 26, 1869, *The Swinburne Letters,* ed. Cecil Y. Lang (New Haven: Yale University Press, 1959), 2:46–47; Swinburne's italics. In the same letter Swinburne expresses his outrage at Austin's attack on Browning.

# "I stop somewhere waiting for you": Whitman's Femininity and the Reader of *Leaves of Grass*

KAREN OAKES

I MET WALT WHITMAN in an undergraduate course in American Literature. The professor, an eclectic scholar whom I admired for his beautiful mind and beautiful hair, tried to impress on us Whitman's status: first great American poet and world-class innovator. Nevertheless, I was bored and frustrated by the poet whose primary talents seemed to lie in interminable lists and inflated claims of self-importance. My response to the week we spent on "Song of Myself" was "I am the woman, I suffered, I was there."[1]

Later, reading Sandra Gilbert and Susan Gubar for a paper on Whitman and Dickinson, I could hardly disagree with their assessment of the former: "He didn't need to put his name on the title page of his poem, because he and his poem were coextensive: the poem itself *was* in a sense his name, writ large and bold." It seemed I would be forever distracted by what Virginia Woolf calls "the dominance of the letter 'I' and the aridity, which, like the giant beech tree, it casts within its shade."[2]

And then I discovered D. H. Lawrence's frightened and frightening vision of Whitman's poetic self:

> Your mainspring is broken, Walt Whitman. The mainspring of your own individuality. And so you run down with a great whirr, merging with everything. . . . Oh Walter, Walter, what have you done with . . . your own individual self? For it sounds as if it had all leaked out of you, leaked into the universe.

Lawrence gasps at the prospect of a writer losing his autonomy, and he sees this loss as "Death," calling Whitman the "post mortem poet." Furthermore, he explicitly names the poet's impulse to relinquish the self as a desire to regain the feminine: "Everything was female to him: even himself. . . . Always wanting to merge himself into the womb of something or other."[3]

Lawrence's "mourning" blurred my habitual response to Whitman, then refocused it with new clarity.

"Merging" is a radical act for all poets, who, as Gilbert and Gubar argue, traditionally write from a stance of autonomy; and women, they suggest, have historically been excluded from the creation of poetic discourse because the conventional, self-effacing feminine self is antipathetic to a genre that demands a strong, individuated creator. The lyric poet must be *subjective*: "the poet, even when writing in the third person, says 'I.'" This "I" is "strong and assertive," "a central self that is forcefully defined, whether real or imaginary." The idea of poet as divinity, as Emersonian "Namer or Language-Maker" seems at first to correspond to Whitman's self-portrait in "Song of Myself" as a "kosmos."[4]

Nevertheless, to define Whitman's vision of the "central self" poses extraordinary problems, as witnessed by the sheer volume of writing on the subject. At one extreme, Roy Harvey Pearce, with Gilbert and Gubar, views Whitman as a powerful, centered, Adamic self; at the other, June Jordan emphasizes the poet's intimacy and equality with the reader.[5] The work of Nancy Chodorow will help untangle the knot of divergent opinion. Chodorow argues that the feminine self, where "feminine" represents a cultural (not a biological) term and where "feminine" and "masculine" occupy a continuum, achieves its most authentic shape in the context of personal relationships: "The basic feminine sense of self is connected to the world, the basic masculine sense of self is separate"; hence, "[m]asculine personality . . . comes to be defined more in terms of denial of relation and connection (and denial of femininity), whereas feminine personality comes to include a fundamental definition of self in relationship."[6] This emphasis on relationship contrasts with the "masculine" autonomy that Gilbert and Gubar attribute to the poetic self, and specifically to Whitman.

Historical context and situation in patriarchal culture circumscribe the continuum of psychological gender for an individual. As Carroll Smith-Rosenberg has observed, "an abundance of manuscript evidence suggests that eighteenth- and nineteenth-century women routinely formed emotional ties with other women," and "[s]uch deeply felt same-sex friendships were casually accepted in American society," even those that represented "sensual avowals of love by mature women."[7] Similarly, John D'Emilio and Estelle B. Freedman point out that the "modern terms *homosexuality* and *heterosexuality* do not apply to an era that had not yet articulated these distinctions"; and it was only by the 1880s that the potential sexual content of single-sex relationships became widely known. Nevertheless, they indicate:

> Whitman's life embodied the tension between romantic and sexual love among same-sex friends in the nineteenth century. He championed manly love as a form of intense, romantic friendship, yet at times, he struggled to suppress his erotic desires for men.

We witness this struggle in Whitman's muffled and agonized remarks about his relationship to a young friend, Peter Doyle. In a coded notebook entry with the gender changed, he wrote with double underscoring: "*Remember where I am most weak,* & most lacking. Yet always preserve a kind spirit and demeanor to 16. *But pursue her no more.*"[8]

Whitman's search for what D'Emilio and Freedman call "intense, romantic friendship" suggests both his culturally "feminine" desires and their suppression by patriarchal standards of what behavior is appropriate to males—or at least to males who would be considered "masculine," that is, "normal." As Frank Lentricchia points out, one form of "patriarchal oppression . . . consists of imposing certain social standards of masculinity on all biological men, in order precisely to make us believe that the chosen standards for masculinity are *natural.*" Hence, an urgent need for critics of both sexes is to "disentangle [the] confusion [between masculinity and male]." One of the purposes of this study of Whitman will be to explore what Elizabeth Langland and Laura Claridge call "the possibility that maleness exists in relation to patriarchy as a third term of gender discourse, whose terms are woman, man and patriarchy."[9]

Given his cultural situation, Whitman enacts his "feminine" need for the other—and his homoeroticism—as much on a literary as on a social stage. For the poet, unequipped with the "characters" of narrative fiction who can enact a displaced interpersonal drama, the reader may become the other actor in the drama of "relationship." Nevertheless, patriarchy constrains him not just socially and personally but also artistically, as it formalizes literary style and convention. Whitman's struggle with gender identity and his explosions against the constraints of patriarchy influence the terms and shape of this relationship with the reader, its hospitality or distance, and ultimately define the peculiar power of his voice.

Because "Song of Myself" addresses the reader directly and because it represents the poet's movement toward self-definition, it brings into relief issues of autonomy and hierarchy, fluidity and equality; hence, my discussion in the first section of this essay will focus on the 1891–92 edition of "Song." As I explore Whitman's self-concept I will pay particular attention to moments that evince an especially acute attentiveness to the reader.[10] I will argue that although Whitman struggles with a psychologically "feminine" fear of detachment from and loss of the beloved other, his "masculine" fear of merging predominates, and it leads him to imagine the poet as incorporator or consumer and the reader as detached interpreter.

The second section will focus on the first version of "Song" and the important changes Whitman made in *Leaves of Grass* as he developed his ideas. The poet's earlier poems, written in a more "feminine" voice, imagine a more generous, subtle, and intimate relationship with his reader than do his later poems or revisions of early poems. These poems in effect "feminize" the reader, requiring of us a more kinetic, participatory response to the poet's gestures.[11] Whitman's later work, I will suggest, has been valorized by the critical community because it privileges a culturally "masculine" voice at the expense of this earlier "feminine" voice. Finally, in the third section I gesture toward a possible source for this repressed voice, namely, Whitman's status as homoerotic other in an increasingly homophobic culture. Throughout the study I will ask: "What does it mean to be a male poet with "feminine," even feminist, desires in a patriarchal culture?[12]

## "Both in and out of the game"

Closing my ears for a moment to Whitman's boasts, I try to listen more carefully to his private voice. Evidence of the blinding importance to him of human connections in his daily life proliferates: his relationship with his brother Jeff; his work in the Civil War hospitals; his enigmatic notebook entries to young male friends. His reaching out to others explicitly includes the reader. In "A Backward Glance o'er Travel'd Roads" (1889) he writes:

> The reader will always have his or her part to do, just as much as I have had mine. I seek less to state or display any theme or thought, and more to bring you, reader, into the atmosphere of the theme or thought—there to pursue your own flight.

The reader must not merely interpret fixed "meaning" but be a parallel creator sailing to his or her own "flight."[13]

In the 1891–92 version of "Song of Myself," this flight is not without hazard. As the poem begins, Whitman's outdoor lover appears to challenge the traditional separation of reader and poetic speaker:

> I celebrate myself, and sing myself,
> And what I assume you shall assume,
> For every atom belonging to me as good belongs to you.
>
> I loafe and invite my soul,
> I lean and loafe at my ease observing a spear of summer grass.
>
> [1, lines 1–5]

To "celebrate" and "sing" the self is to make the private a public event; here Whitman uncovers and even parodies the machinery of poetry, for what gives it movement and shape is a generous human consciousness, not a disembodied divine voice. As June Jordan remarks about other lines in Whitman, his voice "is intimate and direct at once: It is the voice of the poet who assumes that he speaks to an equal and that he need not fear that equality" (*Passion,* xiii). Whitman seems to dissipate his own boundaries as creator, imagining us as collaborators and playmates, at our ease: "For every atom belonging to me as good belongs to you." Nevertheless, while he critiques and evades the patriarchy's constraint of his voice, he simultaneously enacts this constraint and confirms the power it confers: "shall assume" commands our presence, as the speaker "assumes" a position of divine power, vision, and masculinity focused in and by the "I."

In section 2 of the poem we undergo a similar process of involvement, then detachment and analysis. At first, Whitman appears to assume a distinctly feminine posture, merging with nature:

> The atmosphere is not a perfume, it has no taste of the distillation, it is
> odorless,
> It is for my mouth forever, I am in love with it,
> I will go to the bank by the wood and become undisguised and naked,
> I am mad for it to be in contact with me.
>
> The smoke of my own breath,
>
> . . . . . . . . . . . . . . . . . . . . . . . . . . . . . . . . . .
>
> My respiration and inspiration, the beating of my heart, the passing of blood
> and air through my lungs,
>
> . . . . . . . . . . . . . . . . . . . . . . . . . . . . . . . . . .
>
> The sound of the belch'd words of my voice loos'd to the eddies of the wind[.]
> [2, lines 17, 21, 23, 25]

In the American literary tradition, nature has from the beginning been accorded the diminished power and status of the female.[14] Here the poet makes love with nature, seeking a oneness that seems to promise an equal, feminine melding of the self into the other. Any reader, male or female, cannot help but be seduced by this passage's ecstatic arousal.

At the same time, however, we must hear echoes of Whitman's mentor, for Emerson writes, "Thus in art does Nature work through the will of a man filled with the beauty of her first works. The world thus exists to the soul to satisfy the desire of beauty" (*Selected Writings,* 14). Nature serves as a sexual object for the willful male artist. Furthermore, he affirms, "How does Nature deify us with a few and cheap elements" (10); like Woolf's woman, Emerson's Nature serves as a looking glass that magnifies man (Woolf, *Room of One's Own,* 35). He continues, "Spirit is the Creator . . . And man in all ages and countries embodies it in his language as the FATHER" (*Selected Writings,* 15). By means of language, "man" appropriates creative power from female to male, from Mother Nature to God the "FATHER."

The issue of power becomes more evident when Emerson reflects, "Nature is thoroughly mediate. It is made to serve. It receives the dominion of man" (*Selected Writings,* 22). Hence, when Whitman continues, "Creeds and schools in abeyance . . . I harbor for good or bad, I permit to speak at every hazard, / Nature without check with original energy" (1, lines 10, 12–13), the very idea of "permission" implies "dominion" over nature, incorporation into the divine body, rather than merging with nature on her own terms. From this perspective, as he rewrites Genesis with his own myth of origin, Whitman invites the reader to share his power and privilege by identifying with him. Once again, the poet expresses his ambivalence about the gender norms of patriarchy (and, here, his tension with his "Master"), by at once relinquishing and reinforcing the self.

At the end of section 2, the poet affirms even more explicitly that our access to the experience offered by "Song" will come not through detachment and interpretation but through our enactment of its vision:

> Have you practis'd so long to learn to read?
> Have you felt so proud to get at the meaning of poems?
>
> Stop this day and night with me and you shall possess the origin of all poems,
> You shall possess the good of the earth and sun, (there are millions of suns left,)
> You shall no longer take things at second or third hand, nor look through the eyes of the dead . . .
> You shall not look through my eyes either, nor take things from me,
> You shall listen to all sides and filter them from your self.
>
> [2–3, lines 31–37]

The speaker confronts directly our assumptions about reading. While "practicing" implies numbing repetition, "get at" emphasizes the hostility and potential violence with which a reader approaches a poem whose "meaning" she or he considers concealed and detachable. Whitman claims that the reader creates "meaning," for even the poet represents an unreliable source of knowledge; we shall not perceive the world through his eyes, or through his "I."

Nevertheless, an edge of coercion emerges in the imperative "stop" and in the "shall" (Hollis, *Language and Style,* 98). The anaphora underlines the divine power of the visionary, creative speaker, who seems to "possess the origin of all poems" and "the good of the earth and sun." Section 4 makes his stance overt:

Apart from the pulling and hauling stands what I am,
Stands amused, complacent, compassionating, idle, unitary,
Looks down, is erect, or bends an arm on an impalpable certain rest,
Looking with side-curved head curious what will come next,
Both in and out of the game and watching and wondering at it.
[5, lines 75–79]

This speaker indicates his simultaneously involved and detached perspective; he assumes the "normal" masculine stance of the poet in patriarchy: autonomous, hierarchical, and "transcendent," "look[ing] down" from a position of power, yet "in" "the game" as well. The "game" is a telling choice, for it suggests Whitman's simultaneous absence and presence, his seduction and withdrawal; it permits him to have the illusion of intimacy without any of its risks, to soothe his feminine fear of the loss of the other while it assuages his masculine fear of the loss of the self. The duplicity and ambivalence here recur throughout the poem, perhaps most notably at the end of section 19, where he affirms, "This hour I tell things in confidence, / I might not tell everybody but I will tell you" (24, lines 387–88). The ambiguity in the word "confidence" underlines the complexity of our relationship with him; we may be confident of our intimacy, he suggests, yet his playfulness implies the hidden power of the "confidence man."

But in proposing the role of confidence man for himself, in putting the reader at arm's length, he works at odds with his proclaimed purpose in "A Backward Glance," to allow us to "pursue [our] own flight," inviting instead our detachment from the poetic experience; his own "game" of hide-and-seek first seduces and then challenges us "to get at the meaning" of the poem. That is, he in effect defines *us* as masculine: Autonomous and separate, we are invited to seek coherence and conclusion. He re-creates us in his own image, offering the feminine reader a chance to enjoy vicariously the power of the incorporating Father. Ultimately, while the 1891–92 edition of "Song" gestures toward escaping patriarchal norms for the poetic self, it confirms their power.

## Making Room for the Reader

I imagine Whitman smiling across "Space and Time" (43, line 710) as he acknowledges his playfulness with respect to the reader in an unsigned review of 1855: "He comes to no conclusions, and does not satisfy the reader" (778). Like a lover who will not commit himself beyond pleasure, younger Whitman leaves me wishing for more. Nevertheless, though our verbal intercourse may lack something of the certainty and security of a marriage, it has a (troubling) freedom: Without the definition imposed by a formal relationship, I must be creative in my own right; I must invent my role rather than enacting the role he has imagined for me as "wife."

If patriarchy mediates between male and female, masculine and feminine, by affirming their discontinuity, their radical otherness, Whitman struggles with patriarchy's idea that males must be masculine and females feminine.[15] One marker of his challenge to this idea appears in his enhanced attentiveness to process in the first version of "Song." Extrapolating from Chodorow's work on fluid feminine selfhood, Judith Kegan Gardiner argues that "female identity is a process"; hence, she says, women's writing "may . . . defy completion."[16] Though we should revise the emphasis on women's writing to feminine writing, Gardiner's ideas about process illuminate the differences between Whitman's later and earlier work.

In its alterations, the 1891–92 edition evinces Whitman's shift from a more feminine to a more masculine perspective, from a fluid, other-directed voice whose concerns are intimacy, relationship, and process to a more detached and self-centered one whose concerns are autonomy, self-consolidation, and conclusion. The addition of an "introductory" section, "Inscriptions," illustrates this shift. Whereas the first version of "Song" immerses us in the experience of the poem, the later one states the intention of the poet: "to define America, her athletic Democracy" ("To Foreign Lands," 417, line 2). Another poem speaks of his remoteness from the "intellect," his indirect method, full of "latencies" ("Shut Not Your Doors, 456, lines 3–6); but because of their attempts at self-definition, these poems ironically encourage the reader's analysis, not identification and participation with a fluidly defined speaker.

"Starting from Paumanock" also suggests the more constrained, formal, acculturated quality of the final "Song," for it appears to be Whitman's attempt to answer the implicit question of beginnings and origins that the poem raises. The egocentric speaker imagines himself as the pivot for future readers: "See, projected through time, / For me an audience interminable" (274–75, lines 29–30). "Paumanock" reveals to these readers what the goals of the speaker-poet will be: to connect with past and future (section 5); to sing for all (sections 7, 8, 10); to connect body and soul (sections 6, 13). In general:

> I will not make poems with reference to parts,
> But I will make poems, songs, thoughts, with reference to ensemble,
> And I will not sing with reference to a day, but with reference to all
>   days,
> And I will not make a poem nor the least part of a poem but has reference to
>   the soul[.] [283, lines 172–75]

This section explains what the 1855 "Song" attempts to enact. By distancing him from us, by emphasizing his self-centered project, the introductory apparatus as a whole enhances the speaker's masculine status.

Furthermore, Whitman's choices in sectioning the poem suggest his increased desire for masculinity. To the original text, he adds the "explanation" of lines 6 to 13, indicating the speaker-poet's history and, perhaps more significantly, his goal: to "permit to speak at every hazard, / Nature without check with original energy" (1, lines 12–13). These additional lines foreground a view of meaning defined in terms of the Poet's genesis and experience. In contrast, the first opening, which moves directly from "I lean and loafe at my ease" to "Houses and rooms are full of perfumes," entices readers to draw from their own sensual experience, to share as equals in a kinetic process of self-discovery.

Two other crucial locations at which Whitman separates sections are 21 and 24, which he begins with himself: "I am the poet of the Body and I am the poet of the Soul" (26, line 422); and "Walt Whitman, a kosmos, of Manhattan the son" (31, line 497). These breaks center the poem's experience in the speaker, not the reader, and they emphasize his power. Whitman claims to be "no stander above men and women or apart from them," even on the page, but here he isolates and individuates himself (31, line 499). The many section divisions that foreground the "I" require analysis, not participation. The first line of section 44 encourages this approach: "It is time to explain myself—let us stand up" (70, line 1134).

Of course, the "explanation" does not provide the insight that a reader bent on "meaning" might wish, as the speaker continues his wide-ranging and playful route. Nevertheless, the first version's omission of such signposts as an "introduction," titles, and even a closing period on the road toward self-definition suggests the younger poet's concern with process over product, with journey over destination, with voice over form, with reader over Reader.[17] The earlier version gestures toward our role; the poet merges with us without privilege, rather than incorporating and in effect "consuming" us. The masculine voice informed by patriarchy—Gilbert and Gubar's "strong and assertive I"—assumes a kind of power and autonomy that Whitman's feminine voice declines; it provides the "coherence" and "unity" necessary for the poem's canonization.

Although Whitman gradually represses the femininity of the early "Song," other poems in the original *Leaves* confirm more directly the poet's concern with intimacy and his feminine hospitality to dialogue with the other. In "There Was a Child Went Forth," the speaker lists parts of the child's domestic world, then moves outward into the world at large:

The hurrying tumbling waves, quick-broken crests, slapping,
The strata of color'd clouds, the long bar of maroon-tint away solitary by itself, the spread of purity it lies motionless in,
The horizon's edge, the flying sea-crow, the fragrance of salt marsh and shore mud,
These became part of the child that went forth every day, and who now goes, and will always go forth every day. [152, lines 36–39]

The first edition includes one more line: "And these [lines] become [part] of him or her that peruses them now" (152n.).

Similarly, in "Who Learns My Lesson Complete?" the poet excises the closing gesture to the reader. The 1891–92 version ends:

And that the moon spins round the earth and on with the earth, is equally wonderful,
And that they balance themselves with the sun and stars is equally wonderful. [154, lines 25–26]

The first version envisions our role in the creation of wonder:

Come I should like to hear you tell me what there is in yourself that is not just as wonderful,
And I should like to hear the name of anything between Sunday morning and Saturday night that is not just as wonderful. [154n.]

These endings domesticate and familiarize his relationship with the reader. By deleting these final lines, Whitman makes each poem more "universal"; he indicates his alienation from the feminine reader and from his own feminine self. These later, canonical versions privilege the masculine autonomy of the Poet; the literary patriarchy values "universality" over relationship with the reader.

Whitman's detachment has a more physical component. For example, he diminishes his emphasis on the body and on the sexual relations between poet and reader at the beginning of the 1891–92 "Song for Occupations" in favor of a presumably more "poetic" tone:

A song for occupations!
In the labor of engines and trades and the labor of fields I find the developments,
And find the eternal meanings. [83, lines 1–3]

In contrast, the first version underlines the speaker's intimacy with the reader:

Come closer to me,
Push close my lovers and take the best I possess,
Yield closer and closer and give me the best you possess. [83–84n.]

Here the speaker's physical, literal proximity strikes us with the force of a sexual encounter; he assumes an interactive and generous intercourse of "give" and "take." The revised version subordinates this relationship to transcendence, to "find[ing] eternal meanings."

The trend toward universalization and away from the feminine voice of proximity and invitation continues with "I Sing the Body Electric." The original reads:

> The bodies of men and women engirth me, and I engirth them,
> They will not let me off nor I them till I go with them and respond to them and
> love them. [121n.]

Again we find ourselves plunged into literal and loving intercourse and passion, whereas the final version depicts a depersonalized speaker–reader relationship centering on the "I":

> I sing the body electric,
> The armies of those I love engirth me and I engirth them,
> They will not let me off till I go with them, respond to them,
> And discorrupt them, and charge them full with the charge of the soul.
> [121, lines 1–4]

By adding the first line, Whitman announces a "project" and his own bardic status; by changing "bodies" to "armies," he prohibits the reader from loving, intimate interaction.

All of these changes highlight the poet's increasing concern with masculine self-definition and legitimacy, engendered perhaps by his need to gain acceptance by the literary establishment, by his literary "fathers." In an inversion of Harold Bloom's "anxiety of influence," Whitman seems to suffer from what we might call an "anxiety of paternity."[18] Hence, the 1891–92 version of "Song of the Answerer" underscores his project and his privileged status as Poet:

> Now list to my morning's romanza, I tell the signs of the Answerer,
> To the cities and farms I sing as they spread in the sunshine before me.
> [137, lines 1–2]

In spite of the folksy tone of "romanza," the Poet surveys his domain as if from a great height and distance. By foregrounding his project and goal, he distances himself from the process in which he engages the reader in the first version by beginning with the story itself:

> A young man came to me with a message from his brother,
> How should the young man know the whether and when of his brother?
> Tell him to send me the signs. [138n.]

The final version capitalizes the "Answerer," who in a new section 2 proclaims his greatness and power as creator:

The maker of poems settles justice, reality, immortality,
His insight and power encircle things and the human race.
[141–42, lines 58–59]

Although later in the same section the speaker affirms that the "Poet" (again, capitalized) will "balance ranks, colors, races, creeds, and the sexes" (143, line 77), his privileged status emerges quite clearly when we contrast these statements to the excised closing lines from the first version:

You think it would be good to be the writer of melodious verses,
Well it would be good to be the writer of melodious verses;
But what are verses beyond the flowing character you could have? . . . . or beyond beautiful manners and behavior?
Or beyond one manly or affectionate deed of an apprenticeboy? . . or old woman? . . or man that has been in prison or is likely to be in prison?
[141n.]

Whereas in the later version the speaker-poet indulges in separate meditation, in the first version he inspires us to feminine, even feminist, dialogue and exchange, privileging the other's perspective with his own: We are cocreators.

## "(Be not too certain but I am now with you.)"

"Now, dearest comrade, lift me to your face, / We must separate awhile—Here! take from my lips this kiss; / Whoever you are, I give it especially to you; / *So long!*—And I hope we shall meet again."[19]

Why did you leave this intimate gesture out of *Leaves,* Walt? Was "merging" too frightening? Did it prevent you from being a "real poet" (or a "real man")? Why did you repress your feminine desires?

I imagine the scorn and disregard with which you were greeted. The tenuousness of your place in patriarchal poetry emerges as I remember first Lawrence's mourning accusation, then F. O. Matthiessen's comment about one part of "Song":

> [I]n the passivity of the poet's body there is a quality vaguely pathological and homosexual. This is in keeping with the regressive, infantile fluidity, imaginatively polyperverse, which breaks down all mature barriers, a little further on in "Song of Myself," to declare that he is "maternal as well as paternal, a child as well as a man."[20]

To be fluid, to break down "barriers"—and most of all, to be feminine—is to be perceived as "infantile," "regressive," and even "pathological."

The tension that informs *Leaves*—between masculine and feminine voices, between the poet's urges to embrace or to revise the stringent standards of the patriarchy, the Father—emerges most explicitly and most strikingly, perhaps, in the contrast between "Children of Adam" and "Calamus." In the "Children of Adam" poem, "From Pent-up Aching Rivers," Whitman identifies himself as potent masculine poet; "From my own voice resonant, singing the phallus" comes his song (353, line 4). Later in the poem, though, he claims his intimacy with a reader who must assume a position as Eve, claiming, "I love you, O you entirely possess me," and swearing "[t]he oath of the inseparableness of two together, of the woman that loves me and whom I love more than my life" (354, 355, lines 28, 32). Similarly, in "I Sing the Body Electric," he affirms the equality of male and female repeatedly (127, 126, lines 84, 68–71).

Nevertheless, in "A Woman Waits for Me," his emphasis on male potency in these relationships becomes transparent:

> I draw you close to me, you women,
> . . . . . . . . . . . . . . . . . . . . . . . . . . . . . . . . . . .
> I am stern, acrid, large, undissuadable, but I love you,
> I do not hurt you more than is necessary for you,
> I pour the stuff to start sons and daughters fit for these States, I press with slow rude muscle,
> I brace myself effectually, I listen to no entreaties,
> I dare not withdraw till I deposit what has so long accumulated within me.
> [239–40, lines 20, 26–30]

In effect, the speaker-poet consummates a rape, claiming his own superior knowledge. Female readers of this poem especially are asked to participate in their own violation, as Whitman proposes his dominance over the feminine by emphasizing the centered "I."

In contrast to the self-contained confidence, even brutality, of the masculine voice in "Children of Adam," the repressed feminine voice finds its analogue in the voice of Whitman's homoerotic self, which emerges in "Calamus." Aware of and admitting to his vulnerability, the speaker-poet confesses in "Here the Frailest Leaves of Me": "Here the frailest leaves of me and yet my strongest lasting, / Here I shade and hide my thoughts, I myself do not expose them, / And yet they expose me more than all my other poems" (407, lines 1–3). Hence, he approaches his "lover and perfect equal" "by faint indirections" ("Among the Multitude," 405, lines 5–6). One such indirection is to place outside himself (and outside his relationship to the reader) the adhesiveness he longs for:

> . . . two simple men I saw to-day on the pier in the midst of the crowd, parting the parting of dear friends,
> The one to remain hung on the other's neck and passionately kiss'd him,
> While the one to depart tightly prest the one to remain in his arms.
> ["What Think You I Take My Pen in Hand," 399–400, lines 5–7]

The relationship between equals finds one of its fullest expressions in "I Saw in Louisiana a Live-Oak Growing." The poet-tree is "uttering joyous leaves all its life without a friend a lover near," and the poet-person affirms, "I know very well I could not" (390, lines 12–13). This connection with the other offers an elaboration of the poet's repressed feminine voice: In "Calamus," we discover a speaker who is wistful, tentative, and subdued. The poem ends here, with meaning located in this relationship between equals, not in some "transcendent" vision of the poet who emphasizes his emotional and physical autonomy.

However much Whitman concealed or denied this repressed voice, others recognized it. Lawrence heard it; Matthiessen heard it; John Addington Symonds heard it; his early female readers heard it and responded far more positively than their male counterparts (Kaplan, *Walt Whitman,* 45 ff.; Guttry, "Whitman and the Woman Reader," 104–5). The feminine text that Whitman creates and then obscures has several crucial features: first, an enhanced attentiveness to the body and, in particular, to sexual "intercourse" with the reader; second, a concern for the process of reading rather than its conclusions; third, a more fluid, less sharply defined sense of poetic speaker as Poet.[21] In "Calamus" perhaps even more than in the 1855 *Leaves* Whitman's feminine readers embrace him on the grounds of our shared marginality—except that here the "margins" fill the page.

We are left to speculate about the sources of the poet's metamorphosis. Many detachments or emotional consolidations were required in his personal life—a split from his favorite brother Jeff after the latter's marriage; a suppression of his own homoerotic desires. The Civil War made imperative certain adjustments in his vision of America. Most importantly, Whitman's earliest readers' responses surely influenced his withdrawal from intercourse and his need for recognition by the male literary establishment. His difference from other masculine voices was so vivid that he felt compelled to assert his "legitimacy" as a son of patriarchy by re-creating himself as the autonomous Poet.

A comparative study of Whitman's late and early work, throughout which he struggles toward an authentic gender definition, underscores the idea that patriarchy is not identical to maleness but, rather, that it represents a way of thinking informed by a polarized and polarizing masculine standard, even though very few men fit the norm of masculinity. By his example, Whitman teaches us that masculinity is not necessarily negative, but what is negative is the patriarchy's definition of it as the desirable goal and its exclusion of both sexes from the qualities "normally" found in the other. In a culture that circumscribes difference, Whitman manages, though not without hesitation and pain, to embrace feminine otherness in his early work, ending "Calamus" even in the final edition with quiet reassurance: "(Be not too certain but I am now with you)" ("Full of Life Now," 408, line 8). This voice, though it speaks in whispers, speaks loudest to his feminine readers.

## Notes

This chapter contains segments of my Ph.D. dissertation, "Reading the Feminine: Gender Gestures in Poetic Voice" (Brandeis University, 1986).

1. See Walt Whitman, "Song of Myself," in *Leaves of Grass: A Textual Variorum of the Printed Poems,* ed. Sculley Bradley et al., 3 vols. (New York: New York University Press, 1980), 51, line 832. All subsequent references to the poetry of Whitman will be to this text and to the 1891–92 edition of *Leaves of Grass,* except where otherwise noted.
2. Sandra M. Gilbert and Susan Gubar, *The Madwoman in the Attic: The Woman Writer and the Nineteenth-Century Literary Tradition* (New Haven: Yale University Press, 1979), 556; Virginia Woolf, *A Room of One's Own* (San Diego: Harcourt Brace Jovanovich, Harvest, 1957), 104.
3. D. H. Lawrence, *Studies in Classic American Literature* (New York: Viking Press, 1961), 165, 169, 166, 168. See also Ralph Waldo Emerson, "The Poet," in *The Selected Writings of Ralph Waldo Emerson,* ed. Brooks Atkinson (New York: Modern Library, 1950), 328, 332.
4. Gilbert and Gubar, *Madwoman,* 548; 539–650 passim, 16–19, 48, 64 ff., 72–73. See Margaret Homans, *Women Writers and Poetic Identity: Dorothy Wordsworth, Emily Brontë, and Emily Dickinson* (Princeton, NJ: Princeton University Press, 1980), 33; Lionel Trilling, *Sincerity and Authenticity* (Cambridge, MA: Harvard University Press, 1972), 98–99; Sandra Gilbert, "The American Sexual Politics of Walt Whitman and Emily Dickinson," in *Reconstructing American Literary History,* ed. Sacvan Bercovitch (Cambridge, MA: Harvard University Press, 1986), 127, 130, 140. Emerson, *Selected Writings,* 329; Whitman, "Song of Myself," 31, line 497.
5. Roy Harvey Pearce, *The Continuity of American Poetry* (Princeton, NJ: Princeton University Press, 1961), 69–83, 164–74; June Jordan, "For the Sake of a People's Poetry: Walt Whitman and the Rest of Us," *Passion* (Boston: Beacon Press, 1980), xiii, xv, xxii. See also E. Fred Carlisle, *The Uncertain Self: Whitman's Drama of Identity* (East Lansing: Michigan State University Press, 1973), xi–xv, 11, 44–45, 75, chap. 8; Richard Lebeaux, "Walt Whitman and His Poems, 1856–60: The Quest for Intimacy and Generativity," *Walt Whitman Review* 25 (Dec. 1979): 146–63; Jerome Loving, *Emerson, Whitman, and the American Muse* (Chapel Hill: University of North Carolina Press, 1982), 147–90; C. Carroll Hollis, *Language and Style in "Leaves of Grass"* (Baton Rouge: Louisiana State University Press, 1983), 164, 167, 193; Eric R. Birdsall, "Translating the Hints: Whitman's Theory of Poetry," *Walt Whitman Review* 26 (Sept. 1980): 117, 120, 122; Paul Zweig, *Walt Whitman: The Making of the Poet* (New York: Basic, 1984), 174 ff., 188, 227–75, 286–87; Lottie L. Guttry, "Walt Whitman and the Woman Reader," *Walt Whitman Review* 22 (Sept. 1976): 106, 109; Donald Kummings, "Whitman's Voice in 'Song of Myself': From Private to Public," *Walt Whitman Review* 17 (Mar. 1971): 10–15; Agnieszka Salska, *Walt Whitman and Emily Dickinson: Poetry of the Central Consciousness* (Philadelphia: University of Pennsylvania Press, 1985), 77, 110, 118 ff., 172, 190.
6. Nancy Chodorow, *The Reproduction of Mothering: Psychoanalysis and the Sociology of Gender* (Berkeley: University of California Press, 1978), 169. See Carol Gilligan, *In a Different Voice: Psychological Theory and Women's Development* (Cambridge, MA: Harvard University Press, 1982), 39, 147; Jean Baker Miller, *Toward a New Psychology of Women* (Boston: Beacon, 1977), 83.

7. Carroll Smith-Rosenberg, *Disorderly Conduct: Visions of Gender in Victorian America* (New York: Knopf, 1985), 53.
8. John D'Emilio and Estelle B. Freedman, *Intimate Matters: A History of Sexuality in America* (New York: Harper and Row, 1988), 121, 128. Whitman, in Justin Kaplan, *Walt Whitman: A Life* (New York: Simon and Schuster, 1980), 316. See Zweig, *Walt Whitman,* 194; Kaplan, *Walt Whitman,* 86, 233–40, 286–87, 311–16, 359–64.
9. Frank Lentricchia, "Patriarchy against Itself: The Young Manhood of Wallace Stevens," *Critical Inquiry* 13 (Summer 1987): 774; Laura Claridge and Elizabeth Langland, cited in Lentricchia, "Andiamo!" *Critical Inquiry* 14 (Winter 1988): 413.
10. See Walter J. Ong, "The Writer's Audience Is Always a Fiction," *PMLA* 90 (Jan. 1975): 11, 12. I do not mean to suggest that masculine writers have written without the idea of audience; rather, the audience has been secondary to the poetic vision: T. S. Eliot's "voice of the poet talking to no one, or to himself" ("The Three Voices of Poetry," *On Poetry and Poets* [London: Faber and Faber, 1957], 89, 97).
11. See Judith Fetterley, *The Resisting Reader: A Feminist Approach to American Fiction* (Bloomington: Indiana University Press, 1981), xi–xxvi, on the "immasculation" of the female reader of American literature.
12. I am assuming that from this point the reader will continue to be aware that my account is based on a cultural and psychological paradigm for a continuum of *gender,* not on a biological polarization of *sex,* and hence that she or he will imaginatively supply quotation marks enclosing the slippery terms "feminine" and "masculine."

    In his recent book, M. Jimmie Killingsworth argues that the older Whitman systematically censored and diluted his early poems on the body, particularly those with homoerotic themes. Although he focuses on sex difference rather than psychological gender difference, his argument parallels and reinforces mine concerning the poet's diminished femininity (as revealed in or metaphorized by his homoeroticism). The timing of his book's appearance (as this essay was going to press) precludes the fuller discussion that it merits. M. Jimmie Killingsworth, *Whitman's Poetry of the Body: Sexuality, Politics, and the Text* (Chapel Hill: University of North Carolina Press, 1989). For another view of Whitman's self-censorship, see Robert K. Martin, *The Homosexual Tradition in American Poetry* (Austin: University of Texas Press, 1979), 7, 61, 49–50.
13. Walt Whitman, "A Backward Glance O'er Travel'd Roads," in *Leaves of Grass,* ed. Sculley Bradley and Harold W. Blodgett (New York: Norton, 1973), 570. All subsequent references to Whitman's prose will be to this text. Emile Benveniste argues that the pronoun "you" engages the reader in a process; *Problems in General Linguistics,* trans. Mary Elizabeth Meek (Coral Gables, FL: University of Miami Press, 1971), 218, 221. Of course, the mere presence of "you" in a poem does not guarantee reader–poet or reader–speaker intimacy. Whitman defines the "you" of "Song" as the reader–listener, as he states in lines 31–32, 1321.
14. Annette Kolodny, *The Lay of the Land: Metaphor as Experience and History in American Life and Letters* (Chapel Hill: University of North Carolina Press, 1975), 3–9 and passim.
15. Simone de Beauvoir, *The Second Sex,* trans. H. M. Parshley (New York: Random House, Vintage Books, 1974), xix–xxxv passim.
16. Like many writers, Gardiner appears to equate female with feminine, a problem given the psychologists' cultural use of the latter term. Although her context is prose, the gender differences she specifies may be enhanced in poetry, given the traditionally autonomous poet. "On Female Identity and Writing by Women," in *Writing and Sexual Difference,* ed. Elizabeth Abel (Chicago: University of Chicago Press, 1982), 184–85. For a critique of Gardiner, see Carolyn G. Heilbrun, "A Response to 'Writing and Sexual Difference,'" in Abel, *Writing,* 295–96. For Whitman and process, see also Pearce, *Continuity,* 72–82.
17. Of course, revision of the poem itself may imply that Whitman viewed the poem as fluid and processual—or that he viewed it as a perfectible object. Some readers argue that the omission of the final period in the 1855 "Song" was a "typographical error." Arthur

Golden, "The Ending of the 1855 Version of 'Song of Myself,'" *Walt Whitman Review* 3 (Spring 1986): 29.

18. Whitman's self-review in 1855 emphasized his masculinity but, more importantly, his departure from literary forefathers (Bradley and Blodgett, *Leaves of Grass*, 777–79). Harold Bloom, *The Anxiety of Influence* (New York: Oxford University Press, 1973).
19. "To the Reader at Parting," in Bradley and Blodgett, *Leaves of Grass*, 604. Whitman excluded this poem from the 1871 edition of *Leaves*.
20. F. O. Matthiessen, *American Renaissance: Art and Expression in the Age of Emerson and Whitman* (London: Oxford University Press, 1941), 535.
21. In some sense, his explicit, positive connection between mind and body feminizes him, as he refuses what Adrienne Rich calls our perception of "ourselves as polluted" and "Our tendency to flesh-loathing"; Adrienne Rich, *Of Woman Born: Motherhood as Experience and Institution* (New York: Norton, 1976), 94, see 97, 90 ff. Dorothy Dinnerstein, *The Mermaid and the Minotaur: Sexual Arrangements and Human Malaise* (New York: Harper Colophon, 1976), 128, 148–49, chap. 7.

# Rewriting the Male Plot in Wilkie Collins's *No Name:* Captain Wragge Orders an Omelette and Mrs. Wragge Goes into Custody

DEIRDRE DAVID

WHETHER WILKIE COLLINS was a feminist, deployed popular literature for feminist ideology, or even liked women is not the subject of this essay. My interest is in something less explicit, perhaps not fully intentional, to be discovered in his fiction: an informing link between restlessness with dominant modes of literary form and fictional critique of dominant modes of gender politics. In what follows, I aim to show how the narrative shape of one of Collins's most baroquely plotted, narratively complex novels is inextricably enmeshed with its thematic material. I refer to *No Name,* a novel whose subversion of fictional omniscience suggests Collins's radical literary practice and whose sympathy for a rebellious heroine in search of subjectivity suggests his liberal sexual politics.[1] To be sure, there are other Collins novels as narratively self-reflexive as *No Name, The Moonstone,* for one; and *Man and Wife,* for example, mounts a strong attack on misogynistic subjection of women (particularly when exercised by heroes of the Muscular Christian variety). But no Collins novel, in my view, so interestingly conflates resistance to dominant aesthetic and sexual ideologies as *No Name,* even as it ultimately displays its appropriation by the authority that both enables its existence and fuels its resistance.

Challenging authoritarian, patriarchal-sited power in his interrogation of form and theme, Collins collapses a binary opposition between the two, a separation assumed in Victorian criticism of the novel and still, perhaps, possessing a lingering appeal in these deconstructive times. The intense dialogism, the insistent relativism, of *No Name* makes it impossible to align in one column what is represented and in another the *ways* in which representation takes place. Neither is it possible to construct a neat alignment of fictionality and representation, to say that at this moment the novel performs self-reflexive cartwheels and that at another we are in the realm of strict mimesis. Mimesis, one might say, is always simultaneous with semiosis in *No Name,* so much so, in fact, that representation, say, of a character obsessed with the record keeping which is the means of his social survival, becomes a field for self-reflexive fictionality; and, to a lesser extent, fictionality is sometimes the ground on which Collins maps his persuasively realistic narrative.[2] Collapsing the neat polarities of literary analysis, upsetting the conventions of omniscient narrative, showing a woman's struggle for survival as she is both exiled from and enclosed within patriarchal structures—all this is the business of *No Name,* in my view an exemplary novel for "naming" Collins's disruptive place in the tradition of Victorian fiction.

The original publication of Collins's novels covers some forty years, from *Antonina* in 1850 to *Blind Love,* left unfinished at his death in 1889, and his career encompasses two distinct periods in the history of Victorian fiction: At the beginning we are in the age of Dickens and Thackeray; at the end we enter a new generation composed of Hardy, Stevenson, Moore, Gissing, and Kipling.[3] With *Antonina,* a historical romance set in fifth-century Rome and owing much to Gibbon and Bulwer-Lytton, Collins established himself as a powerful storyteller with a commendable eye for detail, and by the time of his fifth novel, *The Woman in White,* he emerged as a master of diegesis with a narrative something for everyone: omniscience, free indirect discourse, autobiography, diary, letter, newspaper story, ledger book, memoranda. *No Name* appeared during the 1860s (Collins's stellar decade of literary production) between his two best-known novels, *The Woman in White* and *The Moonstone,* and was first published in Dickens's weekly magazine *All the Year Round* from March 1862 to January 1863 and published in three volumes at the end of 1862. Divided into eight dramatic "scenes," punctuated by groups of letters which are, in turn, interpolated with newspaper stories and journal entries, *No Name* was phenomenally successful. Collins received 3,000 pounds for the first edition, sold nearly 4,000 copies on the day of publication, netted 1,500 pounds for American serial rights, and obtained 5,000 guineas from Smith Elder for his next novel before having written a word.[4]

Unlike most Collins novels, however, *No Name* discloses no secrets, rattles no nerves with sensational excitement; rather, as he observes in his preface, "all the main events of the story are purposely foreshadowed, before they take place—my present design being to rouse the reader's interest in following the train of circumstances by which these foreseen events are brought about."[5] For some critics, the absence of suspense seriously impairs *No Name*'s success. Jerome Meckier, in particular, finds "the biggest mistake" to be "procedural" and believes Collins "sadly misjudges his own strengths" in forgoing surprise. From another perspective, however, one can argue that even before it begins *No Name*, a story about an unconventional female response to legal disinheritance, seeks to demystify the power of conventional, one might say inherited, Victorian narrative discourse. Rather than demanding from the reader acquiescence in a controlled revelation of plot, the narrator collaboratively offers a chance to see how plot comes into being, an opportunity to experience plot-in-process, so to speak, rather than plot-as-product. What's more, as several contemporary critics perceived, in forgoing narrative suspense for readerly collaboration, Collins situates his narrative practice in contention with the sort of instructive discourse perfected by George Eliot, whose *Adam Bede* and *The Mill on the Floss*, with their exemplary narrative discursions into questions of social responsibility, artistic representation, and cultural change preceded *No Name* by several years.[6]

As it is difficult to discuss any Collins novel without summarizing what happens, I shall do that briefly before showing how *No Name* disrupts conventional narrative discourse in the process of interrogating Victorian gender politics. On the death of their father Andrew Vanstone, eighteen-year-old Magdalen and her older sister Norah are unable to inherit his considerable fortune. As a young officer in Canada, he married impetuously, repented quickly, and returned to England, where he met the mother-to-be of Magdalen and Norah, a woman courageous enough to live with him. In the opening chapter, Vanstone and his forty-four-year-old pregnant not-wife learn of the death of his legal wife and quickly go off to London to marry. But a few days later Vanstone is killed in a railway accident, and the now legal second wife rapidly declines into death after childbirth, leaving her orphan daughters to discover that, although they are now legitimate, they are disinherited because Vanstone made his will before marrying their mother. They are named "Nobody's children," and their inheritance goes to a mean-spirited uncle who quickly departs the novel—leaving his puny son Noel immensely rich and vulnerable to Magdalen's considerable attractions. A born actress, she undertakes numerous disguises with the assistance of one Captain Horatio Wragge (a scoundrel who achieves respectability by the end of the novel), marries Noel under an assumed name, is unmasked by her husband's craftily intelligent housekeeper, falls desperately ill after the death of Noel, and is dramatically rescued by the son of a friend of her father, a Captain Kirke—whom she marries in a symbolic reconciliation with the father figure who left her legitimate yet disinherited at the beginning of the novel. Exiled from patriarchal protection in the opening chapters, she is enfolded within patriarchy's embrace by the end. And to complete this story of return to one's heritage, her sister marries the man who inherits the estate from Noel Vanstone.

*No Name* is notable for Collins's bold delineation of a heroine who sells her sexuality to regain her rightful fortune. An outraged Mrs. Oliphant (always good for a scandalized response) declared in 1863 that Magdalen engages in "a career of vulgar and aimless trickery and wickedness, with which it is impossible to have a shadow of sympathy," that she is tainted by "the pollutions of . . . endless deceptions and horrible marriage."[7] The "horrible marriage" part distressed almost all reviewers, and even now, in our far less prudish time, it is difficult not to be troubled, even embarrassed, by Collins's sexual frankness. He describes a young woman bursting with "exuberant vitality," possessed of "a figure instinct with such a seductive, serpentine suppleness, so lightly and playfully graceful, that its movements suggested, not unnaturally, the movements of a young cat . . . so perfectly developed already that no one who saw her could have supposed that she was only eighteen," undergoing "the revolting ordeal of marriage" to a frail little man with a miserable moustache, the complexion of a delicate girl, an appalling habit of screwing up his pale eyes, and a forehead that is always crumpling "into a nest of wicked little wrinkles."[8] But the chilling picture of sexual bargain between vibrant young woman and sickly older man, undisguised as it is by the cosmetic of Victorian piety, serves its political purpose: Collins makes us see that disinherited middle-class women, deprived of paternal protection, assume an identity that is both inscribed and concealed by the gender politics of their social class—that of sexual object. We also see how the literal incarceration of women to be found in Collins's earlier novel *The Woman in White* becomes, in *No Name,* an incarceration formed of rigid laws, of patriarchal injunctions.

In his focus upon the "sensational" aspects of *The Woman in White,* the ways that this novel (and others in the "sensation" genre) elaborates "a fantasmatics of sensation," D. A. Miller observes that Laura Fairlie "follows a common itinerary of the liberal subject in nineteenth-century fiction: she takes a nightmarish detour through the carceral ghetto on her way *home,* to the domestic haven where she is always felt to belong."[9] In *No Name,* Magdalen Vanstone also makes that journey. But whereas Laura is essentially passive, the quintessentially pale and quivering victim, Magdalen is aggressive, robustly in rebellion against the law that confines her to impecunious humiliation. What's more, Magdalen's awesomely vibrant performances (first in legitimate roles as Julia and Lucy in an amateur production of *The Rivals* at the beginning of the novel, then in illegitimate impersonations of her former governess and a parlormaid) constitute energetic difference from the passivity of women in *The Woman in White* (excluding, needless to say, that fascinating pioneer woman detective, Marion Halcombe).

Magdalen possesses a frightening ability to lose her own self in the assumption of other identities,[10] and her first strategy for survival when she finds herself "Nobody's" daughter is to leave home and seek out the manager of the amateur theatricals, who, amazed by her talent for mimicry, had given her his card and declared her a "born actress." Unable to find him, she is befriended (or, rather, appropriated) by Captain Wragge: He will turn her into a professional and will be compensated when Magdalen recovers her rightful fortune. Wragge's recounting (in one of his numerous Chronicles, which I shall discuss in a moment) of her first appearance in an "At Home" (a performance featuring one actor assuming a series of extraordinarily different characters) indicates some of the larger meanings of gender politics in the novel. Wragge devises "the Entertainment," manages "all the business," writes two anonymous letters to the lawyer authorized to find her, fortifies her with sal volatile as antidote to unhappy memories of her family, and sends her on stage:

> We strung her up in no time, to concert pitch; set her eyes in a blaze; and made her out-blush her own rouge. The curtain rose when we had got her at red heat. She dashed at it . . . rushed full gallop through her changes of character, her songs, and her dialogue; making mistakes by the dozen, and never stopping to set them right; carrying the people along with her in a perfect whirlwind, and never waiting for the applause.[11]

Endowed with a natural vitality which is "managed," disciplined, and shaped by Wragge, Magdalen, during the actual performance reasserts her naturally vital, rebellious female self in "out-blushing" her own rouge, thereby suggesting how the novel, in general, addresses the way woman's "natural" talent is shaped by patriarchal culture, society, and the law. If Wragge, then, as stage manager operates as an omnipotent string puller, let us see how his other activities strongly suggest the omnipotence associated with narrative omniscience. Wragge may be seen as parodic emblem, as Collins's embodied and symbolic critique of prevailing literary form in the Victorian period.

Omniscience, according to J. Hillis Miller, finds its authority and its origin in the unsettling of established religious beliefs: "The development of Victorian fiction is a movement from the assumption that society and the self are founded on some superhuman power outside them, to a putting in question of this assumption, to a discovery that society now appears to be self-creating and self-supporting, resting on nothing outside itself."[12] As remedy for the profound unease occasioned by such a discovery, society turns to/authorizes the fictionally omniscient/omnipotent narrator to fill the void, retard slippage from belief to skepticism. Through his unrelenting insistence on diegetic relativism, which is expressed in the multiple narrative perspectives we encounter in almost all his fiction, Collins refuses to perform the consolatory functions Miller identifies. Very much like Thackeray in *Vanity Fair,* who interrogates all forms of authority and wants us to examine the unthinking ways we accept fictions of various sorts, how, especially, we believe in a novelist's total knowledge of the world, Collins insists that we see the subjective, arbitrary nature of fictional representation, the hubristic nature of novelistic omnipotence.

Defining himself as a "moral agriculturalist; a man who cultivates the field of human sympathy," Wragge scoffs at being labeled a "Swindler": "What of that? The same low tone of mind assails men in other professions in a similar manner—calls great writers, scribblers—great generals, butchers—and so on."[13] Identifying himself with "great writers" who cultivate "the field of human sympathy," he becomes, of course, both like and unlike Wilkie Collins, the Victorian inheritor and reviser of conventional narrative discourse. But this is not all; Wragge's deft talent for inventing characters and identities also associates him with the creation of fiction. For example, one of the books in his "commercial library" (a repository of reference works in roguery and deception) is entitled "Skins to Jump Into." Concocting plausible identities for himself, Mrs. Wragge, and Magdalen in the plot to attract and snare Noel Vanstone, he selects the "skins" of a Mr. Bygrave, Mrs. Bygrave, and niece Susan and instructs Magdalen as follows:

> My worthy brother was established twenty years ago, in the mahogany and logwood trade at Belize, Honduras. He died in that place; and is buried on the south-west side of the local cemetery, with a neat monument of native wood carved by a self-taught negro artist. Nineteen months afterwards, his widow died of apoplexy at a boarding-house in Cheltenham. She was supposed to be the most corpulent woman in England; and was accommodated on the ground floor of the house in consequence of the difficulty of getting her up and down stairs. You are her only child; you have been under my care since the sad event at Cheltenham; you are twenty-one years old on the second of August next; and, corpulence excepted, you are the living image of your mother.[14]

His imperative omniscience, his persuasive attention to detail, his energetic keeping up of numerous journals and ledgers that record assumable identities, characteristics of different "districts," narratives of successful and unsuccessful swindles—all affirm his status in *No Name* as parodic narrator, as emblem of convention, order, and legitimacy (despite and because of his vagabond status).

Insisting "he must have everything down in black and white," announcing that "All untidiness, all want of system and regularity, causes me the acutest irritation,"[15] in a manner worthy of Conrad's accountant in *Heart of Darkness,* he writes his narratives of deception in precise pages of neat handwriting, obsessively aligns rows of figures, and permits no blots, stains, or erasures. To complete this empire of fiction making, of fabrication of identity, he has, quite literally, authorized himself; everything, he proudly declares, is verified by "my testimonials to my own worth and integrity." In sum, Wragge performs a kind of burlesque of Victorian narrative discourse, of the sovereign omniscience that dominates the period—and this, of course, is the mode of arbitrary narrative from which Wilkie Collins implicitly disinherited himself in his persistent interpolation of omniscience with the relativism of diary, letter, journalistic fragment, and so on. Bakhtin's observation that the novel form "is the expression of a Galilean perception of language, one that denies the absolutism of a single and unitary language," is richly borne out by the dialogism of *No Name.*[16]

If Captain Horatio Wragge serves as vehicle for Collins's restlessness with dominant modes of literary form, then it is his wife, Matilda Wragge, who, absolutely unconsciously, expresses Collins's critique of dominant modes of gender politics. *No Name,* thick with the inherited themes of Victorian fiction—marriage, family, money, wills, female desire, male governance—contains an irregular, disruptive episode that functions as an important signifier for Collins's indictment of patriarchal law. Mrs. Wragge is the alarming center of this episode, an illegitimate, irregular, symbolically political action that molests the attempts at omnipotence practiced by her husband. She is affiliated more with modes of signification, with interrogations of fictionality, than with the events of the signified, with what is being represented. I'm going to name this episode "Captain Wragge Orders an Omelette." And to explain what I mean by this, let me take you to the scene where Magdalen meets Matilda for the first time.

Characterized by her husband as "constitutionally torpid" and declared by Lewis Carroll to be an uncanny anticipation of his White Queen,[17] Mrs. Wragge is a physical marvel. A gigantic six feet, three inches, she has an enormous, smooth, moonlike face, "dimly irradiated by eyes of mild and faded blue, which looked straightforward into vacancy,"[18] and complains constantly of a "Buzzing" in her head. This buzzing is not helped by her husband's compulsion to bark orders like a sergeant major: Confiding to Magdalen that he is a "martyr" to his own sense of order, Wragge shouts, "Sit straight at the table. More to the left, more still—that will do,"[19] and "Pull it up at heel, Mrs. Wragge—pull it up at heel!"—this occasioned by the sight of her worn slippers. The buzzing, she explains, began before she married the Captain and was working as a waitress in Darch's Dining Rooms in London: "The gentlemen all came together; the gentlemen were all hungry together; the gentlemen all gave their orders together."[20] Years later she is still trying to get the gentlemen's orders sorted out; becoming "violently excited" by Magdalen's sympathetic questioning, she begins to repeat the orders retained in her muddled mind:

> Boiled pork and greens and peas-pudding for Number One. Stewed beef and carrots and gooseberry tart, for Number Two. Cut of mutton, and quick about it, well done, and plenty of fat, for Number Three. Codfish and parsnips, two chops to follow, hot-and-hot, or I'll be the death of you, for Number Four. Five, six, seven, eight, nine, ten. Carrots and gooseberry tart—peas pudding and plenty of fat—pork and beef and mutton, and cut 'em all, and quick about it—stout for one, and ale for t'other—and stale bread here, and new bread there—and this gentleman likes cheese, and that gentleman doesn't—Matilda, Tilda, Tilda, Tilda, fifty times over, till I don't know my own name."[21]

In this City chophouse, eerily suggestive of Harold Pinter's *Dumb-Waiter* where two hit men attempt to fill orders for steak and chips, jam tarts, and so on, Matilda, disoriented by the barrage of gentlemen's orders, does not know her own name, feels herself deprived of identity by the incessant discipline of male directions; she becomes, in a sense, somewhat like Magdalen, a woman deprived of her identity as inheriting daughter and disciplined by laws that legislate legitimacy and correct irregularity.

It is at Darch's Dining Rooms that Mrs. Wragge meets the Captain, "the hungriest and the loudest" of the lot. Once married, her servant duties are transferred from a multitude of hungry and demanding gentlemen to one: She shaves him, does his hair, cuts his nails, presses his trousers, trims his nails, and, misery of miseries, cooks his meals. This latter duty requires constant recourse to a "tattered" cookery book, and when Magdalen meets her, she is attempting to master the directions for making an omelette (ordered by the Captain for breakfast the next day). As I'm going to suggest, this is an omelette with many fillings.

Here's how she interprets the recipe to Magdalen:

> "Omelette with Herbs. Beat up two eggs with a little water or milk, salt, pepper, chives, and parsley. Mince small" There! mince small! How am I to mince small, when it's all mixed up and running? "Put a piece of butter the size of your thumb into the frying pan."—Look at my thumb, and look at yours! whose size does she mean? "Boil, but not brown."—If it mustn't be brown, what colour must it be? . . . "Allow it to set, raise it round the edge; when done, turn it over to double it . . . Keep it soft; put the dish on the frying-pan, and turn it over." Which am I to turn over . . . the dish or the frying-pan? . . . It sounds like poetry, don't it?[22]

Probably not, I think is our response, but Mrs. Wragge's innocent deconstruction of a recipe generates a kind of narrative poetics and gender politics for *No Name*. On the level of narrative, her contention with the cookery book implies female subversion of male-authorized texts or laws (the cookery book written by a woman for the instruction of other women in filling male orders); on the level of story, her resistance to accepted interpretation intimates the larger battle in this novel between legitimacy and illegitimacy, between male governance and female revenge. And she doesn't let up. Grandiosely introducing Magdalen to the Wragge way of life, the Captain offers "A pauper's meal, my dear girl—seasoned with a gentleman's welcome"; his wife begins to mutter, "Seasoned with salt, pepper, chives, and parsley." Negotiating terms with Magdalen for her dramatic training, the Captain begs her "not to mince the matter on your side—and depend on me not to mince it on mine"; his wife (of course) mutters that one should always try to "mince small." Her "torpid" yet disruptive presence not only prefigures Lewis Carroll's White Queen but also anticipates the interrogation of arbitrary systems of signification that we find in *Alice in Wonderland*. If her husband's attitudes, despite his raffish demeanor and picaresque career, represent conformity and conservatism, then Mrs. Wragge's attitudes represent resistance and interrogation.

And what of Mrs. Wragge's omelette? Well, she makes it, but, as she says, "It isn't nice. We had some accidents with it. It's been under the grate. It's been spilt on the stairs. It's scalded the landlady's youngest boy—he went and sat on it."[23] Her interpretation of male orders results in something not "nice," and certainly illegitimate as an omelette. And what of Captain Wragge? Abandoning "moral agriculture" for "medical agriculture," he goes in for the manufacture and sale of laxatives. Turning his talent for narrative to the production of stories about "The Pill," his skill in creating identities to the fabrication of testimonials about its dramatic effects, he becomes very rich. Meeting Magdalen at the end of the novel, "the copious flow of language pouring smoothly from his lips," he declares, "I merely understand the age I live in."[24] It seems as if his attitudes no longer *represent* conformity and acceptance (as I suggested earlier); speaking the dominant sociolect of "the age," which will never be understood by his wife, he ceases to function as parody or burlesque and becomes the thing itself. In other words, he goes legit. And instead of shouting at his wife, he appropriates her astonishing physical presence for the narrative that makes him rich: She is, he says, "the celebrated woman whom I have cured of indescribable agonies from every complaint under the sun. Her portrait is engraved on all the wrappers, with the following inscription beneath it:—'Before she took the Pill, you might have blown this patient away with a feather. Look at her now!!!' "[25] Just as Magdalen's story of return to legitimate social identity in marriage assumes conventional narrative form, so Mrs. Wragge's story of respectable celebrity puts an end to her disruption of parodic omnipotence. No longer the resisting reader of a recipe, like the Captain she becomes the thing itself and is read by others, engraved and inscribed as she is on all the wrappers for "The Pill." Mrs. Wragge is in custody, just as, one might venture, Collins's interrogations of narrative form, patriarchal law, misogynistic sexual politics are (must be) eventually placed in the demanding custody of his serialized novel. They are disciplined by the contingent demands of his career, by the male-dominated directives of his culture. In sum, the subversiveness of *No Name* must ultimately be contained by the structure that enables its existence. Shall we say real life as opposed to fiction? But perhaps we should remember Noel Vanstone's astonished response to the revelation of Magdalen's plot for revenge: "It's like a scene in a novel—it's like nothing in real life."[26] In deconstructing Collins's literary practice and gender politics in *No Name,* we should not try to break the dialectical bond between theme and form, life and novel.

## Notes

I am grateful to Gerhard Joseph for pointing out to me that Mrs. Wragge "goes into custody."

1. Comparing *No Name* with *Great Expectations* (which it followed in Dickens's periodical *All the Year Round*), Jerome Meckier finds Collins's novel inferior. Meckier's interest is in the way these two novels address barriers to "social progress," their meaning as "serious, philosophical critique of shortcomings traceable to the very nature of things." Meckier's tendency to focus exclusively on informing connections between the private plight of Pip and public disorder blinds him, I think, to the very real social difficulties experienced by women in Collins's novel. Jerome Meckier, *Hidden Rivalries in Victorian Fiction: Dickens, Realism, and Reevaluation* (Lexington: University Press of Kentucky, 1987), 129.
2. For stimulating discussion of relationships between mimesis and semiosis, I am indebted to Michael Riffaterre's lecture series at the University of Pennsylvania, February 1988.
3. Norman Page, ed., *Wilkie Collins: The Critical Heritage,* Critical Heritage Series (London: Routledge and Kegan Paul, 1974), i–xvi.
4. Ibid., 169.
5. Wilkie Collins, *No Name* (1864; rpt. Oxford: Oxford University Press, 1986); preface pages are not numbered.
6. An unsigned review in *Dublin University Magazine* in February 1861 observes that "a writer like George Eliot may look down from a very far height on such a dweller in the plains as he who wrote *The Woman in White.*" For this critic, Collins's novel is infected by "the spirit of modern realism." In 1863, Alexander Smith in the *North British Review* more neutrally noted that Collins was "a writer of quite a different stamp from George Eliot." Page, *Wilkie Collins,* 104, 140.
7. Page, *Wilkie Collins,* 143.
8. Collins, *No Name,* 6, 357, 205.
9. D. A. Miller, *The Novel and the Police* (Berkeley and Los Angeles: University of California Press, 1988), 172.
10. Jonathan Loesberg makes the interesting point that "sensation novels evoke their most typical moments of sensation response from images of a loss of class identity. And this common image links up with a fear of a general loss of social identity as a result of the merging of the classes—a fear that was commonly expressed in the debate over social and parliamentary reform in the late 1850s and 1860s." Part of the implicit threat to estab-

lished gender and class politics posed by Magdalen's protean ability to switch roles may be ascribed to such a fear. Jonathan Loesberg, "The Ideology of Narrative Form in Sensation Fiction," *Representations* 13 (Winter 1986): 117.

11. Collins, *No Name*, 175.
12. J. Hillis Miller, *The Form of Victorian Fiction: Thackeray, Dickens, Trollope, George Eliot, Meredith, and Hardy* (Notre Dame, IN: University of Notre Dame Press, 1968), 30.
13. Collins, *No Name*, 153.
14. Ibid., 235–36.
15. Ibid., 147.
16. Mikhail Bakhtin, *The Dialogic Imagination*, trans. Caryl Emerson and Michael Holquist, ed. Michael Holquist (Austin: University of Texas Press, 1981), 366.
17. Page, *Wilkie Collins*, 245.
18. Collins, *No Name*, 146.
19. Ibid., 151.
20. Ibid., 148.
21. Ibid.
22. Ibid., 150.
23. Ibid., 161.
24. Ibid., 529.
25. Ibid., 526.
26. Ibid., 403.

# Fictions of Feminine Voice: Antiphony and Silence in Hardy's *Tess of the d'Urbervilles*

MARGARET R. HIGONNET

IN PUBLISHING the first edition of *Tess of the d'Urbervilles: A Pure Woman, Faithfully Presented,* Hardy explained that he had made a sincere "attempt to give artistic form to a true sequence of things" (xv).[1] One of the "truths" maintained by Hardy's artistic sequence is the controversial paradox that his pastoral heroine—an unwed mother and murderess—remains, as much as Keats's urn, a "still unravished bride of quietness." Silent and cold as a "marble term" while Alec imprints a kiss on her cheek, Tess resists the imprint of men's values and actions; as a "term," she marks the limits of conventional understanding and points to her own unspoken experiences. The text at once claims to express the true sequence of her life and requires the fictional suppression of her voice in order to anchor its own artistic sequence.

The question of Tess's voice has social and historical significance, in addition to the major critical difficulties it unleashes. In one sense, the public's irate reaction to the language of the subtitle—"a pure woman"—confirmed Hardy's contention in the preface that his heroine had been muted by what he calls there the "merely vocal formulae of society" (xvii). Warding off such censorship both in the fictional past and in the future reception of his book, Hardy tried to present a "faithful" echo of his heroine's voice. He maintains the authenticity of his written evocation of her elusive oral presence. In short, Hardy focuses through his female protagonist on the ancient Platonic problems of the value of fiction and the power of the written word. In addition, by identifying his story of emblematic femininity with the philosophic problem of discerning truth, he created a novel that was representative of contemporary intellectuals' strategies, most notably in the works of Nietzsche and Freud.

Confident as the claim of his title seems, Hardy wrestled with the difficulty of giving voice to a woman's story, in *Tess* as in his other fiction. One aspect of that difficulty lies in his own gender: Can a man implicated in patriarchy speak for a woman constrained by it? As the manuscript history of *Tess* will show, such a project is not free of social entanglements. Hardy indeed "got into hot water," as he puts it, for his attempt to give words to Tess's story, encountering first censorship and then critical outrage.[2] Because he was so conscious of the problem, Hardy's exploration of a woman's voice in *Tess* sheds light on two matters of broader import: first, the difficulty of defining a character's voice (faced not only by authors but also by critics), and, second, the centrality of the female protagonist to nineteenth-century narrative experiment.

As a way of framing these problems, it should be said first that the autonomous selfhood and therefore voice of a literary character are always no more than useful fictions within the fiction. Narratorial language mediates our illusion of hearing a singular character's voice, as it mediates our perception of a singular narrative voice. Slipping between the two, critics have tended to subordinate the theory of a character's voice to that of narrative voice, even as they take for granted some definition of a character's voice in order to talk about narrative personae. Postmodernist theory further forces us to interrogate the singularity of subjectivity: Can we speak of Tess as a unitary person, or of "the" narrator? If we think of the self as a site of social production, an intersection of discourses rather than a pure origin of expression, then the goal of giving voice to a woman's story comes to seem more like a dream.

*Tess of the d'Urbervilles* can be read as a nineteenth-century prelude to such twentieth-century questioning. Hardy underscores his desire to recover Tess's "true" voice, not only by the subtitle but by the device of the comic intercalated tale about Jack Dollop, a " 'hore's-bird" of a milker ensnared by a widow-woman who neglects to warn him that her pension will expire on her remarriage. "The ghost of her first man would trouble him." While others laugh, Tess flees in silence from Dairyman Crick's jocular account of the affair, for "This *question of a woman telling her story*" is to her "the heaviest of crosses" (29:232–33; my italics). One reason it is so hard for women to tell their story may be that men won't listen; certainly this is Tess's experience. But beyond that, women's pains and feelings may be "indescribable by men's words," as Hardy wrote in *Desperate Remedies (DR)*. At times of intense misery,

> a woman does not faint, or weep, or scream as she will in the moment of sudden shocks. When lanced by a mental agony of such refined and special torture that it is indescribable by men's words, she moves among her acquaintance much as before, and continues so to cast her actions in the old moulds that she is only considered to be rather duller than usual. [*DR*, chap. 13][3]

Similarly, Bathsheba finds herself speechless: "I cannot tell you. It is difficult for a woman to define her feelings in language which is chiefly made by men to express theirs" (*Far from the Madding Crowd*, chap. 51).[4]

Hardy addresses the "question of a woman telling her story" in part by directly quoting the words of Tess's hypothetical voice—her dialogue, her letters—to which he gives distinctive traits that reflect her specific values and experiences. More problematic material lies in the intermediate domain of "free indirect discourse," the mediated summaries of Tess's thoughts and conversations. Hardy's *narrator,* moreover, swiftly outlines a set of events that constitute Tess's story—a story that she herself then tries to tell. This banal narrative order produces a woman's "voice" that will always necessarily be belated.

Hardy differs, however, from the traditional realist writer's attempt "faithfully" to present a heroine in his own stress on the construction (and misconstruction) of Tess's story. As in *Jude the Obscure,* Hardy offers in *Tess* "a series of seemings," the illusory schemata by which Tess, as well as those around her, reads her life. Among those readers we must include the narrator himself, for Hardy avails himself of the artist's last resource, the reflexively ironic presentation of his narrator, in order to grapple with this problem of representation.

Hardy also goes beyond the familiar narrative pose of empathy with his heroine. For the story of Tess implies that voice takes on full, phenomenological, existence only in its reception and repetition or assimilation. To be sure, empathetic imagination is one of the traits Tess shares with the narrator.[5] Thus, in the extraordinary scene when she awakens on the heath to the palpitating gasps of pheasants in their last agony, Tess both identifies with them and controls their fate: "'Poor darlings—to suppose myself the most miserable being on earth in the sight o' such misery as yours!' she exclaimed, her eyes running down as she killed the birds tenderly" (41:335). Tess here incarnates the tenet by which an author claims identity with the creatures whose fates are spun out within the text.

Yet an even more central bird image underscores Tess's reciprocity (rather than identity) with the narrator: the scene in which, by whistling, she gives voice to the bullfinches—and does so before a hidden, eavesdropping audience. The birds "go back" in their singing unless Tess whistles for them; just so, Hardy implies, Tess's fluty voice would be lost without a narrator's elicitation of it.[6] It is in Hardy's interest, of course, to suggest a subliminal identity between his heroine and his narrator as an anchor for the authenticity and "reality" of his tale; apparently contradictory, Ciceronian claims of inadequacy simply invoke another code of realism. But, as we shall see, Hardy turns this problem of representation inside out by focusing it on Tess's voice.

My study of voice in Hardy's novel falls into two sections. In the first, I note that voices in this novel are gendered. Hardy, like any other author but more consciously than most, constructs his own gender code to define the differences between the voices of men and women. Mary Jacobus has already shown that Hardy stressed certain gender differences between Tess and her two lovers Alec and Angel in their physical descriptions; similarly, Penny Boumelha has found masculine traits in the narrator's descriptive language, applied to the feminine Tess.[7] To their general analyses of gender, this paper will add specific instances in which Hardy encodes Tess's voice as feminine. Furthermore, Hardy (not unlike George Eliot) opposed the unnatural laws and maxims of men, the voice of society at large, to Tess's individual voice, what Angel calls her "actualized poetry."

Second, Hardy plots two intersecting trajectories: An elective affinity between Tess and Angel leads eventually to a convergence not only of their views but of their voices into a harmony beyond gender. "All the while they were converging, under an irresistible law, as surely as two streams in one vale" (20:165).

Their developing relationship, in turn, becomes Hardy's model for that of the teller to his tale. Through the course of the novel, the dialectic between a variable, one might even say "polyglot," narrative voice and Tess's quoted or echoed voice becomes an explicit theme and problem. Narrative re-presentation always puts into question the singular identity of a character; identity recedes into the abyss of silence. Yet the dynamic mutability of the character Tess, with her gradually evolving voice, can only be recorded through shifts in the narrative voice, or through "narrative androgyny." In this dynamic interplay between Tess and the narrator, I focus on their vocal reciprocity or "antiphony."[8]

From the outset, Hardy maps a repressive set of discourses that are inadequate to true morality and inimical to the development and expression of Tess's selfhood. Hardy encodes most of the "merely vocal formulae" of the Bible or "ordinances of civilization" as masculine, though he shows their inhuman effects on men as well as women. The wisdom of "sundry gnomic texts and phrases" profits us naught without the experience it would prevent; Tess "might have ironically said to God with Saint Augustine: 'Thou hast counselled a better course than Thou hast permitted' " (15:124). Tess repeats mechanically the words of Ecclesiastes, "All is vanity," "till she reflected that this was a most inadequate thought for modern days. . . . If all were only vanity, who would mind it? All was, alas worse than vanity—injustice, punishment, exaction, death" (41:353). When Angel asks her if she doesn't want to learn anything, she replies, "I shouldn't mind learning why—why the sun do shine on the just and the unjust alike. . . . But that's what books will not tell me" (19:162).

Notably, the narrator opposes men who follow the Word to women who reject it for the truths of their heart. On her son's return, we are told, Mrs. Clare cared no more for "the stains of heterodoxy which had caused all this separation than for the dust upon his clothes." "What woman, indeed, among the most faithful adherents of the truth, believes the promises and threats of the Word in the sense in which she believes in her own children, or would not throw her theology to the wind if weighed against their happiness?" (53:470).

The inadequacy of received texts seems universally applicable, but the focus of moral formulas on chastity orients their attack against women. One voice oppressing women, for example, is the "trade voice" of the man who paints Mosaic laws on barns: "THOU, SHALT, NOT, COMMIT ———." What he calls the "tex" links Tess to sex, and though unjustly applied to "dangerous young females" like herself, "the words entered Tess with accusatory horror" (12:101–2). Their "hideous defacement" damages not only the surface on which they are painted but the person whose image they defile. An Augustinian at heart, for whom chastity is a matter of the will and not of the body, Hardy also takes to task the Clare family's Pauline doctrine.[9] The cult of chastity, which in Paul's own era opposed the cult of the many-breasted Artemis of the Ephesians, in the novel vilifies the heroine, for Tess is a Diana of the Crossroads, virgin, mother, and goddess of death in her successive phases.[10] Tess's human complexities not only resist the stereotype of the "simple" or "unsullied country maid" that Angel and then his parents take her to be but make it difficult "to apply the words" of King Lemuel in Proverbs 31 to her genuine virtue.

Hardy, of course, will not allow Tess to remain a totally passive object of description by his male characters—including the narrator. Yet when she does speak up, her individual words are reductively interpreted through men's codes about women. In one of the most dramatic scenes of the novel, Alec argues that women don't mean what they say.

> "I didn't understand your meaning till it was too late."
> "That's what every woman says."
> "How can you dare to use such words!" she cried, turning impetuously upon him, her eyes flashing as the latent spirit (of which he was to see more some day) awoke in her. "My God! I could knock you out of the gig! Did it never strike your mind that what every woman says some women may feel?" [12:97]

She leaves Trantridge (in the manuscript version) because "They called me your—your—I won't say the horrid word" (MS f. 106).[11]

She likewise resists Angel's stereotypes of femininity, whether idealizing or degrading. When Angel idealizes her as Demeter and Artemis, she responds, "Call me Tess."[12] Angel, "yet the slave to custom and conventionality," like Alec takes her *no* for *yes:* "his experience of women was great enough for him to be aware that the negative often meant nothing more than the preface to the affirmative" (28:224). In one of Hardy's more ironic passages, Angel attempts—and fails—to interpret Tess's melancholy and "self-suppression," as if he were interpreting a text.

> "She is a dear dear Tess," he thought to himself, as one deciding on the true construction of a difficult passage. "Do I realize solemnly enough how utterly and irretrievably this little womanly thing is the creature of my good or bad faith and fortune? I think not. I could not, unless I were a woman myself." [34:278]

Ellen Moers has observed that stereotypical images, from milkmaid to murderess, both idealize and debase "this little womanly thing."[13] Just as Angel must learn at the outset of his stay in Talbothays to differentiate the typical and unvarying country man "Hodge" into "beings of many minds, . . . men every one of whom walked in his own individual way the road to dusty death," so he must learn to "disintegrate" the falsifying projections by men onto individual women (18:152). Misreadings of Tess sum up for Hardy our misreading in general of what today one might call the subaltern.

Hardy's rebellion against such constraining social codes generates his view of women in history. For the past as masculine event ironically names the present. Each time the past is voiced—whether in Tess's descent from aristocratic philanderers or her seduction—Tess is displaced, often physically, and wrenched from her pursuit of selfhood. Tellingly, Tess tends to suppress allusion to her supposed aristocratic forebears, except in a mistaken if brief move to accommodate the prejudices of Angel's family. Though John Durbeyfield, Joan, Alec (who poses as an ancestor), and Angel all refer to the d'Urberville connection, it is the narrator who alludes to it most insistently. In a spectacular instance, the narrator comments on the unspeakable violence done to Tess by Alec in the well-named woods of The Chase. In this symbolically darkened and dimmed setting, the narrator ironically suggests that historical justice somehow visits the sins of the fathers upon the daughters, whereas a closer examination of that maxim suggests instead a historical repetition of the sins of powerful men against simple peasant girls. Here we find one of the cruxes in interpretation of the novel, for giving voice to the historian is one of the narrator's functions that splits the narrative voice asunder.

Opposed to men's maxims, then, lies a complex womanly truth, given form in Tess's voice, one of Hardy's most brilliant inventions. Fluty, murmuring, quavering, stammering, panting, its breaks and stops evoke a systematically conceived linguistic code of femininity. Hardy reminds us of the nineteenth-century origins of a theory such as Julia Kristeva's *semeiotike,* that fluid, contradictory, disruptive, and silent preoedipal language, which critics like Margaret Homans have applied to female modernists' linguistic experiments.[14] Hardy's narrator assimilates three features above all to the feminine: Tess's "native phrases," her emotional fusion of body and words, and her silences.

In the opening chapters Hardy links Tess's voice to her mother's through their love of song and use of dialect. As Ralph Elliot suggests, Hardy's "reliance upon archaic or local language seems like a deliberate attempt to free contemporary English of its more inhibiting, 'male' associations."[15] The manuscript evidence shows that Hardy initially added dialectal phrasing, heightening his heroine's links to an archaic, rural society. The figure called Love or Rosemary (before she became Tess) started off in the first pages of Hardy's draft speaking standard English even at home; manuscript changes then added dialect for Tess, especially in states of emotion, "when excited by joy, surprise, or grief" (MS f. 19). In the later versions, dialect took on class and intellectual connotations: Tess, who plans to become a schoolteacher, speaks "ordinary English abroad and to persons of quality" (3:21).[16]

The narrator seems to present superstition as if it were a feminine interpretive code; women, we are told, retain "Pagan fantasy" (16:134). We first encounter superstition in Joan Durbeyfield's use of the casting or divining book, which she keeps appropriately enough on the margins of her household, in the outhouse.[17] Out of a "curious fetishistic fear," this women's language of diagnosis must be exiled. Hardy tells us that "a gap of two hundred years" lies between Joan's folklore and the "standard knowledge" of Tess, but the narrative assimilation of superstitious signs to critical moments in Tess's life suggests otherwise. Among the moments with ominous signs that Tess, "steeped in fancies and prefigurative superstitions," takes to be an ill omen, we may include the rose prick on her first return from Trantridge, the cockcrow on her departure from Talbothays, and most important, the sound of the d'Urberville coach.

One curious aspect of these incidents is that many are introduced or observed by men; indeed, they tend to record the "ghosts" or power of men over women. Yet women believe in these prefigurations that almost inevitably designate them as "figures." Angel and Alec recount the myth of the d'Urberville coach without faith, whereas Tess is credulous. Similarly, Dairyman Crick takes the cockcrow to signify a change in weather, whereas for his wife it may foreshadow sickness or death; we shortly hear of Retty's suicide attempt and Marian's bout with alcohol, not to mention Angel's dream projection of Tess's death. (The narrator's attitude toward these events is suggestively ambiguous, even split. When Tess somehow knows the coach, perhaps from a dream, the narrator maintains distance unimplicated by any confession of faith. Yet, by introducing the superstitious sign *qua* sign and by shaping the turn of events, the narrator lends credence to the superstition.) If Tess speaks the language of superstition throughout, it is certainly no accident that the narrator describes her murder of Alec as marked by a stain in the shape of an ace of hearts—inviting us to *read* through the code of superstition.

Like the links between women and divination, the literary allusions that surround Tess—the Childe ballad about a maid that had done amiss, her Shakespearean intuitions—lend her a poetic power of prophecy.[18] Though Tess's reactions to the Bible are explicit and negative, these literary echoes are indirect and unconscious. Only by dramatic irony do they permit Tess to narrate proleptically her own story.

Bilingual by training, once Tess leaves home she speaks a more refined "Sixth Standard" English, close to that spoken by the better-educated characters of the novel, though less abstract and complex in its constructions, and through Angel she acquires the repertoire of a more educated, disillusioned middle-class man. Indeed, later editions stripped dialect from Tess's speech after she leaves Marlott, a process that Laird attributes to Hardy's desire to dignify Tess.[19] These changes created a problem: how to mark Tess's voice as that of a woman.

Hardy dealt with that problem, I think, by foregrounding features that he could encode as feminine. He counterbalanced the more universal and sophisticated features in Tess's acquired language by assimilating her speech to her body and to nature. Hardy's notebooks record the semiotic truth that "there are looks, & tones, & gestures, which form a significant language of their own."[20] Hardy enumerates bits of her body and, as he does so, introduces the notion of body language: "her mobile peony mouth and large innocent eyes added eloquence to colour and shape." Not her words but her peony mouth, displaced from speech into a flower of speech, has "eloquence." Likewise, Tess's "eloquent" eyes "flash" and confess. "Every seesaw of her breath, every wave of her blood, every pulse singing in her ears was a voice that joined with nature in revolt against her scrupulousness" (28:228).

Of a woman's speaking "parts," the heart is one of the most important. When Tess baptizes her dying child Sorrow, she speaks "boldly and triumphantly in the stopt-diapason note which her voice acquired when her heart was in her speech" (14:120).[21] Here, the musical term "stopt-diapason," for the muffled, higher note reached when an organ pipe is stopped, evokes harmonious sublimity. Subliminally, the phrase suggests that "stopping" or muting Tess's voice may help the narrator create a higher harmony. At the same time, it reminds us of the "stops" in Tess's speech, the breaks that mark the difference between her use of Sixth Standard English and the controlled linearity typical of Angel's or Alec's speech.

Tess's fragments and her fusion of body with language typify Hardy's representation of her voice as a vehicle of poetic truth, whose breaks fall naturally rather than according to the dictates of art and grammar. During her engagement, for example, Tess speaks in ecstatic fragments, dictated by the "leapings of her heart," the voice and laughter of a woman in love:

> Some of the dairy-people, who were also out of doors on the first Sunday evening after their engagement, heard her impulsive speeches, ecstasized to fragments, though they were too far off to hear the words discoursed; noted the spasmodic catch in her remarks, broken into syllables by the leapings of her heart, as she walked leaning on his arm; her contented pauses, the occasional laugh upon which her soul seemed to ride—the laugh of a woman in company with the man she loves and has won from all other women—unlike anything else in nature. [31:249]

This "articulatory physiology" (Elliot, *Hardy's English,* 340) links natural, spontaneous poetry to the feminine. It is not surprising to find the pair set their marriage date amid the "liquid voices" of the weir and landscape, assimilating passion to nature.

One of the most extraordinary passages in which Hardy uses body language to express Tess's feelings is the lunch break during the Marlott harvest, when she suckles the infant Sorrow who has been brought to her.

> When the infant had taken its fill the young mother sat it upright in her lap, and looking into the far distance dandled it with a gloomy indifference that was almost dislike; then all of a sudden she fell to violently kissing it some dozens of times, as if she could never leave off, the child crying at the vehemence of an onset which strangely combined passionateness with contempt. [14:114]

Such preverbal communication with the preverbal Sorrow links the woman's sexual and linguistic roles in a quite traditional way. More interestingly, it also mirrors the mixture of sexual passion and contempt that disfigured her relationship to Alec. Furthermore, Tess's violence here evokes a particular form of "maternal anger" not often recognized in literature written by men. Hers is certainly the anger of the repressed voice, but it is also the anger of the exploited body, of a maternity whose pleasures have been fatally contaminated by rape.[22]

Essential to Hardy's presentation of Tess as a young woman who yearns to leave her body behind while stargazing is the treachery of a woman's body as voice. Holes in your stockings "don't speak," says her mother, Joan, but her "developing figure" does—and it "belies" her age. Angel, when he wishes to decode Tess's rejection of marriage, "conned the characters of her face as if they had been hieroglyphics" telling him what he wants to hear (28:225). Tess finally mutilates her eyebrows to prevent men from "conning" the hieroglyphs of her face and taking it as a screen for their projections.

In order to compensate for the misspeech of her feminine body language, which falsifies her desires and intentions, she first does violence to herself and then has resort to physical violence against Alec with instruments traditionally identified with men—a gauntlet, a knife. In ominous foreshadowing, Hardy makes Alec watch Tess castrate swedes in the swede cutter. In the manuscript, her violation of both gender and class rules, when she knocks Alec off his horse, is punished by her own violation.

Beyond body language lies silence as a feminine form of speech, whose multiple moral and sexual meanings underscore its significance as a way for Tess to voice herself.[23] For Tess is "impressed" by soundlessness "as a positive entity rather than the mere negation of noise" (19:157). When she forces Alec to let her out of the gig, her "strategic silence" tells him she has lost her hat on purpose (8:66). Later, Tess's silence compounded by negatives when Angel presses her to marry him bespeaks her moral choice to efface herself, on behalf of her friends and what she perceives as his well-being (31:246). Still later, during their engagement, Tess's silence concerning her past voices her irrepressible desires as well as her mother's advice. At different moments, then, silence gives voice to her conscience and her erotic drives.

Yet finally, her silence, her vow not to write Angel until written to, bespeaks "dumb and vacant fidelity" (35:296). Such imposed silence is the badge of woman's subjection and the sign of her vacancy, her chastity. The moment when Tess finally speaks out is catastrophic; as the title of the next "phase" reveals, if she speaks, "the woman pays." Tess knows this economy of speech: "She would pay to the uttermost farthing; she would tell, there and then" (34:284). Ironically, when she and Angel are finally united, it is she who urges him to mute the past: "Don't think of what's past!" She has become like one of the polar birds at Flintcomb-Ash:

> gaunt spectral creatures with tragical eyes—eyes which had witnessed scenes of cataclysmal horror in inaccessible polar regions of a magnitude such as no human being had ever conceived, . . . but of all they had seen which humanity would never see, they had brought no account. [43:367]

"Dumb impassivity" records the journey of such travelers through life.

To record silence necessitates a narrator's voice. "She thought," writes Hardy, "without actually wording the thought, how strange and godlike was a composer's power, who from the grave could lead through sequences of emotion, which he alone had felt at first, a girl like her who had never heard of his name" (13:107). If the composer proleptically directs the future, the author divines the unspoken past.

To speak for Tess means to define a particular woman's voice. Herein lies a problem. For to present Tess in her womanhood, the phases of maiden, mother, wife, mistress, and murderess, means to assimilate her to conventions about different feminine voices. Conversely, to distinguish Tess in her particularity seems to entail—for Hardy at least—assimilating her to masculine discourse.

Tess "herself," as we have already seen, rejects the body language conventionally assigned to women. After her confession, she rejects the feminine hysterics and "feminine" strategy of intimacy that might have enabled her to hold Angel. "It would have denoted deficiency of womanhood if she had not instinctively known what an argument lies in propinquity. Nothing else would serve her, she knew, if this failed." Yet Tess is Angel's best advocate, for she knows, "It was wrong to hope in what was of the nature of strategy" (36:311; see 37:323). Joan's earlier stratagems to entrap a gentleman husband for her daughter shock Tess, who tries to silence her mother. Tess's attempts to distinguish herself from the conventions of femininity elicit D. H. Lawrence's explanation of her plight as "despising herself in the flesh, despising the deep Female she was."[24]

Part of Tess's development, as even Alec notices, consists in her adopting Angel's "vocabulary, his accent" (28:225). "She had caught his manner and habits, his speech and phrases, his likings and his aversions" (32:260). She proves her "reverential fidelity" to her husband—a model for the narrator's fidelity—by repeating verbatim Angel's syllogisms in "crystallized phrases." She learns and repeats his songs. She also, however, turns his words to serve her own insights, as Adrian Poole has rightly observed:

> "Our tremulous lives are so different from theirs, are they not?" he musingly observed to her, as he regarded the three figures of her milkmaid-companions.
>
> "Not so very different, I think," she said.

> "Why do you think that?"
> "There are very few women's lives that are not—tremulous," Tess replied, pausing over the new word as if it impressed her. [29:235]

For Angel's complacent polarity between the doubts of the philosophical questioner and the calm of the unthinking masses, she substitutes a more accurate polarity between the secure lives of men and "tremulous" lives of women. Likewise in the baptism passage, when she usurps male language and male rites, she achieves "almost regal" grandeur, authenticating her own existence and that of her child.

From the start, of course, before she ever meets Angel, one may catch in Tess's vivid, metaphoric speech about blighted worlds as "stubbard trees" certain philosophic turns of phrase and questioning. These were not learned "by rote," as Angel wrongly suspects—"And as he looked at the unpractised mouth and lips, he thought that such a daughter of the soil could only have caught up the sentiment by rote" (19:162). In fact, as Angel subsequently reflects, Tess knows "the ache of modernism" because

> advanced ideas are really in great part but the latest fashion in definition—a more accurate expression by words in -logy & -ism, of sensations which men [& women] [*sic*] have vaguely grasped for centuries. [MS f. 137–38; 19:160]

Tess has had ample opportunity to learn this ache through her "troubles."

Yet in the course of the novel Tess does become more articulate in her pessimism. Hardy intensified the fluency and depth of her voice in his revisions "by increasing our sense of the different languages she speaks" (Poole, "Men's Words," 341, 342–43). More technically, the different linguistic repertoires she masters complicate our sense of Tess's voice. If our multiple discourses "speak" us, at the same time we hear her transferring codes to make them fit better the actualities she observes.

The last phase in this development is to pass from voice to *écriture,* from oral to written form. Technically, the comparatively late location of Tess's letters to Angel, which we read first broken off, then transcribed in full, supports the illusion that Tess has developed from a meditative milkmaid into an articulate subject capable of verbalizing in writing her sense of selfhood. The late letter that follows Angel in his peregrinations is indeed passionate and eloquent, sufficiently powerful to wrench Angel out of himself and to call him back to her. Fragmentary echoes of her writing (when Hardy describes its reception by Angel) confirm the hermeneutic pattern discussed at the outset of this essay: Her voice by passing from oral to written form acquires the necessary substantiality to be "heard," to be repeated and understood.

This leads into the second part of my argument: An exchange of voice lies at the very heart of Tess's relationship to Angel Clare. At the outset, Angel is drawn to Tess precisely because she seems to echo his own thoughts, in a different register. He recognizes his own skepticism in her remarks, which distinguish her voice for him from among those of the other dairy folk. We may detect a certain narcissism in his very respect for her:

> At such times as this, apprehending the grounds of her refusal to be her modest sense of incompetence in matters social and polite, he would say that she was wonderfully well-informed and versatile—which was certainly true, her natural quickness, and her admiration for him, having led her to pick up his vocabulary, his accent, and fragments of his knowledge, to a surprising extent. [28:225]

Nonetheless, Angel is also drawn by the "soft and silent Tess" (24:190), and his embrace "stills" her (25:197). He deflects her attempts at confession, interrupting with belittling assumptions or deferring the moment of her truth: "No, no—we can't have faults talked of . . . you shall tell me anything . . . not now" (33:269). And she responds with "mute obedience." Their courtship, then, is marked by a conflict between his attraction to her conventionally feminine Otherness, including her muteness, and his sympathetic identification with her intimations of philosophic alienation (his own form of Otherness).

In a development that inverts the development of Tess, Angel acquires the body language of a farmer, more expressive eyes, and phrases like "a drop of pretty tipple," much to the horror of his superfine clerical brothers. He assimilates a cottager's "tone" in a way that his brothers interpret as "growing social ineptness." Yet this process of mutual adaptation comes to grief with the climactic double confession on the wedding night. Angel "seemed to be her double" (34:285) in telling Tess his story—but he cannot be her double until he realizes that his story is indeed hers. Her own "re-assertions and secondary explanations" have no meaning for him (35:291). The story of Angel's development shows us he must draw closer to the phenomena of nature, he must learn to recognize the "mutely Miltonic" among the countryfolk and come to hear "the voices of inanimate things" (18:152–53). He must discern the new note of Tess in the babble of conventions in order to respond; symbolically, he cannot receive her letters until he is psychologically ready to answer.

Only Angel's sojourn in Brazil reveals to him his own "parochialism," for it is there that he tells not only his story but that of Tess to the stranger.[25] Only then, after this retransmission of Tess's story, can Angel truly modulate his voice to hers. Then his illness and emotion make his voice husky and broken, his sentences interrupted by pauses and dashes, much as Tess's have been in the past. " 'Ah—it is my fault!' said Clare. But he could not get on. Speech was as inexpressive as silence" (45:484). At Stonehenge finally, he learns to console Tess by renouncing speech altogether: "Like a greater than himself, to the critical question at the critical time he did not answer; and they were again silent" (58:504). The two lovers become assimilated to the mute history of the monumental stones that surround them.

The narrative traces these two main intersecting lines, the masculinization of Tess's voice and the feminization of Angel's.[26] A glance at Alec suggests that Hardy used him as a mirror as well as a foil to Angel, reinforcing some of these same themes. Hardy shows us that Angel's verbal fluency at critical moments masks his religious doubts and that Alec's language as seducer and preacher constitutes abuse; we may set their oral arts against Tess's silences. Significantly, Alec is converted by Angel's "crystallized phrases" as transmitted by Tess, a form of communion between the two men over Tess's body that suggests the type of homosocial relationship Eve Sedgwick has analyzed.[27] "She repeated the argument, and d'Urberville thoughtfully murmured the words after her" (46:410). Alec, even before Angel, finds his voice changed by his liaison with Tess; even if we set aside his first half-feminized letter to her, under his mother's forged signature, his pagan discourse of seduction becomes a Pauline sermon of conversion; then, amid the Satanic, mocking phrases with which he entraps Tess once again, moments of straightforward desire and respect find expression on his lips. When Tess tells him of the birth of their child, "D'Urberville was struck mute" (45:396). Indeed, he grasps Tess's purity better than Angel does:

> No, by my word and truth, I never despised you; if I had I should not love you now! Why I did not despise you was on account of your being unsmirched in spite of all; you withdrew yourself from me so quickly and resolutely when you saw the situation; you did not remain at my pleasure; so there was one petticoat in the world for whom I had no contempt, and you are she. [46:411]

Though Alec still thinks of Tess as a "petticoat," he has been forced to respect her independence.

I might add that Hardy uses the symmetrical structure of the novel to reinforce the theme of language and silence. The most important symmetry balances Angel's banal confession against Tess's socially unacceptable one, showing their intrinsic similarity—"tis just the same!" This expansive scene, split over a major section break, acquires symbolic resonance through the images of reflected warmth and distorted shadows. Just as striking are certain verbal echoes in other parts of the novel. Tess's inexpressible combat between conscience and desire at Talbothays wrenches from her a cry, "O-O-O" (28:229). At Sandbourne that same "O-O-O" recurs in the lower note of unspeakable despair (56:486). Tess's first, unread, four-page "succinct narrative" to Angel is paralleled by the letters that she starts but does not mail, and by those that must go to Brazil and back before he receives them.

Although the evidence is somewhat more tenuous and complex, there are suggestive parallels between Tess's voice and certain aspects of the narrator's polyglot voice. To be sure, the narrative is punctuated by images of penetration and inscription, images that lead Boumelha to comment, "The passionate commitment to exhibiting Tess as the subject of her own experience evokes an unusually overt maleness in the narrative voice" (*Hardy and Women*, 120). At the same time, a number of critics have noted a "feminine principle" in the narration.[28] Hardy appears to have constructed deliberate parallels between what the narrator says and what Tess says or thinks. This convergence bears on Tess's development. Hardy, Mary Jacobus says, "starts with an unformed heroine, and shows us the emergence of a reflective consciousness close to his own" ("Tess's Purity," 324). The congruence between Tess and the narrator also bears on Hardy's basic project, his desire to create the ventriloquistic illusion that for once we can hear a woman's story—hence the ambiguous parallel between the narrator's use of superstition and the heroine's inclination to lend it credence, or between Hardy's notorious penchant to formulas of philosophic fatalism (called "Tessimism" by one reviewer) and Tess's view of life on this "blighted" star.[29]

In addition, we may point to a number of close verbal echoes that assimilate her prophetic knowledge to a narrator's control and omniscience. Tess is permitted to foresee Angel's complaint that she is not the woman he has been loving: "she you love is not my real self, but one in my image; the one I might have been!" (33:273). Similarly, the narrator tells us that "the intuitive heart of woman" knows that her husband's "own fastidious brain" may be the source of reproaches he imputes to strangers—a critique of Angel that forms an obvious parallel to Tess's insight that "you might get angry with me for any ordinary matter, and knowing what you do of my bygones you yourself might be tempted to say words, and they might be overheard" (36:312–13). Tess's ability to enter into another resembles her sensitivity to the voices of nature; commenting on those crepuscular moments when she intensifies natural processes until they seem a part of her own story, the narrator declares that her pathetic projections are not a fallacy but in a sense true: "For the world is only a psychological phenomenon and what they seemed they were" (13:108). Implicitly, Tess becomes a figure for the imagination.[30]

The poetry of her ecstatic speech and of her flavorful analogies (the lords and ladies, the stubbard trees) actualizes one aspect of the author's own craft. Her relationship to the implied author, then, may be turned inside out—as the narrator at one point turns Tess's skin inside out, in order to give voice to the sensuality that she represses. For when he tells us "She was not an existence, an experience, a passion, a structure of sensations, to anybody but herself" (14:115), Tess's isolation underscores the implied author's underlying claim of identity with her. As Hardy says elsewhere, "Art consists in so depicting the common events of life as to bring on the features which illustrate the author's idiosyncratic mode of regard" (*Early Life,* 294).

Briefly, by way of a conclusion, I want to identify three problems directly related to my stress on the complexity of Tess's voice. First, the complexity—even inconsistency—of the narrative voice: Hardy's effort to wrestle with the codes of masculinity and femininity ironically traps him in their repetition. In narrating Tess's struggle against the "tex" of womanhood, Hardy attempts to break the hold of such discourses over the individual. Yet at the same time, in proposing to represent Tess "faithfully" as a "pure" woman, he inexorably falls subject to other, equally conventional discourses. Within Hardy's system of polarities, "sex and nature are assigned to the female" in an ideological tragedy that forces Tess to play the conventional passive role (Boumelha, *Hardy and Women,* 123; cf. Boone, *Tradition*).

Hardy's divided view of conventions about the feminine continuously complicates the narrative representation of Tess. Not the least of Hardy's successes, for example, is his paradoxical depiction of Tess wandering at dusk, hearing "formulae of bitter reproach" in the gusts of oncoming night. Vividly as this scene attests to her imagination and to a psychological truth, the narrator turns back from the claim "what they seemed they were" to reject Tess's self-condemnation. For she mistakenly internalizes, he explains, the "moral hobgoblins," the "shreds of convention" that accuse her, just as later she will unquestioningly accept Angel's condemnation of her (13:108). This structure re-creates the kind of hierarchy Hardy wishes to undo and undermines the autonomy of his subject.[31] By permitting his narrator first to approve, then disapprove Tess, Hardy puts back into question the whole project of narrative fidelity. The only possible fidelity seems to lie in acknowledging inevitable misrepresentation.

The second problem: gender categories, I suspect, contaminate our criticism too. Many readers privilege the more sensually expressive (i.e., more "natural") heroine of the manuscript (Love, Cis, or Rosemary) as the true Tess. Her sensuality and attachment to her rural roots seem to them to make her a more "responsible" and therefore more credible woman than the Tess of the final version, which therefore appears to falsify Hardy's "original intention" (Jacobus, "Tess's Purity," 331). This search for the original Tess is not unlike the impulse to identify Tess with Tryphena Sparks, Hardy's early fiancée, who may have borne his illegitimate child (Laird, *Shaping of "Tess,"* 118–22). Yet temporal priority does not give Love greater "truth" than Tess. Such confusions have extended to discussions of Tess's language, which tend to slip between questions of sexual explicitness and those of linguistic repertoire. Some have seen in the purging of dialect from Love's voice a bowdlerization of her sensuality, part of Hardy's self-censorship in response to early criticism that continued into the latest editions. It would be more accurate to say simply that Hardy's revisions both muted and heightened Tess's sensual entanglements. The New Wessex Tess speaks in a mixed voice that links her to "the fieldwoman" as well as to Angel and the narrator—and at both ends of this spectrum we are dealing with repertoires, that is, with the reproduction of linguistic stereotypes.

Precisely this intersection of conflicting repertoires may help us to assess the meaning of what I've called antiphony, the responsive dialectic between the voices of Tess and of the narrator. Reading the novel as a metanarrative about voice helps us see in greater detail not only problems Hardy encountered in his narrative but his achievement. For I think Tess's postulated voice permits a creative extension of Hardy's own voice. For the nineteenth-century male writer who centers his fiction on a female protagonist does so not only in order to expose the contradictions of bourgeois, particularist individualism or the inequities of existing gendered hierarchies. In the process of "faithfully" representing his heroine's voice and experience, Hardy seeks access to an unrepresented zone of experience and language.

The narrative pattern of deferral, for example, has often been read as a gesture of fatalism; it also, however, typifies narratives of female desire.[32] Recall that Tess desires "a perpetual betrothal" (32:256). From the first, Angel defers the telling of their two stories, and at the end the two live their idyll in a temporally incomplete world where "every idea was temporary and unforefending, like the plans of two children" (57:494). Deferral is the obverse of belatedness, of course, and that is one of the central themes of a novel whose title until publication was "Too Late, Beloved." If it is belatedness or *déjà vu* that draws Angel to Tess, it is also belatedness that separates the two, suspending them in perpetual courtship with only the briefest "fulfilment" (title of the seventh "phase," which traces their journey from Sandbourne to Stonehenge).

Most significant, Hardy's narrative gaps have provoked debate. The unseen rape, the missing four-page note to Angel, the omitted double confession, all have been condemned as Hardy's suppression of Tess's voice and experience, or even his censorship of moments when his male rivals possess his beloved heroine.[33] In a review by Mowbray Morris in the *Quarterly Review* (1892), we hear, "The gaps that represent bad work are too large and too frequent." Franz Stanzel suggests that Hardy censored his own text to prevent readers from reaching an independent (negative) opinion of his heroine.[34]

From a feminist perspective, Childers has charged that Hardy "takes away from Tess all power to speak what she means" ("Thomas Hardy," 329). Boumelha finds Tess's consciousness all but edited out, part of a larger tragic pattern, "the ideological elision of woman, sex, and nature." This elision means that Tess is "most woman" when she is "dumb" (*Hardy and Women*, 122–23). Perhaps inadvertently, Hillis Miller complains in *Fiction and Repetition* about the "effacement" of Tess's violation and "the similar failure to describe directly all the crucial acts of violence which echo Tess's violation before and after its occurrence" (118). Such charges are particularly ironic, given Hardy's own struggle against the gaps imposed by censorship. His "Explanatory Note" to the first edition complains of the "piecemeal mode of parturition" and his need to rejoin limbs and trunk. Again, in the *Life*, he describes the struggle in virtually sexual terms, as one to preserve "the novel intact," not "mutilated" by censorship to eliminate "improper explicitness" of certain passages (*Early Life*, 291).

Interpreted as an assimilation of Tess's "feminine" language, Hardy's pauses acquire fresh complexity. In one sense, the blank pages between "phases" constitute a silent "body language" for Hardy's text. Such breaks, of course, have no single meaning, as the interplay between the two central examples makes clear. The gap between Alec's discovery of the sleeping Tess and the beginning of the second phase symbolically renders the tearing of flesh that it literally does not describe; such a gap is a pure literary convention for the socially taboo or the unspeakable. When Hardy, however, repeats this narrative gap on the wedding night, at the moment when Tess reveals her innermost secret (that is, the secret moment that we know as the previous gap in the narrative), he ironically plays upon an (absent) hymeneal rupture, the unconsummated marriage, and points us toward another initiatory knowledge, for which Angel is not ready. The result is that Hardy brings to the foreground the sexuality of storytelling, the rupture enacted by women's storytelling.

Hardy's silence also reproduces Tess's difficulty in coming to speech. We have been asked whether her story will "bear" telling, a burden, it seems, that Tess alone must take on. Curiously, an inversion has taken place: The narrative becomes the margin for her silently spoken secret, raising the question of the propriety of narrative-making itself. Important as the problem of giving voice to a woman's story may be, it also becomes a figure for the problem of giving voice to experience and to the Other at all. The controversial conclusion, in which Tess's double Liza-Lu joins hands with Angel and goes on, strangely enacts Tess's desire to rewrite her own story, for Tess would "share" in her sister's marriage to Angel. Yet the projected, unwritten story is itself disturbingly ambiguous; it evokes not only a resurrection but a repetition "shrunk to half [the] natural size" of the original.

Finally, Hardy's silences may, I suggest, be read as experiments with what he considered a feminine discourse, a discourse similar to the broken line that Virginia Woolf would describe in *A Room of One's Own*. Such experiments are typical of nineteenth-century men's fiction. At the same time, the construction and then figurative transposition of a "feminine" discourse contain the seeds of its own destruction. For resistance to the social code of gender is undermined by the reinscription of a gendered linguistic code. In turn, one may want to challenge the perpetual displacement of woman as figure. The violence and other costs of both silence and speech for women are absent from the male narrator's domain; the presence or absence of choice marks a critical difference. Ultimately, then, Hardy forces us back upon the question whether silence expresses the ineffable or more simply records the unspeakable, and the most pervasive form of violence against women.

## Notes

In writing this paper, I have profited from comments by the editors of this volume, Joseph Boone, Elisabeth Bronfen, Carol Christ, U. C. Knoepflmacher, James Kincaid, and David Sonstroem.

1. All quotations from *Tess* refer to the Wessex Edition of *The Works of Thomas Hardy in Prose and Verse* (1912; rpt. New York: AMS, 1984), by chapter and page.
2. "I have for a long time been in favour of woman-suffrage. . . . I am in favour of it because I think the tendency of the woman's vote will be to break up the pernicious conventions in respect of women, customs, religion, illegitimacy, the stereotyped household (that it must be the unit of society), the father of a woman's child (that it is anybody's business but the woman's own) . . . and other matters which I got into hot water for touching on many years ago." Letter of Nov. 30, 1906, to Mrs. Fawcett, cited in Gail Cunningham, "Thomas Hardy: New Women for Old," *The New Woman and the Victorian Novel* (London: Macmillan, 1978), 115. A. O. J. Cockshut, however, believes that "the attempt to turn Hardy into a feminist is altogether vain"; cited in Elaine Showalter, "The Unmanning of the Mayor of Casterbridge," in *Critical Approaches to the Fiction of Thomas Hardy,* ed. Dale Kramer (Totowa, NJ: Barnes and Noble, 1979), 101.
3. There is for any modern reader an obvious irony in giving these lines about the incapacity of men's words to a narrator who, though anonymous, by his elaborately wrought, semireligious language assimilates himself to the highly educated and confessional, masculine, roles of artist and priest. Whereas the narrator's omniscient condescension to the species "woman" here may not betray Hardy's conscious deployment of irony, U. C. Knoepflmacher suggests that by the time he wrote *Tess* such contradictions are probably deliberate, for they constantly rend the text.

4. Adrian Poole, "Men's Words and Hardy's Women," *Essays in Criticism* 31 (1981): 328–45, in discussing these passages stresses Hardy's sensitivity to "the effort of men's words to circumscribe and describe, confine and define, women's bodies" (329). Hardy thematizes the difficulty throughout his oeuvre, as in *A Pair of Blue Eyes,* where Knight, who lacks "the trick of reading the truly enigmatical forces at work in women," "could pack them into sentences like a workman, but practically was nowhere" (20:226; 18:193).
5. Many readers have observed that the narrator's contradictory philosophy distantly echoes the conflicting attitudes that burden Tess's heart. J. Hillis Miller finds in all Hardy's novels "an ultimate convergence of the protagonists' point of view with the narrator's point of view." In the case of Tess, he thinks Hardy "even obscurely identified himself with her" (*Thomas Hardy: Distance and Desire* [Cambridge, MA: Harvard University Press, 1970], 119): Tess, "c'est moi." For Bernard J. Paris, "Hardy is Tess's apologist: he sees her and everything else in her terms" ("'A Confusion of Many Standards': Conflicting Value Systems in *Tess of the d'Urbervilles,*" *Nineteenth-Century Fiction* 24 [1969]: 76–77). Or, to cite Mary Childers, "Thomas Hardy, the Man Who 'Liked' Women," *Criticism* 23 (1981): 326, "projection does not balk at transvestism."
6. Furthermore, the stage of her re-creation depends upon its veiling and, as James Kincaid suggests in an unpublished essay, upon the reader's lubricious participation.
7. Mary Jacobus, "Tess's Purity," *Essays in Criticism* 26 (1976): 318–38; Penny Boumelha, *Thomas Hardy and Women: Sexual Ideology and Narrative* (New York: Barnes and Noble, 1982). See also Joseph A. Boone, *Tradition Counter Tradition: Love and the Form of Fiction* (Chicago: University of Chicago Press, 1987); Childers, "Thomas Hardy"; Vernon Lee, "Hardy," in *The Handling of Words and Other Studies in Literary Psychology* (New York, 1923), 222–41; Tony Tanner, "Colour and Movement in Hardy's *Tess of the d'Urbervilles,*" *Critical Quarterly* 10 (Autumn 1968): 219–39.
8. Repetition, especially in narrative representation, is the focus of Hillis Miller's chapter on Hardy in *Fiction and Repetition: Seven English Novels* (Cambridge, MA: Harvard University Press, 1982). "Narrative androgyny," Penny Boumelha's term, refers to the ambiguous relation of the narrator to Tess: "she is not only spoken by the narrator but also spoken *for*" (*Hardy and Women,* 120). Elizabeth Ermarth (*Realism and Consensus in the English Novel* [Princeton, NJ.: Princeton University Press, 1983]) stresses the ideological control exercised by the temporality of narrative discourse, to which one could add many other aspects of narrative voice. U. C. Knoepflmacher helped me see how Hardy splits and multiplies the narrator's discursive sets, as he wrestles with the problem of the narrator's filtering voice.
9. Compare Augustine's *City of God,* book 1, chaps. 19–32, to Hardy: "Who was the moral man? Still more pertinently, who was the moral woman? The beauty and ugliness of a character lay not only in its achievements, but in its aims and impulses; its true history lay not among things done but among things willed" (49:433).
10. Hardy drives the point home when he describes the ironically sexual, barren landscape of Flintcomb-Ash "as if Cybele the Many-breasted were supinely extended there" (42:358).
11. References to the manuscript are drawn from *Tess of the d'Urbervilles: A Facsimile of the MS,* ed. Simon Gatrell (New York: Garland, 1986). Adrian Poole observes of her exchange with Alec in the gig, "She is taking possession of a cliche, and this is inseparable from the taking possession of her own body at this moment. In the face of men's threat to dispossess the woman of her own body, of the right to speech—to reduce her to physical and linguistic cliche—, Tess re-claims that body and that right to speech, repossessing the discarded and supposedly empty shell" ("Men's Words," 342).
12. Yet she does not escape from stereotypes herself. She herself idealizes Angel as an Apollo of wisdom or an Abraham on the American plains.
13. Ellen Moers, "Hardy Perennial," *New York Review of Books,* Nov. 9, 1967, 31–33.
14. Margaret Homans, *Bearing the Word* (Chicago: University of Chicago Press, 1986), 16–20.

15. Though I admire Elliot's work, we differ in interpreting the evidence: "It cannot truthfully be averred that Hardy's women have in any important sense a language of their own. Nor, strictly speaking, have his men. The traits that distinguish Hardy's characters cut across sexual division; nor is language used by Hardy consistently to create idiolects" (Ralph W. V. Elliot, *Thomas Hardy's English* [Oxford: Blackwell, 1984], 337). Adrian Poole, commenting on Tess's use of dialect in different editions, notes "Hardy's uncertainty about stressing or unstressing a linguistic distance between Tess's dialect and Angel's Standard English" ("Men's Words," 345, n. 24).
16. A scrupulous examination of these changes reveals that Hardy also localized the vocabulary of John Durbeyfield, as well as that of Joan and Tess (see the edition of 1892). Significantly, however, the comments of the narrator stress *women's* use of dialect rather than that of John.
17. Though this book might have been written by a man, Hardy presumably has in mind the post-Renaissance identification of women with "primitive" sciences, as opposed to the institutions of modern learning controlled by men.
18. Marlene Springer, *Hardy's Use of Allusion* (Lawrence: University of Kansas Press, 1983), argues that these allusions "intensify her intellectual development, minimise her mistakes" (142).
19. John Tudor Laird, *The Shaping of "Tess of the d'Urbervilles"* (Oxford: Clarendon, 1975), 184.
20. *Literary Notebooks of Thomas Hardy,* ed. Lennart A. Bjork, 2 vols. (New York: New York University Press, 1974, 1985), 1:103.
21. This passage raises the question of the narrator's shifting relationship to Tess, for it adds that the voice "will never be forgotten by those who knew her." To explain the vocal mosaic of a narrator at times close to Tess, at times distant, Rosemarie Morgan (*Women and Sexuality in the Novels of Thomas Hardy* [London: Routledge, 1988]) argues for splintered narrative personae, U. C. Knoepflmacher for multiple narrators.
22. My thanks to Marianne Hirsch and Mieke Bal for first bringing the theme of maternal anger to my attention. In a paper presented at the Harvard Center for Literary Studies, Hirsch wrote, "Anger may well be what defines subjectivity whenever the subjective is denied speech." E. B. Browning's "Runaway Slave at Pilgrim's Point" offers a woman poet's analysis of the class and racial components in such maternal anger.
23. Mary Childers comments on Hardy's recognition that silence may express power ("Thomas Hardy," 322). She goes on to suggest that the muting of his female characters "suggests Hardy's own submission to censureship [*sic*] and sensitivity to criticism" (333).
24. D. H. Lawrence, "The Male and Female Principles in *Tess of the d'Urbervilles,* in *Thomas Hardy, "Tess of the d'Urbervilles": An Authoritative Text,* ed. Scott Elledge, 2d ed. (New York: Norton, 1979), 409.
25. Angel is both a shadow of the narrator and a projection of the reader; his poeticisms and conventionalism echo apparently deliberate misreadings of Tess by the narrator and our own problems of reception, which prevent us from hearing Tess's story. More positively the reader and the narrator, of course, strive like Angel to receive Tess's wounded name into our "bosom."
26. Showalter ("Unmanning") notes generally that for Hardy's heroes "maturity involves a kind of assimilation of female suffering, an identification with a woman which is also an effort to come to terms with their own deepest selves" (101).
27. Eve Kosofsky Sedgwick, *Between Men: English Literature and Male Homosocial Desire* (New York: Columbia University Press, 1985). D. H. Lawrence noted this homosocial mutualism: "It is inevitable for Angel Clare and for Alec d'Urberville mutually to destroy the woman they both loved" ("Male and Female," 410).
28. Irving Howe finds "a curious power of sexual insinuation, almost as if he were not locked into the limits of masculine perception but could shuttle between, or for moments yoke together, the responses of the two sexes" ("Let the Day Perish," in *Thomas Hardy, "Tess of*

*the d'Urbervilles": An Authoritative Text,* ed. Scott Elledge, 2d ed. [New York: Norton, 1979], 109). Showalter considers Hardy "one of the few Victorian male novelists who wrote in what may be called a female tradition" ("Unmanning," 99) and finds in his work "a consistent element of self-expression through women" "as screens or ghosts of himself" (101).

29. Cf. Florence Emily Hardy [Thomas Hardy], *The Early Life of Thomas Hardy* (London: Macmillan, 1928), 285–86.
30. Hardy takes the similar projections of paranoia to be poetic: "Apprehension is a great element in imagination. It is a semi-madness, which see enemies, etc., in inanimate objects" (*Early Life,* 294).
31. Boone, *Tradition,* argues that the linear seduction plot repeats through its relentless rhythms of pursuit and flight the violations it describes. As for the recurrent masculine and feminine symbolisms of the novel, Boumelha comments on "Hardy's increasing interrogation of his own modes of narration. The disjunctions in narrative voice, the contradictions of logic, the abrupt shifts of point of view . . . disintegrate the stability of character as a cohering force, they threaten the dominance of the dispassionate and omniscient narrator, and so push to its limit the androgynous narrative mode that seeks to represent and explain the woman from within and without" (*Hardy and Women,* 132). Whereas David Lodge complains that Hardy "undermines our trust in the reliability of Tess's response to Nature, which is his own chief rhetorical device for defending her character" ("Tess, Nature, and the Voices of Hardy," *Language of Fiction* [New York: Columbia University Press, 1966], 76), James Kincaid revalues "the large and the local gaps" as evidence of creative "tentativeness and inconsistency," i.e., of openings rather than foreclosures ("Hardy's Absences," in *Critical Approaches to the Fiction of Thomas Hardy,* ed. Dale Kramer [Totowa, NJ: Barnes and Noble, 1979], 202).
32. Margaret R. Higonnet, "Writing from the Feminine: *Lucinde* and *Adolphe,*" *Annales Benjamin Constant* 15 (1986): 22, 28.
33. John Bayley, *An Essay on Hardy* (Cambridge: Cambridge University Press, 1978), 183.
34. Mowbray Morris, "Culture and Anarchy," *Quarterly Review* 174 (1892): 317–43; Franz Stanzel, "Thomas Hardy: Tess of the d'Urbervilles," in *Der moderne Englische Roman: Interpretationen,* ed. Horst Oppel (Berlin, 1963), 38–40.

# Henry James and the Uses of the Feminine

WILLIAM VEEDER

HENRY JAMES'S RELATION to the feminine has concerned critics at least since the publication of *The Portrait of a Lady* when the *Dial* reviewer, H. A. Huntington, called Isabel Archer "only Mr. James in domino."[1] Critical approaches both finer and more diverse than Huntington's have enabled recent scholars to analyze James's art revealingly and to ask questions important both methodologically (about the relative efficacy of psychological and cultural analyses) and evaluatively (Is James a feminist or a patriarchal force?).[2] I want to take as my starting point an insight of John Carlos Rowe.

> What makes James's identification with women so successful . . . is his tendency to transform the social psychology of women into the formal esthetics as well as the psychohistory of the author. Even as this identification marks James as singularly sympathetic to the larger social issues of feminism, it is based on James's own inevitable defense: that process by which Henry James, the Master, *uses* feminism, uses the "other sex" as part of his own literary power for the sake of engendering his own identity as Author.[3]

Rowe effectively demonstrates how James uses the feminine to defend against professional dangers—the influence of such strong predecessors as Hawthorne, and the challenge of popular women writers. I want to explore dangers more exclusively psychological and more resolutely archaic, dangers that threaten Henry James's very existence as a human being. Woman he uses here too as defense and compensation.[4]

To see James's relation to the feminine as therapeutic is of course not new. Numerous biographers and critics—most prominently Leon Edel—have read James's art in terms of the management of childhood trauma and adolescent depression. I want to go beyond previous interpretations, both in the nature and in the scope of what I claim. James's childhood, his first major masterpiece, his subsequent fiction and particularly the novels of his so-called Major Phase, and ultimately the shape of his whole career are affected profoundly by his need to represent himself through two traditional figures. What these two share is what the culture has traditionally defined as woman's essence—negation, absence, lack. The first figure is *not* gendered: the orphan. The second is woman herself, as heroine. Why should Henry James who was manifestly a male child in a family of seven persons conceive of himself—and in a sense conceive himself—as a female orphan?

I will ask this question three times: of James's childhood, when the figures of the orphan and the woman take on their enduring significance; of James's first major masterpiece, *The Portrait of a Lady,* where the female orphan as heroine functions as defense and compensation; and of the later fiction, where the pattern established in *The Portrait* is obsessively repeated and, quite amazingly, transformed finally. I in effect see James's long professional life as the acting out of a boast made early on to his family: "If I keep along here patiently I rather think I shall become a (sufficiently) great man" (Edel, 2:105). That greatness would require an interaction with gender intricate enough to transform the traditional notion of the Great Man, that greatness as an artist and a human being would require James to use and finally to transcend the figure of the female orphan—this is a drama even James's own perspicacity could not have anticipated.

## Figures of Fantasy: Defense and Compensation

With his "imagination of disaster" Henry James felt threatened from his earliest years to his final days—threatened by an intimation of absence, a sense of lack at the center of human being, a fear of castration and extermination. Danger emanated both from within his family and from the culture outside. Against each danger James defended himself by developing a compensatory fantasy.

At home young Henry felt threatened—as Edel has convincingly shown—by the lethal weakness of Henry Sr., by the smothering strength of his mother, Mary, and by the frenetic intrusiveness of his brothers.[5] How does Henry defend himself? He fantasizes a bizarre version of what Sigmund Freud called Family Romance.[6] James says of himself as a child, "I seemed to have been constantly eager to exchange my lot for that of somebody else."[7] Normally, when a child imagines himself somebody else, he imagines somebody grand, some crown prince whose real parents are the king and queen. Though young Henry James occasionally engages in such fantasies,[8] his core family romance is more bizarre.

In describing a cousin, Henry exults that "this genial girl, like her brother, was in the grand situation of having no home" (*SB,* 188). The homeless orphan: here is the ideal. In James's negative version of the family romance, parents are replaced not by monarchs but by corpses—or, rather, by absences. "I think my first childish conception of the enviable lot, formed amid these associations, was to be little fathered or mothered" (*SB*, 14). James clarifies what is idyllic about orphanhood when he explains why "cousin Albert, still another of the blest orphans" (*SB*, 120), surpasses even the genial girl, for she was encumbered by a sibling.

> If it was my habit, as I have hinted, to attribute to orphans *as* orphans a circumstantial charm, a setting necessarily more delightful than our father'd and mother'd one, so there spread about this appointed comrade [Albert], the perfection of the type, in as much as he alone was neither brother'd or sister'd, an air of possibilities that were none the less vivid for being quite indefinite. [*SB*, 120–21]

Again and again the fantasy recurs: the "rare radiance of privation" experienced by orphaned cousin Gus (*SB*, 173), "the undomesticated character at its highest" enjoyed by orphaned cousin Bob (*SB*, 188).[9] James thus idealizes a negated role, a position of lack (father *less*, mother *less*, home *less*), so that he can defend against, can in fact negate, the negating forces of experience. In thus beating reality at its own game, young Henry is taking a page from his father's book. Henry Sr. told Ralph Waldo Emerson that "he wished sometimes the lightning would strike his wife and children out of existence"—because he loved them so much, of course.[10] Henry Jr.'s core fantasy of the orphan enacts this project. He exterminates his family before they can get him.

Since Henry Jr. is most entangled emotionally with his mother, she causes him additional difficulties, which he defends against more extensively by elaborating in young adulthood the exclusionary fantasy of his childhood. When Mary writes to him in London that "your life must need this [my own] succulent, fattening element more than you know yourself" (Edel, 1:47), Henry knows about himself that he must forgo his cake and eat it too. So he gains *dozens* of pounds in London, then informs Mary that "I am as broad as I am long, as fat as a butter-tub and as red as a British *materfamilias*" (Edel, 2:343). The once skinny son has thus incorporated maternal nurturance while escaping mother. London as "a good married matron" fosters "British stoutness" (Edel, 1:295, 419). Surrounding himself with a barrier of fat—"my flesh hangs over my waistband in huge bags" (Edel, 2:343)—Henry keeps the world at distance. Obesity constitutes the physical equivalent of his family romance of exclusion.

Such a physical articulation of fantasy is something that Henry had sought since childhood.

> Our general medium of life in the situation I speak of [playing with neighbor children] was such as to make a large defensive veranda, which seems to have very stoutly and completely surrounded us, play more or less the part of a raft of rescue in too high a tide. . . . it must really have played for us, so far as its narrowness and exposure permitted, the part of a buffer-state against the wilderness immediately near, that of the empty, the unlovely, and mean. [*SB*, 37]

Again protection is imagined "stoutly," a "buffer-state." In childhood, alas, architectural buffers failed to prove stout enough, as James's lifelong friend T. S. Perry testified.

> Those unhappy [James] children fight like cats and dogs. . . . [Henry] was trying to obtain solitude in the library, with the rest of the family pounding at the door, and rushing in all the time. He so far forgot himself at one time as to try to put and lock me out of the house. It was a terrible sight, and I can assure you I pitied poor Harry, and asked him to come and stay with me. [Edel, 1:43]

Only in adulthood does the expatriate James find an adequate geographic buffer, as the Atlantic Ocean provides a supplementary moat to his wall of fat.

A second source of threat was social—the negating force of American commercial culture. "Disconnected from business we [Jameses] could only be connected with the negation of it" (*NSB*, 71). Familial negation inevitably marks the small boy. "I never dreamed of competing—a business having in it at the best, for my temper, if not for my total failure of temper, a displeasing ferocity" (*SB*, 176). The word "business" here does not mean commerce specifically, but its appearance in James's sentence underscores his lack of competitive ferocity.[11] William James's famous taunt—"*I* play with boys who curse and swear!"—is followed by lines less often quoted but singularly appropriate to Henry's sense of self-negation: "I had sadly to recognize that I didn't, that I couldn't pretend to have come to that yet. . . . It wasn't that I mightn't have been drawn to the boys in question, but that I simply wasn't qualified" (*SB*, 259, 260).

Negation is especially threatening because the small boy's chief buffer against the commercial environment—his father—seemed to him egregiously negated. "That the head of our family was *not* in business" struck the small boy as "tasteless and even humiliating" (*NSB*, 71); that his father espoused no organized religion meant that "our pewless state . . . involved, to my imagination, much the same discredit that a houseless or cookless would have done" (*SB*, 234); that Henry Sr. "cared only for virtue that was more or less ashamed of itself" (*SB*, 216) meant that he was compromised even as a moralist. Besides the obvious physical sign of lack—the amputation of his right leg—Henry James, Sr., with his "almost eccentrically home-loving habit" seemed to his son "afraid to recognize certain anxieties, fairly declining to dabble in the harshness of practical precautions or imposition" (*SB*, 72, 200).

Negation is gendered in bourgeois culture. Henry James inevitably sees himself not only as an orphan but also as a woman. Let me begin with a gender opposition that was made sometimes by James himself and has been formulated succinctly by Edel. "Downtown was the world of the money-makers that he [James] didn't know and couldn't write about. Uptown represented leisure, largely feminine (since the males were Downtown making the money), and this world was useable in his books" (1:103).[12] I want to complicate considerably this gender opposition, but first I need to foreground what is useful in it—the association of Henry James and the feminine. Virtually everything about young Henry seemed to him to bespeak woman. Take, for example, "my long fair curls," which are described early in *A Small Boy* (12). On the same page James presents an aunt featuring "long light 'front' ringlets, the fashion of the time and the capital sign of all our paternal aunts." One of these aunts is Catherine James, "whose fair hair framed her pointed smile in full and far-drooping 'front' curls" (*SB*, 40). In addition to other ladies, like a Mrs. Rogers with her "long black glossy ringlets" and a Miss Emily Mestayer "coifed in a tangle of small, fine, damp-looking short curls" (*SB*, 17, 156), there are the artistic women—various female authors "glossily ringleted" and an actress with "very tight black curls" (*SB*, 59, 108). When the small boy who grows up with the women Uptown chooses a literary vocation far removed from Downtown business, the last thing he wants to hear is that his prose is effeminate. William James thus finds a nerve when he says of Henry's early travel sketches, "the style ran a little more to *curliness* than suited the average mind" (Edel, 2:71).

Since James's adult vocation carries on his childhood associations with femininity, why does the Downtown–Uptown opposition need to be complicated? Because gender cannot be equated, finally, with either genital endowment or professional status. Indicative of James's prescience about gender is his recognition

> that scarce aught but disaster *could*, in that so unformed and unseasoned society, overtake young men who were in the least exposed. Not to have been immediately launched in business of a rigorous sort was to *be* exposed—in the absence I mean of some fairly abnormal predisposition to virtue; since it was a world so simply constituted that whatever wasn't business, or exactly an office or a "store," places in which people sat close and made money, was just simply pleasure, sought, and sought only, in places in which people got tipsy. [*SB*, 48–49]

The basic distinction here is less between man and woman than between business and pleasure. To explain why *this* distinction complicates—to the point of subversion—the Downtown–Uptown gender opposition, what I must *not* do is claim that James resists the implicit association here of pleasure and women. Indeed he insists upon the association. After establishing "the wondrous fact that ladies might live for pleasure, pleasure always, pleasure alone," Henry focuses upon his aunt Catherine who "was distinguished for nothing whatever so much as for an insatiable love of the dance; that passion in which I think of the 'good,' the best, New York society of the time as having capered and champagned itself away" (*SB*, 40). Woman is as evanescent as champagne bubbles, as transitory as waltz music. Aunt Catherine proved it by dying young.

Rather than resisting the association of the feminine with pleasure and death, James emphasizes it by implicating himself. He has opted, like woman, for pleasure over business, so he must face the music when his two principal sources of pleasure—art and Europe—prove fatal all around him. Cousin Bob

> seemed exposed, for his pleasure—if pleasure it was!—and my wonder, to every assault of experience. . . . it was all in the right key that, a few years later, he should, after "showing some talent for sculpture," have gone the way of most of the Albany youth . . . and died prematurely and pointlessly. [*SB*, 188]

"Exposed" next is "another slim shade, one of the younger and I believe quite the most hapless of those I have called the outstanding ones . . . succumbing to monstrous early trouble after having 'shown some talent' for music" (*SB*, 189). The danger inherent in an inclination to the arts is compounded by an attraction to Europe. Death is again the reward of pleasure as James catalogues the family fatalities. First, "a young collateral ancestor who died on the European tour" (*SB*, 123). Then cousin Albert, "a small New York Orestes ridden by the furies" whose "early Wanderjahre" ended as soon as he "disembarked in England. . . . He just landed and died" (*SB*, 133, 142, 143). Cousin J.J. makes it back to New York, "but he had verily performed his scant office on earth [being one of] those to whom it was given but to toy so briefly with the flowers" (*SB*, 192, 193).

Why must the Downtown–Uptown gender opposition be complicated? Because Bob, Albert, J.J., the musical cousin, and the collateral ancestor are all male. Pleasure is fatal to men as well as to women. And not merely to a few aesthetes and Anglophiles like the Jameses. Henry James understood what recent feminist scholars have insisted upon—that gender is socially produced. When his society equates business with men-life-presence and pleasure with women-death-absence, James recognizes that a puritanical capitalism is presenting as a "natural," "essential" opposition what is in fact a defense against anxiety, a reaction formation. What is most prominent for me in the prescient passage from pages 48 to 49 of *A Small Boy* is not the manifest opposition of the sexes but the barely latent anxiety underlying that opposition. "Exposed . . . exposed" intimates the menace of castration that awaits anyone who fails to "sit tight." "Exposed" was the term used with artistic Cousin Bob, yet here it appears twice with his supposed antitheses, the young men of business. No less doomed than Catherine James was her youthful bridegroom who survived her by less than two years. "It is at all events to the sound of fiddles and the popping up corks that I see even young brides, as well as young grooms . . . vanish untimely" (*SB*, 42). By turning the wedding waltz into the *danse macabre*, James is saying not so much that women die of pleasure but that anyone, everyone does.

Henry James does not resist the equation of women with pleasure and death because he sees that women do enjoy and do perish. But he insists that men also enjoy and also perish. "Business" is no more than a defense against a vulnerability endemic to human being. "Woman" as a gender construct is a social fate available to persons of either sex. *Everyone* is "feminine" because anyone can be effeminated by the negating force of mortality. The only valid opposition is between those who admit their vulnerability and those who do not. James thus subverts that basic opposition of the sexes upon which patriarchal hegemony is based, for he insists upon lack, "castration," at the very heart of commercial America. Caspar Goodwood, for example, the archetypical American entrepreneur in *The Portrait of a Lady*, becomes "quite as sick, in a different way, as [the Europeanized expatriate] Mr. Touchett"[13] once he ceases to sit tight and travels to Europe.

Henry James thus provides a compelling variation upon the insight of Claridge and Langland that "maleness exists in a relation to patriarchy as a third term of gender discourse, whose terms are woman, man, and patriarchy."[14] In James's variation, a three-term structure counterpoints patriarchy off against both those women (and men) who are capable of pleasure and are therefore seen as "feminine," effeminated, and fatal and those men (and women) who are committed to the puritanical repressiveness characteristic of business and are therefore safely "masculine" so long as they sit tight and expose nothing. To establish that the latter group is no more restricted to men than the former is to women, to establish in other words that the crucial factor is one's attitude toward pleasure rather than one's genitals or profession, Henry James reveals in two early heroines the anxiety that pleasure can generate. Mary Garland is the flower of New England womanhood in *Roderick Hudson*. She puritanically fears the allure of Europe and ventures across the sea only to try to rescue the expatriated Roderick. Mary then experiences what American business is configured to defend against. " 'I used to think . . . that if any trouble came to me I should bear it like a stoic, But that was at home, where things don't speak to us of *enjoyment* as they do here. . . . This place has destroyed every scrap of consistency that I ever possessed."[15] Isabel Archer is much more cosmopolitan than Mary, but she too is a daughter of the Puritans (as

Osmond points out contemptuously), and she too fears pleasure: "There was a terror in beginning to spend. If she touched it, it would all come out" (4:18). Isabel is explicitly referring to her inheritance here, but, as Carren Kaston points out, James is deploying unmistakably a "figure for orgasm." Kaston goes on to show persuasively how this "old and tired figure" is "revitalized by being made to echo the overall concerns of the book." Another type of revitalization is operative as well. What is old and tired about the figure of spending is that it is everywhere in the nineteenth century, but everywhere it is applied to men. Capitalist culture feared that spending too much semen in pleasurable Eros would deny men the energy necessary to succeed in the daytime—paramount—world of business.[16] That Henry James can apply an ejaculatory image to a woman indicates that anyone, everyone, in bourgeois culture is threatened with "castration," effeminization. Not the sex but the attitude toward pleasure is what matters.

This distinction is, I feel, what Joyce W. Warren is overlooking when she attacks psychological explanations of James's empathy with women. "One problem with these explanations is that James did not identify only with his female characters. To conclude that he saw himself as a woman is no more valid than to say that he saw himself as an impoverished London bookbinder."[17] But James *did* see himself as Hyacinth Robinson in *The Bostonians*—and for the same reason that he saw himself as Isabel Archer. Hyacinth too is culturally "feminine." Though he does "work" for a living, Hyacinth's trade of bookbinding indicates his inclination to literature and the arts rather than to commerce, and it prepares us for his ravishment by beauty when he at last reaches Venice. After such pleasures, death is inevitable for this surrogate James who was provided with "an office or a 'store,' places in which people sat close and made money," but who could not sit still.

More than this needs to be said, however. Henry James was far more alive to experience—more affirmative in his responses, more resilient before setbacks, more daring as an artist—than I have indicated so far. Despite the menace of death inherent in exposure to pleasure, James was committed to life—to travel, art, above all to the play of consciousness—with a quiet ferocity that was finally undaunted by the anxieties of capitalist patriarchy. Even as a small boy he believed deep down, deeper than anyone at the time could guess, that *he* was marked by presence, that he had a productive genius. His defenses were thus compensations as well, facilitations. The fantasy of the orphan freed him from domestic menace so that he could be free for achievement. But the orphan role could not produce that achievement. It was too thoroughly negative, negated. For James to become "a (sufficiently) great man," he had to find a second role that would make practicable the freedom garnered by the fantasy of orphanhood. Fortunately, he hadn't far to look.

Especially in America, the figure of Woman had positive as well as negative aspects. Freedom and daring of mind (and even of action) characterized the American girl long before she debuted in James's fiction. In the society around him, in other words, young Henry James saw not only active male figures who could never express his self but also active female figures who could.[18] Woman's capacity to resist anxiety and embrace pleasure is dramatized by Mary Garland, who goes beyond her puritan fear of "enjoyment" in Europe and exclaims, "but even if I must myself say something sinful I love it!" Henry James particularly needed a compensatory affiliation with the figure of woman as heroine because he had to defend against one additional threat—from the "feminine" nature of his own sexuality.

Henry's erotic inclinations toward William have been suggested by various biographers.[19] If the younger brother was "in love with" the older, what are the causes and the effects of this emotion? Causation in Henry's case seems virtually paradigmatic of one type of homosexual object choice defined by Freud: A son prevented—by paternal ineffectuality and maternal oversolicitude—from accomplishing the oedipal transfer from mother to father seeks men for two reasons. On the one hand, his failure to bond with father means that the boy remains joined to mother and thus "feminine" sexually. He desires what she desires: men. The most dominating male presence in Henry's immediate view was the dynamic William. On the other hand, the son who has failed to affiliate with the father lacks a role model and thus seeks perpetually a male figure to incorporate as the ego ideal that would solidify his conception of himself as masculine. Again William stands forth inescapably. What complicates the paradigm, of course, is that the male chosen by Henry abides *within the family.* To one taboo—homosexuality—is thus added another: incest. A young man whose orphan fantasy shows him already wary of all relationships will of course repress such desires, but he must deal with the narcissism involved in loving someone who is both of his sex and in his family. If solipsism is obviously the danger of Henry's family romance of negation—obliterating everyone but himself—the addition of narcissistic object choice only worsens matters.

How long Henry could have gone on managing these conflicting forces becomes suddenly moot in 1878. William James, at the age of thirty-seven, announces his decision to wed Alice Gibbens. In the same year, 1878, Henry James begins to write novels about heroines instead of about heroes.[20] If passive Henry, already "feminine" in his self-perceived negation, functions as "the girl" in his unconscious homosexual bond with active William, he becomes the girl rejected, the woman scorned, when William weds. Henry compensates by projecting his female self outward: He enacts through his fiction what no longer works as private fantasy. Moreover, the change in Henry's narrative pattern coincides with the other major change of 1878. His enormous gain in weight occurs precisely at this time, the fall and winter of 1878–79. Henry is using body as well as art to buffer himself against the shock of William's rejection. Body could never compensate enough, however. James must tell himself a story—over and over. How he uses fiction-as-fantasy to enact the feminine orphan we can see in his first major masterpiece.

## *The Portrait of a Lad(d)y*

When Henry James was eight years old, he endured in the studio of Matthew Brady a portrait session described, like so much in *A Small Boy,* in terms of negation. "Sharp again is my sense of not being so adequately dressed as I should have taken thought for had I foreseen my exposure" (87). Again the threat of "exposure," emphasized this time by the photography pun. Henry James never exposed himself in fiction so vulnerably as he did in Brady's head brace.

*The Portrait of a Lady* contains much autobiographical data,[21] but it also contains traps for any unwary equator of life and art. Edel in his discussion of cousin Minny Temple's tuberculosis maintains that "she became, nine years after her death, the heroine of *The Portrait of a Lady*" (1:331). There is indeed a death from tuberculosis in *The Portrait,* but the victim is Ralph Touchett. Isabel Archer evinces traits of Minny, as she does of Henry James, but Isabel is *not* Minny, any more than she *is* Henry. The small boy who grew up too wary of exposure to entrust himself to any one personal relationship became a novelist whose distaste for "the terrible fluidity of revelation"[22] precluded one-to-one correspondence with any character. Studying *The Portrait* as autobiography is useful precisely because it requires us to see how diverse James's self-representation is, how many characters reflect him. His "problem [of how] to live in England, and yet not be of it" (35) challenges Daniel Touchett; his awareness that parents attempt to atone through their children for their own lives having "failed so dreadfully" (503) is dramatized with Pansy; the "selfishness" inherent in "the preference for a single life" (282) marks Gilbert Osmond; and the Jamesian fear of "exposure" is expressed through three women. Isabel feels "the fear of exposing—not her ignorance; for that she cared comparatively little—but her possible grossness of perception" (243); Lydia Touchett parodies James's fussiness about his health when she affirms "her wisdom in not exposing herself to the English climate" (35); and Pansy's sense of the inadequacy of her dress recalls James's anxiety at Matthew Brady's as she asks Merle, "why should I expose it beside your beautiful things?" (249).

James's self-portrayal in *The Portrait* achieves coherence not because of any one-to-one correspondence with life but because of the consistency with which he represents three of the things we saw in *A Small Boy*—the negating threat of mortality, the realization that men as well as women are marked by emasculation and lack, and the Jamesian defenses against and compensations for such a situation. Attention to these essential matters will, I hope, enable us both to gain new insight into a complicated novel and to confront the notoriously difficult end of *The Portrait* in a way that will help account for—though by no means explain away—its difficulties in terms of James's core fantasy of negation.

*The Portrait* opens with the threat of mortality articulated in terms of transience. By its very placement in midafternoon, the "ceremony" of tea (5) becomes part of, rather than a buffer against, the flux of time. "The shadows . . . long upon the smooth, dense turf . . . lengthened slowly" (5). Inexorably. By the time Isabel awaits the death of the tea ceremony's host, "the shadows [had] deepened" (160). She has just met Madame Merle whose introduction of Gilbert Osmond will darken life more. "Then the shadows began to gather; it was as if Osmond deliberately, almost malignantly, had put the lights out one by one" (392). Isabel's final scene in *The Portrait* begins amid "shadows [that] were long upon the acres of turf" (539) and ends in "darkness" (544). The flux of time is reflected in transient life styles. As children, Ned, Ralph, Isabel, Merle, Gemini, and Gilbert were all whisked—like the James children—back and forth across the Atlantic and around the Continent. As adults, Lydia, Merle, and Ned continue their restless search for pleasure, while Henrietta roves professionally, Caspar and Warburton pursue Isabel, and Ralph flees death. James's international theme derives not simply from his knowledge of the expatriate community in Europe. Expatriation represents for him the human condition of transience.

This transience marks characters as negated from the opening of *The Portrait*. Daniel Touchett "was not likely to displace himself" (7); Ralph "was not very firm on his legs" (8). That James is representing not physical invalidism but an ineluctable human vulnerability is established by the fact that the robust Lord Warburton is sick too. "He is sick of life" (10). Warburton's negation is political, for "he doesn't take himself seriously . . . and he doesn't know what to believe in. . . . [He] can neither abolish himself as a nuisance nor maintain himself as an institution" (66, 67). Warburton admits, "I don't approve of myself in the least" (119). That political negation constitutes, in effect, the condition of "woman" is confirmed when Warburton goes on to equate himself, however ironically, with his powerless sister: "We neither of us have any position to speak of" (120). Association with another powerless woman is prepared for in the first scene. Here Warburton wears "a hat which looked too big for him" (7–8); later Pansy Osmond will wear a "hat [which] always seemed too big for her" (326). That "she does not really fill out the part" (340) is equally true of Warburton, as Isabel confirms: "I said she [Pansy] was limited. And so she is. And so is Lord Warburton" (380).

Emasculate men inhabit the condition of the "feminine" in the opening description of the tea drinkers. "They were not of the sex which is supposed to furnish the regular votaries of the ceremony" (5). In the face of woman's traditional definition as the nonmale, men here in *The Portrait* are defined as the nonfemale—*at the very moment that the females are marked as absent.* Lydia, who should preside over the tea ceremony, is not here; Isabel, who could substitute for her, has not yet arrived on the lawn. To be the negative of the absent does not give presence to men. " 'A woman, perhaps, can get on. . . . But the men . . . what do they make of it over here? I don't envy them, trying to arrange themselves. Look at poor Ralph Touchett. . . . "An American who lives in Europe." That signifies absolutely nothing' " (181–82). Negated like Ralph who " 'does nothing' " (36) are his servant, who " 'is good for nothing; he is always looking out the window' " (524); Mr. Luce, who "was the most unoccupied man in Europe, for he not only had no duties, but he had no pleasures" (196); and Ned Rosier, who " 'can't go home and be a shopkeeper . . . can't be a doctor . . . can't be a clergyman . . . can't be a lawyer' " (199–200).

To such negation a Gilded Age businessman might react: "What do you expect? Of course men who don't work become dysfunctional." But Henry James, as we have seen, resists this reaction formation. Everyone is negated. Warburton and Goodwood are men of the world, actively engaged in politics and industry. Yet we have seen that Caspar " 'is as sick, in his way, as Mr. Touchett' " and that Warburton is "sick" too. At stake is not what you do but what doing means. As soon as you expose yourself to the vast life outside any vocation's narrow confines, you enter the relays of mortality. Moreover, and finally more important, if business is no better off than leisure in terms of health, leisure is not superior morally. What James found distasteful about business—its competitive ferocity, its determination to appropriate, acquire—is equally true of leisure. Predation is coeval with living. Osmond confines Isabel as tightly as Warburton and Goodwood would. Her mistake is not in rejecting the ostensibly active men but in accepting the apparently passive one. Essential to the acquisitive *I* is the appropriating *eye*. To understand what *The Portrait* is saying about negation, in other words, we must go beyond profession to perception itself.

" 'You look at things in a way that could make everything wrong' " (169). This sounds like a fair criticism of Gilbert Osmond, but the "you" is Ralph Touchett.[23] It could be anyone in *The Portrait,* for endemic to seeing is desiring. Reification, that paradigm motion by which capitalism reduces all value to exchange value, is the staple of the leisured characters in the novel. Turning persons into objects is unmistakable with Osmond, who defines Isabel as "a young lady who had qualified herself to figure in his collection of choice objects" (279), but it also characterizes Ralph, who initially sees Isabel as " 'a Titian, by the post, to hang on my wall' " (59). Moreover, gender is not a factor here. Long before Osmond asks Merle, " 'what do you want to do with her' " (222), Ralph asks Lydia, " 'what do you mean to do with her . . . what do you mean to do with her . . . what do you mean to do with her . . . what [do] you intend to do with her?' " (39, 41). Though Ralph's mother responds properly—" 'Do with her? You talk as if she were a yard of calico' " (41)—Lydia is already tarred with her own brush. " 'For a woman of my age there is no more becoming ornament than an attractive niece' " (40). That Isabel is an object for women as well as for men is evident when Ralph says,

> "I shall have the entertainment of seeing what a young lady does who won't marry Lord Warburton."
> "That is what your mother counts upon too," said Isabel.
> "Ah, there will be plenty of spectators!" [138–39]

The "gaze" is not exclusively masculine in *The Portrait.* When Merle says to Isabel, " 'I want to see what life makes of you' " (174), she foresees direct entertainment for Osmond and indirect profit for herself. Both sexes are unable *not* to treat human beings as objects because both sexes sense their own essential reification. Without a positive sense of one's own subjectivity, one cannot value the other as subject, as sacredly *other.* Being essentially negated is what expatriation represents for both sexes. " 'If we are not good Americans we are certainly poor Europeans; we have no natural place here' " (181).

Isabel attempts to maintain traditional sex divisions when she asserts that "I am not an adventurous spirit. Women are not like men" (140). But in fact no one in *The Portrait* is "like men." Everyone is "woman" because no one is truly "adventurous."[24] No one can get beyond the " 'mere spectatorship' " (137) that marks Ralph and mars Osmond. Gilbert's litany—" 'I have neither fortune, nor fame, nor extrinsic advantages of any kind'" (287)—is echoed by Merle. "'What have I got? Neither husband, nor child, nor fortune, nor position, nor the traces of a beauty which I never had'" (184). Distinctions of sex vanish in a wash of negatives as relentless in *The Portrait* as in *A Small Boy*.

> "I never do anything," said this young lady [124]. . . . "I don't come up to the mark" [136]. . . . "No; the best part is gone, and gone for nothing" [184]. . . . "What have my talents brought me? Nothing but the need of using them still" [185]. . . . Nothing tender, nothing sympathetic . . . no wind-sown blossom, no familiar moss [204]. . . . "I teach nothing" [212]. . . . He seemed to intimate that nothing was of much consequence [236]. . . . "there is nothing, nothing, nothing" [251]. . . . "I have nothing on earth to do" [266]. . . . "He does nothing. But he doesn't like me" [450]. . . . "Do you mean that without my *bibelots* I am nothing?" [486]. . . . "It has not been a successful life" [525].

The spirit that prompted James's core fantasy prompts Ralph Touchett to say, "I think I am glad to leave people" (530).

Having defended against the threat of extirpation by engaging as a small boy in the fantasy of orphanhood, James enacts this fantasy as an adult by filling *The Portrait* with orphans. In addition to Warburton who "had lost both parents" (64) and Henrietta who is "without parents and without property" (49), there is Ned whose mother is never mentioned and whose "father was dead and his *bonne* was dismissed" (198), Merle who never refers to her mother and praises her father in the past tense (162), and Gilbert and Gemini whose "mother had died three years after the Countess's marriage, the father having died long before" (258–59).[25] It is left to Isabel to articulate that attractive potential of orphanhood that James fantasized about in his family romance. She achieves the status of James's chief autobiographical resource in *The Portrait* because she knows the *attraction* to negation, which the other characters cannot ever know because they are defined absolutely *as* negated. Isabel says, "'I belong quite to the independent class. I have neither father nor mother'" (149).

The freedom of orphanhood is associated in *The Portrait* with another obsession of *A Small Boy*, as Isabel goes on to say, "'I am poor.'" She experiences the Jamesian opposition between business, which necessitates restrictions, and pleasure, which promises liberation. This opposition originates in her life where it did in Henry's own. Her father too exhibits "occasional incoherency of conduct" (32). On the one hand, Isabel represents that isolation from the world of money that marked the children of Henry James, Sr. Since business is "everything" in America, Isabel, like Henry James, Jr., is inevitably characterized by "nothing."

> Isabel of course knew nothing about bills. . . . "I don't know anything about money." . . . "she has nothing but the crumbs of that feast [her father's spending of his capital] to live on, and she doesn't really know how meagre they are." [22, 171]

Economic naiveté is only one aspect of Isabel's psychic economy, however, because she functions in *The Portrait* as more than a replication of Henry James. She is also the wish fulfillment that assures him compensation. Isabel is thus endowed with a childhood free of the anxiety over paternal incoherence and financial uncertainty that scarred Henry's own youth. "If he [Mr. Archer] had been troubled about money matters, nothing ever disturbed their [his children's] irreflective consciousness of many possessions" (32). Wish fulfillment then persists into adulthood. Isabel avoids the financial anxieties that James knew in his twenties and early thirties because *The Portrait* presents—apparently—a fairytale solution to such anxieties. First a good witch whisks Isabel away to Henry's cherished refuge, England. Then an ideal father surrogate absolves her of all financial worry. Isabel has achieved material independence without having to grub for it in business.

What makes the ending of *The Portrait* so difficult is that wish fulfillment proves finally incompatible with fairytale. If James were writing a storybook romance, the now rich princess would marry her Prince Charming and live happily ever after. Instead, Isabel marries disastrously. To understand how such an anti-fairytale can function compensatorily as a wish fulfillment, we must understand why James's protagonist chooses a Prince Uncharming. " 'I am marrying a nonentity. . . . a person who has none of Lord Warburton's great advantages—no property, no title, no honours, no houses, nor lands, nor position, nor reputation, nor brilliant belongings of any sort. It is the total absence of all these things that pleases me' " (305, 321). Part of the attraction here is Isabel's power to launch Gilbert's boat, the "maternal" power to *make* him, which many critics have noticed. But the words " 'nonentity' " and " 'absence' " and all the negatives indicate that more is involved—or, rather, less.

Osmond is for Isabel the quintessence of absence, the essential nullity. And why would that attract her? "Of all liberties, the one she herself found sweetest was the liberty to forget" (208). Here is where the freedom of the orphan leads ultimately: not to action but to nada. James knows well the limitations of his family romance of extirpation. It is at best a local, provisional solution because the ultimate threat is not external, nor familial or even social, but internal. What is mortal about us is our own mortality; we will die even if no one kills us. Thus, for a person obsessed with vulnerability, the only way to deal with the fear of being killed is to kill it.

Which means to kill the self. In the animal world, the dog bites the wounded paw that is wounding him; in the human world, thanataphobia leads to suicide. Isabel Archer expresses Henry James's desire to escape from suffering altogether. Gilbert Osmond constitutes the ultimate nada. He has expressly defined his life to Isabel as a negative surrender. " 'Not to worry—not to strive nor struggle. To resign myself' " (245). That these words do not in fact characterize competitive, emulous Gilbert is irrelevant to Isabel's charmed reception of his words. What Gilbert offers her is what she wants, negation. And she is willing to pay a high price for it. "It was *not* that, however, his objecting to her opinions; that was *nothing*. She had *no* opinions—*none* that she would *not* have been eager to sacrifice in the satisfaction of feeling herself loved" (395; my italics).

Thus, when we see Isabel mastered by negativity after her marriage—"there was nothing to gape at, nothing to criticize, nothing even to admire" (362)—we must not jump to the melodramatic conclusion which Ned reaches and which Isabel tries to persuade herself of: that this is all Osmond's doing. Of course, he has sought a certain type of "nothing" in his wife. But Isabel too has sought "nothing." The tragedy, almost the comedy, is that they have not meant the same thing by nothing. Negatives saturate the portrait of Isabel after her marriage:

> she appeared now to think there was nothing worth people's either differing about or agreeing upon [363]. . . . she was resolved to assume nothing. . . . she would recognize nothing [387]. . . . she answered nothing. . . . She answered nothing [389]. . . . Nothing was a pleasure to her now [400]. . . . "I have heard nothing of it." . . . Isabel could say nothing more; she understood nothing [489]. . . . "I have guessed nothing. . . . I don't know what you mean" [499]. . . . "I don't know why you say such things! I don't know what you know" [515]. . . . Nothing seemed of use to her to-day [516]. . . . "She asked nothing" [517]

We would succumb to the temptation to blame Gilbert for Isabel's negation if we were to ignore the fact that the desolating negatives that proliferate after her marriage derive not simply from that marriage but from the years of her life before it. Isabel has always been afraid—of knowing.

> "I don't know—I can't judge" [18]. . . . "I don't know what you are trying to fasten upon me, for I am not in the least an adventurous spirit. Women are not like men" [140]. . . . "She doesn't know what to think about the matter at all" [193]. . . . "I don't want to know anything more—I know too much already" [237]. . . . "I would rather hear nothing that Pansy may not!" [329]

Fear of knowledge involves what James fears most—exposure. "A large fortune means freedom, and I am afraid of that. . . . I am not sure that it's not a greater happiness to be powerless" (206). In expressing her specific fear about inherited wealth, Isabel is giving voice to the larger fear and the larger issue of freedom itself, the orphan's legacy. It necessitates exposure. It flaunts those very risks against which James's virtually pathological sense of vulnerability defends. Gilbert Osmond as negation is the ultimate defense against and compensation for the negating forces of experience.

He is also more. He is compensation for the terrible year of 1878. To indulge through *The Portrait* his homoerotic love for William, Henry must do more than switch from male to female protagonists and invest Isabel with aspects of himself. He must also project aspects of William onto Gilbert. This is no untoward endeavor, for in his last big novel, *The American* (1877), Henry had already portrayed unflattering aspects of his elder brother, both in the coldness of the elder Bellegarde and (as William himself recognized) in the hypercritical morbidity of the little American tourist, Rev. Babcock.[26] The recurrence of these features in Osmond is not therefore surprising. What is startling is how much more obvious and extensive the portrait of William becomes by 1881.

> He was a man of forty, with a well-shaped head, upon which the hair, still dense but prematurely grizzled, had been cropped close. He had a thin, delicate, sharply cut face, of which the only fault was that it looked too pointed; an appearance of which the shape of his beard contributed not a little. [211]

Born in 1842, William James is on the threshold of "forty" in 1881. Although his hair would not grizzle until later, the other features of Isabel/Henry's portrait of Gilbert are accurate enough. The well-shaped head; the hair cropped close; the face thin, delicate, and sharply cut; its pointed quality emphasized by the beard: these features are all suggested in William's self-portrait reproduced by Feinstein (246). In body type, William shares Gilbert's "light smooth slenderness of structure" (242). The intellectual acuity of each man is signaled in "his luminous intelligent eye" (211). And temperamentally, William as well as Gilbert "was certainly fastidious and critical" (242). Isabel adds to her portrait that "he was *probably* irritable" (242; my italics) because she does not know *yet* what her creator had already suffered from for years—how punishingly irritable William's fastidiously critical sensibility could be. What the younger brother said about the elder in the very year of the composition of *The Portrait*—"he takes himself and his nerves and his physical condition too seriously" (Edel, 2:419)—is said about Osmond in the novel: " 'He takes himself so seriously' " (319).

Probably most aggressive is Henry's implication of William in one other trait conferred upon Osmond. " 'In itself your little picture is very good. . . . But as the only thing you do it's so little' " (224). Both William and Gilbert are amateur painters of some talent. By denying to Gilbert all true creative genius, Henry can take revenge upon the artistic and scholastic superiority that William flaunted throughout their school years. The genius evident in *The Portrait* allows Henry to take the high ground here. And high ground is essential for wish fulfillment. As the woman scorned by William, Henry expresses through Isabel a double triumph. Her marriage with Osmond is the realization of Henry's courtship of William, while the public revelation of Osmond's marital failure constitutes Henry's revenge upon the one who had failed him by marrying another.

More than such nastiness is involved, however. The year 1878 confirmed Henry James in renunciation: There would be no more intimate relationships. For *The Portrait* to function as truly compensatory wish fulfillment, James must handle not only Isabel's marriage to and rupture with Osmond but also her days afterward. She must walk the narrow line between two types of negation presented in the novel. She must avoid the deadening lovelessness of Gilbert, Merle, and Lydia, who end up cut off from life; yet she must not succumb to the deadening self-effacement inherent in unions like Warburton's with " 'Lady Flora, or Lady Felicia—something of that sort' " (526). To effect the ultimate wish fulfillment, James returns Caspar Goodwood to the stage of Gardencourt.

For all his phallic puissance, Caspar too is marked by lack. " 'There *is* nothing left for Mr. Goodwood.' . . . The future had nothing for him. . . . He was hopeless, he was helpless, he was superfluous. . . . 'I have nothing else to do,' . . . 'I can't understand, I can't penetrate you' " (464, 467, 468, 471). Caspar, " 'quite as sick, in a different way, as Mr. Touchett' " and Lord Warburton, has not learned *The Portrait*'s lesson about negation. He holds to patriarchal stereotypes that credit the male with presence and reduce the woman to absence. Having said early on that " 'an unmarried woman—a girl of your age—is not independent. There are all sorts of things she cannot do' " (149), Caspar continues at the end to give the negative constructions to Isabel and now bestows the positive on himself. " 'You don't know where to turn. Now it is that I want you to think of me. . . . You don't know where to turn; turn to me!' " (542, 543). What Caspar offers Isabel is a future not of sexual liberation but of perpetuated inequality. Freedom is not the watchword here, because the absence of any truly egalitarian viewpoint characterizes Caspar's empty rhetoric. He emphasizes his paternalism by incorporating Isabel into that exchange of women which Lévi-Strauss defines as the origin of patriarchy—" 'he [Ralph] left you to my care' " (541). Caspar for his sins then becomes the butt of something close to outright sarcasm from the Jamesian narrator: " 'my care,' said Goodwood, as if he were making a great point" (541).

Freedom abides finally for the adult Isabel where it did for the orphan Henry: not in relationships but in isolation. What is usually said about Isabel's final state is that "she has gone back to her husband." In fact, *The Portrait* ends not with Isabel having gone back to her husband but with her *going* back. By setting the last scene of the novel on the morning of Isabel's departure from England—rather than, say, on the next day when she would already have reached Rome—James leaves his protagonist suspended between departure and arrival, poised between separation and commitment. Isabel is neither with the pair who represent the bondage of advocated adultery—Caspar and Henrietta—nor with the pair who represent the bondage of conventional domesticity—Gilbert and Pansy. Isabel is alone yet not solipsistic, neither exposed nor dead. Her train ride is a timeless suspension. Like the figures on Keats's Grecian Urn, Isabel is preserved in midmotion: ". . . do not grieve; / She cannot fade . . . forever young; / All breathing human passion far above" (18–19, 27–28).

> To cease utterly, to give it all up and not know anything more—this idea was as sweet as the vision of a cool bath in a marble tank, in a darkened chamber, in a hot land. She had moments, indeed, in her journey from Rome, which were almost as good as being dead. She sat in her corner, so motionless, so passive, simply with the sense of being carried, so detached from hope and regret, that if her spirit was haunted with sudden pictures, it might have been the spirit disembarrassed of the flesh. There was nothing to regret now—that was all over. [516]

Immediately a fact must be faced: This passage presents Isabel's emotions on the ride *to*—not *from*—England. If withdrawal represents James's ultimate ideal, why is there no rearticulation of Isabel's emotion on the ultimate ride—the one *back* to Italy?[27] Any answer to this question must confront Ralph Touchett's intervening admonition to Isabel: "life is better; for in life there is love. Death is good—but there is no love" (530). The power of these lines seems to me incontestable. At issue is not whether Ralph speaks for Henry James here but whether he says all that is on James's mind. One possibility is that he does, that James finally sides unilaterally with life and allows Ralph's words to redeem Isabel from the death-in-life represented by the tank image. Another possibility is that James must have things both ways.

The tank image represents what Sigmund Freud would later call the Death Drive,[28] the organism's determination to return to the condition of nonexistence. Suicide cannot be countenanced as the resolution of either James's novel or his family romance. He shares Ralph's belief in life. What is the fantasy of the feminine orphan but a way to stay alive? Thus James's lifelong dilemma is Isabel's now: how to love and yet maintain enough distance to escape the exposure inevitable with intimacy; how to remain in life but not of it. The ending of *The Portrait* allows James, I believe, to have both life and isolation. Ralph's words and Isabel's return to Pansy and to marriage are James's pledge to life. But this pledge he does not require himself to honor. Isabel need never reach Italy—life—*in this narrative.* James get both the pleasure of his good intentions and the pleasure of fantasized isolation. His formal artistry assures both that Isabel's train will never arrive and that her acts of commitment to relationships will suffice as a rejection of suicide. Like Ralph, she can do without the people, yet unlike Ralph she is saved from the death feared by Henry James and us all.

## Teleology and Transformation

To chart in detail the recurrence and eventual transformation of James's wish-fulfillment figures after *The Portrait* is a task too extensive for the pages remaining to me. I can, however, suggest this crucial development—suggest a shape to his career and a congruent interpretation to his late fiction—by drawing again upon Carren Kaston and Leon Edel.

Readers for generations have been troubled by the ending of *The Portrait* (and *The Ambassadors*), the renunciation practiced by Isabel (and Strether). Though Kaston does not of course discuss these endings in light of James's negating fantasy of the feminine orphan, she does discuss them in terms of renunciation. Her approach is daringly teleological. *The Golden Bowl* is the climactic achievement of James's career because Maggie Verver constitutes a new order of protagonist. Kaston, fully aware of the dangers of teleological argument, grounds herself in a developmental view articulated by James himself in his preface to *The Ambassadors.*

> My poor friend [Strether] . . . would have . . . imagination galore. . . . [But] this personage of course, so enriched, wouldn't give me, for his type, imagination in *predominance*. . . . So particular a luxury—some occasion, that is, for study of the high gift of *supreme* command of a case or of a career—would still doubtless come on the day I should be ready to pay for it; and till then it might, as from far back, remain hung up well in view and just out of reach. [4–5]

The two types of imagination distinguished by James here—in "galore" and in "*predominance*"—are deployed by Kaston evaluatively. "In light of James's desire for 'imagination in *predominance*,' Maggie's ability to fuse consciousness with material presence and profit provides a standard against which to see James's other major characters implicitly ranged as they retreat from or renounce material experience" (10). Characters who do not get beyond imagination galore remain actors in some other character's drama and thus remain immaturely part of "the melodrama of loss and withdrawal" (14).

| | | | |
|---|---|---|---|
| Imagination galore | Character as actor | as immature | in melodrama |
| Imagination *predominant* | Character as author | as adult | in high art |

Teleology becomes explicit in James's passage when he speaks of "*supreme* command" coming "on the day I should be ready . . . for it." Hope for the dawning of such a day is warranted for Kaston by James's career-long awareness of the limitations of renunciation: "James spends so much energy making the suffering appear supererogatory, willful, or perversely gratifying" (16). The new day finally dawns with "*The Golden Bowl*—in which the dialectic of mastery and subordination is superceded" (1). Maggie achieves, for Kaston, the feminist ideal of maturity, "that fusing of consciousness with presence [which] will bring them [Jamesian characters] back into the world to live out, with those they no longer need to renounce, reciprocally satisfying compositions of experience" (14).

Kaston's argument is powerful for several reasons. She suggests coherence to a career in which certain themes and situations and images recur so compulsively that James must be attempting again and yet again to resolve a dilemma basic to his being. Moreover, Kaston articulates many readers' sense that *The Golden Bowl* does indeed constitute a special achievement—one beyond simply being James's *best* novel. Despite the admirable daring, energy, and insightfulness of Kaston's argument, however, there is work remaining to be done—in four areas. Kaston discusses teleology without speculating on causation. Then, regarding the actual teleology of James's career, Kaston moves from *The Ambassadors* and *The Golden Bowl* without accounting for the intervening, vexing presence of *The Wings of the Dove*. Also, her account of *The Golden Bowl* itself—and thus the specific teleology she envisions—seems problematic to me in various ways. More generally, and more important, Kaston's teleology does not explain *why* James's new day dawns at last, *how* he manages to move from Isabel/Strether to Maggie Verver.

Kaston cannot include causation in her speculations about development because she locates the problem of renunciation at the level of the character, whereas it originates, I believe, at the level of the author.[29] The renunciation enacted in the narration is reenacted twice within James himself—on the conscious level where he avoids enduring sexual union and chooses an expatriate life; and on the unconscious level where he lives through the fantasy of the feminine orphan. Thus the ideal of "*supreme* command of a case or of a career" entails supreme command of the ultimate case, James's own career. Command would consist of sustaining that sense of the limitations of renunciation which surfaces in every important work of James but which shapes unambiguously the end of no work before *The Wings of the*

*Dove*. In other words, James must come to see steadily and fully the archaic quality of his core fantasy of rejection, the regressive immaturity of his use of the feminine orphan.

To explain how I see James maturing to "*supreme* command," I will begin with Edel's interpretation of the career between 1895 and 1903, between the trauma of the Theater Phase and the beginning of the Major Phase. James in Edel's view responds to humiliation by regressing to childhood. He reenacts his sense of himself as abused child by dramatizing the abuse of young protagonists who proceed in age from the child Morgan Moreen of "The Pupil," to Maisie Farange who reaches puberty by the end of *What Maisie Knew,* to Nanda Brookingham who passes from adolescence to young womanhood in *The Awkward Age.* (Edel could have added Fleda Vetch who embodies the next stage of womanhood beyond Nanda's, though *The Spoils of Poynton* appears two years before *The Awkward Age* [1899]). The therapeutic process of this "working through" of trauma enables James to finally close his wound, close the Therapy Phase, and resume adult concerns with Lambert Strether and the successor protagonists of the Major Phase.

Persuasive about Edel's account is the model of healing he provides: The successive ages of the young protagonists show James effecting self-therapy in the very decade that Sigmund Freud was engaged in his own epoch-making course of self-analysis. Edel thus points us toward an explanation of the developmental process that was lacking in Kaston's teleological perspective—a way of understanding *how* James could move to supreme command. Edel does not, however, actually provide such an explanation—for two reasons. In terms of James's psychology, a more complicated explanatory mechanism is needed; in terms of James's career, an extension of the Therapy Phase.

Psychologically, James is doing more than simply empathizing self-pityingly with beset children. He is exemplifying a truism of psychoanalysis: The more dire the threat, the more prominent the defense. At the darkest moment of James's life, darker even than the perfidious year of 1878, the feminine orphan takes center stage. This figure, let me remind my readers, derives causally from a two-part sequence in *A Small Boy.* Young Henry feels so beset—so already orphaned psychologically due to parental dereliction—that he fantasizes about being an orphan literally. He is then free to fantasize himself a feminine orphan capable of dealing, however renunciatorily, with the world. The narratives of the Therapy Phase enact both parts of this sequence.

Morgan-Maisie-Nanda dramatize why James felt orphaned psychologically. They experience abandonment, not because of parental death but because of parental dereliction and dysfunction. Morgan is sold to his tutor by his mother in order to augment the family's faltering finances; Maisie is shuttlecocked among parent surrogates to facilitate parental philandering; and Nanda is shuffled off for both the financial and the sexual convenience of her mother. Such are the parents who prompt James's family romance of extirpation. How he takes pleasure from the ensuing fantasy of the feminine orphan becomes clear in the final states of Maisie, Nanda, and Fleda. All three protagonists end, like Isabel Archer, on journeys that ensure psychological distance from alternatives unacceptable to their author. Maisie is safely at sea between France where sexuality has arrived with puberty and England where she will have to begin functioning as an adult; Nanda is set to retreat to the countryside where Mr. Longdon will provide an alternative to both a home life that has become impossible and a future that would require her to assume responsibility for herself; Fleda reenacts Isabel's train ride most exactly, for she ends en route, poised on a railway platform between the embers of the Poynton past and the uncertainty of the future. In each case, the protagonist is safely removed from a male whose intense sexual presence has proved as enticingly threatening as Caspar's did to Isabel. Sir Claude, Vanderbank, and Owen *must* be things of the past if James's wish fulfillment of isolation is to be satisfied.

James's Therapy Phase extends, I believe, beyond *The Awkward Age*. The lineage Morgan-Maisie-Nanda-Fleda continues on to Lambert Strether. "Working through" involves bringing the protagonist surrogates up through middle age to James's present situation. Strether resembles his immediate predecessors in important ways because the similarities that Kaston and many other readers have seen between him and Isabel are in fact similarities shared among all the feminine orphans. Strether is an "orphan" since he is bereft of living relations; he is "feminine" culturally in his isolation from business and his devotion to literature. (His business counterpart, Waymarch, resembles Caspar Goodwood in that he too becomes vulnerable once he ceases to sit close and is "exposed" to the pleasures of travel and Europe.) Most of all, Strether, like Isabel and his immediate predecessors, ends poised for flight. Between two worlds—one dead, the other not required to be born—he is now safely beyond the Eros of Marie/ Maria and yet still safely distant from a presence as indomitable as Osmond's. The negation inherent in renunciation is articulated in Strether's famous statement of nonpurpose which constitutes the ideal of the feminine orphan. " 'Not, out of the whole affair, to have gotten anything for myself' " (12.5).

Strether is, however, different in one important way from his immediate predecessors. Feminine though he is in gender, he is male in sex. Strether can thus constitute, as Maisie-Nanda-Fleda cannot, the end of the Therapy Phase. This phase began with a male protagonist. Morgan succumbed to experience because James at the beginning of his therapy was too devastated to imagine any pleasure but the fantasy of completely escaping from and thus thoroughly spiting a world grossly unappreciative of its small boys. Morgan dies of James's self-pity. Healing begins when James can appropriate through the *female* orphan enough energy and resilience to survive the necessary stages of maturation. The male orphan then reappears as Strether when healing is sufficiently advanced that James can survive the situation from which his regressive flight took off, the threshold of old age. What *The Ambassadors* announces as maturity's project—and thus as the antidote to the orphan ideal of getting nothing—is the famous "live, live, live." Strether, like John the Baptist, can announce what he cannot enact because he brings James up to the point where living maturely is possible in the Master Phase. The question is what living, what mastery, entails.

*The Wings of the Dove* is the hinge moment in James's career. For the first time he sustains to the end of a major work the reservations about renunciation that have surfaced throughout his fiction.[30] James accomplishes this by presenting *two* feminine orphans. Through doomed Milly Theale, James continues to indulge in those pleasures of renunciation that were provided by Morgan and his beset brethren. James is thus assured enough wish fulfillment that he can for the first time face—and face down—his need for it. Merton Densher is positioned at the end of the novel as Isabel-Maisie-Nanda-Fleda-Strether were: in between. He abides safely between death (Milly) and life (Kate). What is new about *The Wings* is that James unsparingly lays bare the self-serving convenience, the immaturity and self-deception and solipsism, of his cherished position of negated safety. Since my interpretation of Densher differs severely from the critical consensus that he is "redeemed" by Milly's transforming love,[31] I will—however briefly—examine his final scene.

The word "denture," meaning false teeth, was sufficiently current in late-Victorian England that it appeared with this signification in the popular *Pall Mall Gazette* in 1891.[32] In 1902 Henry James names his male protagonist "Densher" because Merton depicts the toothlessness that James recognizes in renunciation. Densher can neither unite with woman nor acknowledge what rejecting her means. Having passively followed Kate's lead throughout the novel, he manages now to make two decisions that preclude further activity. He falls in love with Milly as soon as she is safely dead. Then he disposes of Kate by offering her a choice that is no choice, since she can, he knows, decide only one way. Densher resembles Strether in that he too ends up safely suspended between polar women, but unlike *The Ambassadors, The Wings* ends insisting upon the inadequacy of any Strether-like determination to get nothing out of affairs. Negation marks Densher in the final scene. He who "'saw' nothing" says "I do nothing," and, despite admitting that he has created a test for Kate, insists "I put you up to nothing." She on the other hand is marked by presence, "she, supremely who had the presence of mind." Densher is where he has always been, "in your power." And his shift of allegiance to Milly assures that he'll now remain in woman's power forever. When Kate charges that "you desire to escape everything," Densher concedes her point, but only with an echo ("everything"), so that he does not even have to articulate his responsibility for renunciation. Being "in love with her [Milly's] memory" assures Densher a contact with affection and yet a safe removal from it. "You're one for whom it will do. Her memory's your love. You *want* no other." Wanting, indeed, is what Densher is, toothless and safe.

*The Golden Bowl* takes the final step. Having faced in *The Wings* the inadequacy of flight as a response to the threat of human relationships, James is now ready to face the threat itself, relationship itself. In Maggie's final embrace of Amerigo, James embraces the reality that he had ambivalently drawn to and pushed away from himself for forty years of writing. At issue is what this embrace finally *means*. How benignly can we read the end of *The Golden Bowl?* Kaston answers this question carefully. She first sets up, as we have seen, "the possibility that fusing consciousness with presence will bring them [characters] back into the world to live out, with those they no longer need to renounce, reciprocally satisfying compositions of experience." Kaston then adds: "if James never completely realized this conception of human relations in his fiction, he tested it over and over" (14). The most serious test, the best try, is clearly *The Golden Bowl,* toward which Kaston directs her book-long argument. "While Maggie and Amerigo's final embrace appears to perpetuate the dualism of mastery and submission, it also points toward a fusion of passion and surrender so complex that the distinction between these motives seems almost to disappear" (178). What Kaston sees as a fusing together I see as a solidifying apart.

In *The Golden Bowl,* James gives the alternatives to his family romance—marriage and procreation—their greatest dignity and opportunity for success. Maggie fights for what most readers hold sacred: "love." And "love" triumphs. Maggie banishes the adulterous threat and reconstitutes the nuclear family. But to what end?

> "'See?' I see nothing but *you.*" And the truth of it had, with this force, after a moment, so strangely lighted his eyes that, as for pity and dread of them, she buried her own in his breast.

Maggie turns her face away because she realizes that in reclaiming Amerigo for "love" she has reduced them both to " 'nothing.' " Negation marks Amerigo forever, so Maggie too is negated, not simply or even primarily because she is a woman in patriarchy but because neither sex can function without the other. Maggie assumes the condition of castration—she in effect blinds herself—because she does not want to see what she cannot help knowing. Amerigo is already castrated. "Pity and dread," the emotions of Aristotelian tragedy, are inappropriate to any benign reading of James's denouement but are inevitable once we realize that what has perished is relationship itself. " 'Everything is terrible, Cara, in the heart of man.' " *The Golden Bowl* is James's greatest novel because it combines the fullest expression of his vision of negation and the fiercest determination not to escape from that vision into fantasy. Maggie does not end safely enwombed between polar threats, as Isabel and Strether do. She ends hung upon the cross of her husband's dysfunctional body. There are no successful relationships, and there is nothing else.

*The Golden Bowl* thus attests that young Henry James was right all along. Home *is* impossible. By returning to Kaston's quite different view, I can clarify mine: "the distinction between these motives seems almost to disappear." The hesitancy articulated in "seems" and "almost" derives, I have the feeling, not simply from the complexity of James's scene but from Kaston's concern with larger issues of gender. Kaston wants to argue that James is a "feminist" writer. "Collaboration—shared fictionalizing, or the mutual creation of experience—is the essence of feminism. . . . it is better to have power with people than to have power over them" (15). Like most of Kaston's readers, I share her commitment to gender equality. I also share her belief that James is a great feminist writer. But this does not need to mean that James sees particular men and women sharing equally in power. Distinctions of power need not disappear in order for an equality to exist between the sexes. *The Golden Bowl* is a great feminist novel because James treats his heroine with equality: He subjects her to the same unflinching gaze that he has trained on his men, Adam, Amerigo, and Merton Densher. James refuses to patronize Maggie by using her—as another feminine orphan to provide him wish fulfillment by retreating from life. His ability to face fully the core terror of his life enables this heroine to play out her power relations unfettered by any covert authorial agenda.

If everything is terrible in the heart of man, it is no less terrible in woman. James has, in effect, played out with his heroine a scene he staged with a version of himself in *The Portrait*. When Henrietta said to Ralph, " 'You are not in love with her [Isabel], I hope,' " and he quipped, " 'how can I be, when I am in love with another,' " Henrietta spoke to us all when she snapped, " 'you are in love with yourself, that's the other' " (111). That each of us wants to be both lover and beloved in order to deny the very possibility of any true other is a self-negating propensity which Henry James chronicled more extensively, fiercely, delicately than any novelist in our language. In *The Golden Bowl* James comes to accept the other—as a reality outside himself, as a woman seeing rather than fleeing. Of course this acceptance provides, like every act, its own type of pleasure. But it is now the pleasure of maturity.

Regression, James now says in effect, is for businessmen. Rather than sit still and escape exposure, Henry James has dared what scared him most. He has finally become a sufficiently great man by becoming a sufficiently great artist to see through a woman's eyes the human isolation that had threatened a small boy.

## Notes

1. *Henry James: The Critical Heritage,* ed. Roger Gard (London: Routledge and Kegan Paul, 1968), 111. Nearly a century later Quentin Anderson echoed Huntington: "in *The Portrait of a Lady* the bearded young artist had put on skirts and become the fool of experience rather than its master (*The Imagined Self* [New York: Knopf, 1971], 213). Contemporaries who knew Henry James personally were speculating on his relationship with the feminine before Huntington's published remarks. Between 1877 and 1880, E. S. Nadal gleaned from London encounters with James the now widely quoted perception that "he seemed to look at women rather as women looked at them. Women look at women as persons; men look at them as women. The quality of sex in women, which is their first and chief attraction to most men, was not their chief attraction to James" (Leon Edel, *The Conquest of London* [1962], vol. 2 of *Henry James* [Philadelphia: Lippincott, 1953–1962], 359; hereafter cited in text by volume and page).
2. Methodologically, the case against a psychological approach and for a cultural one is expressed most severely by Joyce W. Warren: "To rely on psychological explorations here would lead to the assumption that James' ability to portray strong, independent women is abnormal. In fact this accomplishment is abnormal only in American literature. . . . the explanation for James' ability [to portray female characters as people] is not primarily psychological but cultural; like Hawthorne, James was not typically American in his attitudes" (*The American Narcissus* [New Brunswick, NJ: Rutgers University Press, 1984], 243–44). For a related critical analysis of James and women, see Virginia C. Fowler, *Henry James's American Girl* (Madison: University of Wisconsin Press, 1984). The principal proponent of the psychological approach to James is of course Leon Edel (esp. vols. 1 and 2 of his biography). Recently, Howard M. Feinstein (*Becoming William James* [Ithaca, NY: Cornell University Press, 1984]) and Richard Hall ("An Obscure Hurt," *New Republic,* Apr. 28 and May 5, 25–31, 25–29) have built upon and diverged competently from Edel. My own analysis, like those of John Carlos Rowe (*The Theoretical Dimensions of Henry James* [Madison: University of Wisconsin Press, 1984] and others, will combine the psychological and the cultural, since both forces are obviously at work in James as in every writer. The evaluative question of James's feminism is much debated today. Severest charges against him come from critics of *The Bostonians* who see James espousing Basil Ransom and maligning Olive Chancellor. For corrective responses to such misreadings of *The Bostonians,* see Judith Fetterley *The Resisting Reader: A*

*Feminist Approach to American Fiction* (Bloomington: Indiana University Press, 1978), and Elizabeth Allen, *A Woman's Place in the Novels of Henry James* (New York: St. Martin's Press, 1984). Among the many other critical discussions of James and women over the last forty years, those particularly helpful to me have been: Louise K. Barnett, "Jamesian Feminism: Women in 'Daisy Miller,'" *Studies in Short Fiction* 16 (1979): 281–87; Rachel M. Brownstein, *Becoming a Heroine* (New York: Viking, 1982); Susan Carlson, "Correspondence," *Henry James Review* 6 (1984): 71–73; Ernest Earnest, *The American Eve in Fact and Fiction, 1775–1914* (Urbana: University of Illinois Press, 1974); Paul John Eakin, *The New England Girl* (Athens: University of Georgia Press, 1976); Fowler, *James's American Girl;* Judith Fryer, *The Faces of Eve* (New York: Oxford University Press, 1976); Clare R. Goldfarb, "Matriarchy in the Late Novels of Henry James," *Research Studies* 49 (1981): 231–34; Alfred Habegger, *Gender, Fantasy, and Realism in American Literature* (New York: Columbia University Press, 1982); Stuart Hutchinson, "Beyond the Victorian: *The Portrait of a Lady*" in *Reading the Victorian Novel: Detail into Form,* ed. Ian Gregor (New York: Barnes and Noble, 1980), 274–87; Annette Nientzow, "Marriage and the New Woman in *The Portrait of a Lady,*" *AL* 47 (1975): 377–95; Anna S. Parrill, "Portraits of Ladies," *Tennessee Studies in Literature* 20 (1975): 92–99; Linda Ray Pratt, "The Abuse of Eve by the New World Adam," in *Image of Women in Fiction: Feminist Perspectives,* ed. Susan Koppelman Cornillon (Bowling Green, KY: Bowling Green University Popular Press, 1972); John Carlos Rowe, "Correspondence," *HJR* 6 (1985): 153–54, and *The Theoretical Dimensions of Henry James* (Madison: University of Wisconsin Press, 1984); Elizabeth Sabiston, "The Prison of Womanhood," *Comparative Literature* 25 (1973): 336–51; Mary S. Schriber, "Isabel Archer and Victorian Manners," *Studies in the Novel* 8 (1976): 441–57; John W. Shroeder, "The Mothers of Henry James," *AL* 22 (1950–51): 424–31; Mary Doyle Springer, *A Rhetoric of Literary Character: Some Women of Henry James* (Chicago: University of Chicago Press, 1978); William T. Stafford, ed., *Perspectives on James's "The Portrait of a Lady": A Collection of Critical Essays* (New York: New York University Press, 1967); William Bysshe Stein, "*The Portrait of a Lady:* Vis Inertiae," in Stafford, *Perspectives,* 166–83; Donald David Stone, *Novelists in a Changing World: Meredith, James, and the Transformation of English Fiction in the 1880's* (Cambridge, MA: Harvard University Press, 1972), 219–22; Anne Robinson Taylor, *Male Novelists and Their Female Voices: Literary Masquerades* (Troy, NY: Whitson, 1981); Edward Wagenknecht, *Eve and Henry James: Portraits of Women and Girls in His Fiction* (Norman: University of Oklahoma Press, 1978); Adele Wiseman, "What Price the Heroine?" *International Journal of Women's Studies* 4 (1981): 459–71.

3. Rowe, *Theoretical Dimensions,* 91.
4. In *Male Novelists,* Anne Robinson Taylor summarizes various explanations—especially those of Virginia Woolf and Simone de Beauvoir—for the use of female masks by male writers (esp. 1–4). Taylor goes on to relate James's empathy with women to his sense of physical vulnerability.
5. See particularly the first two volumes of Edel's biography of James (vol. 1, *The Untried Years* [1953] and vol. 2, *The Conquest of London*) and the more recent work by Jean Strouse (*Alice James: A Biography* [Boston: Houghton Mifflin, 1980]), Howard M. Feinstein (*Becoming William James*), and Jane Maher (*Biography of Broken Fortunes* [Hamden, CT: Archon, 1986]).
6. Sigmund Freud, "Family Romances," in *Collected Papers,* ed. James Strachey (New York: Basic, 1959), 5:74–78. For more recent studies of family romances, see: R. C. Bak, "Discussion of Greenacre's 'Family Romance of Artist,'" *Psychoanalytic Study of Children* 13 (1958): 42–43; Helen K. Gediman, "Narcissistic Trauma, Object Loss, and the Family Romance," *Psychoanalytic Review* 61 (1974): 203–15; Phyllis Greenacre, "Family Romance of Artist," *Psychoanalytic Study of Children* 13 (1958): 9–36; Linda Joan Kaplan, "The Concept of the Family Romance," *Psychoanalytic Review* 61 (1974): 169–

202; Christine Van Boheemen-Saaf, "'The Universe Makes an Indifferent Parent': *Bleak House* and the Victorian Family Romance," *Psychiatry and the Humanities* 6 (1983): 225–57, reprinted with minimal changes in Van Boheemen, *The Novel as Family Romance* (Ithaca, NY: Cornell University Press, 1987), 101–31.

7. Henry James, *A Small Boy and Others* (New York: Scribner, 1913), 175. Subsequent references to this volume will be included in the text, abbreviated *SB*. Likewise, the second volume of James's autobiography, *Notes of a Son and Brother* (New York: Scribner, 1914), will be abbreviated *NSB*.

   Recent students of autobiography have argued convincingly a point I want to affirm here: The autobiographical act relates as importantly to the moment of writing as it does to the moment written about. The core fantasy of *A Small Boy* expresses the seventy-year-old James as much as it does his preschool self. Thus the fantasy that James articulates in *A Small Boy* can never be taken as identical with the one he had as a small boy. The chief functions of fantasy—defense and compensation—are in operation for the aged author as well as for his young subject. James creates a "fictional" character through whom he as an old man can discover more about himself as a small boy and as an aged master. Leon Edel, Roy Pascal (*Design and Truth in Autobiography* [Cambridge, MA: Harvard University Press, 1960]), Robert F. Sayer (*The Examined Self* [Princeton, NJ: Princeton University Press, 1964]), and recently Paul John Eakin (*Fictions in Autobiography* [Princeton, NJ: Princeton University Press, 1985]) have shown how the writing of the autobiographical volumes helped James deal with the despondency, ill health, and professional discouragement that oppressed him after 1910. Eakin in particular has argued convincingly that, by studying how the small boy and the young man invented a self to survive into adulthood, the old man could reinvent that self to survive adulthood. Therefore, though I will often speak of Henry James *as* the small boy, the mediating function of the "fictional" persona and the rhetorical and therapeutic role of the autobiographical act are ever in operation. My assumption is only that the young persona is tied sufficiently to "Henry James himself" that he can be seen as expressing emotions felt in some form by Henry James in the 1840s and 1850s.

8. Young Henry James comes closest to this classic version of the fantasy when he describes with empathy and even envy the prince imperial, the baby son of Napoleon III, "borne forth for his airing or his progress to Saint-Cloud in the splendid coach that gave a glimpse of appointed and costumed nursing breasts and laps, and beside which the *cent-gardes,* all light-blue and silver and intensely erect quick jolt, rattled with pistols raised and cocked" (*SB*, 332). The nursing breasts and cocked pistols represent well the imperial parents of fantasy.

9. For other references to orphanhood in *A Small Boy* see 15, 129, 189, 402. Other James children reflect interestingly upon Henry's obsession with orphanhood. Wilkie expresses the classic family romance fantasy when he says, "I became quite convinced by the time I was twelve years old that I was a foundling" (Maher, *Biography,* 12; also quoted in Edel, 1:60).

10. The full quotation from Emerson appears in vol. 1 of Ralph Barton Perry, *The Thought and Character of William James* (Boston: Little, Brown, 1935), 3: "Henry James said to me, he wished sometimes the lightning would strike his wife and children out of existence, and he should have to suffer no more from loving them." An indication of how young Henry felt menaced by parental aggression is indicated by another version of the family romance of childhood, which was also articulated by James in old age. In 1907 James recalls his boyhood fascination with the fairytale "Hop o' My Thumb," "my small romance of yearning predilection" (*Henry James Letters*, ed. Leon Edel [Cambridge, MA: Harvard University Press, 1984], 4: 446–47). He emphasizes "the parents plotting to mislay their brood," and "the small boy, smaller than one's self, who had in that crisis gained immortality" (447). This small boy flees the lethal parents, in effect orphaning himself before he is destroyed by them. For calling my attention to "Hop o' My Thumb," and for much else, I am indebted to Professor Susan M. Griffin.

Feinstein recognizes astutely Henry Sr.'s "death wish" for his children. When the father describes taking his two younger sons to Sanborn School, "significantly, Henry began his letter on a morbid note: 'I buried two of my children yesterday—at Concord, Mass.' He pulled back in mid-sentence from this undefended death wish to a posture of bereaved parent: 'and feel so heartbroken this morning that I shall need to adopt two more instantly to supply their place.' This parental stance matches Robertson's life-long feeling of being unwanted" (*Becoming William James*, 255–56). Henry Sr. cannot sustain the stance of bereaved parent, however, and the death wish resurfaces: "The short of the story is that we left them . . . hoping that they would not die any of these cold winter days" (256). Strouse focuses on the lethal side of Henry Sr. when she discusses his dealing with Alice's suicidal inclinations: "If he was contriving to stop her from killing herself . . . he nonetheless committed an act of moral violence of the sort he practiced on all his children with loving impunity throughout his life" (*Alice James*, 188). That Alice may have harbored some of the homicidal aspect of Henry's desire to *be* an orphan is suggested in a passage from Strouse. "In March, Alice went to Newport, where Aunt Kate was staying with friends. She was escorted on this venture by John Bancroft, a painter and friend from the Newport years (and son of the American historian and diplomat George Bancroft). William reported to Henry that 'Father was loath to let her go without him, but she said to me and mother that her main wish in going was to get rid of him and Mother, and I was very glad to find her understanding so clearly her position.' Alice knew, then that she wanted to 'get rid of' her parents" (139). Strouse goes on to add the necessary qualification: "to 'get rid of' her parents for a vacation." But, as Alice's famous comment about decapitating the benignant pater indicates, she fantasized a moment of a more permanent separation.

11. Young Henry's sense of self-negation was so great that it expressed itself in terms of both the James household and the world outside. Domestically, Henry compares himself unfavorably not only with William's "deeper strivings and braver deeds" (*SB*, 301) but also with Wilkie's gregarious "go[ing] in for everything and everyone. . . . These latter were what I should have *liked* to go in for, had I but had the intrinsic faculties. . . . [I] was to go without many things, ever so many—as all persons do in whom contemplation takes so much the place of action" (290, 25). Whether the subject is novels that he is forbidden to read ("I remember the soreness of the thought that it was I rather who was wrong for the book" [76]) or literary projects planned (for "which I must at that time quite have failed to exhibit a single in the least 'phenomenal' symptom" [35]), the leitmotif is the same. "There indeed was another humiliation" (385).

Humiliations increase when "there" points outside the home. In school, "I should doubtless as promptly add that my own case must have been intrinsically of the poorest. . . . I can't have had, through it all, I think, a throb of assurance or success" (*SB*, 193, 194). Negation marks the entire scholastic enterprise by the very fact that Henry is not where William is, "a place in the world to which I couldn't at all aspire. . . . I never for all the time of childhood and youth in the least caught up with him or overtook him. . . . We were never in the same schoolroom" (8, 9). Henry studies either with teachers "whose benches indeed my brother did not haunt" (16) or with teachers who compare the boys unfavorably. "On my remarking that I didn't see how she could do it [snuff candles with her fingers] she promptly replied that I of course couldn't do it myself (as *she* could) because I should be afraid" (22). Such salvation as graced Henry came from his genius for nullity, for being overlooked. "I think I was never really aware of how little [attention] I got or how much I did without" (226). Socially, he was less fortunate. There were a stage magician who "practised on my innocence to seduce me to the stage and there plunge me into the shame of my sad failure to account arithmatically" (116); an equally adept schoolmate whose tricks "I ingenuously invited him to show me . . . and then, on his treating me with scorn, renewed without dignity my fond solicitation" (227); and a shopgirl who joined with his father to make him feel that "it was only I who didn't understand" (95).

12. James tends to make the man versus woman split especially sharp in *The American Scene,* where his intention is quite different from that of *A Small Boy.* Depicting American society at the beginning of the twentieth century, James is showing what has happened to the country in the more than fifty years since the time of *A Small Boy.* In the autobiographical volume he is presenting both a family situation and a more leisured society—where men and women were not as relentlessly divided as they had become by the turn of the century.
13. My autobiographical orientation to *The Portrait* determines my choice of text (hereafter cited in text by page number). I cite from the original 1881 edition of the novel (New American Library's Signet Classic, 1963) rather than the revised version of the New York Edition (1907). The remark about Caspar's sickness appears on 492. Quotations from *The Ambassadors* will be cited from the New York edition, by volume and chapter.
14. See Introduction to this volume.
15. Mary Garland's words are discussed in Fowler, *James's American Girl,* 35–36. The quotation appears in vol. 1, 457, of the New York edition of *Roderick Hudson.*
16. Carren Kaston, *Imagination and Desire in the Novels of Henry James* (New Brunswick, NJ: Rutgers University Press, 1984), 45. For a detailed discussion of "spending," see G. J. Barker-Benfield's chapter "The Spermatic Economy and Proto-Sublimation," in *Horrors of the Half-Known Life* (New York: Harper and Row, 1976). The "spending" quotation from *The Portrait* appears only in the revised New York edition, indicating that James was more self-conscious about the nongendered nature of sexual spending after the turn of the century than he was in 1881.
17. Warren, *American Narcissus,* 243.
18. Edel and Strouse give proper stress to the enormous contribution that the anima made to James's psyche. " 'All his life,' writes Edel, Henry James harboured within 'the house of the novelist's inner world the spirit of a young adult female, worldly-wise and curious, possessing a treasure of unassailable virginity and innocence and able to yield to the masculine active world-searching side of James an ever-fresh and exquisite vision of feminine youth and innocence' " (Strouse, *Alice James,* 50). In my chapter, "The American Girl," in *The Woman Question: Society and Literature in Britain and America, 1837–1883* (coauthored with Elizabeth K. Helsinger and Robin Lauterbach Sheets [New York: Garland, 1983; University of Chicago Press, 1989], vol. 3), I discuss this figure prior to James's presentations of her. Taylor speaks for many critics when she observes that, "in the fiction of Henry James, the female characters often seem much more 'masculine' than the males. In all his fiction it is the women who dare to act, who move about . . . who simply *live*" (*Male Novelists,* 157). Though Taylor also stresses a second link between James and women—what she calls "physical vulnerability"—I am finally making a different argument when I maintain that *no one* in James is in fact "masculine," that everyone is effeminated by culture and mortality.
19. James's homosexual inclinations were first given serious treatment by Edel in connection with the novelist's relationship with the Scandinavian sculptor Henrik Anderson in the 1890s (*The Treacherous Years* [1969], vol. 4 of *Henry James,* 306–16). In 1979, Richard Hall traced these inclinations back to the 1870s in connection with Henry's relations with his brother William ("An Obscure Hurt"). In addition to Feinstein's subsequent work on identification and twinship, see B. D. Horwitz's unfairly neglected study of the forces that produced James's homosexual inclinations ("The Sense of Desolation in Henry James," *Psychocultural Review* 1 [1977]: 466–92). In a recent essay, "Henry James: Interpreting an Obsessive Memory," Hall quotes a letter from Edel: "your entire chain of evidence is certainly convincing to me" (*Literary Visions of Homosexuality,* ed. Stuart Kellogg [New York: Haworth, 1983], 85). Edel later added that, "once we agree on Henry's love fixation on William, that explains a lot of things" (86). As early as 1962, Maxwell Geismar discusses "The Pupil" in terms of male bonds and implicates William James (*Henry James and the Jacobites* [New York: Hill and Wang, 1962], 115–16).
20. Edel first noticed this fact about James's protagonists; Hall then took it up. Warren

correctly notes that, "of course, *Daisy Miller* was written before the marriage" (*American Narcissus,* 306 n.). Her additional criticisms of the Edel–Hall position seem weaker, however. "Christina Light was created four years earlier. Furthermore, some of his best male protagonists—Lambert Strether, Hyacinth Robinson—came long afterward. To draw such conclusions on the basis of the tenuous evidence available (most of which relies upon a personal interpretation of the fiction, e.g., the novel *Confidence*) overlooks other forces active in James's life at the time, including his reading and his European experience" (306 n.). Christina Light is not the *protagonist* of *Roderick Hudson.* Moreover, Edel and Hall are not of course pretending that after 1878 Henry James never again presented male protagonists. Their focus is upon Henry's *immediate* response to abandonment by William. Finally, Hall and Edel would surely agree that only by combining a psychoanalytic perspective with others—which would include not only James's reading and European experience but also his prescient recognition of gender as a social construct—can we understand so overdetermined a phenomenon as his personality and creativity.

21. James himself connects Isabel's childhood to his own (*SB,* 9). Edel notes several autobiographical aspects of *The Portrait:* Isabel is given one of Henry's earliest memories—the taste of peaches in his Albany grandmother's garden (1:86); more generally, his grandmother and her house (1:85); Isabel's schooling in Albany, or rather the lack of it (1:61); the role reversal of Ralph's parents paralleling that of Henry's (1:51); Lizzie Boott as the model for Pansy Osmond and Minny Temple (1:237, 332–33) for Isabel. More can be made than Edel does of the similarities between Henry James, Sr., and Mr. Archer: They share both an erratic way of educating their children and an inclination to escape life through death. "Before Isabel was fourteen, he had transported them three times across the Atlantic, giving them on each occasion, however, but a few months' view of foreign lands; a course which had whetted our heroine's curiosity without enabling her to satisfy it . . . and in his last days his general willingness to take leave of a world in which the difficulty of doing as one liked appeared to increase as one grew older" (32).
22. From the preface to *The Ambassadors,* in *The Art of Criticism,* ed. William Veeder and Susan M. Griffin (Chicago: University of Chicago Press, 1986), 372.
23. Although Kaston has recently reaffirmed the view that Ralph is indeed authoring a different scenario from Osmond's, and although I would certainly accept Isabel's distinction between the two men ("Ralph was generous and her husband was not" [400]), I agree with many readers who see little to choose between the two men early in the novel. Ralph is terribly proprietary. Ralph's Osmond-like view of Isabel as "an entertainment of high order" (58) is contested first by Daniel ("you speak as if it [changing the will] were for your entertainment" [171]), then by Henrietta ("Is that why your father did it—for your amusement?" [205]), and finally by Isabel herself: "You say you amused yourself in planning out my future. . . . Don't amuse yourself too much, or I shall think your doing it at my expense" (318).
24. Two exceptions might seem to be Henrietta and Caspar. Both, however, are unable to sustain their adventurousness. Isabel's disappointment of Henrietta's succumbing to marriage is supported by the name James gives to Henrietta's fiancé—"Bantling" means "baby." Caspar is active in the factory and would have been valiant on the battlefield, but love for Isabel makes fantasy life meaningless, and Caspar was—emblematically—born too late to fight in the Civil War.
25. No mention is made of Caspar's mother; his father is referred to in ways that make it unclear whether the factory proprietor is still alive (107).
26. For William's recognition of himself in Babcock, see Perry, *Thought and Character,* 1:371.
27. This question, which dogged many early drafts of my essay, was put to me with kindly rigor by Professor Lyall Powers. Whether or not my eventual answer satisfies him, Professor Powers's insistence upon the facts of the narration has required of my argument a complexity it heretofore lacked.
28. See particularly sections 5–7 of *Beyond the Pleasure Principle* in vol. 18 of *The Standard*

*Edition of the Complete Psychological Works of Sigmund Freud,* ed. James Strachey (London: Hogarth, 1955).

29. Before I proceed, one caveat. In explaining why, psychologically, James resorts to fantasy, I may seem to be belittling him artistically. I am not. I believe that Henry James is the greatest writer in English since John Milton—given as criterion the quantity of quality work produced in diverse genres. James's fiction featuring the feminine orphan dramatizes with emotional power and formal innovation the inclination we all feel for renunciation. Every writer engages in wish fulfillment as he or she works out obsessions and memories; every writer could be analyzed as I do James; few writers would fare so well. If I see *The Golden Bowl* as James's supreme achievement, I do so in the belief that, if he had died after *The Ambassadors,* Henry James would still be America's greatest artist of fiction.
30. I am grateful to Professor Alfred Habegger for pointing out to me that the development which I posit from *The Ambassadors* to *The Wings of the Dove* occurs in fact with "The Beast in the Jungle," which is written *between* the two novels. Marcher is clearly another of James's renunciatory males, but just as clearly the folly of renunciation—Merton Densher's folly—is acknowledged by James. "The Beast" is thus a stalking horse for the novel that follows it in every sense.
31. For a testament to the transcendent quality of redeemed Densher's love, see Cargill's paean (*The Novels of Henry James* [New York: Macmillan, 1961], 35). David H. Hirsch critiques this view effectively, maintaining that, "far from being capable of love, Densher has been transformed from a slave of *eros* to a slave of *thanatos,* and far from being redeemed he is damned to hopeless necrophilism" ("Henry James and the Seal of Love," *Modern Language Studies* 13 [1985]: 53).
32. The *OED* lists, in addition to the 1891 *Pall Mall Gazette* mention of dentures, an 1882 Worchester "exhibit of specimens of dentures in wax before vulcanizing."

# Gesturing toward an Open Space: Gender, Form, and Language in E. M. Forster's *Howards End*

ELIZABETH LANGLAND

**E**. M. FORSTER is a difficult writer to approach because he appears simple. His work presents none of the stylistic resistance and technical virtuosity characteristic of his notable contemporaries like Joyce and Woolf. Further, he seems to have recourse to a nineteenth-century liberal humanism in resolving his novels, an emphasis that sets at naught the complexities of literary modernism.[1] So, at best, Forster claims a precarious stake in the twentieth-century canon. But Forster accomplished something difficult and important in his novel *Howards End* that a gendered politics of reading can uncover. In his personal embattlement with gender and his embattlement with patriarchal culture, Forster exposes the constructed nature of gender and his own ambivalent relationship to traits coded "masculine" and "feminine" in his culture.

This gendered politics of reading begins with an acknowledgment of Forster's homosexuality and outspoken misogyny, a textual politics that is tied to a sexual politics. There is substantial evidence that Forster was deeply troubled and preoccupied by his own gender identity during this period. He had spent his childhood largely in the female company and sheltering presence of his mother and aunt, who no doubt gave him his "knowledge" of women and female friendship. At the same time, he was uncertain of his own sexual orientation and uncertain of even the basic facts of male/female reproduction, which Forster claimed he never fully grasped until his thirties. The conviction of his homosexuality came shortly after publication of *Howards End* when George Merrill, the working-class homosexual lover of Forster's friend Edward Carpenter, "touched Forster's backside 'gently and just above the buttocks.'" Forster continued: "The sensation was unusual and I still remember it. . . . It seemed to go straight through the small of my back into my ideas, without involving my thoughts."[2] That touch conceived *Maurice,* Forster's novel about homosexual love published only posthumously.

It wasn't until 1916 that Forster found "total sexual fulfillment—or, as he put it, 'parted with respectability' "[3]—and not until 1917 that he finally fell in love: with an Egyptian tram conductor, Mohammed-el-Adl. After that fulfillment, Forster wrote to Florence Barger: "It isn't happiness. . . . it's rather—offensive phrase—that I first feel a grown up man."[4] The offensiveness lies in the implication that a man becomes grown up through sexual mastery.

Thus, in 1910, while composing *Howards End,* Forster was in a great deal of confusion, which we can understand more fully if we consider the Victorian notion of homosexuality: *anima mulieris in corpore virile inclusa* or "a woman's soul trapped in a man's body."[5] Ironically, that confusion and dissatisfaction precipitated a misogynistic homosexuality, which I suggest we see in light of Forster's fear of the feminine in himself.[6] This understanding also gives us some insight into the process by which the confusions that produced this misogyny in Forster also fueled a desire for something other than the classical opposition between male and female, masculine and feminine, and so initiated his embattled relationship with patriarchy. In *Howards End* we see this relationship played out through the narrator, the leading female characters, certain thematic oppositions, and the connections between all of these and the dramatic structure of the novel.

At a first glance, Forster appears to offer neither a radical literary practice nor a liberal sexual practice in this story of a younger woman's conventional marriage to an older and successful businessman, who looks upon women as "recreation." But textual evidence suggests that this conventional image is an anamorphosis reflecting Forster's attempt to manage a site of conflict in himself. A close analysis of the textual maneuvers in *Howards End* discloses a radical sexual politics that has been obscured by psychobiographical approaches and by assumptions about Forster's literary allegiance to the nineteenth century. We may begin to excavate the layers of the text through its narrative stance, which is ambiguous, uneasy, and defensive. The following passage from the middle of the novel first brought me to examine *Howards End* because of the ways it makes problematic the omniscient narrator's voice:

> Pity was at the bottom of her [Margaret's] actions all through this crisis. Pity, if one may generalize, is at the bottom of woman. When men like us, it is for our better qualities and however tender their liking, we dare not be unworthy of it, or they will quietly let us go. But unworthiness stimulates woman. It brings out her deeper nature, for good or for evil.[7]

The problem emerges from the "us," which initially appears to refer back to "woman," used to essentialize all women, with whom the narrator seems to identify.[8] A closer reading suggests that "us" simply refers to all people, that is, "when men like people. . . ." The temporary confusion arises here because, previously, the events have been focalized through the female protagonist, Margaret Schlegel, and "us," the first-person-plural pronoun, invokes the feminine perspective.[9]

The "us" feels problematic, too, because the narrator's previous narrative intrusions have been characterized by an uneasy authority that hovers between irony and sympathy, creating an overall impression of indefiniteness.[10] The narrator opens deferentially: "One may as well begin with Helen's letter to her sister" (3). Shortly thereafter we are told: "To Margaret—I hope that it will not set the reader against her—the station of King's Cross had always suggested Infinity" (12). The special pleading is intrusive here and later: "That was 'how it happened,' or, rather, how Helen described it to her sister, using words even more unsympathetic than my own" (25). Comments on the underprivileged seem to attempt sarcasm but end up sounding defensive: "We are not concerned with the very poor. They are unthinkable" (45); or, "take my word for it, that [poor woman's] smile was simply stunning, and it is only you and I who will be fastidious, and complain that true joy begins in the eyes" (48). Later addresses to the reader fail to achieve either authority on the one hand or familiarity on the other: "It is rather a moment when the commentator should step forward. Ought the Wilcoxes have offered their home to Margaret? I think not" (98); and, "Margaret had expected the disturbance. . . . Good-humour was the dominant note of her relations with Mr. Wilcox, or, as I must now call him, Henry" (177).

Forster is more assured when he avoids omniscient comment and focuses on Margaret Schlegel, from whose perspective we see the events of the novel. It is not merely that we share the point of view of a woman here (although that is important to Forster's ends) but also that we tend to take her perspective as representative of the female point of view in general. As the novel develops, Forster complicates this identification of Margaret with the "female" or the "feminine," but initially it undergirds the binary oppositions informing the novel. The novel is built upon a dialectical opposition between male and female, under which several others are subsumed.[11] The most significant oppositions for this analysis are those of class—rich and poor; those of philosophy—logic and vision; and those of language—word and intuition. Under the male side of the equation fall wealth, logic, and the word; under the female, poverty, vision, and intuition. These oppositions are worked out on the level of theme and plot.

On the level of theme, that resolution is fairly straightforward, although we should note that those terms subsumed under the aspect of male and female perpetuate a hierarchical tradition that relegates women to an inferior status. We may want to applaud Forster for attempting to redress the balance by privileging the feminine, but we are still caught in a net of stereotypes that perpetuate hierarchy and binary opposition, ideas that inscribe male perspectives in the world, as we shall see in a moment.

Although I have relegated wealth to the male side of the equation and poverty to the female, in fact, the female protagonists of the novel, Margaret and Helen Schlegel, are well-to-do women. Their sympathy with the poor, however, initiates Forster's interrogation of class distinctions. The Schlegels are distinguished from the Wilcoxes, the masculine protagonists, by their recognition of the privilege that money confers. Margaret asserts that the rich "stand upon money as upon islands" in the sea of life (61). As a result of this perception, she and Helen are able to look beneath the social surface of a poor individual like Leonard Bast to the "real man, who cared for adventure and beauty" (316).

Yet, even as the novel attempts to redress the imbalance between rich and poor, it cannot transcend certain class attitudes which are implicit in Forster's uneven characterization of the workingman and explicit in Margaret's discovery that Jackie Bast has formerly been Henry Wilcox's mistress. She writes to Helen that "The Basts are not at all the type we should trouble about" (241), and Helen, who is ready enough to sympathize with Leonard Bast, condemns Jackie as "ready enough to meet" Henry Wilcox and laments that such women "end in two ways: either they sink till the lunatic asylums and the workhouses are full of them . . . or else they entrap a boy into marriage before it is too late" (253). That Jackie is a victim of patriarchy is understood imperfectly, although Margaret strenuously criticizes Henry's double standard. Helen's disclaimer, "I can't blame her," sounds unconvincing as the novel seeks to deconstruct sexist and class values on the level of theme, which it then reconstructs on the level of plot when Helen has a sexual relationship with Leonard—a woman's classic offering of her body in sympathy—and then arrogantly seeks to compensate him with cash, admitting that "I want never to see him again, though it sounds appalling. I wanted to give him money and feel finished" (313). Both of these episodes play out basic patriarchal expectations about relationships between men and women, between the rich and the poor. The pattern we see here, where plot reconstructs what the theme interrogates to deconstruct, will be replicated in working out Forster's other binary oppositions.

Thematically, vision is privileged over logic, intuition over word. Of course, logic and the word are related: They are in this novel the logos, the word of the fathers. Forster is committed to an ideology that seeks to defy the phallic mode and, from the novel's opening, logic and the word are made to appear irrational. Charles Wilcox's blustering question to his brother, Paul, about his engagement to Helen Schlegel—"Yes or no, man; plain question, plain answer. Did or didn't Miss Schlegel"—is corrected by his mother's response: "Charles, dear Charles, one doesn't ask plain questions. There aren't such things" (22). When Henry Wilcox confronts Margaret over Helen's seemingly irrational behavior at the end of the novel, he echoes his son: "Answer my question. Plain question, plain answer" (284). Henry's plan to trap Helen like some hunted animal and Margaret's resistance provoke her recognition that the plan "is impossible, because—. . . it's not the particular language that Helen and I talk" and his counterclaim that "No education can teach a woman logic" (284). Margaret's later rejoinder—"leave it that you don't see. . . . Call it fancy. But realize that fancy is a scientific fact"—refuses Henry's reductive dichotomies. Margaret is given the final word in the novel as she reflects that, "Logically, they had no right to be there. One's hope was in the weakness of logic" (339), and she is vindicated in the conclusion as the Wilcox clan gather to hear the word of the father—"And again and again fell the word, like the ebb of a dying sea"—which belatedly, yet inevitably, affirms the intuitive vision of the mother in seeing that Margaret is the "spiritual heir" she seeks for Howards End.

And yet Margaret's "final word" is problematic because definitive answers belong to the male-inscribed discourse the novel seeks to deconstruct. We might want to argue that the apparent difficulty is only a matter of semantics. But, in fact, my introduction of a teleology of final word here anticipates the deeper problems we discover on the level of plot.

Forster's central opposition between man and woman would seem, initially, to be played out between Henry Wilcox and Margaret Schlegel. It begins on the level of houses. Margaret recognizes that "ours is a female house. . . . It must be feminine and all we can do is to see that it isn't effeminate. Just as another house that I can mention, but I won't, sounded irrevocably masculine, and all its inmates can do is to see that it isn't brutal" (44). This summary prepares us for the dialectic to follow, but Forster's feminist vision removes Margaret as a single term within the traditional dialectic, replaces her with Helen, and reinterprets Margaret as the principle that will complicate the hierarchical oppositions and provide a new kind of connection. That new connection is not the old androgyny, a merging or blurring of terms and traits;[12] it is a condition that preserves difference.

Whereas Henry Wilcox remains inscribed in a male mode of discourse, set within masculine imagery of dominance and conquest, Forster's descriptions of Margaret transcend the traditionally feminine and reinscribe her within a rhetoric of reconciliation and connection. Through Margaret Schlegel, the traditional terms of masculinity and femininity are scrutinized and subjected to the demands of higher integration. Margaret's point of view, then, is ultimately not representative of a view we might code as essentially female or feminine. Forster is sensitive both to essentialist conceptions of the female and to the social coding of the feminine. He subverts both in his characterization of Margaret Schlegel, who can calmly state, for example, "I do not love children. I am thankful to have none" (337–38), thus debunking ideas of a natural, maternal female.

And Margaret remains constantly alert to social expectations of feminine behavior, decoding those expectations. She turns the notion of "reading the feminine" into a lever against the men who are dependent on and limited by its convenient categories. When Henry proposes, Margaret has anticipated his action, but "she made herself give a little start. She must show surprise if he expected it" (164). Later, when a man hits a cat with his automobile and Margaret jumps out of the car, we learn that "Charles was absolutely honest. He described what he believed to have happened. . . . Miss Schlegel had lost her nerve, as any woman might." But the narrator reveals that "His father accepted this explanation, and neither knew that Margaret had artfully prepared the way for it. It fitted in too well with their view of feminine nature" (215). Later, in response to a question, Margaret "knew . . . but said that she did not know" (221) because "comment is unfeminine" (240).

Throughout the novel, Margaret resists being controlled by this dichotomous thinking and instead manipulates the terms with the goal of dismantling and transcending them. From the beginning, she is suspicious of hierarchies, as we discover in her mediation of the English and German claims to superiority. She announces, "To me one of two things is very clear; either God does not know his own mind about England and Germany, or else these do not know the mind of God" (30). The narrator pronounces her, ironically, "a hateful girl," acknowledging that "at thirteen she had grasped a dilemma that most people travel through life without perceiving" (30). That dilemma focuses on the logic of binary thinking. Margaret resists such dichotomous thought and chastises Helen's binary oppositions as "medieval," telling her "our business is not to contrast the two, but to reconcile them" (104). Not surprisingly, it is Margaret who is capable of concluding that "people are far more different than is pretended. All over the world men and women are worrying because they cannot develop as they are supposed to develop" (339).

In his reconceptualization of Margaret, Forster generates a new integrative principle that is associated with a woman but not ideologically coded as feminine.[13] Part of his success here depends, as I have suggested, on using Helen to reevaluate the traditionally feminine by associating her with emotion and the inner life.

Helen Schlegel, in contrast to Margaret, is emotional, impulsive, impatient of logic, impatient of all restraint on her generous impulses. She scoffs at moderation and is incapable of balance; she is first seduced by the Wilcox men and then violently rejects them. She extols the "inner life" and, unlike Margaret, refuses to acknowledge the value of Wilcox energy, which has created a civilized world in which her sensibilities and the inner life can have free play. When Margaret must protect a pregnant and unmarried Helen from the interference of Wilcox men, Margaret herself codes the struggle as a sexual one: "A new feeling came over her; she was fighting for women against men. She did not care about rights, but if men came into Howards End, it should be over her body" (290). Although Margaret prefers not to be locked into a struggle between opposed faces, under duress she will privilege what Helen represents. Forster has anticipated this moment earlier in the novel when Margaret and Helen disagree over the older sister's impending marriage to Henry Wilcox. Their "inner life was so safe," we are told, "that they could bargain over externals. . . . There are moments when the inner life actually 'pays,' when years of self-scrutiny, conducted for no ulterior motive, are suddenly of practical use" (195). The narrator adds that "Such moments are still rare in the West; that they can come at all promises a fairer future." Forster codes the inner life within another set of oppositions—Eastern mysticism versus Western pragmatism—but he reverses the usual hierarchy to privilege the East and the inner life.

In contrast to Helen, Henry is associated with an imagery of war, battle, and self-defense. When Margaret discovers that Jackie Bast was Henry's mistress, the narrator claims that, "Expelled from his old fortress, Mr. Wilcox was building a new one" (244). Margaret is forced to play "the girl, until he could rebuild his fortress and hide his soul from the world" (246). Henry believes that "Man is for war, woman for the recreation of the warrior, but he does not dislike it if she makes a show of fight. She cannot win in a real battle, having no muscles, only nerves" (259). At the end of the novel, in the crisis over Helen, Henry speaks "straight from his fortress," and Margaret at first fails to recognize that "to break him was her only hope." It is only when "Henry's fortress [gives] way" that Margaret can initiate the process that leads to the integration, the connection, she enacts in the novel's conclusion by bringing Henry and Helen together at Howards End.

It is significant in *Howards End* that the most moving scene occurs between two women, Helen and Margaret.[14] When the sisters meet at Howards End and Margaret discovers Helen is pregnant, she asserts, "It all turns on affection now" (291). Although at first they feel themselves in antagonism, unconsciously they move toward communion:

> The triviality faded from their faces, though it left something behind—the knowledge that they never could be parted because their love was rooted in common things. Explanations and appeals had failed; they had tried for a common meeting-ground, and had only made each other unhappy. And all the time their salvation was lying round them—the past sanctifying the present; the present, with wild heart-throb, declaring that there would after all be a future, with laughter and the voices of children. Helen, still smiling, came up to her sister. She said: "It is always Meg." They looked into each other's eyes. The inner life had paid. [299]

In stark contrast stands Charles Wilcox's relationship with his father:

> The Wilcoxes were not lacking in affection; they had it royally, but they did not know how to use it. It was the talent in the napkin, and, for a warm-hearted man, Charles had conveyed very little joy. As he watched his father shuffling up the road, he had a vague regret—a wish that something had been different somewhere—a wish (though he did not express it thus) that he had been taught to say "I" in his youth. He meant to make up for Margaret's defection, but knew that his father had been very happy with her until yesterday. How had she done it? By some dishonest trick, no doubt—but how? [329]

The traditionally feminine mode is clearly affirmed in these final contrasting scenes that sanction the inner life and "voiceless sympathy."

In privileging the inner life, as we have seen, Forster reverses the usual hierarchy in the oppositions of inner/outer, female/male, East/West, intuition/logic. This affirmation is a part of Forster's achievement. More significant, he takes a further step and sets up through Margaret a double reading in which the poles indecidably include each other and the *différance* of this irreducible difference. It is a process made familiar to us by Derrida.[15] We are forced to think or imagine the "inconceivable," what we have seen as mutually exclusive; we are forced to form conceptions of that for which we have no concepts. The novel's epigraph—"Only connect"—stands at the heart of this difficult process through which Margaret hopes to enable Henry's salvation: "Only connect! That was the whole of her sermon. Only connect the prose and the passion, and both will be exalted, and human love will be seen at its height. Live in fragments no longer" (186–87). At Howards End, Margaret senses this connection of comrades between the house and the wych elm tree: "It was a comrade, bending over the house, strength and adventure in its roots, but in its utmost fingers tenderness. . . .

It was a comrade. House and tree transcended any similes of sex" (206). Significantly, Forster has chosen representative terms—a house and a tree—that resist hierarchical placement and the classical oppositional structure of patriarchal thinking. Margaret reflects that, "to compare either to man, to woman, always dwarfed the vision. Yet they kept within limits of the human. . . . As she stood in the one, gazing at the other, truer relationship had gleamed" (206). Margaret also argues for connection—this discovery of mutual inclusivity—in her conception of proportion: "truth, being alive, was not halfway between anything. It was only to be found by continuous excursions into either realm, and though proportion is the final secret, to espouse it at the outset is to insure sterility" (195). Finally, in the novel's conclusion, Margaret looks toward an "ultimate harmony" (330).

To summarize, the connection that Margaret seeks is obviously not born out of an attempt to merge or to blur or reverse oppositions. She fights the "daily grey" of life, the blending of black and white. Rather, she seeks to dismantle the hierarchical privileging of one term over another. She expresses it as a celebration of "Differences—eternal differences, planted by God in a single family, so that there may always be colour; sorrow perhaps, but colour in the daily grey" (338).

Ironically, however, although the resolution thematically insists on connections and although the patriarch Wilcox is unmanned, the plot appears to encode the patriarchal structures that the novel seeks to escape. I began this essay with the narrator's ambiguous sexual identification. I then quoted a paragraph which is followed by one that reads,

> Here was the core of the question. Henry must be forgiven, and made better by love; nothing else mattered. . . . To her everything was in proportion now. . . . Margaret fell asleep, tethered by affection, and lulled by the murmurs of the river that descended all the night from Wales. She felt herself at one with her future home, colouring it and coloured by it, and awoke to see, for the second time, Oniton Castle conquering the morning mists. [243]

We notice the imagery of proportion, of connection, of mutuality monopolizing the paragraph which, nonetheless, concludes with an image of domination, "Oniton Castle conquering the morning mists." It is possible Forster is being ironic because Oniton is not to be Margaret's home and she is, perhaps, mistaken in so valuing it. Yet, if this is irony, it is irony of a very subtle sort.

I suggest instead that the pattern is not ironic; rather, it anticipates the resolution of the novel where the value of connection, represented by the presence of Henry and Helen at Howards End, is enacted in the plot by Margaret's conquest of Henry. Henry, in masculine style, has earlier told Margaret, "fix your price, and then don't budge," and she has responded,

"But I do budge" (155). Nonetheless, on the issue of connection, she, like her masculine counterparts, won't budge: "He had refused to connect, on the clearest issue that can be laid before a man, and their love must take the consequences" (331). And in the novel's closing paragraphs, Margaret reflects, "There was something uncanny in her triumph. She, who had never expected to conquer anyone, had charged straight through these Wilcoxes and broken up their lives" (341). Margaret has triumphed, conquered, and broken up their lives. This conclusion to a novel about connection is ironic although not, I would suggest, deliberately so.

The irony arises because Forster inscribes the value of connection within the patriarchal dialectic of conquest and defeat, domination and submission, and within a narrative form that demands a resolution instead of "continuous excursions into either realm" (195). Although the themes of the novel indicate a desire to deconstruct the patriarchal ideology, ultimately, it seems, Forster is forced to reconstruct that ideology in the structure of the novel, in Margaret's "victory" over Henry. Plot has demanded a hierarchical ordering of terms for a resolution to conflict even though the novel's themes have argued for replacement of conquest with connection. Forster's often trenchant interrogation of patriarchal language and perspectives appears to give way before the resistless temptation to expropriate the authority available to him in patriarchy. What he *wants* to assert, of course, is the value of the feminine perspective as a first step to dismantling hierarchy, but in the *act* of assertion, he affirms the value of the masculine mode, remaining dependent on patriarchy's hierarchical structures for authority, resolution, and conclusion. Ultimately, Forster recuperates an authority that would thematically seem to be repudiated.

Reaching this point in my argument—where the need to conclude a paper definitively is as imperative as the requirement to resolve a novel—I nonetheless stepped back from my own recuperation of authority, stepped from form to language. Perhaps Forster's critique of patriarchal modes and binary thinking was more trenchant and thoroughgoing than I first perceived. Forster had certainly appropriated the language of conquest, but he had also recontextualized it and, in the process, forestalled expropriation by that masculine terminology. A deep suspicion of conquest in its most notable manifestations—imperialism and war—lies at the very heart of *Howards End*. The narrator simply asserts, contrasting the yeoman who is "England's hope" to the Imperialist who "hopes to inherit the earth," that "the Imperialist is not what he thinks or seems. He is a destroyer. He prepares the way for cosmopolitanism, and though his ambitions may be fulfilled, the earth that he inherits will be grey" (323). Strong biblical cadences underline this apocalyptic vision of a world shaped in a masculine mode.

Perhaps, then, Forster is having his joke when Margaret characterizes her success as a conquest. "She, who had never expected to conquer anyone, had charged straight through these Wilcoxes and broken up their lives" (341). In fact, she has not "charged through"; she has simply done what "seemed easiest" (334). "No better plan had occurred to her" (335). She confesses, "I did the obvious things" (339). "Conquer," in this context, is not an act of self-assertion and dominance but is redefined as nonassertion, an opening up of space, a refusal to accept the exclusivity of opposition between Henry and Helen. "Everyone said [living together at Howards End] was impossible" (338), but Margaret defies this patriarchal logic.

The futility of binary thinking appears in the lives of both Henry and Helen, both of whom declare they are "ended." Henry confesses, "I don't know what to do—what to do. I'm broken—I'm ended" (334).[16] As if in echo, Helen rejoins, "I'm ended. I used to be so dreamy about a man's love as a girl, and think that, for good or evil, love must be the great thing. But it hasn't been" (337). The man of action and the woman of emotion reach the bankruptcy implicit in their exclusive positions. Margaret's conquest or victory, then, is not the patriarchal one demanding suppression of an other but one that emerges as the traditional oppositions destroy themselves and clear a space for difference.

Forster has anticipated this conclusion, as we have seen earlier, in identifying a warfare mentality with Henry Wilcox. But we may now discover a further step Forster has taken. While Henry Wilcox persistently refers to casualties such as Leonard Bast as "part of the battle of life" (191) as if such casualties were in the "nature" of things, Margaret decodes his metaphor: "We upper classes have ruined him, and I suppose you'll tell me it's part of the battle of life" (224). Margaret herself is a master of words, as we see in her first encounter with Leonard Bast when her speeches "flutter away from him like birds" (40). But Margaret's strength lies in recognizing the way ideologies are encoded in language and in acknowledging the social privilege behind her "speech." She early argues, "all our thoughts are the thoughts of six-hundred-pounders, and all our speeches" (61), underlining both the intensity and the futility of Leonard Bast's desire "to form his style on Ruskin" (49). Ruskin's style cannot "speak" Leonard Bast's life.

When Margaret rejects Henry's language and metaphor of life as a battle, she rejects his patriarchal ideology and introduces new terms into the novel. She reflects that "Life is indeed dangerous, but not in the way morality would have us believe. It is indeed unmanageable, but the essence of it is not a battle. It is unmanageable because it is a romance, and its essence is romantic beauty" (107). This passage informs the entire novel and encourages us to reread the metaphors of conquest concluding the novel within a romance topos put into play by the figure of Ruth Wilcox, Henry's first wife.

Margaret's own sense of victory is severely qualified when she learns that Ruth Wilcox had "willed" Howards End to her, had designated her as its "spiritual heir," many years earlier: "Something shook [Margaret's] life in its inmost recesses, and she shivered" (342). Ruth Wilcox is introduced into the novel as one who always "knew," although no one "told her a word" (27). Ruth Wilcox is represented as beyond language deployed as power, beyond the words that cripple communication among the other characters, implicated as they are in ideology. Margaret ultimately asserts to Helen: "I feel that you and I and Henry are only fragments of that woman's mind. She knows everything. She is everything. She is the house, and the tree that leans over it" (313).

Miss Avery, who after Mrs. Wilcox's death becomes her representative, prophesies to Margaret: "You think you won't come back to live here [at Howards End], but you will" (272), and Margaret, who has discounted her words, is disturbed to find them fulfilled when she and Helen sleep in the house: "It is disquieting to fulfil a prophecy, however superficially" (302). She will, of course, fulfill it much more deeply, making Howards End her permanent home, as, increasingly, Margaret herself recognizes the "power of the house. It kills what is dreadful and makes what is beautiful live" (300).

As Margaret moves toward insight and vision, she, too, moves away from language. The narrator comments, for example, that Margaret's "mind trembled toward a conclusion which only the unwise will put into words" (205). And later we learn that Margaret "had outgrown stimulants, and was passing from words to things," an inevitable process "if the mind itself is to become a creative power" (262). Finally, Margaret admits to Helen, who calls her life "heroic," "No doubt I have done a little towards straightening the tangle, but things that I can't phrase have helped me" (339).

At best, because of its ideological character, language can take characters to the brink of understanding as it does when Margaret exposes Henry's hypocrisy in committing adultery himself and refusing to forgive it in Helen. Margaret confronts Henry: "I think you yourself recommended plain speaking." And the narrator reveals that "they looked at each other in amazement. The precipice was at their feet now" (307). Language takes them to the abyss, but it cannot reconstruct their lives on a new basis because they cannot form conceptions of that for which there is no concept. Margaret simply relies on "the power of the house."

As we reconsider Forster's resolution in light of Mrs. Wilcox and the spiritual heir she seeks for Howards End, we notice that the novel moves toward resolution, but it is a resolution that existed from the beginning as a "part of Mrs. Wilcox's mind" (315). In that respect, the plot subverts its own commitment to hierarchy and sequence, to prior and subsequent events. In addition, the power that has "defeated" Henry Wilcox, the patriarch, is diffused over the universe. At the end of the novel, Henry Wilcox lies suffering with hay fever, confined to the house, recalling Miss Avery's words with their echoes of battle imagery: "There's not one Wilcox that can stand up against a field in June" (273). The patriarch is "shut up in the house," and his wife pronounces, "It has to be. . . . The hay-fever is his chief objection to living here, but he thinks it worth while" (336).

As previously noted, the novel's last words belong to Helen, who rushes into the house with her child and the neighbor boy accompanied by "shouts of infectious joy": "We've seen to the very end," she cries, "and it'll be such a crop of hay as never" (343). To see "to the very end," in this scene and in the novel as a whole, is to discover the beginning of possibility: "such a crop of hay as never." The last phrase is appropriate, too, concluding with a "never" that has already been subverted. In its closure, the novel gestures toward an open space, like a field in June, that "not one Wilcox . . . can stand up against." It is a "closure" that echoes Hélène Cixous on *écriture féminine*. Though Cixous is speaking of women writers, she describes what I am arguing that Forster has achieved:

> [Writers] must invent the impregnable language that will wreck partitions, classes, and rhetorics, regulations and codes, they must submerge, cut through, get beyond the ultimate reserve-discourse, including the one that laughs at the very idea of pronouncing the word "silence," the one that, aiming for the impossible, stops short before the word "impossible" and writes it as "the end."[17]

This reading seems more true to the narrative and linguistic procedures of Forster's *Howards End*. But it raises further questions. Can Forster thus evade the connection between discourse and power by postulating an unspoken knowledge? Indeed, the pressure of resolution may seem inevitably to produce an evasion as Forster gestures toward an alternative to binary thinking, a "conclusion that only the unwise will put into words." It is, at best, an uneasy truce. And this final inaccessible metaphysics may leave us frustrated by our own continuing embattlement with language, power, and patriarchy.

## Notes

1. After the early, enthusiastic appreciation of Forster's work set in motion by Lionel Trilling, *E. M. Forster* (New York: New Directions, 1943), and Trilling's identification of

*Howards End* as "undoubtedly Forster's masterpiece," because it develops to their full the themes and attitudes of the early books and connects them "with a more mature sense of responsibility" (114–15), other critics have not been content to rest with the thematic coherence of his work and have disagreed with Trilling's assessment. They have located Forster's reliance on nineteenth-century modes as a source of the novel's weakness. See, for example, Frederick Crews, who feels that Margaret's " 'connection' with the Wilcoxes is merely diagrammatic" and that Forster's "plot must finally retreat to an unconvincingly 'moral' ending" (*E. M. Forster: The Perils of Humanism* [Princeton, NJ: Princeton University Press, 1962], 122). See also Wilfred Stone, who claims that "The forces of value do not 'connect,' but pursue each other in a lonely and circular futility. And the circle is especially vicious because Forster seems to see only its 'proportion' and not its 'emptiness' " (*The Cave and the Mountain: A Study of E. M. Forster* [Stanford, CA: Stanford University Press, 1966], 266).

I hope my own analysis identifies a new way to see the narrative strengths and challenges of Forster's novel, to perceive those techniques and questions that align him with other literary modernists. At the same time, my goal in this essay is to give another perspective from which to assess the novel's difficulties, which have been too readily grouped under the rubric of Forster's return to a nineteenth-century liberal humanism.

2. Francis King, *E. M. Forster and His World* (New York: Scribner, 1978), 57.
3. Ibid., 64
4. P. N. Furbank, *E. M. Forster: A Life*, 2 vols. (New York and London: Harcourt Brace Jovanovich, 1977, 1978), 2:40.
5. D. A. Miller, *The Novel and the Police* (Berkeley and Los Angeles: University of California Press, 1988), 154–55.
6. Eve Kosofsky Sedgwick, *Between Men: English Literature and Male Homosocial Desire* (New York: Columbia University Press, 1985), 20, has made an important connection here between misogyny and fear of the feminine. She argues that "homophobia directed by men against men is misogynistic, and perhaps transhistorically so. (By 'misogynistic' I mean not only that it is oppressive of the so-called feminine in men, but that it is oppressive of women)." Sedgwick also notes that, although antihomophobia and feminism are not the same forces, the bonds between them are "profound and intuitable."
7. E. M. Forster, *Howards End* (New York: Random House, Vintage Books, 1921), 243. All subsequent references are from this edition, and page numbers are provided in the text.
8. One critic who has observed that the narrator is female is Kinley Roby, "Irony and Narrative Voice in *Howards End*," *Journal of Narrative Technique* 2 (May 1972), but his argument differs sharply from mine because he uses the evidence that Forster has created a female narrator to argue for Forster's separation from and *condemnation* of the narrator's narrow and biased attitudes: "The contrast between the action of the novel and the narrator's view of that action suggests that the narrator and the group for whom she claims to speak see the world neither steadily nor as a whole. . . . Forster seems to be suggesting that the narrator and those like her cannot have their 'islands,' their illusions and, at the same time, a world worth inhabiting" (123).
9. There is some evidence from contemporaneous reviews that Forster's narrator and the narrative point of view were problematic. Indeed, some reviewers were persuaded that E. M. Forster must be a woman who had adopted a male pseudonym. Elia Pettie of the *Chicago Tribune*, in support of her argument that Forster was female, wrote: "In feeling the book is feminine" (cited in Philip Gardner, ed., *E. M. Forster: The Critical Heritage* [London and Boston: Routledge and Kegan Paul, 1973], 160). Gardner also notes in his introduction that Pettie's conviction had British precedent: "The idea [that Forster was female] had already been whispered in passing" (5).
10. Philip Gardner, *E. M. Forster* (London: Longmans, 1977), has also noted of *Howards End*, identifying Forster with his narrator, that "at times Forster's [comments] to the reader lack his usual authority and aplomb" (25).

11. It is a commonplace to recognize that Forster's novel is built upon oppositions. He himself said about the book's composition: "I am grinding out my novel into a contrast between money and death" (cited in King, *Forster and His World,* 49). Other critics have generally cited the clash between the material and spiritual lives, the seen and the unseen, Bentham and Coleridge, Lloyd George liberalism and classical liberalism. My own interpretation takes the gender conflict as preeminent.
12. The subject of androgyny has become a vexed one in contemporary feminist discourse. In early stages of the feminist movement, the argument for equal treatment of women and men seemed to depend on detecting similarities: the masculine in the feminine and the feminine in the masculine. Then androgyny seemed the ideal. Subsequently, women have wanted to argue for the authority of the female perspective and values, and androgyny as a concept has become less attractive. It is interesting, in this light, that Forster doesn't advocate the merging of traits androgyny implies but instead insists on preserving distinctions. He is, in that regard, closer to the spirit of a contemporary discourse that speaks of escaping hierarchies.
13. Glen Caveliero suggests a similar point but does not develop it in *A Reading of E. M. Forster's Novels* (Totowa, NJ: Rowman and Littlefield, 1979). Caveliero writes: "Although it is possible to detect an anti-female bias in his work, it is really in the interests of feminine values and fulfillment that he writes, and the kind of wisdom he advocates goes well beyond the contemporary sexual polarizations. Even as a homosexual he was ahead of his time" (127–28). Also, Anne Wyatt-Brown, in "*Howards End:* Celibacy and Stalemate," *Psychohistory Review* 12, no. 1 (Fall 1983): 29, argues that Forster lends "his own feelings to Margaret; surely the pressures of virginity that drove her into Henry Wilcox's arms were his own."
14. Contemporaneous reviewers testify to Forster's success at representing female friendship: An unsigned reviewer in the *Atheneum* wrote: "the great thing in the book is the sisters' affection for each other. . . . personal relationships . . . have never, we venture to say, been made more beautiful or more real" (cited in Gardner, *Critical Heritage,* 151). Forster's success here, and I would argue that he does succeed, is the more remarkable if we consider that Virginia Woolf wrote in *A Room of One's Own* (New York: Harcourt Brace and World, 1929): " 'Chloe liked Olivia.' I read. And then it struck me how immense a change was there. Chloe liked Olivia perhaps for the first time in literature" (86). Woolf argues that the representation of female friendship depends on female writers and so seems to forget Forster's novel. But his treatment of women must have impressed her at one time. Vanessa Bell invited Forster, after the publication of *Howards End,* to speak at the Friday Club on "The Feminine Note in Literature." According to Furbank, "Virginia told him [Forster] afterwards it was the best paper the Club had heard so far" (*Forster: A Life,* 1: 193).

    It is an interesting, if small, point that critics Wilfred Stone, *Cave and Mountain,* 239, and Elizabeth Heine, "E. M. Forster and the Bloomsbury Group," *Cahiers d'Etudes & de Recherches Victoriennes & Edouardiennes (CVE)* 4–5 (1977): 47–48, have pointed to Virginia and Vanessa Stephen as models for the Schlegel sisters although Forster himself claimed the three sisters of Goldsworthy Lowes Dickinson as his models ("The Art of Fiction," *Paris Review* 1 [1953]: 37).
15. Although I find *différance* a fruitful concept for allowing us to see Forster's achievement in a new light—for allowing us to perceive a radical dimension to his art obscured by previous insistence that he belongs to a nineteenth-century tradition of liberal humanism—I am not doing a Derridean deconstruction on this text. Indeed, the conclusion I postulate—Margaret's ultimate spiritual insight outside language—Derrida would probably see as a metaphysics. I am, however, inevitably led to see the parallels between Forster's conception of connection and Derrida's notion of *différance,* both of which are crucial to the problem of sexual difference.
16. The tendency among critics has been to pose the Schlegel sisters together in opposition to

the Wilcoxes. Frederick Crews is one critic who appreciates the distinctions Forster has drawn between Helen and Margaret and the similarities between Helen and Henry: "Henry and Helen together are people who isolate and simplify rather than allowing their imaginations to play across a broad range of related circumstances. . . . Both the Wilcoxes and Helen are unwilling to come to grips with prosaic reality" (*E. M. Forster,* 120).

17. Hélène Cixous, "The Laugh of the Medusa," in *New French Feminisms: An Anthology,* ed. Elaine Marks and Isabelle de Courtivron (New York: Schocken, 1981), 256.

# The Resentments of Robert Frost

FRANK LENTRICCHIA

By 1919 Louis Untermeyer—Robert Frost's most assiduously cultivated (if unwitting) literary operative—could declare in the opening sentence to the first edition of his soon-to-be influential anthology, *Modern American Poetry,* that "America's poetic renascence" was more than just a bandied and self-congratulatory phrase of advanced literary culture: "it is a fact."[1] And on the basis of that fact or wish (it hardly matters which) Untermeyer and Harcourt Brace made what turned out to be a lucrative wager on the poetry market through seven editions of the anthology, the latter of which entered the university curriculum and stayed there through the 1940s and 1950s, bearing to more than one generation of faculty and students the news of the poetry of modernism and at the same time establishing well into the sixties a list of modernist musts: Frost foremost, together with strong representations of Pound, Eliot, Stevens, Williams, Hart Crane, and a long list of more briefly represented—and now mostly forgotten—poets. What Untermeyer had succeeded in presenting in his later editions, against his own literary and social values, was a stylistic texture of modern American poetry so mixed as to defy the force of canonical directive. If the poetry of modernism could include Frost, Stevens, Pound, Marianne Moore, and Langston Hughes, then maybe the phenomenon of modernism embraced a diversity of intentions too heterogeneous to satisfy the tidy needs of historical definition.

But the first edition of Untermeyer's book offered no such collagelike portrait of the emerging scene of modern American poetry: no Eliot, Stevens, or Williams, only a token of Pound and the avant-gardists. Untermeyer's anthology of 1919 was in fact heavily studded with names that had appeared a few years earlier in the anthology of his chief genteel competitor, Jessie Belle Rittenhouse's *Little Book of Modern Verse* (1912)—including the name of Rittenhouse herself. The economic interests of Untermeyer and his publisher, as Untermeyer would acknowledge years later, ensured that his declaration of the new be accompanied not by an avant-garde act of rupture but by a conciliating act that veiled his differences with the popular taste that Rittenhouse, then in her second edition, had so well played to.[2] The first edition of Rittenhouse's anthology had sold over 100,000 copies, a fact never apparently lost on Untermeyer, who through all of his editions managed to include poems that Rittenhouse would have admired and which, through no stretch of imagination, would be included under anybody's definition of modernism.

Rittenhouse, a major literary journalist in the American scene in the first two decades of this century,[3] published in 1904 what must have been the first book to attempt a characterization of *modern* American poetry (*The Younger American Poets*), though not one writer she took up has survived in recent accounts of American literary history (not even for a sentence). She made it her business to get to know the literary powers of the day in New York and Boston, interviewing many of them for major northeast dailies; became chief poetry reviewer for the *New York Times;* and a founder in 1910 of the Poetry Society of America. In her various writings and anthologies she could say who was in and who (usually by omission) was out, and though recent historians have not ratified any of her choices and do not know her name, she was a force who represented both in her female person and in her taste the aesthetic grain that the emerging modernist male poets worked against: the principle of "the Feminine in literature," as Eliot put it,[4] which he was none too anxious to give space to in *The Egoist;* the "Aunt Hepsy" that Pound saw as typifying poetry's contemporary audience in the United States;[5] one of those—again Pound—who had turned poetry (for serious people) into "balderdash—a sort of embroidery for dilettantes and women."[6]

Like Stedman's *American Anthology* (1900) and Francis Palgrave's *Golden Treasury* (1867), in its several editions a best-seller in America, Rittenhouse's *Little Book of Modern Verse* sustained an innocent lyric ideal of sweetness, the voice of unadulterated song. Nothing in her anthology contradicted the literary principles announced by Palgrave and Stedman in their respective prefaces, where they characterized lyric by what they excluded: no narrative, no description of local, regional cast; no humor (the antithesis of the lyric mode, according to Palgrave); no intellect at meditation; nothing occasional; nothing dramatic—no textures of blank verse because lyric in its purity excludes the dramatic voice in its speaking cadences; certainly no vernacular. Eliot would say that a real poet could amalgamate his experiences of falling in love and reading Spinoza because a real poet's sensibility was not dissociated; a real poet did not shrink from the impurities of heterogeneous experience.[7] Palgrave, Stedman, and Rittenhouse were champions of the dissociated lyric of exclusion, the homogeneity of the isolate, autonomous, unmixed feeling (no ironists allowed), and their books sanctioned and sustained that lyric ideal through the young manhoods of the modernists-to-be who would in some large part learn how to write a "modern" poetry by writing against "poetry" as it was underwritten by these major taste makers and the mass-circulation magazines that gave space to genteel lyric and precious little else.

Stedman summed up genteel America's poetic ideal most provocatively when, in an I-told-you-so aside, he noted that the Civil War had motivated no "little classics of absolute song."[8] Democratic cultures, as we know, are not supposed to venerate heroic ideals; the big epic literary classic is presumably beyond our reach—which leaves us with the little or lyric classic, but even that is imperiled by the forces of social environment, the penetration of lyric interiority by temporal immediacy. The unhappy result, in the embedded logic of Stedman's lament, is the birth of the impure or "partial" song, song not quite emptied of worldly interests and pressures—lyric too much with the world. Joyce Kilmer thought Rittenhouse had "raised anthology-making to a fine art."[9] Frost thought otherwise. He told one correspondent that her title was "silly."[10] He didn't explain what he meant, but he must have meant that she had no right to the word "modern"; and, of course, by the governing aesthetic dicta of genteel anthology making, she didn't. In the world of Palgrave and Stedman, "modern lyric" is a contradiction in terms, not to mention a besmirching of the category of lyric. Lyric practice by male and female writers seemed to Pound and Frost an effeminate business, and cultural authority in the female person of Jessie Belle must have made it seem doubly so.

Aside from needing to make a buck, Untermeyer needed to make a point or two. If he was at veiled war with Rittenhouse and genteel culture, then he was at open polemics with Conrad Aiken over whose version of the new poetry would achieve cultural authority, which new poets would survive. For Untermeyer the modern moment was peculiarly American, its progenitors his benign versions of Whitman and Dickinson, its vision hopeful and democratic, its formal manner always submissive to its human content: art with positive social function. The decadence of Stevens, the assiduous internationalism of Pound, the tenuous inwardness of Eliot, all represented an unhealthy foreign strain, an elitist art-for-art's-sake plying of the craft for a coterie audience: undemocratic to the core, Untermeyer believed, because an art that only the culturally privileged could make any sense of.[11] *Modern American Poetry* was aimed at a mass audience for economic reasons, but its democratic ideology also demanded a mass audience, and as a perfectly blended capitalist/populist venture Untermeyer's book stood against the coterie anthologies only recently put out by the New York avant-garde, by Pound, and by Wyndham Lewis (*Others, The Catholic*

*Anthology, Blast*). So upon the economic success of *Modern American Poetry* hung Untermeyer's version of the future of the new poetry, his desire for a poetry rooted in diverse American cultures, and his hopes for the reading and dissemination of poetry in a democratic society. Upon the economic success of Untermeyer's anthology hung the cultural authority of the party of Van Wyck Brooks's nativist intellectuals, the cultural politics of "America's coming-of-age," of which *Modern American Poetry* was the anthological representative.

Untermeyer went polemically further in his companion critical volume, *The New Era in American Poetry* (also published in 1919), in which he characterized the work of Pound, Stevens, and their aesthetic companions published by Walter Arensberg's *Others* as "mere verbal legerdemain," effeminate and morbid.[12] Aiken, Eliot's collegemate and long-time correspondent, counterattacked in a review of the book in the *New Republic* with the charge that Untermeyer's celebration in American poetry of "the unflinchingly masculine" (which he glossed with the words "Americanism" and "lustihood") was unwittingly a celebration of the most conservative of poetic and political values.[13] Poetry with the right message—the carefully monitored poetry of the ideal state, good for the education of soldiers—had been welcomed by Plato, after all, poetry's most celebrated historical enemy. Aiken argued that Untermeyer's soft socialist politics, grafted onto a happy version of Whitman, blinded him to the force of the true revolutionaries who were "throwing their bombs into the aesthetic arena": not Frost, Sandburg, Masters, Robinson, and Lindsay (those low modernists who dominated the first edition of *Modern American Poetry*) but the formal innovators, the high modernists of "absolute poetry" to whom Untermeyer had given such short shrift.[14] Untermeyer never managed to, or could, say why the stance of virility or the politics of social democracy required poetic representation, or what difference it could make to virility or democracy that they be imagined in an aesthetic rather than in some other medium. Aiken, on the other hand, who declared himself on the side of literary experimentation as the agency of art for art's sake, never managed to, or could, say what connection obtained, if any, between literary and social experimentation, or why he should be taken seriously when he described the literary avant-gardist as a bomb-throwing radical. What surfaces in this early argument within modernism is one of the most ancient topics in literary theory, that of the relationship of art and the commonweal, here, in the Aiken–Untermeyer clash, given what would become its definitive framing in the critical literature of modernism, where aesthetics and politics are typically forced by rhetorical heat to stand in opposition even as that same rhetoric of modernist polemic causes them suspiciously (because protesting too much) to lean toward one another, as if revolution in poetry and social change could not be imagined outside a relation of strong interdependence.

But if, in Aiken's view, Untermeyer's introduction to *Modern American Poetry* seemed in its immediate polemical context to cherish too chauvinistically the peculiarly American possibilities for poetic renascence and too eager to court insulation from European traditions, if Untermeyer appeared to be replaying Emerson's call in "The American Scholar" for an American literature free from servility to British aesthetic rule, rooted in the American commonplaces, and therefore worthy of the American social experiment, then on Untermeyer's behalf it ought to be remembered that his distinguishing heritage was not Emersonian New England but German-Jewish immigrant stock and that his revision of Emerson's ideas on the relations of literary expression to their cultural matrix was worked out at the high tide of our heaviest period of immigration. What Untermeyer needed to see in the new poetry was aesthetic responsiveness to voices that were never heard at the cosmopolitan finishing schools of genteel America, voices that were virtually unrepresented in poetic traditions before Wordsworth because they were unworthy of the memorialization provided by traditional producers of literature, whose typical objects of representation were people like themselves, with privileged routes to the acquisition of literacy. Alongside genteel authors Untermeyer published a black poet (Paul Laurence Dunbar), several Jews, T. A. Daly, a Philadelphia Irish-American journalist whose speciality was Italian-American dialect, and numerous poets from outside the northeast corner of the United States. In his critical book he devoted an entire chapter to the Italian immigrant socialist admirer of Whitman, Arturo Giovannitti: America was changing and as an untraditional literary voice himself, Untermeyer, the literary historian as anthologist, found himself in the sensitive political position to disseminate his vision of an America in which poetry emerged not from one or two culturally elite centers but from everywhere; a poetry which, in refusing legendary, traditional, and classical poetic materials and their generally economically advantaged authors, in choosing its *materia poetica* from everywhere but the traditional sources, was in effect fashioning itself as a revolutionary literature standing against what literature had been. From the traditional perspective, the new poetry was an antipoetic poetry that even the "conservative *New York Times*,"[15] as Untermeyer put it, had to acknowledge had dislodged poetic traditions in this country in favor of a writing that insisted on prosaic everydayness, not only as subject but as its very medium of expression; a poetry which in following the lead of Howells, Twain, and the new novel would spell the death of genteel aesthetic ideals and at the same time signal a larger death, that of genteel America's cultural and political authority.

Although Untermeyer probably tuned into much of this American cultural and social change on his own—he was a keen observer of the literary scene—his sensibility was nevertheless being shrewdly nurtured and directed by his correspondence with Robert Frost, his favorite poet of the new school, who by the time he returned home from England in 1915 had set himself against Pound and the self-conscious avant-garde and was fully engaged in the entrepreneurial process of staging his own image as a different, an American kind of modernist. The Frostian directives that got into both Untermeyer's anthology and the critical volume of 1919 must have sounded to Aiken like Wordsworth's Preface to *Lyrical Ballads* revisited, an effort to finish off a poetic revolution that had gotten sidetracked by Tennysonian aestheticism and the various moods of the 1890s. What Untermeyer thought he saw emerging in American poetry—the discarding of a "stilted" (he meant a rare, rhetorical, ornate, *writerly*) vocabulary, in favor of what he called a sincere, simple "daily vocabulary" (a vocal language of everyday situation)—appears to overcome the very mediation of print itself, so that we can virtually hear the speaker on the printed page. All of it amounted to the creation of a literature whose most powerful effect lay in the illusion it created of its unliterariness, in its refusal to borrow its verbal modes and tics from official poetic history, from Poetry with a capital letter under the imprimatur of Francis Palgrave.[16] Modern American poetry, Untermeyer thought, would be recognizable by its unliterary (vernacular) borrowing directly from life itself: Like Frost and the realists he meant by "life" the lives of the historically unsung—therein lay the radical, the "modern," and the "American" character of "modern American poetry." But what this account of the new poetry left out (this, perhaps, is the root of Aiken's impatience with Untermeyer's downplaying of the aesthetic dimension) is that such radicality is mainly perceptible only to those with keen awareness of the history of English poetry, because only those (not the unlettered man celebrated by Untermeyer's Whitmanesque ideal) are in a position to grasp basic shifts in literary history; to grasp not a change from "literariness" to "lifelikeness" but a change from established kinds of literariness, and the social bases that supported such writing, to a new kind of literariness, presumably an organic expression of a new kind of social arrangement: literary change, in so many words, as index of social change and proleptic glimpse and push in the direction American society might be heading. The historically startling idea that social change might be reflected in and directed by lyric poetry, of all things, as well as in the grungy bourgeois forms of prose fiction, where accounts of social conflict are to be expected—in a novelized poetry that (Untermeyer's words) "explores the borderland of poetry and prose"[17] and thereby, at that generic crossing, explores fundamental social differences: this was perhaps the most deeply buried issue of the relation of aesthetics and politics that lay unexamined between Untermeyer and Aiken, Frost's line of the modern and Pound's.

In his battle with inherited poetic diction, Frost believed that in *North of Boston* he had scored a decisive victory in literary history because there he had "dropped to an everyday level of diction that even Wordsworth kept above"; there, in *North of Boston,* he had performed "in a language absolutely unliterary" and had barred from his writing all "words and expressions he had merely *seen*" (in books) and had not "*heard* used in running speech."[18] "Words that are the product of another poet's imagination," as he declared in his strongest avant-garde moment, "cannot be passed off again. . . . All this using of poetic diction is wrong."[19] This, he explained, was the essence of his "war on clichés," which he later described as a war on all structure, systems, and system building.[20] But he didn't want to be misunderstood, as he believed Pound had misunderstood him, as "a spontaneous untutored child" because he was not "undesigning."[21] What Frost's design amounted to was an antinomian intention to undo all design (all intention, all structure) in its institutional incarnation and sanction. "What I suspect we hate," he wrote in 1937, "is canons, which are no better than my guidances insisted on as your guidances."[22] For canons are on the side of stabilization and tradition and would give the rule of the dead over the living, once and for all. But literature, Frost thought, is the very spirit of insubordination, as such the anticanonical principle verbally incarnate. If nothing is "momentous," if "nothing is final," then, he concluded, literary canons and the critical generalizations that produce and sustain them are instruments of literary repression wielded by professors in Frost's constant institutional target of literary repression, the university or college.[23]

The logic of Frost's poetics equates literary insubordination with literature itself, and literature with modern literature, not as some specific historical style evolved in the early twentieth century but as something like the very spirit of literature finding its fullest incarnation in an American scene that provided its true (because democratic) political directive: No literature except in radically individualized expression. In his arguments on behalf of the vernacular as an intoned and intransigent locality, the basis of a vital and living literary voice, "entangled somehow in the syntax, idiom and meaning of a sentence," Frost named the multiheaded enemy of literary insubordination—that is to say, the enemy of *literature*—as the professorial sentence, the dead, grammatical discourse taught at school; the poets of classical tradition, fawned over by professors who teach them as literary models but whose sentences in living speech are not accessible to us; and the reiterated poeticisms of English tradition preserved and sustained by contemporary genteel anthologists like Stedman and Rittenhouse: all those enemies of a living (i.e., a "contemporary," a genuinely "modern") literature who come at us from the feminized crypt of manliness, the book.[24]

"Words," Frost said in a striking proverbial moment, "exist in the mouth," their masculine origin, "not in books," their effeminate emasculation.[25] He told his son Carol, in a startling letter of sexual-poetic self-evocation, that Carol had written "No sissy poem such as I get from poetic boys." (And note "poetic boys": The provocatively gendered responses of Frost, Pound, and other male modernists were to a literary style, a cultural feminization, at work in the writing of both sexes.) It seems that Carol (who with a name like that maybe needed to hear this) had managed to "ram" his writing "full of all sorts of things"; the poem he sent his father had been "written with a man's vigor and goes down into a man's depth."[26] The mark of Frost's own manliness lay (this is a frequent boast in his letters) in the success he had in breaking through the genteel lyric, as if through a cultural chastity belt, a vernacular desert from which Stedman and other genteel cultural critics had outlawed the conversational voice. And it lay in his success in "bringing to book" tones never heard before in poetry.[27] Frost's sexual self-image as a writer would define him simultaneously as phallic inseminator (vigorous rammer, which no sissy, feminized male was capable of becoming) and radical female creator ("bringing to book" was his literary turn on "bringing to bed" with child), all for the purpose of penetrating down—now the homoerotic image—into a man's depth.

Frost's ideal audience would not be composed of the Aunt Hepsys contemptuously alluded to by Pound as the real material base of reception for genteel lyric. His ideal audience would be no feminized audience in need of feeling his "prowess" (a favorite term with Frost, describing his feats of literary "performance"); it would be, rather, a skeptical and even scoffing masculinized audience whose American cultural formation had made it resistant to poetic reception but which might receive him in its depth if his was the verse of a writer who is all man and whose poetry does not present itself under the conventional genteel signs of "poetry."[28] Often a sneering coded term in the critical reflections of the emerging poets of modernism, American "poetry" at the turn of the century constantly flies and flees into the circumambient gases, as one of the gurus of modernism, T. E. Hulme, put it in scornful dismissal of nineteenth-century soft lyric ideals.[29] Poetry, Hulme argued, must become instead "hard" and "dry."[30] It must cease being "the great passive vulva," as Hulme's intellectual brother Ezra Pound would write of the London literary scene at the turn of the century.[31] A real man's poetry would not be shamed by confrontation with the real if, as Frost insisted against various nineteenth-century idealist rhetorics of lyricism, he did not "create" but "summoned" voices from the quotidian in all their particularity.[32] The act of summoning voices from the vernacular would be the sign of masculinity in poetry, an invitation to poetic reading that real (economically earnest) men might find seductive because redolent with the odors of a world they knew and the new lyric poet's key technical liaison with the already powerfully emerged realist novel that might win for him, an American male lyricist, social acceptance in an American capitalist context, which typically encoded economic and cultural roles in engendered opposition.

So Frost's struggle against canonical forces was a struggle carried out on behalf of a new lyric diction and therefore new (and low) lyric social materials (below even Wordsworth), for the purpose of reengendering lyric for "masculinity," a word in Frost's and other poetic modernists' lexicons signifying not a literal opening of the lyric to actual male voices and subjects but a symbolic shattering of a constrictive lyric decorum that had the effect, in Frost's America, of denigrating poetry as the province of leisured women in their land of cultural irrelevance. (Frost's experiments in fact often featured at their very center economically disadvantaged female voices.) Unlike the old lyric, the modern lyric (like modern America itself) would be (should be) indecorously open ("full of all sorts of things"); the old lyric, which Frost talked about as if it were coextensive with poetry itself and what it had been, "left to its own tendencies" "would exclude everything but love and the moon" in its decorously pure, homogeneous texture.[33] Frost's struggle against the traditional author and the traditional lyric was simultaneously a struggle against both social and literary exclusion. The new lyric would be "modern" because it would implicitly stand as a political rebuke to traditional literature: revolutionary because heterogeneous in form, style, diction, subject, social origin, and social reference. In Untermeyer's and Frost's America, the new manly lyric would be an expressive medium of the collage of cultures America was fast becoming, the literary resistance to the cultural melting pot, a genuinely American creation, true to the radical spirit of the American social experiment.

Frost made his points in letters, not in essays, but because his thought made an appearance in Untermeyer's critical prose and as the hidden genius of his anthology, it made its historical impact. Concurrent with Frost's gendered, socially expansive, and novelized efforts to rethink and rewrite lyric, Pound and Eliot pursued parallel efforts to open up the lyric, but in more public ways, in essays of immediate critical impact which eventually gave rise to a codified theory of poetry, the critical representation of modernity that came to be known as the New Criticism. In one of its most elegant expressions, Robert Penn Warren in "Pure and Impure Poetry" (1943) provides at once a focus for the issues of the emerging new lyric around 1912 and the ironic costs of the institutional prestige it had achieved by the late 1940s when Warren, Cleanth Brooks, John Crowe Ransom, and Allen Tate had secured the domination of T. S. Eliot's poetics and criticism.

Like Frost, and in a gesture typical of the drastically narrowed idea of poetic types that had taken hold early in the nineteenth century, Warren—following Poe's pronouncement that a long poem is a contradiction in terms—identifies poetry with the singular subjective intensity of the short lyric and its tendency to exclude everything but feeling anchored in nothing but its own self-regard. In a key allegorical moment of alliance with the very aesthetic ideals that he would critically revise, Warren says, "Poetry wants to be pure, but poems do not."[34] The impurity that lyric would exclude—and that Warren would put back into poems—turns out to be coextensive with the world of "prose and imperfection," by which Warren means the everyday world represented in realist fiction—"unbeautiful, disagreeable, or neutral materials," "situation, narrative," "realistic details, exact description, realism in general."[35] Warren's list of excluded impurities is notable for its aesthetic conservatism. He doesn't really disagree with Poe that there is such a thing as poetic decorum: because if there are such things as inherently unbeautiful or disagreeable materials, then there must be an inherently beautiful object toward which "poetry" might properly yearn. And his list is notable as well for its interesting confusion of realms, with some elements in the list referring to things in the world that "poetry" (to its detriment) doesn't wish to take account of and other elements referring to the realist literary medium of their representation. The oddity of Warren's effort to liberate poets from the straitjacketing decorum of "poetry" is that it must grant the genteel aesthete's point—that there is a realm of the beautiful which is poetry's proper object—precisely in order to establish the identity of the "poem," whose character would lie in its act of avoiding "poetry." Strong mixtures of subject, diction, tone, and allusion are the trademarks of the tough-minded modernist poem that Warren and other New Critics admired in Eliot and which they theorized in their essays as signs of highest literary value. But these signs of the new poetics bear a haunted, historical quality—an uneasy consciousness (ironic, nostalgic, sometimes both at once) of the way things used to be, of what can no longer be written but which is nevertheless often evoked in gestures of modernist farewell.

Like Frost's, Warren's account of traditional lyric (via romantic aesthetics) would appear to identify lyric substance with unsituated feelings of love, a subjectivity whose object knows no history. Poe's beautiful dead woman would be something like the logical object and fulfillment of this aesthetic and affective drive, the essence of lyric idealism, not its deviation. Frost calls the traditional lyric object "love and the moon"; Warren's examples of lyric are almost all drawn from the literature of love. So Frost and Warren pursue, because they understand, the issue of lyric purity in its late-nineteenth-century embattled generic context in which the contemporary genteel lyric was being pushed gleefully into the grave by the novel and the polemical defenders of realism. They implicitly define the modernist moment for poetry as the moment of realist pressure upon the lyric; both, but Warren more than Frost, hypostatize a lyric impulse drained of historical specificity in direct proportion to their sensitivity to the generic dominance of a kind of writing (realist fiction) whose central claim to cultural value was its historical density. The struggle for literary liberation in the early modern moment of American poetry was directed against genteel idealism and its Victorian and romantic sources, but the seductive pull of that idealism in the embryonic moments of modernist literary culture turned out to be greater, more insidious, more invasive than might appear at face value in modernist polemic and manifesto.

Frost's effort to destroy what Poe, Tennyson, and Swinburne had wrought (and Palgrave, Stedman, and Rittenhouse had institutionalized) by dramatically adapting rhythms and aural qualities of the traditional lyric to the cacophonous, speaking rhythms of voices in worldly situations is an effort to come to terms with the novel, as is his theory that everything "written is as good as it is dramatic—even the most unassuming lyric," which must be heard as "spoken by a person in a scene—in character, in a setting."[36] His desire to be known as a poet who had summoned (not created) tones and rhythms from actual speech is as good a sign as we have of how far down in prestige traditional notions of "poetry" had sunk in the rankings of the literary genres by the early twentieth century. If in middle-class societies the novel had displaced the epic of traditional culture, and if classic forms of drama were increasingly being "replaced" (Pound's acidic reflection) by more popular and economically feasible forms of theater, then what role could possibly be imagined for the lyric?[37] Only half kiddingly, Wallace Stevens asked Elsie Moll to keep it a secret that he was, some ten years after his Harvard experiments in decadence, returning to the making of verses, a habit he described as "positively lady-like."[38] In a letter of May 2, 1913, Frost expressed similar male discomfort when he remarked on the ease with which English men, as opposed to their pragmatic American counterparts, could attend to their aesthetic inclinations without sparking a scandal of gender decorum violated: "I like that about the English—they all have time to dig in the ground for the nonutilitarian flower. I mean the men. It marks the great difference between them and our men." In the same letter Frost goes on to nominate himself the rare exception among American males—a digger of the wildflower, like a man he knew who "was a byword in five townships for the flowers he tended with his own hand" (pansy!). With sardonic joy he links his cultivation of the poetic with that same non-utilitarian and—this is the American cultural logic—unmanly pursuit ("I have certain useless accomplishments to my credit").[39] So when twenty years later he praises his son for the manliness of his poetic style and adds, "You perhaps don't realize what this means to me,"[40] he is reflecting in the precisest terms possible the crisis in the genteel lyric that such as he, Pound, Eliot, and others had precipitated when they decided (after, in Frost's and Pound's cases, brief flirtations with the novel) to devote their literary energies to producing a new (manly) lyric mode.

This issue of manliness is the historical thread binding Frost and Warren's New Criticism and an index to the difference between the historical situation of the new lyric at its emergence point and the historical situation of its triumphs of the 1920s and 1930s, when it was difficult to see it any longer as new writing in struggle against official forms of literariness, when, in fact, by the early forties, when Warren's essay appeared, the new lyric's open ("impure") and heterogeneous character was fast becoming no longer perceptible as a historically specific discourse because it had been thoroughly institutionalized as the way poems always had been at their best. Brooks's landmark of 1942, *The Well Wrought Urn,* in effect so canonized the modernist lyric by carefully explicating what he offered as examples of poetic discourse from all the literary periods; by projecting the modernist moment backward in time (*Modern Poetry and the Tradition* [1939] is the title of his first critical book), Brooks, in patient elaboration of the argument Eliot had tossed off in a few sentences in the essay "The Metaphysical Poets," thought he had found a poetics good for all time. Warren for his part had inveighed in his essay against locating the poetic in some specific subject which then becomes the sign of poetic essence here and everywhere and forever (love and the moon), but he ended by reifying, like his coauthor Brooks, the heterogeneous lyric (contra all canons of decorum, presumably) as itself a poetic essence, the standard of a new ("modernist") literary decorum no less constraining than the old decorum enforced by Palgrave, Stedman, and Rittenhouse. And no less canonical in its effect, as the revolt of the Beats and various poets of the sixties in so many words testifies.

If love is lyric poetry's purest inherent tendency—in Warren's terms, lyric's "soft" subject, and the exclusionary principle par excellence—then the principle of impurity is embodied, in Warren's most resonant example, by Mercutio, the spirit of hard masculine wit who brings love back from the far empyrean to bawdy earth.[41] Mercutio, in lines cited by Warren, by carrying the news of the unrequited phallic urge to Romeo and Juliet becomes the representation of the principle of impurity who transforms "poetry" into a *complex, ironic,* and (key new critical word) *mature* "poem." In terms closer to the effete literary culture that the American modern poets would have understood because they grew up in it: the genteel yearning for a desexualized Keats—a superb blue moth as Stedman would have him, the genteel representation of the poetic itself, free from the Victorian scandal of the Fanny Brawne letters—this fairylike Keats must be surrounded by an unidealized consciousness that so far from doing in and doing away with the purity of "poetry" actually acts as its world-toughened shield, the realist protector of airy romantic ideality, "poetry" safely tucked away inside the "poem"—Keats made safe for modernist tough guys. No poet dare not make his peace with Mercutio who, if he is not invited inside, will do his bawdy debunking work destructively from without, relegating "poetry" for the males who take it up to the self-embarrassed sphere of the ladylike (Stevens), the work of sissy boys (Frost), and societies of leisured ladies who have nothing better to do, having left business and politics to their men, as Pound once roughly put it in allusion to Jessie Belle Rittenhouse.

So the lyric is culturally sanctioned in modernist polemic when what is culturally branded (and denigrated) as essentially female is not done away with but is married to the male principle: Such marriage is the mark, for Warren, of heterogeneous or impure lyric *tout court* and not only of the historically circumscribed modernist lyric which is lyric's most recent incarnation. In context, however, the issue of poetic manliness in the first decade of the twentieth century in the United States was not just another chapter in a historical battle of genders and genres, and not just another testament of patriarchal authority asserted (though Warren's essay is open to this last charge). For Frost and other young poetic modernists, manliness was quite simply the culturally excluded principle in a life given to poetry that made it difficult for the modern American male to enter the literary life with a clean conscience. In the young Frost's case the prospect of a literary life in poetry could raise only the most bitter of issues. For his assumption of the culturally imposed, feminine lyric posture as seeker of the beautiful not only cut against the authoritative and rapacious male models of vocation that culture in the Gilded Age offered him, as ironic gifts of social acceptance, but also cut severely against the actual lives of the females closest to him: his mother and his wife, neither of whom was blessed with the role of privileged-class woman upon whom ideals of cultural feminization in America are typically based. Neither Frost's mother nor his wife could qualify in the technical sense as working-class, but both were tied to toiling joylessly and without hope of respite in jobs of no glamour and to lifetime grooves of family obligation that permitted no life in high cultural activity for themselves; no life certainly in the leisured-class work of cultural promulgation and the taming of the materially driven spirit of men in the values of religion, poetry, and domestic commitment; no life, in other words, in the cultural work enshrined in America's sentimental nineteenth-century feminine tradition.

The accolade of manliness that Frost gave to his son and his desire to get rid of poetic diction altogether are the related acts of insubordination and resentment of an economically marginal American college dropout who enjoyed none of the social privileges of the great English poets he admired, and whose class formation permitted him not even the easy pleasures of idealizing the life of his womenfolk, for the women he knew best knew only the hardest of times. For Frost the fashioning of a new lyric mode was an opening to all that his social identity had declared out of bounds. The cultural issue of manliness had for him immediate, personal impact; it was what structured his relationship to his family, to himself as a male, and to literary history. It was not, as it would become for the institutionally powerful practice that Warren helped to initiate, a symbolic issue concerning associated sensibilities and the course of English literary history in the seventeenth century.

In his earliest efforts to open lyric by rejecting the heritage of official lyric diction preserved and passed on to his generation of poets by his Anglophiliac genteel culture, Frost in effect predicted the shape that his literary career would take. It was to be a career committed to nativist values. The struggle of any young American poet who would be an original, he often argued, must be against those custodians of culture who betray the American scene by directing him to write in a banalized, special language found only in books (and English books at that), a language with no sources in the "cave" of the "mouth," a language that "everybody exclaims Poetry! at."[42] The American sounds and rhythms in running speech would constitute Frost's newfound virgin land, the uncanonized territory that gave him refuge of aesthetic freedom because he could refuse, as "no one horse American poet" after Keats could refuse, the mimetic idolatry of Keats's yearning romantic diction. Frost offered the endlessly echoed word "alien" from the Nightingale poem as the exemplary piece of ironic evidence of American self-alienation, a denaturing of the American thing by poets who could not help but indenture themselves to Keats, and a continuing display of aesthetic servitude to British rule that Emerson and many others had lamented in the 1820s and 1830s in their call for literary emancipation.[43]

The generally conservative lyric practice of Frost's first volume, *A Boy's Will* (1913), was followed by the dramatic and narrative experiments in the blending of dialogue, storytelling, and a vocality "lower" than Wordsworth's in his second volume, *North of Boston* (1914), which was in turn followed by his final major transformation into the sententious poet of public fame who comes to dominate most of what he writes after the publication of his third volume, *Mountain Interval* (1916). These neat divisions of Frost's career tell the familiar modern American tale of youthful genius emancipated from convention only to be seduced by capital and heavy media attention. But in this case it is a story that partially misrepresents because it segregates what at Frost's most original was the fusion from early on, in a single literary impulse, of lyrical, narrative, dramatic, and didactic moods. (In fact, all of *North of Boston* and some of *Mountain Interval* were written in the long apprenticeship preceding the publication of *A Boy's Will.*) His most radical moment as a new lyric poet is discernible not in the dramatic and narrative successes of *North of Boston* ("Mending Wall," "The Death of the Hired Man," "A Servant to Servants") but in the deceptive poems of *A Boy's Will* where in a context of tame, historically recognizable lyric practice, which won him (before he traveled to England) some acceptances in mass-circulation magazines, we come across "Mowing," a poem in which the thought he had gotten so close to getting down everything he wanted to get down that he despaired of ever matching that effort again:

> There was never a sound beside the wood but one,
> And that was my long scythe whispering to the ground.
> What was it it whispered? I knew not well myself;
> Perhaps it was something about the heat of the sun,
> Something, perhaps, about the lack of sound—
> And that was why it whispered and did not speak.
> It was no dream of the gift of idle hours,
> Or easy gold at the hand of fay or elf:
> Anything more than the truth would have seemed too weak
> To the earnest love that laid the swale in rows,
> Not without feeble-pointed spikes of flowers
> (Pale orchises), and scared a bright green snake.
> The fact is the sweetest dream that labor knows.
> My long scythe whispered and left the hay to make.[44]

Beginning with his title Frost plunges us into a poetry of work interrupted and obligation briefly stayed ("But I have promises to keep / And miles to go before I sleep"), aesthetic satisfaction wrested from a context of labor which is at once the antagonist of the aesthetic moment and the trigger of its gratification. Labor: the grudging basis for poetry for those who have no traditional means of economic and cultural support for the writing of lyric—those whose lyricism, like Frost's, had better somehow be supported *by and in* the course of the actual tasks of daily work because there is no alternative system of literary support available; those who somehow must be simultaneously poets and laborers. Frost's penchant for titles that feature the present participle promotes the biographically telling fiction that his is a writing coincidental with the actual processes of work it describes ("Mowing," "Going for Water," "Mending Wall," "After Apple-Picking," "Putting in the Seed"). These poems obliquely focus the biography of a writer who from his childhood was required by circumstances to work: Between eight and eighteen as newspaper carrier, waiter, gatekeeper at a mill, farmhand, and, more than once, as assembly-line worker—first at twelve years old in a shoe factory, the second time at a woolen mill, at seventeen, for sixty-three hours per week.

Wordsworth often composed in his head, wandering at his leisure in the Lake District, and Stevens did likewise, walking purposively through the districts of Hartford, Connecticut, to his executive desk at the insurance company. Frost's most intriguing poems imply a different fiction about their author's social origins: that he did it *as* he worked, that their written forms are unnecessary—the gratuitous recordings of an act, antecedent to writing, of labor aesthetically intersected for a laborer who may never actually write, either because he will have no time for it or because he will have no skill to do so. The implicit poetics of Frost's lyric poetry of work makes the statement that this is a kind of writing that claims nothing special for its being written, or for the values of writing as such: an antipoetics of work for those who may never have heard of poetics, or read a poet; a highly literate poetry, nevertheless, that needed, in sly guilt, to efface itself as literature—as if poetry were a highfalutin indulgence, yet for some reason necessary—and in such effacement give us access to life in the here and now, access, in other words, to "modernity."

Unlike Wordsworth's "Solitary Reaper," upon which Frost's "Mowing" mounts a critique empowered not a little out of resentment, there is no separation in Frost's poem of poetic and laboring voices. Wordsworth, a third-person observer, coolly notes "yon" Highland lass, reaping and singing. His poem's key rhetorical directives ("Behold her . . . / Stop here or gently pass!") tell us that his physical distance from the reaper is an aid to the distance required for imaginative reflection. And distance, physical and contemplative, is in turn a figure for the class difference, hierarchy, and privilege that define Wordsworth's relation to the working presence named in his title. These social distances produce the very possibility of this poem and also this, its pivotal question: "Will no one tell me what she sings?" Frost, a first-person participant, answers Wordsworth's innocent question with a parodic allusion to it that amounts to a workingman's joke on a comfortable outsider whose purpose is manipulation of pastoral conventions, not knowledge of labor: "What was it it whispered? I knew not well myself." The reaper is the occasion for Wordsworth's imaginative excursion; Wordsworth is in part recollecting his experience as a literal tourist who doesn't speak the language, but it hardly matters. In fact, his outsiderly perspective (linguistically, economically, and educationally inflected) is all to the good: He is not obligated to communication, only to searching his own inwardness. So just as fast as he can, and while seeming to honor the mesmeric power of the reaper's song, Wordsworth moves in his second stanza from the site of the reaper's work to faraway romantic places, "Arabian sands," "the farthest Hebrides." Through Frost's lens Wordsworth's poem becomes everything that Frost's is not: "a dream of the gift of idle hours." Frost's poem, in this dialogue of literary history, claims that this man who writes *is* working; he *is* the solitary reaper.

Wordsworth's polished displays of highly regularized rhythm and intricate rhyme pattern, sustained flawlessly from beginning to end, sound monological next to Frost, who moves between the effortless lyric grace of his opening two lines (with anapests, trochees, and iambs fluidly integrated), to the sudden interruption of an unscannable talking (not singing) voice at line three ("What was it it whispered?) and its playful prosy surmises (perhaps, perhaps), then on to the flat declarative and epigrammatic (yet still musical iambic) moment for which he will become famous in the penultimate line: "The fact is the sweetest dream that labor knows." Never a poet of discontinuities and fragments in the sense made famous, and made synonymous with modernist collage, by Pound and Eliot, Frost is yet, in his subtlest vocal experiments, a maker of the quiet vocal collage, which more than anything else in his repertory of strategies is the mark of his mixed identity as writer-worker and of his difference from the traditional poet represented by Wordsworth.

Frost did what Wordsworth never had to do (worked lower-class jobs), but also what all those represented by Wordsworth's female reaper were not likely to do (write poems of literary sophistication). Frost's virtuoso vocal changes, worked through a heavily Anglo-Saxonate diction, flaunt his difference with Wordsworth, whose nondramatic, regularized lyric voice, bodied forth in high literacy, highlights the critical social difference between the poet who imagines and the object that is the cause of his imagining. The socially and economically comfortable male poet builds visionary stanzas tranquilly upon his recollection of a female laborer, who becomes a peculiarly modern muse for a socially sympathetic English lyricist, the very same who had gone officially on record in his famous polemical Preface that he intended to honor ordinary voices but who is himself no ordinary voice and whose poem "The Solitary Reaper" unintentionally acknowledges his privileged relation to the base of rural labor that inspired him.

Though the poverty and the sex of the solitary reaper doubly and drastically inhibit her access to the ease of literacy that might eventuate in a career like Wordsworth's, and though Frost's male mower performs roughly the solitary reaper's kind of work—therein lie the connections of class across gender—at the same time Frost's male mower can do what Wordsworth's female reaper cannot (this is Frost's pact with Wordsworth): make knowing allusion to literary tradition, here to a Shakespearean song in part about work ("Perhaps it was something about the heat of the sun"), thereby revealing his learned, bookish ways in the very voice of the ordinary worker. This laborer is an American who has had the advantage conferred by democratic commitment to education. And his whispering scythe talks not only Shakespeare but also more than a little Andrew Marvell, whose "Damon the Mower" Frost recalls in order deftly to send up—in his critical allusion to "fay or elf"—a patently literary device, an artifice out of touch with the quotidian of farm labor ("The deathless Fairyes take me oft / To lead them in their Danses soft"). No fairies are taking Frost's poet-laborer anywhere.

More urgently, and closer to literary home, Frost's whispering scythe implies, through a criticism of W. B. Yeats, the dominant living poet in English in the first decade of the twentieth century, Frost's own self-critique: In denying "dream" and the work of "fay or elf," Frost, in the directness of his vernacular voice, mounts an internal commentary on the ninetyish poetic diction of a number of his own early dreamy lyrics in *A Boy's Will* while forecasting the colloquial richness and unpretentiousness of *North of Boston*. Frost stakes his claim to difference not only from Wordsworth's elite position but also from Yeats and Yeats's overt celebration of dream in his early poetry and plays which Frost knew intimately, having produced the plays of heart's desire while a teacher at Pinkerton Academy in 1910; difference from the Yeats who had famously declared in flight from the world of fact that the "dream" of the poets "alone is certain good." So "dream" becomes in Frost's poem a doubly coded term of criticism signifying both the leisured idleness of the British poetic classes and an unmanly contemporary aestheticist fashionability, a world-fleeing imagination whose diction Yeats would purify from his writing with the help of Pound's editing, but which Pound himself would have trouble getting out of his own system until after Frost, in his early-century obscurity at the Derry, New Hampshire, farm, had succeeded in doing so, though without the proper critical organs at his disposal to declare his triumph of having made it new.

Boring from within Wordsworth's pastoral territory and Yeats's domain of dream-as-imagination, Frost reduces visionary dream to vision (as in visual) and imagination to the purest act of perception (as in image making), a precious because fleeting knowledge of fact, and fleeting because labor will not permit leisurely lingering in aesthetic pleasure of natural detail strictly irrelevant to the task of labor. And it is a knowledge that Frost comes to have not as independent agent—the laboring agent knows little freedom—but as agent of *labor's* action. Labor, not Frost, in Frost's most radical identification of literature with work, "knows" "the fact," which is also and at the same time the ultimate dream of imagination; Frost may know only insofar as he labors. The act of labor as an act of imagination rescues dreaming (Yeats's synonym for poetry) from both Wordsworth and Yeats, in this context impractical "dreamers" in the worst sense of the word.

Frost routes dream into a riveted attention to the incidental fact unveiled in work: a glimpse of fact for itself alone opened briefly, in a throwaway moment of syntactical subordination, as if it would be a desecration of work to permit those images of flowers (only parenthetically named) and the "bright green snake" to take over center stage and distract the laborer from his real task. This moment of syntactical subordination in "Mowing" is the expressive sign of a culturally subordinated aesthesis, an American guilt of poesis, the image garnered for no profit, stolen from the process of work which—by opening the possibility of aesthetic experience, of a consciousness momentarily off the groove of its utilitarian routine—becomes the necessary economic ground of aesthesis. So: work, a ruthless end-directed activity, not in hostile opposition to an activity valuable in itself—as the story of nineteenth-century idealist aesthetics would have it—but work as both constraining and productive context of the aesthetic for those, unlike Wordsworth and Yeats, who find work inescapable, whose own labor, not someone else's, is their peculiarly modern muse.

Yet what comes seeping through this effort to write out of a sympathetic antipastoral of work—a sympathy that would mark his difference from the social and sexual hierarchy of Wordsworth's pastoral performance—is a social arrangement similar to the object of Frost's critique of Wordsworth. Social distance and its corollary attitude, the sentimentalizing of common country labor—an attitude virtually demanded by traditional pastoral—make a subversive return in "Mowing" in order partially to trip up Frost's intention and to reveal his own sentimentalizing impulse in his would-be realist antipoetics and his subtly conventional stance above labor. This literate farmer is more literate than farmer, but uneasily so. This is guilty pastoral, written not out of leisure-class privilege but out of American social constraint by a man who wanted his work to be writing, not those other jobs he did that qualify officially in our culture as work—including farming—and that he found so dissatisfying. The "earnest love" of this farmer's "long scythe" that "laid the swale" (not just any meadow but a low-lying, moist depression of a meadow), this farmer's productive phallic love throws into even greater subordination the moment of aesthetic vision as an interiorized moment of pathos, a moment freed from the act of labor (which makes hay while the sun shines)—unproductive, masturbatory, the indulgent feminine moment. In "Mowing," the literal parenthesis of lyric impression.

The didactic force of Frost's difficult penultimate line yields its statement best against the background of the huge cultural claims for poetic function made by traditional theories of poetry from Aristotle to Wordsworth. The role of poetry for a poet who is constricted by inescapable labor, a poet without the classic advantages, is perhaps a diminished thing in light of the portentousness of those earlier claims. But perhaps poetic function is newly enhanced, after all, in this kind of modern setting of work. Poetry now becomes a pragmatic personal urgency, an aid to getting by in a social setting which for Frost (in this he is representative of the modern American writer) doesn't make getting by very easy. Frost's implied comparative and his explicit superlative condense a story of literary and social history: Dreams sweet and sweeter, the dreams of Marvell, Wordsworth, and Yeats—the easy poetic gold of idleness—yield to dreams sweetest. Sweetest dream—the best dream of all—is a form of laboring consciousness, somehow and oddly identical with "facts"—what is presumably raw, informational, objectively there. But "fact" in that ordinary sense is turned by this poet into an extraordinary thing; this constricted laborer just happens (an American happening) to be schooled in Latin etymologies of English ordinariness. *Factum:* a thing done, or produced, a matter revealed by and for a laboring consciousness, for no end beyond the momentary refreshment of its own act. *Factum:* a feat, a kind of performance, a display of prowess, the virtuosity, the poetry of work, but also (How could aesthetic contemplation be otherwise for a practical American male?) a kind of crime, as in an accessory after the fact.

## Notes

1. Louis Untermeyer, ed., *Modern American Poetry: An Introduction* (New York: Harcourt Brace, 1919), vii.
2. *From Another World: The Autobiography of Louis Untermeyer* (New York: Harcourt Brace, 1939), 327–32.
3. For the relevant information, see Margaret Widdemer, *Jessie Rittenhouse: A Centenary Memoir–Anthology* (South Brunswick, NJ, and New York: Banner, 1969).
4. *The Letters of T. S. Eliot: vol. 1. 1898–1922*, ed. Valerie Eliot (New York: Harcourt Brace Jovanovich, 1988), 204.
5. *Literary Essays of Ezra Pound*, ed. with an introduction by T. S. Eliot (New York: New Directions, 1968), 17.
6. Ezra Pound, *Selected Prose, 1909–1965*, ed. with an introduction by William Cookson (New York: New Directions, 1972), 41.
7. T. S. Eliot, *Selected Essays* (New York: Harcourt Brace, 1932), 247.
8. E. C. Stedman, ed., *An American Anthology, 1787–1900* (Boston: Houghton Mifflin, 1900), xxxi.
9. Quoted in Widdemer, *Jessie Rittenhouse*, 23.
10. *Selected Letters of Robert Frost*, ed. Lawrance Thompson (New York: Holt, Rinehart and Winston, 1964), 174.
11. Louis Untermeyer, *The New Era in American Poetry* (New York: Harcourt Brace, 1919), 206, 209–10, 317.
12. See Conrad Aiken, "The Ivory Tower—I"; Louis Untermeyer, "The Ivory Tower—II," *New Republic*, May 10, 1919, 58–61.
13. Ibid.
14. Ibid.
15. Untermeyer, *Modern American Poetry*, viii.
16. Ibid., viii–ix.
17. Ibid., ix.
18. Frost, *Letters*, 84, 102.
19. Louis Untermeyer, *Interviews with Robert Frost* (New York: Holt, Rinehart and Winston, 1966), 26.
20. Frost, *Letters*, 343.
21. Ibid., 84.
22. Ibid., 444.
23. Ibid., 181, 191, 234.
24. Ibid., 106–8, 140, 159, 181, 191, 234.
25. Ibid., 108.
26. Ibid., 390.
27. Ibid., 191.
28. Ibid., 138.
29. T. E. Hulme, *Speculations* (New York: Harcourt Brace, 1924), 120.
30. Ibid., 126.
31. Ezra Pound, *Pavannes and Divagations* (New York: New Directions, 1958), 204.
32. Frost, *Letters*, 80.
33. Ibid., 182.
34. Robert Penn Warren, "Pure and Impure Poetry," in *Critiques and Essays in Criticism*, ed. Robert W. Stallman (New York: Ronald, 1949), 86.
35. Ibid., 86, 87, 99.
36. *Selected Prose of Robert Frost*, ed. Hyde Cox and E. C. Lathem (New York: Holt, Rinehart and Winston, 1966), 13.
37. See Pound's "Hugh Selwyn Mauberley": "The pianola 'replaces' / Sappho's barbitos."
38. *Letters of Wallace Stevens*, ed. Holly Stevens (New York: Knopf, 1966), 180.

39. Frost, *Letters,* 71–72.
40. Ibid., 390.
41. Warren, "Pure and Impure Poetry," 87, 90.
42. Frost, *Letters,* 191, 141.
43. Ibid., 141.
44. *The Poetry of Robert Frost,* ed. E. C. Lathem (New York: Holt, Rinehart and Winston, 1969), 17.

# Faulkner's Fictional Photographs: Playing With Difference

JUDITH L. SENSIBAR

A SOUTHERN GENTLEMAN knew better than to be an artist. "The *forte* of the Old Dominion," said a pre–Civil War news editor, "is to be found in the masculine production of her statesmen . . . who have *never* indulged in works of imagination" (my italics).[1] By declaring himself an artist, William Faulkner openly threatened one of his culture's most firmly entrenched gender classifications: "Real" southern men did not write.[2] Moreover, for American southern writers, the difficulty of freeing themselves from a culturally imposed requirement to serve as polemicists for southern patriarchal values, "to pacify the autocratic voice of [the] ruling classes or established ideas," was especially pronounced.[3] Anne Goodwyn Jones and Louis D. Rubin, Jr., have detailed and analyzed the cultural pressures placed upon both sexes not to create at all or, at most, to write fiction and poetry reflecting the fantasies of the South's Narcissa Benbows, Ellen Coldfields, and Drusilla Sartorises. Such propaganda, which passed for art, was relegated to women "in the equation of women, beauty, literature, and irrelevance" (Jones, *Tomorrow,* 44). Since the Civil War, writers who forthrightly questioned the status quo had been judged traitors and banished. Through the examples of her fictional artists, Mme. Pontellier and Mlle. Reisz, Kate Chopin (whose personal experience informs these portrayals) shows what happened to southern women who took their talents seriously: They were silenced as hysterics or marginalized as insane.

While, as Jones notes, imaginative realms were off limits to southern males, the three respectable occupations for genteel white women were teaching, sewing, and writing (*Tomorrow,* 34). In fact, the South praised and venerated its women writers, for the most part, because they conformed to cultural strictures that guaranteed "a fundamentally nonserious literary tradition" (44), a tradition Faulkner simultaneously immortalizes and challenges with *Absalom, Absalom!* Paradoxically, however, the disruption of southern patriarchy began in the South's historical endorsement of women writers (45). I draw your attention to this paradox because such connections among creativity, the feminine, and the patriarchal values of his own late nineteenth- and early twentieth-century Lafayette County play importantly in Faulkner's artistic beginnings, particularly in his use of real and imaginary photographs.

And I suggest that we can arrive at a more fruitful understanding of the relation among gender issues, creativity, and desire in Faulkner's fiction if we start where he did—with his assumption that, for a southerner, art was an exclusively female occupation. Practically, what did this mean? Because my space here is limited, I will focus on one way in which this issue manifested itself in Faulkner's work throughout his career: his experiments in expressing illicit and unspeakable longing by merging language, first with his own drawings and photographs and later with fictional photographs—that is, photographs he describes in his fiction. This is not to argue either that he was a feminist or that he wished to appropriate feminine space in order to extend the patriarchy's hegemony. Faulkner's ambivalence toward the feminine manifests itself frequently in both life and art. But his fiction is immersed in gender issues and, as I have written elsewhere and will elaborate here, his response to patriarchal definitions of those issues was extremely complicated.[4] Yet, in these experiments, Faulkner consistently uses drawings and photographs to figure desire in ways that challenge conventional language and the binarism of gender and to explode patriarchal tenets and assumptions about difference. And, particularly at the beginning of his career, the questions of difference he poses with drawings and photographs have to do with the meaning and relation of gender to his chosen vocation.

Not surprisingly, in these early visual experiments, his debt and attachment to the lived and the imaginative realities of two of the first artists in his life, Maud Butler, his mother, and Estelle Oldham, his wife and childhood friend, reveal themselves most clearly.[5] Artists themselves, and born of women who maintained lifelong artistic commitments (Maud's mother to sculpting and painting and Estelle's to music) in the indifferent, if not hostile, communities of Kosciusko and Oxford, Mississippi, they were adepts of disguise. And they passed on their skills to their son and lover, teaching him how to mask his subversive activities and use marginalization to his advantage in order to enjoy serious art's forbidden pleasures.[6] Maud and Estelle did not make William into a writer and their art was not comparable to his. However, these two women to whom Faulkner was closest were artists and, under the circumstances, this had an impact on him.

As their memoirs show vividly, the iconoclastic Maud Butler Falkner impressed upon all four sons a familial, feminine, and artistic tradition of rebellion. As a young girl, Maud's mother, Lelia Dean Swift, had outwitted her father, a "hard-shell" Arkansas Baptist "who thought that any creation which came out of thin-air, like painting, was the work of the Devil." Replacing the painting supplies he had confiscated and forbidden her "ever to touch . . . again," she began painting in secret. To make sure "no one could tell what she was doing," she either crawled under her family's farmhouse or rowed out "in the middle of a nearby lake."[7]

William's mother, Maud, and his maternal grandmother, Lelia (who lived with them), were, perhaps, gifted. His three brothers remembered both women for the intensity with which they sculpted and painted.[8] In 1890, shortly after Lelia's husband had deserted her, she turned down an art scholarship to study abroad. She could not afford the luxury. To support them both, Maud then dropped out of the State College for Women, where she was enrolled in the three-year business program.[9] Mother and daughter moved to Texarkana, where Maud worked as a stenographer.[10] Lelia Butler continued her art, sculpting in laundry soap, an affordable and available medium. When Maud arrived home from work, she was often greeted with unmade dinner and unwashed dishes. Sculpting with soap was considerably more interesting than washing with it.[11]

Talented herself, Maud Butler didn't marry until 1896 when, at twenty-five, she was looked on as an "old maid." Within a year she bore William, the first of her four sons. As far as is known, she did not paint seriously until she was in her sixties and living, for the first time in her life, on her own. And then she painted almost full-time until her death.

Estelle Oldham's family background and her involvement in art and music follow a similar chronology. Her mother, Lida Allen, studied at the New England Conservatory of Music.[12] She wrote and performed her own music, first in her hometown, Kosciusko, and later in Oxford, where she also taught piano. Letters record her sending composition portfolios to and receiving criticism from a Cincinnati music publisher.[13] Estelle wrote music too. A good pianist, she had "what amounted to total musical recall, a very visual, I suppose you might say, photographic memory and could play almost anything she had ever heard."[14] She also wrote short stories, and, in the last decade of her life when she, too, was living on her own for the first time, she began to spend most of her days painting.[15]

Though their culture classified them, safely, as amateurs, both Faulkner's mother and his wife were, in fact, primitives, in John Berger's sense of these terms.[16] Their art (and in more subtle ways their lives) displays the strengths of that origin—an individualism and freedom from convention and tradition that they apparently passed on to Faulkner. Although Berger's remarks are intended to describe European male primitive artists, they work equally well for describing Maud Butler and Estelle Oldham. Like most primitive painters, both began painting seriously, that is, full-time, in late middle age. Therefore, as Berger notes, "their art derives from considerable personal experience and, indeed, is often provoked as a result of the profundity or intensity of that experience."[17] Because their paintings were the creations of a mature vision, they also reflect fully formed and somewhat stabilized perceptions of reality and so can be read as an accurate summation and ordering of how the world seemed to these two very different women. Equally important, because primitive artists are either self-trained or trained in maturity, they have adapted to being marginalized as different or other:

> The primitive begins alone; she inherits no practice. . . . She does not use the pictorial grammar of the tradition—hence she is ungrammatical. [She refuses the tradition] because she knows already that her own lived experience which is forcing her to make art has no place in that tradition. . . . She knows it because her whole experience is one of being excluded from the exercise of power in her society. . . . The will of primitives derives from faith in their own experience and a profound skepticism about society as they have found it.

Thus Berger argues that primitive art is saying what "was never meant, according to the cultural class system, to be said" ("Primitive," 68; I have changed "he" to "she" in this quotation).

Maud Butler saw herself as a primitive and therefore different and unclassifiable.[18] A Memphis journalist raised her ire when he compared her to Grandma Moses, and she was even more displeased when Robert Coughlan wrote in *Life* magazine that she was a joiner and an amateur painter: "He said I was a church-goer—I haven't been in a church in ten years, except for funerals. As for my painting, I am not one of these little old Southern ladies who paints porcelain or greeting cards. Women come to me to have their china painted or to get greeting cards. I tell them to go somewhere else. I am a picture painter. I sell my paintings; I make money on them."[19]

Faulkner became an artist in a culture that defined art as a feminine occupation. Women painters and musicians were his role models. In his literature he used first his own drawings and, later, fictional photographs, which in their nonfictional form encode the essence of modernist and postmodernist epistemology, to question masculinist racial and gender classifications and to figure desire. Against this backdrop of a southern tradition of art as a feminine pursuit, one exemplified in the lives of two generations of Faulkner and Oldham women—women who worked in wordless media (art and music)—I want to set Faulkner's wordless signs, his actual and fictional photographs.

## Actual and Fictional Photographs

In the film *Shy People,* a Cajun woman uses her photograph album to tell their family's history to her city cousin, a New York journalist. Consistently, one person's face has been blanked out. The city cousin asks who he is. "My dead son. He's a sinner. . . . He went against us," the Cajun mother answers. "But he is your son!" protests her city cousin. "He's *dead!* That's all," the Cajun mother says stonily. We watch the two women's expressions; we look at them looking at the album, open across their laps; we see the city cousin's shock. There is something violent and taboo about destroying a photograph. To destroy it is to erase that irrefutable proof of what was: A photograph is "at once the past and the real."[20]

Memory is flawed: It distorts; it forgets. I cannot recall my beloved grandmother's face. I can hear her voice, taste her wild plum jam, remember the feel of her fingers lifting the skin of my scalp as she braided my hair; but her features blur when I try to call them up.

My father-in-law comes to visit. He is eighty-three and has a hole in his heart. I take over a dozen snapshots. Constantly I frame father and son, grandfather and grandson—shoring up against the end, the not-exist. After he leaves, I finish the roll and open our camera. It is empty. Instantly, intensely, I feel bereaved. It is irrational. Still, I grieve.

Photographs don't lie. Our great-aunt says she needs her hip replaced. "I don't want a second opinion. I saw the X rays. Even a layperson could see my pelvis is like tissue paper." Legally, she is blind. But she believes (sees) the X ray.

Barthes asserts that no writing can authenticate as definitively as a photograph: "language is, by nature, fictional; the attempt to render language unfictional requires an enormous apparatus of measurements: we convoke logic, or, lacking that, sworn oath; but the Photograph is indifferent to all intermediaries: it does not invent; it is authentication itself; the (rare) artifices it permits are not probative; they are, on the contrary, trick pictures: the photograph is laborious only when it fakes." A photograph can lie about its referent's meaning but never about its existence; "the power of authentication exceeds the power of representation" (*Camera Lucida,* 87, 89).

As those who write about photographs and our own experiences have shown us, the actual photograph encodes the essence of the modernist and postmodernist experience of knowing or, rather, not knowing.[21] Its teasing false reality (in contrast to other frankly interpretive mimetic forms); its use as a device for fragmenting reality; as a tool of aggression, acquisition, power; as witness, evidence; its surrealistic ability to freeze time—"The reading of the photograph is thus always historical"[22]—and yet blur the lines between art and life as it demarcates the chasm separating sight from speech; its unquestioned ability to testify to, as Barthes says, "*what has been*" (*Camera Lucida,* 85); its outrageous voyeurism that "makes everyone a tourist in other people's reality and eventually in one's own";[23] and paradoxically, its ability to do all this *without language*—to speak with its body—these are some of the qualities that make the photograph, particularly the photograph of desire, so compelling to us and to Faulkner's fictional men and women.

In general, those who have written about photographs and photography focus on actual photographs.[24] If, like Sontag, they allude to fictional photographs, they do not distinguish between the actual and the imagined.[25] Even Wright Morris, who illustrates some of his novels with real photographs, has never explored the epistemologically dazzling vista presented by the fictional photograph.[26] But it is precisely this vista that Faulkner's fiction exploits. Since his photographs are fictional rather than actual, we never literally see them. A step is left out; their episteme is further complicated. We know that, for their fictive spectators, the people pictured exist or existed, but for us this information is only connoted. With the literal camera image removed, we are denied the "objective" record with which to measure for ourselves the reflections of each spectator/speaker's desire, his or her wish for what will be or what was. Only the actual photograph can denote. But as we read fictional photographs, we are not aware of this lack or gap; the fictional spectator's gaze has become, for the moment, our own.

Photographs seem to exert tremendous erotic power in Faulkner's fiction. In "The Leg" (1925), an early short supernatural tale, a photograph created by a jealous lover's ghost drives his girlfriend mad, nearly causes his rival's murder, incites the girl's brother to murder, and causes the brother's death. In the first Yoknapatawpha novel, *Flags in the Dust* (1926), Bayard Sartoris burns the photograph of his dead twin brother in a desperate effort to free himself from his obsession with his idealized double. *Sanctuary* (1931) and *Absalom, Absalom!* (1936) are Faulkner's most stunning invocations of the photograph's multiplicity of meanings and its wordlessness to figure desire in ways that transgress and thus transcend patriarchy; there it becomes a subversive presence, challenging the boundaries of language and the binarism of gender.[27] In these novels the force of this image reaches beyond the conventions of the literal photograph. The epistemological issues double as he uses fictional photographs to question and critique phallocentric ways of seeing, speaking, and acting out desire. In *Sanctuary,* Horace Benbow's forbidden fantasies of lust, incest, and pedophilia all coalesce as he gazes on a stolen photograph of his nubile young stepdaughter. In *Absalom, Absalom!* Rosa Coldfield articulates the essence of absence and desire encoded in a picture of someone else's lover. Throughout Faulkner's work, even as late as *The Fable* (1954), fictional photographs are images for epistemological conundrums of forbidden love.

Objectively, literally, the photograph is an undistorted, frozen mirror image of what has been. Yet, paradoxically, in the act of possessing the photographic image, of giving meaning to it with words, the viewer's vision begins to blur and distort. Faulkner replicates this process precisely. As the failed artist, failed lawyer, failed lover Horace Benbow gazes hungrily at a photograph of his stepdaughter's "small face," it "seemed to swoon in a voluptuous languor, blurring still more, fading, leaving upon his eye a soft and fading aftermath."[28] And Barthes confirms, "photographs are signs which don't *take,* which *turn,* as milk does. Whatever it grants to vision and whatever its manner, a photograph is always invisible: it is not it that we see."[29] Instead, the spectator's words (the captions) record a visual image that replicates the carnival theater of emotions released by his or her desire to possess the image in the photograph. Language transforms the photograph from a record of an external reality of the other (its subjects) to an image of the speaker/perceiver's internal reality and so seems to confirm the impossibility of an objective perception of reality. There is a shift in meaning from what the photograph denotes to what the spectator connotes: Barthes claims that "in no other treatment does connotation assume so completely the 'objective' mask of denotation."[30] How the Faulknerian spectators transform this carnival image and what they do with it signal both the extent of their bondage to patriarchal constructs of desire and their ability to subvert and/or break those same bonds.

As I will illustrate, Faulkner consistently uses the fictional photograph to question certain culturally gendered erotic responses and to probe the reasons for their being gendered. Our not being able actually to see the photograph—its fictionality—gives it a greater intensity than either straight fantasy or an actual photograph. Faulkner's characters capitalize on the photograph's multiplicity of meanings and its wordlessness to imagine desire and use it or fail to use it either to challenge or to accept the prescribed binary boundaries of their lives.

## Artistic Precursors to Faulkner's Fictional Photographs

"Seeing comes before words."[31] It is a long way from Faulkner's imitative 1920 dreamplay *The Marionettes* to *Sanctuary* and *Absalom, Absalom!,* but this play, which Faulkner illustrated with his own drawings that swerve dramatically yet silently from his written text, signals the beginning of his revolt as the southern male artist. For a southern man, to write or paint challenged the status quo. In writing, illustrating, binding, and selling five copies of *The Marionettes,* Faulkner did both. His drawings here are perhaps the most subtle challenge, for they say, in concrete images, what he cannot say in words.[32] A fictional photograph serves a similar purpose for Faulkner's fictional characters: It offers them the chance to free themselves from silence, without imprisoning themselves in language.

*The Marionettes*' central protagonist is the young Faulkner's favorite persona, Pierrot, that amoral, often inebriated hero of the nineteenth-century French pantos whom, as Robert Storey has taught us, modernist novelists and poets adopted and reinvented to serve their own imaginative yearnings. At the opening and throughout *The Marionettes,* Faulkner has drawn him sprawling side-stage, his head resting on a spindly café table. There, immobilized and insensible and thus not morally responsible for his thoughts, he dreams the two dreams that are this play. These uninhibited "fermented" dreams and the drawings that often turn from their text reflect truly how Pierrot/Faulkner sees and says himself in the world. They may be thought of as his way of appropriating the language of the body—his mother's tongue. For he says here, with his drawings of Pierrot's, his "moon-mad" mother's, and Marietta's bodies what he dares not say in words.[33]

The drawings reveal that Pierrot wants to merge with and possess the two artists in his life, his mother, who controls the power of "song," and a young virgin, who offers adult passion. Faulkner's concluding drawing illustrates that such coupling will kill Pierrot's lover and leave him voiceless, staring solipsistically in a mirror (see fig. 1). But only Faulkner's drawing says this. His text never alludes to this drawing, which is, as you can see, the play's "Curtain" image. His silence on this drawing of death and mirror images is so disturbing that it erupts beyond the curtain—denying the closure signaled by this word.

This and the other surreal drawings, which compose *The Marionettes*' countertext, also reflect the ways in which he has been stimulated by and attempted to merge Maud's and Estelle's mutually antithetical imaginative realities. Maud's paintings were deliberately realistic—she speaks of herself as a realist; Estelle's "dream" paintings, as she calls them, are impressionistic and sometimes surreal.[34] Describing Maud's son John's equally realistic paintings, Estelle clarifies, "The difference between John's style and mine is that he painted trees as trees. . . . He was a realist. My paintings are not realistic. . . . All my subjects are unconscious things. All are pure fantasy."[35] "I never paint from nature. . . . I never paint still-lifes. I think God

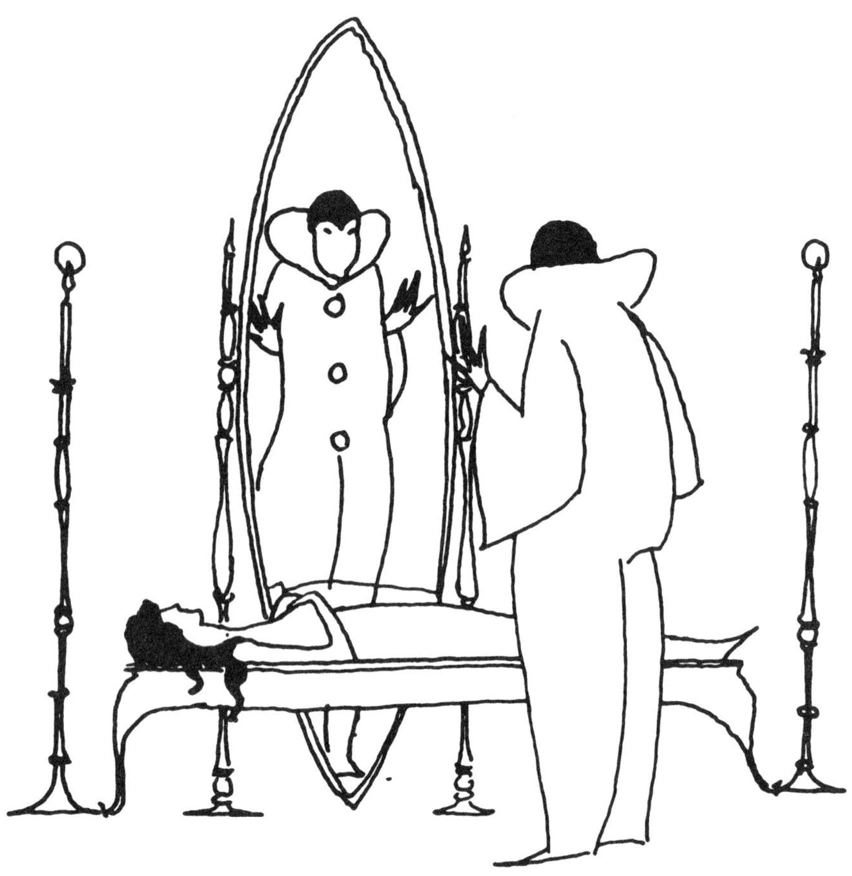

**Figure 1.** Faulkner's drawing of the silenced Pierrot standing beside the dead Marietta but watching himself in a mirror. From the author's dreamplay, *The Marionettes,* c. 1920. Courtesy of Jill Faulkner Summers and the William Faulkner Collection (Acc. No. 6271 aj), University of Virginia Library.

can make flowers better than I can."[36] Though Faulkner's highly stylized *Marionettes* drawings are self-consciously antirealistic, Marietta, the play's female protagonist, whom Pierrot seduces and abandons, bears an uncanny resemblance to contemporary photographs of Estelle Oldham (see figs. 2 and 3).[37] I will point out that a photograph of Estelle, perhaps even this one, is the only image of his lover William would have had when he was writing this play. The actual Estelle was then living in Honolulu with her first husband. Thus surrealism masks realism, creating another aspect of the play's hidden psychological tension; his drawings' nonserious imitative style screens a deeply serious and disruptive content—Pierrot's desire to be an artist and to become that by possessing the silent imaginative language of both mother and lover.

**Figure 2.** The virgin Marietta and her reflection being seduced by Pierrot's "moon-mad" mother. From *The Marionettes*. Courtesy of Jill Faulkner Summers and the William Faulkner Collection (Acc. No. 6271 aj), University of Virginia Library.

**Figure 3.** Lida Estelle (née Oldham) Franklin, c. 1920. Courtesy Jill Faulkner Summers.

Faulkner's early experiments with actual visual images extended to self-photographs as well. As early as 1918 he had begun what was to be a lifelong manipulation of the camera eye as he played with the power of actual but trick photographs to alter viewers' perceptions. Posing for a series of snapshots of himself as wounded war hero, Faulkner created a firmly masculine image, an acceptable front behind which he could practice his art (see fig. 4). Here he used photographs to manipulate reality to his own advantage, to appear as he wished to be viewed by his family and fellow townspeople.[38] But the military cover was not sufficient for his purposes. He needed, as well, to play the fool. Thus he alternated his flier's pose with the ridiculous costumes of dandy and tramp. I have not seen photographs of Faulkner in these other roles, but the nickname they earned him—Count No' Count—a linguistic photograph attesting to the success of his posing, survives. His deliberately outrageous but essentially harmless behavior distracted the townspeople's attention from his potentially more disturbing pursuit, one that threatened prescribed gender classifications: becoming an artist. These experiments in altering his own visual image while simultaneously teaching himself to write and draw show the writer moving from the relatively powerless position of actor/fool in spectacles of frustrated desire to creator of actors in spectacles of desire.

**Figure 4.** William Faulkner posing as wounded war hero, c. 1919. Courtesy Jill Faulkner Summers.

These origins of Faulkner's interest in the fictional photograph suggest that it was an extension of his earliest emotional and aesthetic solutions to writing beyond sexual difference. His dialogue with this mimetic visual image in one of his earliest imaginative creations, this dreamplay, and with his staged wounded-war-hero photographs reveals, in part, why its fictional counterpart served so well to challenge the prescribed binary boundaries of the lives of his fictional characters.

## Reading Faulkner's Fictional Photographs

Barthes speaks of the power of the camera's eye to make him feel like an impostor and (thus) specter:

> In front of the lens, I am at the same time: the one I think I am, the one I want others to think I am, the one the photographer thinks I am, and the one he makes use of to exhibit his art. . . . I do not stop imitating myself, and because of this, each time I am (or let myself be) photographed, I invariably suffer from a sensation of inauthenticity, sometimes of imposture (comparable to certain nightmares). In terms of image-repertoire, the Photograph (the one I *intend*) represents that very subtle moment when, to tell the truth, I am neither subject nor object but a subject who feels he is becoming an object.

In this "parenthesis," he says, "I am truly becoming a specter."[39]

Barthes's choice of verb voice pinpoints the difference between his response to being photographed and Faulkner's. Barthes feels manipulated by the camera: "I am (or let myself be) photographed." Even though he plays a role in front of the camera, the photographer is in charge of him. Faulkner's staged photographs elicit the precisely opposite sensation. He fakes for the camera lens to provide and control the spectacle. In contrast to Barthes, he seems to enjoy that in-between space. He deliberately plays the eerily Chaplinesque figure of the wounded war hero or fool—Count No 'Count—to clear space for his forbidden career. To the people of Oxford he was a joke.

It is no accident, then, that Rosa Coldfield, an expert at reading photographs of desire, appears to the doomed Quentin and his lost father as a joke as well. Quentin's and others' descriptions of Rosa "frame" her in ways that, opposite to Faulkner and his photographs of himself, diminish her strength and stature and make her an object rather than a subject. Much of the force of *Absalom, Absalom!* comes from her eruption out of that image—her refusal to be "framed." Not surprisingly, father's and son's framing language assaults her gender and her sexuality. They view her as a foolish old spinster caught in a forty-three-year-old time warp by an insult to her maidenhood. Rosa Coldfield understands the role she is supposed to play as Jefferson's penniless and slightly mad piece of "lonely thwarted old female flesh," a role apparently confirmed as we view her through Quentin's eyes in the novel's opening paragraphs.[40]

There she sits like a life-sized puppet, "bolt upright in the straight hard chair that was so tall for her that her legs hung straight and rigid as if she had iron shinbones and ankles, clear of the floor with that air of impotent and static rage like children's feet" (7). Dehumanized, infantilized, treated as property by her father and as a potential broodmare by her brother-in-law, Thomas Sutpen, Rosa Coldfield uses the one title she has garnered because she *is* so marginalized—poetess laureate of Yoknapatawpha—to move from silence into speech and from object of spectacle to projector of spectacle. Cast by the patriarchal values of her family and community in the role of fool (foolish child and hysterical virgin), she becomes self-conscious fool, thereby taking control of the text of the house of Sutpen and releasing it, in all its madness and frenzy, to the world at large.[41]

Like a photograph, whose function in the play and tug of desire she so perfectly understands, Rosa was there and can testify to what has been. But, just as she recognizes the underlying instability of the meaning of the photographic image, so she believes that the past is subject to reinterpretation. She speaks to open up the past, a past that is fragmented, dynamic, violent, and disjunctive and always focused on the constantly shifting relationships and the gender disruptions and racial conflict in the House of Sutpen.

When Quentin is faced with Rosa's oral portraits of the man he calls "the ogre-shape," his "two half-ogre children," and his wife "who had conceived to the demon in a kind of nightmare," he insists this is just a normal family. He

> seemed to see them, the four of them arranged into the conventional family group of the period, with formal and lifeless decorum, and seen now as the fading and ancient photograph itself would have been seen enlarged and hung on the wall behind and above the voice and of whose presence there the voice's owner was not even aware. [14]

But the frame he wants to put around the Sutpens, the photograph he wants to see, won't stabilize, won't bend to his need to preserve convention. No sooner does he imagine its formal and lifeless decorum than it becomes "a picture, a group which even to Quentin had a quality strange, contradictory and bizarre; not quite comprehensible, not (even to twenty) quite right—" (14). The image Quentin frames is bizarre because he has erased its emotional content, its meaning. The only relationship between the figures is their formal sitting arrangement. Faulkner fills this novel with photographic imagery and loads it with theatrical and cinematic scenes that for both Quentin and Mr. Compson are "just incredible. It just does not explain. . . . They are there, yet something is missing; they are like a chemical formula . . . you bring them together again and again and nothing happens: just the words, the symbols, the shapes themselves, shadowy inscrutable and serene" (100–1).[42] For Quentin's father and the rest, the scenes don't add up because they do not understand the relation of the scenes to their meaning. These scenes, like photographs, "offer appearances—with all the credibility and gravity we normally lend to appearances—prised away from their meaning. Meaning is the result of understanding functions."[43] Rosa's marginalized position as artist and fool paradoxically privileges her intelligence and her voice. She does not know everything, but she knows and understands a great deal more than any fictional listeners or many real readers have given her credit for because, rather than listening to her, they look at her and listen to her from Quentin's, Mr. Compson's, and Shreve's perspectives.

One indicator of Rosa's brilliance and clarity of imagination is her ability to read a particular kind of Faulknerian photograph of desire. While the town of Jefferson makes her a subject for jump-rope ditties—as she says herself, "Oh yes, I know: 'Rosie Coldfield, lose him, weep him; caught a man but couldn't keep him' " (168, 171)—she is busy inventing serious art, the story she tells Quentin. Like Faulkner, and many southern women, she conceals her art-making with masks; "I was not only a Southern gentlewoman but the very modest character" (169).[44] She appears as a proper lady, producing quantities of polemical art, over 1,000 poems—"ode, eulogie, and epitaph"—to fallen Civil War heroes (11, 83). These "beautifully safe and patriotic productions"[45] establish her as "the poetess laureate" of Yoknapatawpha before she tells the tale that questions all the values those polemics support. Furthermore, she makes sure that her real art will have national circulation. A pauperized spinster, *she* may not leave the South, but she can tell her story to a young man who is leaving:

> "Because you are going away to attend the college at Harvard they tell me," Miss Coldfield said. "So I don't imagine you will ever come back here and settle down. . . . So maybe you will enter the literary profession . . . and maybe someday you will remember this and write about it." [9–10]

Rosa cannot escape the physical confines of her culture and is locked in other ways within its patriarchal constructs. But her imagination is free, and she uses it to communicate and question.

Quentin recognizes part of Rosa's motivation: "*It's because she wants it told.*" But he fails to see that (as the narrator notes in a rare intrusion) Rosa can be "cold, implacable, and even ruthless"—attributes Faulkner claims are essential for a great writer (10).[46] Rosa can tell a good story; her personal life may be a shambles, but still she is a successful artist who uses fantasies evoked by a photograph of desire to elicit new meanings. By understanding the content of a photograph of desire, Rosa Coldfield lays claim to her own reality and enlarges ours. Articulating to another the absence in her life leads her to understand it and then use it to create art.[47] Thus, while Rosa's life remains circumscribed (the novel's other narrators nourish the melodramatic belief that she dies because the source of her outrage has been destroyed), her story takes on a life of its own. In similar circumstances Horace Benbow will use language to obfuscate; here Rosa uses language to create and illuminate:

> *I had never seen him (I never saw him. I never even saw him dead. I heard a name, I saw a photograph, I helped to make a grave: and that was all). . . . (I did not love him; how could I? I had never even heard his voice, had only Ellen's word for it that there was such a person) . . . because I had not even seen the photograph then.*

As she talks to Quentin, her inner vision begins to clarify:

> *I dont know even now if I was ever aware that I had seen nothing of his face but that photograph, that shadow, that picture in a young girl's bedroom: a picture casual and framed upon a littered dressing table yet bowered and dressed (or so I thought) with all the maiden and invisible lily roses, because even before I saw the photograph I could have recognized, nay, described, the very face. But I never saw it. I do not even know of my own knowledge that Ellen ever saw it, that Judith ever loved it, that Henry slew it: so who will dispute me when I say, Why did I not invent, create it?*

Rosa has raised the question: Is the existence of the photograph material? That is, if the feelings that it evoked in her and she describes feel true to the listener, isn't that emotional reality more valid than a physical object? And, of course, this is what she is asserting as she then reveals her marvelous invention:

> *—And I know this: if I were God I would invent out of this seething turmoil we call progress something (a machine perhaps) which would adorn the barren mirror altars of every plain girl who breathes with such as this—which is so little since we want so little—this pictured face. It would not even need a skull behind it; almost anonymous, it would only need vague inference of some walking flesh and blood desired by someone else if only in some shadow-realm of make-believe.* [146–47]

At first Rosa asserts to her audience—Quentin—that she could not have loved Charles Bon because she only knew him from his photograph. But as she describes what Bon's picture connotes, she realizes why his photograph both created and fed her desire. This realization allows her to move on to an elegant and imaginative insight about the kinds of people who crave this kind of desire, what its essence is—absence and illicitness—and what lack it fills. We never know what Bon looks like—his features, hair color, his eyes. These are facts, and they don't interest Rosa. All she cares about are how and why photographs—images of another reality—work as they do upon the spectator's imagination. Rather than losing herself, like Horace, in lustful fantasies of illicit, forbidden, incestuous, and unattainable desire, she frankly acknowledges her wishes to her audience and then uses them and her own experience to abstract and generalize.[48] Her idea is wonderfully playful, amusing, and true. It's also an accurate reading of adolescent sexuality. As Susan Sontag notes,

> The sense of the unattainable that can be evoked by photographs feeds directly into the erotic feelings of those for whom desirability is enhanced by distance. The lover's photograph hidden in the married woman's wallet, the poster photograph of a rock star tacked up over an adolescent's bed, . . .—such talismanic uses of photographs express a feeling both sentimental and implicitly magical: they are attempts to contact or lay claim to another reality.[49]

Unlike Horace, Rosa is not fantasizing silently and alone in a dark and empty house. She shares her feelings as she creates a story she knows cannot be written in the South, and that perhaps has not been written anywhere. It is a story in which a woman, not a man, is doing the gazing, and she is looking at a man. As Berger, in his essay on the convention of the female nude in Western painting, points out,

> Women are depicted in a quite different way from men—not because the feminine is different from the masculine—but because the "ideal" spectator is always assumed to be male and the image of the woman is designed to flatter him.

In these nude scenes,

> the principal protagonist is never painted. He is the spectator in front of the picture and he is presumed to be a man. Everything is addressed to him. . . . It is for him that the figures have assumed their nudity. But he, by definition, is a stranger—with his clothes still on. . . . This picture is made to appeal to *his* sexuality. It has nothing to do with her sexuality. . . . (The woman's sexual passion needs to be minimized so that the spectator may feel that he has the monopoly of such passion.) Women are there to feed an appetite, not to have any of their own.[50]

Unlike the male protagonist, who keeps his clothes on, Rosa has, metaphorically, disrobed. By doing so, she demystifies this kind of desire. Unlike Horace, she *wants* to communicate and she wants to understand relationships. Mastery of the photograph's message renders Rosa's telling a success. She achieves a coherence Horace never can experience. Rosa's tale disrupts because, in its larger sense, it lays bare the polemics of conventional southern fiction, thereby causing its readers to rethink the racial and gender distinctions imposed by southern patriarchy. By telling her tale to Quentin, Rosa breaks forty-three years of silence.

Both Horace Benbow's and Rosa Coldfield's talismanic use of photographs of desire question, frustrate, and disrupt gendered notions of sexuality. For each, the photograph is a trope for a thematics of desire that feeds on frustration, absence, incestuous wishes, and voyeurism. But whereas Rosa's intent is (in this instance) to demythologize desire for herself and her listener, Horace's is opposite. Rosa, who imagines herself as Macbeth and Hamlet, at first seems to appropriate Judith's photograph of Charles Bon, as Horace has Little Belle's. But Rosa never literally steals Judith's photograph. She doesn't need to because what she really wants to appropriate is an understanding of her desire. Possessed of that, she does indeed become "all polymath love's androgynous advocate," an artist (146).

Much has been written about *Sanctuary* as a Wasteland novel. The unnoticed "wasteland" Faulkner paints here is that wrought by culturally imposed class, race, and gender distinctions. Each major character represents a Type in the panorama, but a Type developed to its logical and most horrendous extreme. Thus Narcissa, draped always in white, is the ice maiden, that aristocratic image of the Southern Lady "born in the imaginations of white slaveholding men" and therefore "linked directly to fundamental southern questions of race, class, and sex."[51] Horace is the Southern Gentleman, sworn from birth to protect and worship but never to have sexual thoughts about this maiden ideal; Temple and Little Belle, the dark side of the virgin image, the Southern Lady turned whore; and Popeye, the "black man," that Other through whom Faulkner ironically caricatures the patriarchal myth of blacks' unbridled licentiousness and sexual potency. Horace's reading of Little Belle's photograph reveals the desires and fears those culturally imposed gender distinctions are designed to mask and control. His designs on the photograph he steals are purely pornographic, onanistic, and acquisitive. But because Faulkner's purpose is to question Horace's way of seeing, Horace's designs are disrupted.

Horace (and Popeye, his underworld double) appears to conform to Berger's description of the male spectator in front of the picture of the female nude. That spectator's expectations are Horace's. But, unlike Berger's spectators, Horace's expectations are constantly frustrated. For example, Little Belle's gaze continually eludes him: "He stood before it [the photograph], looking at the sweet inscrutable face which looked in turn at something just beyond his shoulder" (162, 163). While he owns her photograph, he cannot own her gaze. Like Rosa, he makes the photographed object less, not more, real. But unlike her, he doesn't realize what he's done, that "a photograph is both a pseudo-presence and a token of absence."[52] If he were to understand, his desire would be too threatening.

Horace dramatizes the destructive power of the patriarchal gaze—for both the gazer and the gazed upon. In a novel where everyone sees or is seen in frames, Horace's act of unframing and snitching not his wife's but his stepdaughter's picture as he flees to his sister's "sanctuary" may be seen as the first step that leads to the greatest frame-up in the novel—Lee Goodwin's lynching. In this sense Horace destroys or maims everything his eyes touch. He tries to use his position as spectator-owner of Little Belle's photograph in a traditional way. But Horace's appropriation, like Popeye's voyeuristic framing of Temple to sate his hunger (Temple develops a passion for Red that Popeye can't control), fails. Horace's gaze triggers fantasies of desire that literally make him sick. Desire cannot be contained or framed. Faulkner's phallic imagery here is wonderfully ironic. With the thick smell of honeysuckle writhing "like cold smoke" outside his darkened bedroom window, Little Belle's face "appeared to breathe in his palms in a shallow bath of highlight, beneath the slow, smokelike tongues of invisible honeysuckle."[53] The "infinitesimal movement of his hands, his own breathing" make her "small face seem to swoon in a voluptuous languor, blurring still more, fading, leaving upon his eye a soft and fading aftermath of invitation and voluptuous promise and secret affirmation like a scent itself" (215–16). Like Rosa, Horace never describes this voluptuous promise. Little Belle's actuality holds no interest for him. She is a fetishized object that he imagines raping. But his fantasied rape of this object climaxes in vomiting, not orgasm, as (now self-transformed to the impotent Popeye) he

> leaned upon his braced arms while the shucks set up a terrific uproar beneath her thighs. . . . She was bound naked on her back on a flat car moving at speed through a black tunnel, the blackness streaming in rigid threads overhead, a roar of iron wheels in her ears. The car shot bodily from the tunnel in a long upward slant, . . . toward a crescendo like a held breath. . . . Far beneath her she could hear the faint, furious uproar of the shucks. [216]

Horace's gaze is undermined as a potential feast becomes a violent retching scene. His spectatorship leaves him totally unmanned—and empty. His words will also prove empty for he loses his case, his client is lynched, and the uncomprehending Horace remains trapped within the confines of a power structure he claims to despise. Silence results from using others as objects.

Rosa succeeds where Horace fails not because she is a woman and he a man. She succeeds because, although she turns what we would call a masculine gaze upon Judith's photograph of Charles Bon, a gaze which transforms Bon from subject to object, her gaze is, finally, self-conscious. This self-consciousness, her desire to know why she sees the way she does and to analyze her motives and to abstract and learn about this gaze and then to share her knowledge with another, questions all the premises upon which such objectification is based. It changes her and makes us, if we listen to her voice, see desire in a way that questions the conventions of Rosa's (as well as our own) culture. Faulkner may be suggesting that because Rosa is a woman she is better equipped to make that challenge. But her gender alone is no assurance of success, and her success is very limited because, in so many other ways, her behavior meets cultural expectations. But Rosa is unlike either her sister Ellen, who retreats into a harmless and culturally acceptable madness, or Temple Drake and Eula Varner who, like Horace, know how to use language creatively but choose instead to become exemplars of various patriarchal sexual myths. In contrast, Rosa takes one of those myths—that of the sex-starved, hysterical spinster and lady poet—to camouflage her subversive voice.

Faulkner's portrayal of Rosa's and Horace's desire is complicated and compelling. The roots of its complexity lie deep in his own, always very self-conscious, conception of himself as an artist in a culture devoid of and hostile to homemade art, a culture so hostile that it had relegated what art it did foster to its women. As a young man claiming to be an artist, Faulkner threatened tightly held convictions about masculinity and femininity and so put his own gender classification at risk. We see him exploring his anxiety and fear of being silenced/feminized in early poems like "After Fifty Years" and "The Dancer," or in *The Marionettes,* where a young man is imprisoned by the stories, dancing, or music of old and young women. We see his fear more subtly imaged, and better understood, in the men obsessed by Caddy's voice in *The Sound and the Fury* and in the men obsessed by Rosa's in *Absalom, Absalom!*

Many writers begin as visual artists. Experiments in several media and genres are not unusual. Nor was feminization of American artists limited to our southern regions—one has only to read Emerson or Hawthorne to see the anxiety such labeling produced in nineteenth-century New England. But as Jones and Rubin have shown, and as Faulkner himself observed, this attitude reached its extreme in the South.[54] What is unusual was Faulkner's imaginative response. In the beginning of the second decade of this century, when he began his career as an artist, he cared as much about exploring the visual arts as he did about becoming a poet. Like literature, painting and music were also feminized. The years during which first Maud Butler and then Estelle Oldham painted occurred long after their actual painting could have had any effect on Faulkner's fiction. But their aesthetic values and perceptions, their means for coping in a culture that suppressed and trivialized art, and their privileging of art as a vocation were a constant that dated from Faulkner's earliest childhood. It was from them that he learned how to use literal visual images to say first with bodies what he could not say with words, how to expect and cope with marginalization as the price of being an artist, and finally how to encode all he had learned in these fictional photographs in novels that constantly undermine culturally imposed racial and gender classifications. Faulkner's imaginative training begins in and is supported by this female tradition.

## Notes

My research for this essay was supported by a 1988–89 American Council of Learned Societies Fellowship (partially funded by NEH). I want to thank Minrose C. Gwin for her careful and responsive reading when it was most needed. An earlier version was given at the summer 1988 "Faulkner and Popular Culture" Conference sponsored by the Center for the Study of Southern Culture and the English Department of the University of Mississippi, and will appear in the conference papers.

1. Louis D. Rubin, Jr., quoting from a Virginia newspaper editor's welcoming speech to Charles Dickens, 1842, in *The Writer in the South* (Athens: University of Georgia Press, 1972), 12. See also Anne Goodwyn Jones, *Tomorrow Is Another Day: The Woman Writer in the South* (Baton Rouge: Louisiana State University Press, 1981), 42.
2. See Jones's excellent summary, analysis, revision, and extension of Ann Douglas's, Louis D. Rubin's, Eugene Genovese's, and Louis Simpson's explanations for this anomalous situation and its resulting "flawed literature"—"the literary Sahara that was the South"—in *Tomorrow Is Another Day,* 41–46, and her notes to those pages. See also Ann Douglas, *The Feminization of American Culture* (New York: Knopf, 1977); Eugene Genovese, *The World the Slave Holders Made: Two Essays in Interpretation* (New York: Pantheon, 1969).
3. See Rubin quoting from George W. Cable's 1883 commencement speech, in *Writer in the South,* 10. Rubin notes that, until Faulkner, the only writers who seriously challenged the status quo—Samuel Clemens and Edgar Allen Poe—left the South. Faulkner's male friends who wished to be artists and writers—Ben Wasson, Lyle Saxon, William Spratling, and Stark Young—followed their example. Certainly, Faulkner was not the only writer working in the South in the 1920s. The Nashville Agrarians represent, as Rubin notes, an "essential stage in the history of Southern literature" (82). Besides Allan Tate, Robert Penn Warren, and the others, Thomas Wolfe published *Look Homeward, Angel* in 1929, and first novels by Erskine Caldwell and Hamilton Basso appeared the same year. Ellen Glasgow, James Cabell, and other novelists had been publishing steadily throughout the early twenties. But Faulkner's challenge and achievement seem even more exceptional and unique when he is read in their context.
4. See Judith L. Sensibar, *The Origins of Faulkner's Art* (Austin: University of Texas Press, 1984), and "'Drowsing Maidenhead Symbol's Self': Faulkner and the Fictions of Love," in *Faulkner and the Craft of Fiction,* ed. Doreen Fowler and Ann Abadie (Jackson: University Press of Mississippi, 1989), 124–47.
5. The first two artists in Faulkner's life were his mother and her mother, Lelia Dean Swift Butler (Mar. 5, 1849 to June 1, 1907). Faulkner and Estelle Oldham became friends when both were about seven years old. An equally important and early teacher was his black

nurse Caroline Barr who lived with him from his birth until her death in 1940. Her aesthetic legacy is oral. For a brief discussion of Barr's contribution, see Sensibar, "'Drowsing Maidenhead.'" See also Sensibar, *Origins*, chap. 12, and "'Drowsing Maidenhead'" for discussion of southern women artists Faulkner chose as friends and lovers.

6. In her book, Jones shows how certain southern women writers used similar tactics. Faulkner's fictional southern "authoress," Rosa Coldfield, reveals his great interest in an intimate understanding of such women. Despite this well-documented tradition and despite Faulkner's Great-grandfather Falkner's careful trivialization of his own poetry and fiction, this relative is still routinely cited as the novelist's chief familial artistic progenitor and model. For example, see Joseph Blotner, *Faulkner: A Biography* (New York: Random House, 1974, 1984); Michael Grimwood, *Heart in Conflict: Faulkner's Struggles with Vocation* (Athens: University of Georgia Press, 1987); Frederick Karl, *William Faulkner, American Writer* (New York: Weidenfeld and Nicolson, 1988); David Minter, *William Faulkner: His Life and Work* (Baltimore: Johns Hopkins University Press, 1980); Stephen B. Oates, *William Faulkner, The Man and the Artist* (New York: Harper & Row, 1987). That Faulkner showed little interest or skill in emulating the Colonel's polemical literary style, his much admired legal and financial wizardry, or his public displays of physical violence is simply ignored. For another view of Colonel Falkner as an ego ideal for his great-grandson, see Sensibar, *Origins*, chap. 4. The Colonel's attitude toward his writing confirms C. Hugh Holman's observation that "literature was almost an avocation to the [male] Southern writer before the Civil War, something that he did for ladies' books" (quoted in Jones, *Tomorrow*, 42). Jones adds, "It is plausible that a man's taking literature seriously would threaten still more profoundly his already ambiguous sense of sexual identity, an ambiguity whose anxiety he staved off by worshipping woman and deferring to her mysterious beauty and goodness" (*Tomorrow*, 42). Colonel Falkner succeeded because he fulfilled the ideals of his community. Faulkner succeeded despite ignoring or violating them in important ways. Most importantly, he dared to assume a woman's role in order to become an artist. See Sensibar, "'Drowsing Maidenhead,'" 126–28. Concerning self-representation, see also Erving Goffman, *The Presentation of Self in Everyday Life* (New York: Doubleday, Anchor, 1959). For a discussion of the role theatricality played in Faulkner's life and art, see Sensibar, "'Drowsing Maidenhead,'" and *Origins*, chaps. 1 and 4.

7. John Faulkner, *My Brother Bill* (New York: Trident, 1963), 123–24. Faulkner's youngest brother Dean's wife and daughter say that Maud told them Lelia crawled under her father's house (Louise Meadow and Dean Faulkner Wells in interviews with author, May 1989). Murry ("Jack") Falkner's first memory of Lelia, who died in 1907, is of her "always busy at her easel when not helping Mother run the house or watch over my brothers and me. Mother told us that shortly after the War, some northern art society, noting her mother's talent, had offered to send her to Italy to study," which she declined (Murry C. Falkner, *The Falkners of Mississippi: A Memoir* [Baton Rouge: Louisiana State University Press, 1967], 8–9). It's possible, but not likely, that she was offered this scholarship before her marriage at nineteen to Charlie Butler (August 2, 1868); see *Lafayette County Marriage Bonds, Book 2*. That their two children, Sherwood and Maud, were born in 1869 and 1871 suggests that, if she declined somewhat later, her reasons were more personal than nationalistic.

8. A journalist interviewing Maud Butler Falkner in 1956 writes, "On the day of our visit, Miss Maud seemed disconsolate, for, as she expressed it, 'I've been unable to do a lick of work for two weeks.'" Discussing her routine, Maud Butler explained that after breakfast, "'If I feel like painting, I leave the dishes and go at it. If the spirit is moving, I paint right on through dinner—but once I get tired, I just walk out and leave it.'" Asked whether she painted when her children were growing up, she said that the only painting she could remember "for a 35-year span consisted of a few pictures she worked on while standing at the living room mantle with her equipment safely above" her children's reach.

Margaret T. Silver, "A Visit with Miss Maud," typescript for *McCall's* article (Oxford: University of Mississippi Library), 2.

9. Joseph Blotner differs from Murry Falkner. He writes that in 1890 Lelia turned down an art scholarship to study in Rome (*Faulkner* [1974], 57). Maud is registered as a student in the three-year business course for 1889–90 and 1891–92 as well as for 1894–95 when she and Lilla Franklin (who would later become Estelle's cousin by her first marriage to Cornell Franklin) were in the same drawing class. See the catalogues for Mississippi State College for Women at Mississippi University for Women, Registrar's Office, Columbus, MS. The gap in 1890–91 supports the notion that this is when she dropped out to go to work. She may have returned to Texarkana or gone to work again elsewhere from June 1892 to September 1894, when she returned to school for the third time.
10. Blotner, *Faulkner* (1974), 58. According to one account, Lelia's family came from Arkansas, so she and Maud may have gone to relatives in Texarkana.
11. John Faulkner, *My Brother Bill,* 123–24.
12. No date given. *Lafayette County Heritage,* Lafayette Historical Society, Oxford, MS, 202. Lida also enrolled in the same degree program as Maud. See the 1887–89 catalogues for the Mississippi State College for Women, as Mississippi University for Women was then called.
13. For listings of some of Lida's performances and other activities, see *Yearbooks* of the Kosciusko 20th Century Club, Kosciusko Public Library, and the *Attala Democrat,* July 18, 1899, Aug. 4, 1899, Aug. 28, 1900, Kosciusko, MS, and Oxford Women's Book Club Yearbooks and minutes, private collection, and the *Oxford Eagle.* Letters, private collection.
14. Jill Faulkner Summers, interview, Oct. 17, 1989.
15. Summers, interview, Mar. 6, 1990. For more on Estelle's own writing and on her imaginative collaborations with her husband, William, see Sensibar, " 'Drowsing Maidenhead.' "
16. John Berger, "The Primitive and the Professional," *About Looking* (New York: Pantheon, 1980), 64. In 1941, Maud Butler had her only "formal" lessons with the exception of a college Industrial Arts class. "The instructor insisted her technique was all wrong, that she should sketch the whole portrait before painting. But Miss Maud said she would 'paint one eye and if that was right, I really went to town.' Finally, she was left to her own devices" (Silver, "Visit with Miss Maud," 2). For more discussion of Estelle Oldham's imagination, see Sensibar, " 'Drowsing Maidenhead.' "
17. Berger, "Primitive," 64.
18. Berger argues that the word "primitive" has been traditionally used "to put in its place the art of men and women . . . who did not leave their class by becoming artists" (ibid., 64).
19. Maud Butler Falkner, interview, summer 1953; quoted in James Dahl, "A Faulkner Reminiscence: Conversations with Mrs. M. F. Falkner," *JML* 3 (Apr. 1974): 1028.
20. Roland Barthes, *Camera Lucida: Reflections on Photography,* Richard Howard trans. (New York: Hill and Wang, 1981), 82.
21. The critical literature on the aesthetics, practice, and power of photography is vast and varied and derives from a rich variety of disciplines. A partial listing of books and articles I found useful for understanding how and speculating why Faulkner used both actual and imaginary photographs in his life and art includes the following: Richard Arnheim, "On the Nature of Photography," *Critical Inquiry* 1 (Sept. 1974): 149–61; Roland Barthes (see my references to various Barthes essays throughout); Walter Benjamin, "A Short History of Photography," in *Classic Essays on Photography,* ed. Alan Trachtenberg (New Haven: Leete's Island Books, 1980), 199–216; John Berger (see references to specific essays and books throughout); Jefferson Hunter, *Image and Word: The Interaction of Twentieth Century Photographs and Texts* (Cambridge, MA: Harvard University Press, 1987); W. J. T. Mitchell, *Iconology: Image, Text, Ideology* (Chicago: University of Chicago Press, 1986); Neil Walsh Allen and Joel Snyder, "Photography, Vision, and Representation," *Critical Inquiry* 2 (Autumn 1975): 143–69; Susan Sontag (see refer-

ences throughout); Alan Spiegel, *Fiction and the Camera Eye: Visual Consciousness in Film and the Modern Novel* (Charlottesville: University Press of Virginia, 1976); Wendy Steiner, *Pictures of Romance* (Chicago: University of Chicago Press, 1988); John Szarkowski, *Looking at Photographs: 100 Pictures from the Collection of the Museum of Modern Art* (New York: Museum of Modern Art, 1973), and *The Photographer's Eye* (New York: Museum of Modern Art, 1966), as well as numerous novelists and poets. Though many of these critics and artists disagree about what a photograph is/does/signifies, all concur on its centrality to current arguments about aesthetics, mimesis, representation, and cognitive perception.

22. Roland Barthes, "The Photographic Message," in *A Barthes Reader,* ed. Susan Sontag (New York: Hill and Wang, 1982), 206–7.
23. Susan Sontag, *On Photography* (New York: Farrar, Straus and Giroux, 1977), 57.
24. I have found little discussion of the fictional photograph as a distinctly separate aesthetic, political, and perceptual question. Françoise Meltzer's exploration of how and why literature plays with portraiture begins to touch on some of the questions I think fictional photographs pose. See particularly her chapter "Still Life," in *Salome and the Dance of Writing* (Chicago: University of Chicago Press, 1987), 113–58.
25. See Sontag, *On Photography,* 161–67 and passim; and Spiegel, *Fiction and the Camera Eye.*
26. Henry James's New York Edition is perhaps the most famous example of the use of actual photographs to illustrate fiction. But as James himself points out, the purpose of Coburn's photographs was very different. Speaking disdainfully of traditional means of illustrating literature, James wrote, "the frame of one's own work no more provides place for such a plot than we expect flesh and fish to be served on the same platter. One welcomes illustration, in other words, . . . with the emphatic view that . . . it would quite stand off and on its own two feet and thus, as a separate and independent subject of publication, carrying its text in its spirit, just as that text correspondingly carries the plastic possibility, become a still more glorious tribute" (Henry James, Preface to *The Golden Bowl,* quoted in Ralph F. Bogardus, *Pictures and Texts: Henry James, A. L. Coburn, and New Ways of Seeing in Literary Culture* [Ann Arbor: UMI-Research Press, 1984], 52). The twenty-four plates for the New York Edition were to serve as "complementary, non-interfering, and generalizing illustrations" for his novels and short stories and "to stand on their own as beautiful pictures" (5). While James's intentions and their results are a fascinating aspect of the larger subject—the relations between fictional and actual photographs—they are not directly relevant to a discussion of how Faulkner's or any other novelist's or poet's fictional photographs function. James's own fictional photographs are another matter entirely and relate directly to questions raised by Faulkner's fictional photographs.
27. Gender in Faulkner's fictional world is a slippery affair. The constant sexual and racial transformations in *Light in August* and *Absalom, Absalom!* are two obvious examples. Most characters know neither who nor what they are. A major source of confusion is their blind belief in the strict racial and gender classifications imposed by their culture. Elizabeth Fox-Genovese includes a useful chapter on this subject in *Within the Plantation Household: Black and White Women of the Old South* (Chapel Hill: University of North Carolina Press, 1988); see "Gender Conventions," 192–242.
28. William Faulkner, *Sanctuary* (New York: Random House, Vintage Books, 1931, 1958), 215–16.
29. Barthes, *Camera Lucida,* 6.
30. Barthes, "Photographic Message," 200.
31. John Berger, *Ways of Seeing* (London: British Broadcasting Corporation, 1972, 1987), 7.
32. For a more detailed discussion of the two texts, see Sensibar, *Origins,* 19–40.
33. Pierrot/Faulkner's intensely erotic relationships with both mother and lover figures are discussed in Sensibar, *Origins,* and in my introduction to Faulkner's *Vision in Spring* (Austin: University of Texas Press, 1984). Robert Storey notes that the stylized guise of

Pierrot permitted the nineteenth-century French pantomimists to pursue an order of realism far in excess of the naturalists themselves. He quotes Zola's review, "La Pantomime," where the author says he can imagine "with what an angry outcry a work of ours, of the Naturalistic novelists, would be received if we were to push so far the analysis of the human grimace, the satire of man in the grips of his passions" (*Pierrots on the Stage of Desire: Nineteenth Century French Literary Artists and the Comic Pantomime* [Princeton, NJ: Princeton University Press, 1985], 186). Faulkner's drawings of Pierrot serve a similar autobiographical purpose: His fictional photographs permit his characters to release unspeakable emotions as well.

34. Estelle Oldham Faulkner, interview, *Charlottesville Daily Progress*, Jan. 26, 1969, 3-C1. Maud Butler's realistic imaginative perception reveals itself in her paintings and her comments about her own and William's art. Speaking of her painting of Caroline Barr, she says, "She used to come up here and sit with me to keep me company. In her old rocker, just like my picture" (Dahl, "Faulkner Reminiscence," 1027). In a painting Maud did of the inside of a black sharecropper's cabin, she has painted a photograph of Eleanor Roosevelt on the wall (interview, *Memphis Press Scimitar*, Sept. 14, 1954). Speaking of *The Sound and the Fury*, Maud Butler said: "Now, Jason, . . . he talks just like my husband did. My husband had a hardware store uptown at one time. His way of talking was just like Jason's, same words and same style. All those 'you knows.' And of course Dilsey is Mammy Callie" (Dahl, "Faulkner, Reminiscence," 1028).

35. Estelle Oldham Faulkner, interview, *Richmond News Leader*, Nov. 3, 1964, 11–12.

36. Estelle Oldham Faulkner, interview, *Charlottesville Daily Progress*, Jan. 26, 1969, 3-C1.

37. Not only do Faulkner's drawings of Marietta speak to his text's silences, they also contradict the text. Thus, while Marietta is described as having golden hair (*The Marionettes*, 44), Faulkner draws her as a skinny but bosomy flapper, her dark hair cut in a bob. She looks remarkably like photographs of the young Estelle, who had dark red hair.

38. Blotner, *Faulkner;* Goffman, *Presentation of Self;* Grimwood, *Heart in Conflict;* Sensibar, *Origins*, and "'Drowsing Maidenhead'"; and Harvey Strauss, M.D., "A Discussion of J. L. Sensibar's 'William Faulkner, Poet to Novelist: An Imposter Becomes an Artist,'" *Psychoanalytic Studies of Biography*, ed. George Moraitis, M.D., and George H. Pollock, Ph.D., M.D., Emotions and Behavior Monograph Series of the Chicago Institute for Psychoanalysis, no. 4 (Madison, CT: International University Press, 1987). One photograph Faulkner sent to his mother from his RAF training camp in Canada showed him posing beside "his plane." During his brief service Faulkner never flew. Maud, the realist, did a painting of this trick photograph, which she and others believed (Dahl, "Faulkner Reminiscence," 1027). In the 1960s when she agreed to sell it, her son forbade her to; it was "too personal." William Faulkner wanted control of his own trick photographs, it seems. At that point in his life, judging from his letters to Malcolm Cowley, he appears to have been embarrassed by this early imposture. See *Selected Letters of William Faulkner*, ed. Joseph Blotner (New York: Random House, 1974), and *The Faulkner–Cowley File: Letters and Memories, 1944–1962*, ed. Malcolm Cowley (New York: Viking, 1957).

39. Barthes, *Camera Lucida*, 13–14.

40. William Faulkner, *Absalom, Absalom!* (New York: Random House Vintage Books, 1936, 1972), 14; hereafter cited in text by page number.

41. Minrose C. Gwin first questioned the judgment of the male gaze in *Absalom, Absalom!* and argued that Rosa "is the force which drives the past into the present, which insists on the telling of the tale, which must know why. . . . She is both artist and participant. It is she who insists not only that the story be told, but that it be *understood*." See her *Black and White Women in the Old South: The Peculiar Sisterhood in American Literature* (Knoxville: University of Tennessee Press, 1985), 116. As she notes in her newest book, Rosa's "desire to speak the madness of a culture which makes commodities of white women as well as slaves and which encourages white fathers to sell their white daughters as easily as selling livestock—ties the southern patriarchy to sexual commerce in white females as

well as black human beings, and so blurs the boundaries between racial and sexual arenas in the Sutpen saga." See Gwin, *The Feminine and Faulkner: Reading (beyond) Sexual Difference* (Knoxville: University of Tennessee Press, 1990), 75.

42. Other photographs or photographic images occur on 14, 75, 91, 101, 110, 128–29, 146–47, 150, 358–59, and 377.
43. John Berger, "Uses of Photography," *About Looking,* 51.
44. Slave narratives and southern white women's journals and diaries contain numerous examples of the constant acting required of both subjects for maintaining a sense of self and for survival in a slave culture. This behavior extends into the present. As both southern fiction and cultural studies reveal, southern society privileges the theatrical. For discussion of the importance of theater in Faulkner's life (particularly in his marriage) and his art, see Sensibar, "'Drowsing Maidenhead.'"
45. Jones, *Tomorrow Is Another Day,* 42.
46. "[The artist] is completely amoral in that he will rob, borrow, beg, or steal from anybody and everybody to get work done. The writer's only responsibility is to his art. He will be completely ruthless if he is a good one. . . . If a writer has to rob his mother, he will not hesitate; the 'Ode on a Grecian Urn' is worth any number of old ladies." Faulkner, interview, 1956, reprinted in *Lion in the Garden: Interviews with William Faulkner,* ed. James B. Meriwether and Michael Millgate (Lincoln: University of Nebraska Press, 1980), 136–37.
47. When I speak of Rosa's creativity, I use this term as Gwin defines it—not a thing "but a process engendered by desire which always seeks more than it has. This process resides within the female character who remembers herself and the world through imagination." (*The Feminine and Faulkner,* 25).
48. What Gwin says of Addie is equally true of Rosa. She "becomes woman writing her own body," and, quoting Cixous, "she inscribes what she is saying because she does not deny unconscious drives the unmanageable part they play in speech" ("Sorties," 92). Gwin, *The Feminine and Faulkner,* 28.
49. Sontag, *On Photography,* 16.
50. Berger, *Ways of Seeing,* 64, 54–55.
51. Jones, *Tomorrow Is Another Day,* 8.
52. Sontag, *On Photography,* 16.
53. Faulkner here invokes Eliot for his own purposes. "Writhing" in *Sanctuary* is always associated with illicit sex. Tommy writhes watching Temple; Popeye writhes watching Temple and Red. Miss Reba describes Temple and Red as "nekkid as two snakes." Temple writhes against Red just before he is murdered.
54. In response to Faulkner's remarks about southerners not caring to read his books, a questioner asked if that wasn't universal—that no region likes to be criticized. Faulkner answered, "but didn't the people of his own country have a . . . fierce pride in people like Thoreau and Emerson? Or was that just the educated, intellectual New Englander that felt that? . . . I always thought that everybody—they might not have approved so much of all that Emerson or Thoreau said, but they had a fierce, almost provincial pride in— . . . Can a man write about ideas excepting in the provincial terms of his background?" Describing the southern writer's audience, Faulkner said that for these writers "the publisher, and to an extent his readers, are Northerners. I think that most Southerners know that his home folks ain't going to like what he writes anyway. That he's not really writing to them, and that they simply do not read books. . . . The non-writing Southerner, the non-reading Southerner, he wants the sort of brochure that the Chamber of Commerce gets out. There are things in his country that he's not too proud of himself, but to him it's bad manners to show that in public." William Faulkner, interview, May 13, 1957. Frederick Gwynn and Joseph L. Blotner, eds., *Faulkner in the University: Class Conferences at the University of Virginia, 1957–1958* (New York: Knopf, Random House, 1965), 136–37.

# Mappings of Male Desire in Durrell's *Alexandria Quartet:* Homoerotic Negotiations in the Colonial Narrative

JOSEPH A. BOONE

IT IS HARD to recapture the intense excitement that greeted the publication of Lawrence Durrell's *Alexandria Quartet* in the late 1950s as my parents' generation keenly awaited each successive volume with the sense of participating in the making of a contemporary masterpiece. Not only did the *Quartet* win glowing praise from its audience as well as reviewers, but it triumphed in academic circles, spawning literally hundreds of scholarly articles in the following decade—indeed, the Durrell entries in the MLA Bibliographies for the 1960s vie in number with those accorded longtime male favorites like Lawrence, Joyce, and Faulkner. Simultaneously, the *Quartet* found its way onto Ivy League syllabi; while Albert J. Guerard sang Durrell's praises at Harvard, Walton Litz made the *Quartet* a highlight of his modern fiction course at Princeton. This masterpiece, it seemed clear, was going to be around for a long while.

Durrell's critical stock, ironically, couldn't be lower today; his blend of lush romanticism and existential soul-searching stands at a far remove from current postmodern critical sensibilities. And indeed, at worst, a synopsis of the *Quartet*'s multilayered plots sounds depressingly like the stuff of television serials, offering a panorama of ever-shifting sexual alignments glossed over with a pretense to sophistication—or, as one early detractor put it, "Melodramatic erotica . . . made respectable by epigrammatic catch-phrases."[1] I'd like to suggest, however, that if we employ some of the insights that have marked literary criticism—particularly narrative and gender theory—since Durrell's eclipse, we will find a text very much worth our attention, not so much for its successes as for the way it insistently dramatizes the sexual politics of the colonial narrative, particularly as filtered through the eyes of its desiring male subject, a blocked writer and confused sexual subject for whom issues of erotic perception, masculine subjectivity, and narrative authority are inextricably linked.

The "investigation of modern love" that is Durrell's declared subject matter[2] pivots upon his narrator Darley's negotiation of the labyrinthine mazes of Egyptian—and specifically Alexandrian—sensuality. In the process, Egypt becomes much more than an exotic backdrop to the *Quartet;* rather, its geopolitical reality is transformed into a kind of psychic playground upon which Durrell can project titillating visions of sexual otherness and polymorphous freeplay. Not coincidentally, engaging with libidinous fantasy on this symbolic terrain frees Darley to emerge as mature novelist *and* successful lover at the end of the fourth volume. But Darley's response to the lure of foreign otherness is double-edged: Such figurations of Oriental sexuality, for all their attraction, are also terrifying, not the least because they give vent to possibilities "unthinkable" within a Western construction of the masculine. And, tellingly, within the psychodramatic landscape of the *Quartet* that unthinkability is time and again coded as the specter of homosexuality. The possibility—and fear—of being "unmanned" by homoerotic impulses gives the *Quartet* its deconstructive twist, in that the four novels map out a geography of male desire in which Darley's quest for identity depends on a continual negotiation of the one taboo that threatens its goals of "heterosexual" fulfillment and a "written" text. If the Near East seems to hold the promise of literary inspiration and (dreams of) sexual liberation for Durrell, these discursive manifestations of homosexuality suggest another side to the story, one that points to a specific combination of sexual and authorial anxiety triggered by the very enterprise of colonial narrative. A brief look at Durrell's most significant friendship, recorded in a famous exchange of letters with the author Henry Miller, provides some intriguing clues with which to begin to decipher the ambiguous desires that mark the textual erotics of the *Quartet* and its representations of Egyptian sensuality.

## Epistolary Ejaculations

In 1935 the yet unknown Durrell wrote a gushing fan letter to the current *bête noir* of literary letters, Henry Miller, whose infamously graphic *Tropic of Cancer* Durrell proclaimed to be "the only really man-size piece of work which this century can . . . boast of." Miller, his "man-size" ego no doubt flattered by such praise, quickly wrote back, touting Durrell's views as a mirror of his own: "it's the kind of letter I would have written myself." Thus began a series of narcissistically enabling epistolary exchanges that would bond the two writers, man to man, in a lifelong correspondence.[3] The terms of Durrell's adulation, of course, also reveal the young writer's desire to produce his own "man-size piece of work"—a goal which in terms of sheer bulk, if not in terms of outright sexual explicitness, he accomplished twenty-odd years later with the publication of the *Alexandria Quartet*. It is not surprising, then, to find an echo of this early ambition espoused by the *Quartet*'s one successful writer figure, the larger-than-life Pursewarden, who announces that he wants to write a novel "characterised by a *total lack of codpiece!*" (C 130; Durrell's italics). But precisely how, under Miller's tutelage, did Durrell learn to divest himself of *his* "codpiece," to let it all hang out, as it were, in order to display a "piece of work" that, as he says of *Tropic,* "goes straight up among those books . . . which men have built out of their own guts"?[4]

With this phallic imagery towering before us, we might turn to another of the young Durrell's epistolary homages to his literary master. "In telling anyone about myself these days," he proudly boasts, "I always say I'm the first writer to be fertilized by H.M."[5] If, as one critic puts it, "Miller's seed obviously fell on fallow soil,"[6] we may reasonably wonder what it meant for Durrell to find himself assuming a procreative role so diametrically opposed to his man-size ambitions. "Creative" intercourse this may only be, but the fact, nonetheless, is that Durrell's wording places him in a biologically "feminine" relation to his mentor, one in which the fledgling novelist's proud task is the sexual one of serving as womb (or "fallow soil") to Miller's "seed." Language, one is tempted to deduce, subtly contaminates the platonic terms of this manly friendship.[7]

Even more fascinating, in the light of language's destabilizing potential, is the literary metaphor that Durrell uses when writing Miller from Alexandria, seven years later, to describe Eve Cohen, his future wife and original model for the *Quartet*'s archetypal Woman-Temptress, Justine. Attempting to capture the essence of this "strange, smashing, dark-eyed woman" for Miller, Durrell declares that his enticing new acquaintance "is *Tropic of Capricorn* walking."[8] From Durrell's point of view, it would appear that Miller's "man-size" oeuvre—*Capricorn* having superseded *Cancer*—has grown altogether feminine legs. And with this figurative metamorphosis of one text (Miller's *Tropic*) into a woman (Eve) who will become the basis for another text (Durrell's *Justine*), the younger partner in this literary collaboration adroitly reverses the sexual dynamic inscribed in the earlier letter; it is now Durrell who assumes the male role and Miller, via the agency of this female incarnation of his *Tropic,* who is metaphorically inseminated. For Eve becomes, quite literally, Durrell's means of access to an "inside" of Egyptian sexuality that he penetrates not only as lover but as voyeur and, ultimately, writer: "She sits for hours on the bed and tells me all about the sex life of Arabs," Durrell writes to Miller, proceeding to list what sounds like a précis of the various exotica forming the backdrop of the *Quartet:*

"perversions, circumcision, hashish, sweetmeats, removal of the clitoris, cruelty, murder. . . . [S]he has seen *the inside* of Egypt to the last rotten dung-blown flap of obscenity."[9]

Durrell fertilized by H.M., Miller's *Tropic* penetrated by Durrell: Such metaphorically (t)horny intersections should inspire us to look, once again, at the sexual negotiations that make up the lush romanticism of the *Alexandria Quartet*. On one level, the Durrell–Miller relation that I have been sketching resembles the homosocial pattern of male bonding outlined by Eve Kosofsky Sedgwick.[10] Hence, when Durrell, reminiscing about the closing of the French brothels, laments the loss of some "marvellous encounters," he is talking *not* about encounters with their female clientele but, rather, about those with the other male patrons, particularly his fellow artists: "I spent some fabulous hours with Henry Miller at the Sphinx," he remembers—hours "spent," we are meant to assume, in verbal rather than, as the archaic expression goes, the "criminal conversation" more commonly associated with *maisons closes*.[11] Such homosocial behavior, as Sedgwick points out, is antithetical neither to patriarchal formations (such as brothels) nor to male heterosexual (and often homophobic) norms. And of the sexual orientation of this "priest of heterosexual love,"[12] there is "no homosexual component at all," his friend and critic G. S. Fraser hurries to assure us: "Durrell is an extraordinarily purely masculine creature. . . . He has had three marriages . . . in each case to an extremely attractive woman." Fraser's defense of Durrell, mediated by the evidence of Durrell's wives, indeed provides an apt illustration of Sedgwick's homosocial theory at work: Fraser avoids his own contamination, in speaking of such unsavory matters as homosexual tendencies in writers, while also asserting Durrell's monolithic heterosexuality.[13]

On another level, however, the premise of homosocial bonding, pervasive as it is in the world of the *Alexandria Quartet*, doesn't seem to me the only way to get at the curiously elliptical negotiations of "other" sexualities that not only keep rearing their heads in the Miller–Durrell correspondence but also determine the paths whereby the whole problematic of masculine sexual identification, with all its attendant uncertainties, is continually brought to bear on the act of writing in the *Quartet*. Durrell-as-writer obviously holds to an at least partially phallocentric creed—as his desire to emulate Miller's man-size work attests—but the fact is that the very means of his craft with which he has chosen to experiment in the *Quartet*—language, structure, point of view—work to evoke a flux of libidinous desire which, once freed *into* his text, threatens to overwhelm the coherence of its representations of masculine heterosexual competence. What ensues, as we shall now see, is a profound case of authorial anxiety in which the "imaginary geography"[14] of Durrell's (homo)eroticized Egyptian landscape helps to throw the modernist and masculinist tenets of his text into disarray.

## Relative Perceptions: Representations of Egyptian Sexuality

In the four interlocking volumes of the *Quartet,* issues of sexuality and writing are never far apart: "loving is only a sort of skin language, sex a terminology merely," Darley writes (*J* 177), and the novelist Pursewarden dreams of a novel that will "have the curvature of an embrace, the worldlessness of a lover's code" (*B* 235). Thus *Justine,* the first volume of the *Quartet,* begins with Darley's retrospective and highly subjective attempt to come to grips with his narcissistic love affair with the Egyptian-Jewish beauty Justine Hosani by recording events not in chronological sequence but impressionistically, "in the order in which they first became significant to me" (100). The blinders imposed by his romantic solipsism become painfully clear in *Balthazar,* where Darley is forced to relive the "truth" of the sensations he has recorded in *Justine* from a completely different vantage point, that of the Alexandrian doctor Balthazar, whose "corrected" version of the *Justine* manuscript reveals that Justine has possibly engineered the whole affair to conceal her more important liaison with none other than Pursewarden, Darley's mentor. As if to underline further the instability of sexual and narrative perception, *Mountolive* relegates Darley to the background of its action; the now omnisciently narrated action reveals *all* the love plots of the first and second volumes to have been "false," screens for a greater political plot (involving the attempt of Justine and her husband Nessim to rouse Coptic support for the overthrow of Palestine). Only in the final volume of this quartet, *Clea,* does time move forward, as Darley's first-person narration resumes, recording his return to Alexandria and successful love affair with Clea, another expatriate European artist.

In employing multiple points of view to dramatize the instability of truth and the relativity of known reality, Durrell gestures toward the legacy of literary modernism, whose tenets, he intimates, his formal experiments in the *Quartet* have revivified for a post-Einsteinian nuclear age.[15] Durrell also shares with his modernist forebears the desire to find a way of representing the spatiality of consciousness in narrative form, of capturing the flux of "inner" reality and the drift of subconscious desire. "*I would set my own book free to dream*" (*J* 61), he has one of the *Quartet*'s writers say, and he comes closest to achieving this aim in *Balthazar,* where he uses the surreal night world of Alexandria to create a series of psychodramatic set pieces emblematic of mental states. If the technique sounds familiar, it is because Joyce does much the same thing with Dublin's Nighttown in the "Circe" section of *Ulysses*. But the stakes are quite different, as the following passage illustrates. In this episode, Narouz, one of Darley's many alter egos, wanders through Alexandria's prostitute district on the night of a Moslem religious festival:

> From the outer perimeter of darkness came . . . the hoarse rumble of the approaching procession with its sudden bursts of wild music. . . . From the throat of a narrow alley . . . burst a long tilting gallery of human beings headed by the leaping acrobats and dwarfs of Alexandria, and followed at a dancing measure by the long grotesque cavalcade of gonfalons, rising and falling in a tide of mystical light, treading the peristaltic measures of the wild music—nibbled out everywhere by the tattling flutes and the pang of drums [and] the long shivering orgasm of tambourines struck by dervishes in their habits as they moved towards the site of the festival. . . . The night accommodated them all—a prostitute singing in the harsh clipped accents of the land to the gulp and spank of a fingerdrum, the cries of children, . . . the cock-shies and snake-charmers, the freaks (Zubeida the bearded woman and the calf with five legs), the great canvas theatre outside which the muscle-dancers stood, naked except for loin-cloths, to advertise their skill, and motionless, save for the incredible rippling of their bodies—the flickering and toiling of pectoral, abdominal and dorsal muscles, deceptive as summer lightning.
>
> Narouz was rapt and looked about him with the air of a drunkard, revelling in it all. [147, 149]

As in Joyce's "Circe," this carnivalesque spectacle, with its pulsating rhythms and cacophony of elements, attempts to represent in externalized form an unleashing of the unconscious, a "setting free [of] the polymorphous desires of the city" (*B* 196). On this level, Durrell's modernist and psychological intentions seem to work hand in hand: His multidimensional, dispersive, polyphonic text approximates the fragmented, anarchic, psychic terrain of the component instincts sketched out, for instance, by Freud in *Three Essays on the Theory of Sexuality*. But this equation brings us to a more troubling facet of the passage: the fact that its representation of the polymorphous perverse, of the "dark tides of Eros" (*B* 185), has been literally displaced onto a foreign geography, that of Egypt. As such, the *Alexandria Quartet* participates in the enterprise of colonial narrative, its modernist polemics and its sexual politics inextricably bound to its representation of Egyptian sexuality as an alluring but dangerously foreign other.

Edward Said's *Orientalism* has been invaluable in its uncovering of the discursive paths whereby countries like Egypt have come to represent "one of [the West's] deepest and most recurring images of the Other." The "threatening excess" of this otherness, Said suggests, has most often been gendered as "feminine" and sexually available so that it can be penetrated, catalogued, and therefore contained by the "superior" rationality of the Western mind. The upshot of these representations is an "almost uniform association between the Orient and sex." Said takes Gustave Flaubert's 1849–50 journey to Egypt as paradigmatic of the Western writer's tendency to idealize the East as "a place where one could look for [a degree of] sexual experience unobtainable in Europe" and enjoy "a different type of sexuality, perhaps more libertine and less guilt-ridden."[16] Flaubert's experience provides an extraordinarily illuminating context for evaluating Durrell's comparable fascination with Egyptian sensuality 100 years later, as we shall now see.

First, however, we need to interrogate more precisely the nature of the "unavailable" sexual experience to which Said is referring. In Flaubert's case, Said locates such desire in the writer's affair with the celebrated Egyptian female courtesan and dancer, Kuchuk Hanem. Seeing in Kuchuk's "luxuriant and seemingly unbounded sexuality" a symbol of Oriental fecundity, the young writer-to-be uses his diary to transform her material presence, her fleshly being, into a sheerly *poetic occasion,* making her "dumb and irreducible sexuality" the stage for the exercise of his own creative musings, observations, and flights of fancy. Such appropriation, Said argues, is typical of the Westerner's experience of the East; the latter's exoticism is deliberately experienced at a remove as a titillating spectacle, a "living tableau of queerness" that the traveler can enjoy voyeuristically but nonetheless stand apart from, thus theoretically remaining untouched by its difference.[17]

Yet what Said *forgets* to mention in analyzing the West's sexualized response to the Orient is precisely what his unfortunate wording—"living tableau of queerness"—perhaps subconsciously betrays. For, in Flaubert's case, it is not the female Kuchuk but a homosexual male dancer who first catches the traveler's eye. Said's oversight is of a piece with the apologetic disclaimer that immediately follows his account of Flaubert's association of Egypt and sexuality: "Why the Orient still seems to suggest not only fecundity but sexual promise (and threat) . . . is not the province of my analysis here, alas, despite its frequently noted appearance."[18] And what is it that Flaubert (quite literally) sees but that Said feels it necessary, "alas," to repress? This is how Flaubert expresses it in a letter home to Louis Bouilhet, his closest friend:

> But we have seen male dancers. Oh! Oh! Oh! . . . [I]magine two rascals, quite ugly but charming in their corruption, in their obscene leerings and the femininity of their movements, dressed as women, their eyes painted with antimony. . . . [D]uring the dance, the impressario . . . plays around them, kissing them on the

> belly, the arse, and the small of the back, and making obscene remarks in an effort to put additional spice into *a thing that is already quite clear in itself*. . . . I'll have this marvellous Hasan el-Belbeissi come again. He'll dance the Bee for me, in particular. Done by such a bardash as he, it can scarcely be a thing for babes.[19]

Given the fact that a "bardash" is, in modern terminology, a homosexual, we might cast a second glance at that display of nakedly rippling male flesh, otherwise "motionless" amidst the swirl of the celebrants, evoked by Durrell in the previously quoted passage of *Balthazar* and note that in the following paragraph the dazed Narouz, his footsteps leading him through a brilliantly lit corridor of circumcision booths, comes to a halt before an equally riveting spectacle: a "magnificent-looking male prostitute, whose oiled curls hung down his back and whose eyes and lips were heavily painted," as his breast is being tattooed (149–50). The miniature quest on which Durrell has sent Narouz uncovers Hasan's twentieth-century incarnation.

It hardly needs to be stressed that that which is erotically alluring in these Western male representations of Egyptian sexuality is *not only,* or *necessarily,* female, however, "feminized" these objects may appear. We need merely return to Flaubert's account to confirm this intuition. On the one hand, Flaubert's immediate defense against the "charming corruption" of Hasan and his fellow dancers is to assume the outsider's position of artist-observer, noting that their dance "is too beautiful to be exciting" and that their "ugliness" only "adds . . . to the thing as art" (84). On the other hand, as the excited "Oh! Oh! Oh!" and the wish to have Hasan "come again" to perform "a thing that is already quite clear in itself" indicate, the sexuality of the bardash is less easily turned into a purely aesthetic experience than Flaubert's language first suggests. Indeed, as he continues in his letter to Bouilhet, "Speaking of bardashes, . . . [h]ere it is quite accepted. One admits one's sodomy, and it is spoken of at table in the hotel. Sometimes you do a bit of denying, and then everybody teases you and you end up confessing"; whereupon, this womanizer and compulsive habitué of brothels drolly adds,

> we have considered it our duty to indulge in this form of ejaculation. . . . It's at the baths that such things take place. You reserve the bath for yourself . . . and you skewer your lad in one of the rooms. Be informed, furthermore, that all the bath-boys are bardashes. [84]

What is remarkable here, as Flaubert goes on to narrate an abortive attempt to be serviced by one of these "quite nice young boys," is the sheer *ease* of his transition from hetero- to homosexual banter: When in Egypt, do as the Egyptians . . . seems the prevailing attitude. This is not at all meant to suggest that Flaubert suddenly renounced his heterosexual propensities—to the contrary, his written record enumerates many such encounters with great relish and exacting anatomical detail—but to point to an unexpected opening in his perception of the *conceivable*. The behavior of his traveling companion, Maxime du Camp, might be taken as a paradigmatic example: "Max, the old lecher," is excited by native women at one moment, Flaubert reports of the morning they arrive in Egypt, but the next is "just as excited by little negro boys. By whom is he *not* excited? Or, rather, by *what*?" (43). Nor does Flaubert remain immune to these unexpected sources of titillation, as references scattered throughout his papers reveal; he amusedly records the flagrant displays of male sexuality that mark his journey down the Nile, lavishes a page of erotic description on one of his crew's youthful rowers (on whom he appears to have developed a crush), and cavalierly confesses that he has consummated his "business at the baths" with an ugly "young rascal": "It made me laugh, that's all. But I'll be at it again. To be done well, an experiment must be repeated" (203–4).[20]

This fluid movement across sexual boundaries turns out to be considerably more terrifying to Durrell's Darley, for personal reasons we shall soon investigate; but nonetheless the *possibility* of such effortless transgression remains very real for him, a situation heightened by the continually blurring boundaries of Alexandria itself, a polyglot universe composed, Darley writes at the beginning of the *Quartet*, of "[f]ive races, five languages, a dozen creeds . . . [and] more than five sexes, [with] only demotic Greek . . . to distinguish among them (*J* 4).[21] But this heterogeneity is *also* precisely what attracts Durrell—and, as we have seen, before him Flaubert—to Egypt as a symbolically feminized terrain onto which he can project Western male fantasies of sexual otherness and polymorphous freeplay, that unbridled eroticism supposedly unavailable in more puritanical European society. "The sexual provender which lies to hand is staggering in its variety and profusion," Darley notes in a voice at once envious and justifiably a tad nervous (*J* 4). And although Durrell adds that "for the artist in [one]self . . . some confusions of sensibility [are] valuable" (*B* 46), the defamiliarizing experience of Alexandria's "variety and profusion" is as contradictory for Darley as it is instructive; for the fact is, as I have already suggested, that his quest for sexual identity cannot escape a continual negotiation of the homoerotic, in the guise of foreign otherness, that threatens the status of the personal and public texts he wishes to produce. To make sense of the "confusions of sensibility" that ensue from this homosexual subtext, we need to turn, however briefly, to the overt heterosexuality of the *Quartet*'s love plots and investigate Darley's textual affair with Alexandria the city and his sexual affair with Justine, its representative denizen.

## "Her Infinite Variety": The Riddle of Woman, Narcissus, and Male Desire

The mysteriously strange, always protean world of Alexandria holds a tantalizing allure for Darley, a seductive appeal that he attempts to fend off by assuming, like Flaubert, the role of curious but detached artist-spectator. This pose of uninvolvement, however, swiftly breaks down when he meets and falls "blindly and passionately in love" with Justine—or, rather, with "one of the many selves she possessed and inhabited" (*B* 121), for Justine is the embodiment of Alexandria's protean variety. To Darley's Westernizing imagination, this protean quality makes Justine the eternal feminine, ever evading capture yet hopelessly yearning to be possessed by the right man; simultaneously, this quality renders her a variant of the archetypal Oriental woman, a "voluptuar[y] . . . of pain" (*C* 35) in whom a vast array of apparent contraries meet: sensuality and asceticism, mystery and knowledge, fecundity and sterility, pain and pleasure.[22] So too Alexandria is a combination of clashing elements, its divided origins reflected in its mythic history, variously marked by Alexander's library, Cleopatra's court, and Plotinus's philosophy. A city lacking one unified origin, Alexandria becomes the equivalent not only of Justine but of the *Quartet* itself, whose ever shifting points of view also reveal that there is no single interpretation or representation that will capture its multiple realities.

Neither one thing nor the other, Alexandria functions as a passage, a threshold between different cultures and ways of being; it remains a promiscuous "whore among cities" (*B* 13). Similarly, within Darley's imaginative geography of desire, Justine becomes a sexualized site on his route to manhood—or, in Pursewarden's rudely deflationary, and characteristically misogynistic, rhetoric, "a tiresome old sexual turnstile through which presumably we [men] must all pass" (*B* 105). The degree to which Justine serves as a stationary marker in Darley's quest for self-knowledge also raises the (appropriately Egyptian) specter of the Sphinx whose presence confronts the questioning Oedipus with the riddle of Woman.[23] Both enigma and riddle, Justine becomes the text's overdetermined symbol for the instability of truth and language in an existential world—that belated and bitter knowledge awaiting all the *Quartet*'s male seekers. As such, Durrell's representation of Justine forms a classic illustration of the phenomenon Alice Jardine labels "gynesis," the philosophical setting into motion of the concept of Woman as a symbol of the postmodern crisis.[24] Darley colludes in this process by making Justine's "enigma" the *raison d'être* of his own text, but his very words simultaneously betray what is at stake for him, for all men, in this maneuver:

> There was no question of true or false. Nymph? Goddess? Vampire? Yes, she was all of these and none of them. She was, like every woman, everything that the mind of man (let us define "man" as a poet . . .) *wished to imagine*. . . . I began to realize with awe the enormous reflexive power of woman. [C 47–48; italics added]

Significantly, this conceptualizing of "Woman" as man's mirror/other points to an even more suspect feature of Darley's desires: namely, the degree to which his projections onto Justine are narcissistic, mirroring, as Luce Irigaray would say, the masculine back upon itself ("everything that the mind of man . . . wished to imagine"). Moreover, such male worship of sameness begins to suggest the presence of a homoerotic underside to Darley's passion for Justine and, indeed, to Durrell's plotting of male heterosexual desire.[25] Hence Alexandria—elsewhere feminized as "princess and whore" (*C* 54)—is also figured as "a city of incest," in which the "lover mirrors himself [as] Narcissus" (*J* 82). Not only does Darley meet and fall in love with Justine through her reflection in a mirror; mirrors become the text's metaphor for its own destabilizing, multidimensional refractions of point of view.[26] Thus, when Darley begins *Justine* by warning that the "symbolic lovers of the free Hellenic world are replaced here by something different, something subtly androgynous, inverted upon itself" (*J* 4), his use of the word "androgyny" indicates a likeness that is narcissistic in its intimacy; and when Darley speaks of those lovers who emerge from Alexandria's "great wine-press of love . . . deeply wounded in their sex" (*J* 4), he subconsciously attests to the degree to which Alexandria's mirror inversions have undermined the security of his authority as removed, all-seeing observer. The staged spectacle of Egyptian sexuality has become a reflecting glass, "inverted upon itself," for in a world of fluid boundaries he who gazes ultimately finds himself penetrated in turn by his reflection in the other.

Moreover, as the unsuccessful outcome of Darley's affair with Justine indicates, he has reason to feel "wounded in [his] sex," unsure of his "masculine" status and, by extension, his heterosexual competency. A curious impotence has dogged this would-be writer and dazed voyeur ever since his arrival in Alexandria, leading him to experience a failure in all domains of feeling: "to write; even to make love" (*J* 11). His first Egyptian lover, the nightclub dancer Melissa, will confess that "he never excited me like other men did" (*C* 214). And when Justine sweeps Darley across the borderline of voyeuristic detachment into the anarchy of her interior world, Darley assigns to himself the grammatical position of passive object of her desire: "She had achieved me" (*J* 21). Hence, it comes as no surprise that this "timid and scholarly lover with chalk on his sleeve" (*B* 121), having left

Alexandria for an island retreat where he can lick his wounds in solitude, acquiesces with hardly a word of protest to Balthazar's charge (in the latter's heavily annotated and edited draft of the *Justine* manuscript) that the most important love of his life has been a total sham. The fact that Balthazar argues that Justine has used Darley as a "decoy" (12) to conceal her affair with Pursewarden—already Darley's rival as a successful novelist—only underlies Darley's present authorial and psychic impasse. His entire framework of reality thus radically transformed, he must begin the work of "learn[ing] to see it all with new eyes," accustoming himself "to the truths which Balthazar has added" (12), among which he seems to accept as a given the revelation of his "unmanning" at Justine's hands.

Hence, as Darley begins this process of reevaluation, a series of memories and events repressed from *Justine* spontaneously rise to the surface of his recording consciousness, making up the reader's text of *Balthazar.* And, tellingly, what each of these hitherto repressed "events" obsessively reveals are less instances of Justine's infidelity (which we might expect from a deceived lover) than instances of Darley's own profound uncertainty about his status as a man and about the nature of male sexuality in general. We will now turn to the way in which these "returns of the repressed" engender anxieties that cannot be extricated from the pulsations of homoerotic desire.

## The Return of the Repressed: Slippery Significations

It is no coincidence that *Balthazar* is named after the character whose text—nicknamed the Interlinear—threatens the sexual and narrative authority that Darley has attempted to establish over his passion by writing *Justine.* Unexpectedly appearing on Darley's island "like some goat-like apparition from the Underworld," sporting "dark Assyrian ringlets and the beard of Pan" (*B* 8), Balthazar is the perfect guide to lead Darley to the polymorphous realm of forbidden desire. Not insignificantly, he is also a lover of his own sex, as Darley should well know, since he is "often" prone, he casually notes, to walk in unannounced on Balthazar in bed with various sailors (*J* 78). If Balthazar is the first of a series of homosexuals to flood the psychodramatically charged landscape of *Balthazar,* he is also the only man whose "inversion" Darley claims to admire, since, to Darley's view, it doesn't compromise "his innate masculinity of mind" (*J* 78). Darley's phrasing is worth note; the pronoun "his" obviously refers to Balthazar, but like so much else that is objectified as a third-person observation in this volume, the following description could apply equally to its speaker—"innate masculinity of mind" is precisely that which Darley wishes to claim for himself, as well as that which Balthazar's text has thrown into question.

"And so, slowly, reluctantly," Darley writes at the end of the first chapter of *Balthazar,* "I have been driven back to my starting-point. . . . I must set it all down, in cold black and white. . . . [T]he key I am trying to turn is in myself" (13).

Darley's words prove more prophetic than he knows, for the seemingly objective "facts" that he goes on to record in *Balthazar* are indeed often none other than hidden "keys" to himself. Nothing could make this fact more clear than the series of four triggering events whereby the repressed surfaces to rewrite the story of *Justine:* a recollected photograph, the memory of a kiss, the religious festival of which I have already presented an excerpt, and Alexandria's celebration of Carnival. As soon as Balthazar leaves, Darley turns in chapter 2 to a photograph taken outside Mnemjian's barbershop, the hub of the *Quartet*'s male homosocial world. Examining this random "text" for clues to what which he has hitherto failed to see, Darley fixes on two figures, Toto de Brunel and John Keats—characters who have gone totally unmentioned in *Justine.*[27] First, Darley takes up the case of Toto, an aged and effeminate homosexual whose marginal position in the photograph is tellingly the reverse of Darley's own: "And in one corner there I am, in my shabby raincoat—the perfected image of a schoolteacher. In the other corner sits poor little Toto de Brunel . . . the darling of old society women too proud to pay for gigolos" (*B* 15). As we might suspect from Darley's condescending tone—which contrasts markedly with his *professed* tolerance for Balthazar's sexual practices—Toto has become a projection of the speaker's own inadequate and uncertain self-image. For in serving as the "lapdog" of rich society women, Toto's position uncomfortably reminds Darley of the passive role he has unconsciously assumed as Justine's decoy. The fear of having been emasculated by this experience only intensifies his virulent putdown of Toto as a woman-identified man: "There was . . . nothing to be done with him for he was a woman" (15).

Having thus trashed "poor little Toto," Darley's thoughts move on to "poor John Keats," the newspaper correspondent who has snapped this photograph. As the recording "eye" behind the camera lens, Keats symbolically occupies the position of the invisible but all-knowing author, until Darley quickly moves in to let us know better: "Once he had wanted to be a writer but took the wrong turning" (*B* 16). Yet the more Darley ridicules Keats's counterproductive "mania to perpetuate, to record, to photograph everything!" (16), the more these traits begin to sound suspiciously like Darley's own; he, after all, is the blocked writer whose failure to produce a novel is tied to his disabling belief that he can contain everything within one frame of reference—which of course Balthazar's Interlinear, as a corrective to *Justine,* has already begun to disprove.

As the inaugural event in Darley's imaginative reenvisioning of the past, then, it is no accident that his memory exhumes two figures who, respectively, illustrate the impasse of sexual and narrative authority that has precipitated his own identity crisis. Both Toto and Keats, furthermore, individually illustrate the inextricability of the sexual and literary. Toto's sexual perversion is reflected in his comic perversion of language, for he speaks in "a Toto tongue of his own," composed of three languages, whose destabilizing logic subverts the status quo by undermining the assumed relation between signifier and signified: "whenever at a loss for a word he would put in one whose meaning he did not know and the grotesque substitution was often delightful. . . . In it, he almost reached poetry" (*B* 15–16). A more orthodox yoking of sexual potency and the word recurs in Keats's case. For in *Clea* this nondescript writer undergoes a radical transformation, returning from the war front not only a true writer but a masculine "sex symbol," as Darley learns when he finds his double taking a shower in the bathroom of his former apartment; he is stunned at the sight of the now bronzed, athletic physique of a "Greek god!" standing under the water (*C* 170). Yet as Darley's telltale exclamation point suggests, even this now positive projection of his dual goals of writerly and masculine authority is not without a homoerotic undertone that ever so slightly destabilizes its apparent signification, and this slippage turns us back to the anxieties that keep surfacing to plague Darley throughout *Balthazar*.

The last figure that Darley recalls in Keats's photograph, Scobie, brings to the plane of consciousness yet more thoughts of sexual and linguistic perversion. Nothing could be more authentic, Darley assures us, than this colorful ex-sailor and befuddled employee of the Egyptian Secret Police, who has "the comprehensibility of a diagram—plain as a national anthem" (*B* 19). Yet, curiously, Darley's train of thought reveals that this old friend's signifying capacities are not so apparent, after all: He immediately recollects the day Scobie confessed to him that he has "Tendencies" (23) for which he is not "fully Answerable" (33)—namely, that he is a "Peddyrast" (23). In exile from a puritanical England that has not appreciated his zeal as a scoutmaster, Scobie has found a paradise for his proclivities in the colonized Orient: "Looking from east to west over this fertile Delta what do I see?" Scobie rhapsodizes in words that recall Maxime du Camp's excitement upon landing in Egypt with Flaubert, "Mile upon mile of angelic little black bottoms" (*J* 108). Nothing could better uncover the ambiguous sexual politics of Durrell's colonial narrative than Scobie's wording: Beneath the sexual allure of the Orient's "fertile Delta"—age-old symbol for *female* fecundity—there lurks a hidden penchant for *boys*' "black bottoms."[28] Scobie's transgressive tastes, however, do not stop with boys; with the lyrics of a popular jazz melody, "Old Tiresias," drifting in the background, the old man confesses that he doesn't mind "slip[ping into] female duds . . . when the Fleet's in" (*B* 32–33). The frighteningly swift and altogether convincing transformation of Scobie into "a veritable Tuppenny Upright" that follows (32) exposes Darley to another slippage in signification that, by analogy, raises the haunting possibility of his own metaphoric undoing. Moreover, as in Toto's case, this destabilization in sexual meaning is marked by a subversion of linguistic content; Scobie speaks in so arcane a dialect that his verbal perversions necessitate a glossary at the end of the volume.

The manner in which being metaphorically "unmanned" or female-identified may vitiate one's artistic powers becomes the subject of Darley's thoughts even more explicitly in the next chapter, as Balthazar's reconstructed text forces him to travel back in memory to the inception of Justine's lesbian affair with the artist Clea. This is another known "event" that is all but absent from *Justine,* since it runs counter to Darley's romanticizing vision of his and Justine's heterosexual passion. "Distasteful" as Darley claims to find "this subject-matter," he now dwells on the affair at length, and for reasons not merely voyeuristic. First, because the women's lovemaking literally "interrupt[s]" Clea's artistry, her kisses "[falling] where the painter's wet brush should have fallen" (*B* 41), this tableau serves as a cautionary fable for one whose own creative productivity has been blocked by his love for Justine. Second, Clea's break with Justine provides Darley with a model for avoiding inappropriate desires—the homosexuality that he denigrates as "the consuming shape of a sterile love" (42)—and this model is particularly relevant given that Clea becomes Darley's ideal female love object in the final volume of the *Quartet.* Hence, Darley subconsciously depicts Clea's experience as the complementary inverse of his own: Her naive brush with lesbianism proves "that relationships like these did not answer the needs of her nature," that "she was a woman at last and belonged to men" (46). This investment in maintaining Clea's "innocence" (42) attests to the strength of Darley's pressing need to establish his own "innocence," his untainted masculine integrity, in the midst of the sexual "perversions" that increasingly surround him, threatening the presumed "needs of [his own] nature."

Given the welling up of all the forbidden desires represented by Balthazar, Toto, Scobie, and company, it is fascinating to turn to the next "repressed" event reported for the first time in *Balthazar.* This involves chapter 7's long account of the orgiastic mulid (or religious festival) of Sitna Mariam, whose dreamlike atmosphere I have already cited. It only takes a few jotted words in Balthazar's Interlinear—"So Narouz decided to *act*"—

to "detonate" in Darley's "imagination" (143) his version of Narouz's movements through the nighttime festival, which reads as if it were an excerpt from a third-person omniscient narration. What this attempt at narrative distancing fails to conceal, however, is the fact that the sensations attributed to Narouz, the "desires engendered in the forests of the mind" (157), are actually projections, once again, of *Darley's* own psyche.

But why does Darley choose Narouz to "stand in" as actor in his own imaginative fantasy? Because, it turns out, Narouz in many ways embodies Darley's ideal of masculinity. Clad in loose peasant clothes that "expos[e] arms and hands of great power covered by curly dark hair," possessed of a powerful body that emanates "a sensation of overwhelming strength" (*B* 58–59), Narouz epitomizes a kind of untamed, sensual virility. This is a man who can easily, not to say sadistically, dismember animals with one crack of his whip, and who, D. H. Lawrence-like, experiences delirious orgasm when breaking in a wild horse.[29] Narouz's unrequited love for Clea reinforces his function as Darley's heterosexual role model, outlining the proper route for the latter's wayward drives. From Darley's narrating perspective, then, Narouz looms, in perhaps too many senses of the word, as a man's man—so much so, in fact, that an ambiguously homoerotic element begins to infiltrate the narrator's appreciative descriptions of one who, after all, is supposed to be his guide to heterosexual fulfillment. Not only might Darley's lingering evocation of Narouz's orgasm on horseback sound slightly suspect, but the muted feminization of his subject that infiltrates his description of Narouz's "splendid" eyes, "of a blueness and innocence that made them almost like Clea's," along with the "deep and thrilling . . . magic of a woman's contralto" (59) that he reads into his voice, points—as in Flaubert—to an erotic intensity just barely contained by the appeal to sexual difference. Within Durrell's symbolic geography of desire, masculine heterosexuality, once again, is compromised by its proximity to the homoerotic. The one flaw in Narouz's appearance, the harelip that he considers his "dark star" (59), might seem to run counter to this coded language of attraction, until we remember that Flaubert also emphasizes the facial "ugliness" of his (male) objects of desire: In the colonial narrative, a degree of ugliness, as Sander L. Gilman has argued in regard to representations of Africa, becomes a signifier, paradoxically, of sexual availability itself.[30]

That there is more going on here than first meets the eye is confirmed in Darley's evocation of Narouz's night odyssey through the festival grounds. Narouz's movements culminate, finally, in his feverish intercourse with an aged, fat prostitute, in whose voice and body he imagines Clea's presence: "a voice spoke out of the shadows at his side—a voice whose sweetness and depth could belong to one person only: Clea. . . . The voice was the voice of the woman he loved but it came from a hideous form, seated in half-shadow—the grease-folded body of a Moslem woman. . . . Blind now to everything but the cadences of the voice he followed her like an addict" (*B* 158–59). Having entered a mutable and sightless realm where sexuality takes all forms, Narouz in effect creates his own desired love object out of this amorphous and anonymous body, imbuing the prostitute with his disembodied desires for Clea. When we remember that Narouz's perceptions are being hypothesized by the narrating Darley, this moment becomes absolutely crucial in illuminating the stakes involved in this text's constitution of male sexual identity. For what this encounter reveals about the nature of sexual attraction is the fact that *all* desire is unfixed or, to put it in Freud's terms, that there is no necessary link between sexual instinct and object choice: The only "natural" objects of our desires are those that our fantasies construct.[31] In practical terms, Narouz's example teaches Darley the freedom of choice that is his: He too can put his love for Justine aside and redirect his desire to a more "appropriate" object choice. What Balthazar has said in praise of homosexual relations—"Sex has left the body and entered the imagination now" (*J* 82)—turns out to be true of all negotiations of desire.

And Darley should know something about the constructed nature of sexual fantasy, because—in yet another of this text's revelations of repressed knowledge—it turns out that he has not only been a participant in this festival but has *witnessed* Narouz's copulation with the prostitute first hand: "my memory revives *something which it had forgotten;* memories of a dirty booth with a man and woman lying together in a bed and *myself looking down at them,* half-drunk, waiting my turn" (160; italics added). Waiting his turn, that is, to do the same as Narouz and spend the image of his lost love for Justine on this nameless body, which, literally, also means waiting his turn to take Narouz's place, to *become* his eroticized masculine ideal, a "real" man. Unless, of course, Darley means to take the place of the prostitute, to be *with* rather than become his ideal—a possibility that returns us to the sexual ambiguities that have plagued Darley's quest for manhood throughout.[32] Darley's voyeuristic tendencies, one recalls, are especially acute when it comes to spectacles of male sensuality: visiting Balthazar in bed with his boyfriends; walking in on Keats's newly godlike body under the shower; and, now, interrupting Narouz's orgasm. Given these recurrences, it no longer suffices to explain (away) Darley's obsessive thoughts of homosexual taint solely as an internalized reaction to his "failure" as Justine's lover; it becomes more and more possible that he also actively searches out that which he fears because it speaks to his unspoken desires.

Thus it is ironically but psychologically appropriate that the welter of polymorphous desires unleashed by Darley's vivid re-creation of the mulid of Sitna Mariam in chapter 7 is immediately set against an account of Scobie's murder (which occurs earlier in narrative time) at the beginning of chapter 8. Cruising the docks in his female clothes, the genial old "Peddyrast" is brutally kicked to death in a case of fag bashing. In so manipulating the sequential order of his text, Darley subconsciously uses his narrative authority to serve warning on his analogous potential for perversity: Not only do Scobie's "Tendencies" catch up with the old sailor, but the latent desires that Darley's account of Narouz have expressed have also been, if not literally punished, at least overwritten. This report of homophobic violence, moreover, prefigures the psychodramatic climax of *Balthazar*—the Carnival ball during which the effeminate Toto de Brunel is discovered brutally murdered, his head run through with a hatpin—yet another of the events deliberately suppressed from *Justine*'s text. "Why have I never [before] mentioned this [incident]?" Darley himself muses, "I was even there at the time, and yet somehow the whole incident though it belonged to the atmosphere of the moment escaped me in the press of other matters. . . . Nevertheless, it is strange that I should not have mentioned it, even in passing" (*B* 182).

Even more so than the mad jumble of color, sounds, and human grotesques at the festival of Sitna Mariam, Alexandria's celebration of Carnival assumes the contours of a Freudian dream text. "The dark tides of Eros . . . burst out . . . like something long dammed up and raise the forms of strange primeval creatures—the perversions," Darley says, nothing how "the polymorphous desires of the city" well up "like patches of meaning in an obscure text" (*B* 185, 196). The "ruling spirit" of this three-day-long debauch, Darley continues, is "utter anonymity." Hence, the black costumes and dominos donned by the participants become "the outward symbols of our own secret minds," "shroud[ing] identity and sex," blurring the boundaries "between man and woman, wife and lover, friend and enemy" (182, 186). In this world of dissolving boundaries, of unmoored sexuality and identity, Darley finds an exhilarating freedom implicitly related to the taboo subject that has haunted him throughout *Balthazar:*

> One feels free in this disguise to do *whatever one likes without prohibition*. . . . [W]e are delivered from the thrall of personality, from the bondage of ourselves. . . . You cannot tell whether you are dancing with a man or a woman. . . . Yes, who can help but love carnival when . . . all crimes [are] expiated or committed, *all illicit desires sated* . . . without the penalties which conscience or society exact? [185; italics added]

To do "whatever one likes," for Darley, seems intimately connected to the pleasure of, just perhaps, finding oneself dancing with a member of the same sex. But if Carnival, through its exteriorization of internal desire, seems to make possible the unthinkable by temporarily escaping the socially repressive law of "prohibition," "penalties," and "conscience," the festival is also, simultaneously, the siting for a much more ambiguous reinforcement of repression. For Darley's reference to criminal acts "expiated and committed" takes on a deeper meaning once we remember that it is against this ambisexual backdrop that the costumed Toto, Darley's negative alter ego, meets his doom. The satiation of "illicit desires" also exacts its price.

Significantly, Toto is mistaken for Justine when he is killed; on the way to the Cervoni ball, Justine has given him her well-known intaglio ring to wear, so that she can slip away from the ball unobserved, granting him in the meantime "a miracle long desired: . . . to be turned from a man into a woman" (*B* 195). The unintended result of this substitution assumes several levels of meaning: Metaphorically, it enacts the death of the feminized or "unmanned" man that Darley has feared becoming, while, literally, it marks the death of a scapegoat for Justine herself, the negative love object who has engendered his self-doubts. But the death of Toto also symbolizes the scapegoating of Darley's own homosexual impulses. For just as significant as the fact that Toto dies wearing Justine's ring is the fact that she has marked his black sleeve with white chalk so that she may identify him among the other costumed revelers. Crucially, this signifying mark echoes an image that the narrating Darley has already generated to identify himself as "this timid and scholarly lover with chalk on his sleeve" (*B* 121): He and Toto imagistically become one and the same.[33] Toto is not only Darley's negative foil, not only a scapegoat for Justine, but a double or mirror—in this world of incestuously multiplying mirrors—of Darley himself.

And who is it that kills Toto? None other, of course, than Narouz, the male principle incarnate. Thus, in the act of narrating Toto's death, Darley allows his hypermasculine double (Narouz) to assert itself by slaying his feminine self-image (Toto) and with it the specter of his guilty homoerotic desires. This purgation allows Darley to begin to reorient himself as a sexual being and a productive artist, as the rest of the *Quartet* demonstrates. The primary male task, Durrell would appear to be saying, is to create a love object appropriate to one's desired self-image. But for Darley such a goal involves several paradoxes. For that which Darley is exorcising is any expression of the polymorphous play, the slippages in signification, that Carnival (like the tent-city episode preceding it) has revealed to be the underlying "truth" of all sexual desire. Without Carnival's reign of anarchy, moreover, this knowledge would never have occurred to Darley, nor would this symbolic exorcism have been possible. Finally, to the degree that Darley's male ideal Narouz is responsible for slaying his effeminate self, Darley's narration achieves a perversely metaphoric union with the covert object of his desire *in spite of himself:* Toto/Darley gets "pinned" by Narouz, after all. In "hunting from room to room . . . for an identifiable object to direct our love" (*B* 196), as Darley says of the Carnival revelers, we find that there are no "destined" objects *except* those we construct . . . or those we choose to kill.

## Pygmalion and the Reinstatement of "Phallocentric" Discourse

The quintessential Carnival story of unmasked true love, interestingly enough, turns out to be all about the (quite literal) construction of one's desired sexual object, and as such it sheds light on Durrell's resolution to his protagonist's anxieties in the final book of the *Quartet.* It is at Carnival that the doctor Amaril falls "madly in love" (*M* 133) with a masked lady who disappears without leaving her name; the next year, Amaril meets her again and, after a frenzied pursuit, strips her of her mask, only to learn she has no nose. Undeterred by this revelation, Amaril uses his surgical skills to reconstruct a nose for his beloved—in effect, to replace her lack with his own phallic projections. As Clea, who tells this fable, notes, "You see, he [was] after all building a woman of his own fancy . . . only Pygmalion had such a chance before!" (*M* 137). Once Amaril has successfully "authored" this "lovely nose" (*C* 80), he bestows on his bride a very special wedding present: a doll's surgery, where she can repair children's wounded dolls, static Galateas like herself, the rest of her life. "'It is the only way,' says Amaril, 'to hold a really stupid woman you adore. Give her something of her own to do'" (*C* 81).

It is ironically fitting that Clea narrate this story: Not only has she helped Amaril engineer Semira's transformation by sketching models for the new nose, but Semira's fate becomes Clea's own. As I've already mentioned, *Clea* details Darley's return to Alexandria and the self-confidence that he gains as he lays to rest Justine's dangerously Oriental allure and then redirects his sexual energies toward the serenely virginal, blond beauty of Clea. To become a part of this text's economy of male desire, however, Clea must first be remade by man in his image, no matter how perfect she may appear to be, and this symbolic act of rebirth forms the *Quartet*'s symbolically charged climax. Darley and Clea have been deep-sea diving when Clea's hand is accidentally harpooned to a submerged wreck. Unable to free the harpoon, Darley is forced to hack Clea's arm off with a knife, and then, on shore, he pumps her nearly drowned body back to life (she gasps for air like "a newly born child") in a grotesque "simulacrum of the sexual act—life saving, life-giving" (*C* 244–45). Not surprisingly, even Durrell's most ardent supporters have had problems justifying the heavy-handed construction of this scene. Rather than attempt to justify Durrell's execution, I would suggest its *inevitability,* given his unfolding theme. The acute strain that the text evinces at this juncture has everything to do with the difficulty (and desperation) involved in the attempt of his male subject, Darley, to construct a properly heterosexual object of desire.

Durrell's symbolism, indeed, is painfully obvious; not only is Clea pinioned by one phallic object and castrated by another, not only does a simulated sex act by a man bring her back to life, but it is her painter's arm—her means of independent creative productivity—that she loses: the "necessary sacrifice of a useless member," according to one critic.[34] In turn, Darley's role in reanimating Clea transforms him into a Pygmalion-like "life-giver" (*C* 244) whose powers of creation, in "reversing the sexuality of birth," thereby subsume the threat that women's reproductive powers—like Egypt's emblematic fecundity—have traditionally posed to the questing male.[35] This series of identifications is cinched by the fact that it is none other than Amaril who treats the wounded Clea, replacing her missing hand with a mechanical one that, damningly, paints even better than her original: Her creativity is rendered a product of male instrumentality. Simultaneously, Clea reveals that Amaril was the unnamed lover to whom she has earlier lost her virginity, thus "turn[ing]" her "into a woman" (*C* 249) emotionally and sexually ready for Darley's advances. "I suppose I was even a bit eager to be wounded," she says of her sexual initiation (*C* 101), and wounded she indeed becomes in this final bit of psychodrama.[36] Durrell's narrative, in effect, has (forcibly) fashioned an object that answers to Darley's desired self-image as a heterosexually competent man: Via the agency of Greek myth, a perfect (and perfectly Western) mate is born from his foray into the dangerously torrid zone of Mideastern sexuality.

But in order to construct his female counterpart, Darley must first refashion his own self-image, a process which returns us to the sexual ambiguities that have marked his negotiations of masculine subjectivity throughout the *Quartet.* Just as Darley's internalized doubts have been expressed through externalized self-projections, so too a double figure becomes the measure of his potential for self-fashioning, in this case, the hack journalist Johnny Keats, recently returned to Alexandria from the front (World War II has commenced), newly metamorphosed: "And . . . you know what? The most unaccountable and baffling thing. [War] has made a man of me, as the saying goes. More, a writer! . . . I have begun it at last, that bloody joyful book of mine" (*C* 173). If Keats can undergo such a sea change, there would seem to be hope for Darley yet. Keats's doubling function also explains his pronouncement that he considers himself a competitor for Clea: Manhood, writing, and wooing Clea all seem part of one and the same agenda in the world created by this text. But the actual moment of reencounter between Darley and his double unleashes an extraneous erotic energy that belies the assumed coherency of this formula. This scene, briefly noted earlier, occurs when Darley returns to his old apartment to find Keats in the shower: "Under the shower stood a Greek god! I was so surprised at the transformation that I sat down abruptly on the lavatory and studied this . . . apparition. Keats was burnt almost black, and his hair had bleached white. Though slimmer, he looked in first-class physical condition" (170). While Keats dries himself, the two men make conversation:

> "God this water is a treat. I've been revelling."
> "You look in tremendous shape."
> "I am. I am." He smacked himself exuberantly on the buttocks. . . . "You look in quite good shape, too," he said, and his blue eyes twinkled with a new mischievous light. [170]

Taken out of context, this exchange might seem more the prelude to a soft-porn scene in a gay novel by Gordon Merrick than the encounter of a straight hero with his role model. For under Darley's intense gaze, Keats becomes as much an object of consumption, a living spectacle, as the dancer Hasan el-Belbeissi has been for Flaubert (whose reaction is equally surprised but delighted, his prefactory "Oh! Oh! Oh!" mirrored in Darley's own excited exclamation about this "Greek god!"). But there is a significant difference between these two eroticized objects: This newborn Adonis is as unmistakably English as the Pygmalion-like artist whose vision metaphorically creates him. Just as Justine's dark exoticism has been replaced with Clea's rational clarity, the swarthy foreignness of Darley's former male ideal Narouz—murdered at the climax of *Mountolive*—is overwritten by a newly fantasized masculine self-image whose Aryan good looks perfectly complement Clea's own. Yet even the retreat from Oriental sexuality implicit in this pair of substitutions cannot completely eradicate the homoerotic possibility—or threat—that Egypt has already unlocked in the narrator's psyche. It is thus inevitable that Keats dies in battle almost immediately after this encounter; not only does his death free Darley to become the new Keats, as it were, it also ensures that those lingering glances in the bathroom go no further. Thus, in death, Keats joins those other silenced signifiers of homoerotic taboo, Toto, Scobie, and Narouz. Within the world of Durrell's imaginary, the price of masculine subjectivity is that of repressing the very desires that make such a construction a pressing, immediate necessity.

Given the impact of this restructuring imperative on the psychodramatic level of character, it is reasonable to wonder what effects it has on the narrative's formal trajectories of desire. The concluding pages of *Clea* include a vignette that offers a metaphoric answer. In Darley's last walk about town (it is the eve of his final departure from Alexandria), he comes across a religious procession that echoes the Sitna Mariam festival and Carnival scenes in *Balthazar*. But the erotic and ecstatic energies of those events have been subtly homogenized, routed into one linear trajectory, in this reprise: "And to all this queer discontinuous and yet somehow congruent mass of humanity the music lent a sort of homogeneity; it bound it and confined it. . . . [C]ircling, proceeding, halting, the long dancing lines moved on towards the tomb, bursting through the great portals . . . like a tide at full" (262). This channeling of the many tributaries of desire into one massive tide not only uncannily recalls Freud's description of the way sexual instincts are brought into the service of a single drive but also inscribes the physiological process of male orgasm. And with this climactic ejaculation, the hitherto dispersive energies of this multilayered text are "bound and confined" within a specifically phallocentric model of narrative that has little to do with the polymorphous free play Durrell has hitherto promoted. Ironically, the goal, the aim, of the processional is Scobie's former lodging: for this lecherous old Tiresias has been resurrected by the Moslem population of his quarter as El Scob, a fertility god to whom barren women pray. With this rewriting of the very type of male sexual ambiguity into an emblem of heterosexual productivity, the narrative's homogenizing of its deviant impulses would seem to have finally cleared the way for Darley, now the writer par excellence, to produce, at long last, his "man-size" masterpiece.

So how does the artist feel, proverbial pen in hand and facing the blank page? "[L]ike some timid girl, scared of the birth of her first child" (C 275). Perhaps this return of the feminine whereby Darley identifies himself as a "her"is only a joke, or a slip of the tongue, or an assertion of mastery over his former anxieties. Nonetheless, this age-old conflation of masculine artistic productivity and female reproductivity betrays the shadow of a fear that lingers to disturb Darley's newborn confidence. Perhaps he should join the barren wives who pray to El Scob for succor.

## Writing Couples Redux

This welter of contradictions brings us back to this writer's problematic relation to phallocentric discourse, in this case exacerbated and illuminated by the sexual and representational politics of the colonial narrative. For

Durrell, we have seen, is attracted to Alexandria as the locus of his narrative precisely because its exotic, foreign otherness allows him to indulge in fantasies of, as Said puts it, "a different type of sexuality"—certainly one more open, in Flaubert's noun, to "experiment." Likewise, the polyphonic execution of this work evokes a geography of the instincts at least temporarily freed from constrictions of time and space and, to the writing Western consciousness, from sexual-moral orthodoxy. But such representations of foreign sensuality and freeplay, for all their appeal, simultaneously prove unnerving, because they expose the contradictions and incoherencies embedded in Western culture's traditional plots of masculine maturation and articulation. Hence Darley's compulsion to code the "possible" as "homosexual," the absolute antithesis of Western manhood, and hence his impulse to *colonize* these fantasies by equating them with the "feminine," thereby categorizing their difference within familiar hierarchical terms that allow him to pretend to have control over their subversive attraction.

But this desire to control, to pin down as one thing and not the other, is also what the *Quartet,* with its paean to the relativity of all truths and its repeated illustrations of the slipperiness of all signification, works to counter. For if the multiple, overlapping perspectives engendered by the *Quartet*'s refracting linguistic and formal structures are meant to suggest the subjectivity of all viewpoints, so too its evocations of the Alexandrian night world of the festival and Carnival are meant to suggest that the only "truth" of sexuality and sexual identification is its similarly fluid and individually constructed nature. The irony, then, is that Darley's discovery of the arbitrariness of sexual choice, and the role that imagination plays in creating any object of desire, makes all the more urgent his formulation of a choice toward sexual fixity, toward an absolutism of heterosexual identification and, as it were, "straightforward" artistic productivity. Thus *Clea* ends with an exchange of letters between Darley and Clea, letters tremulous with the anticipation of a not-too-distant reunion on safe European soil, followed, on the last page, with the narrator's declaration that he has just penned the first words of his long-deferred novel: "Once upon a time . . . (265). At this moment, with Clea practically in his arms, Darley has become the apotheosis of the Western writer, and the East his safely colonized other, whose perversities he can survey from the authorizing distance of myth and fairytale.

The catch, though, is that Clea really *isn't* in Darley's arms. Despite the fact that Darley has begun to write, his romantic desires remain in a state of suspension; the concluding exchange of letters gives an illusion of romantic closure where none exists. And with this image of Clea writing from Paris and Darley writing from his island retreat, I inevitably call to mind two other writing couples for whom correspondence whets rather than consummates desire: Miller in Paris, Durrell on one of his Mediterranean islands; Flaubert in Egypt, Bouilhet back home in France.[37] By way of ending this essay, I'd like to return to this latter pair and take note of Flaubert's epistolary comment after describing sex with the exotic dancer Kuchuk Hanem:

> In my absorption in all those things, *mon pauvre vieux,* you never ceased to be present. The thought of you was like a constant vesicant, inflaming my mind and making its juices flow by adding to the stimulation. I was sorry (the word is weak) that you were not there—I enjoyed it all for myself and for you—the excitement was for both of us, and you came in for a good share, you may be sure. [*Flaubert in Egypt,* 130]

In this example of male homosocial desire at its most crystalline, Kuchuk's sexualized body primarily serves to bond the two correspondents: As she stimulates Flaubert's bodily parts, his mind is inflamed by thoughts of Bouilhet. This latter is the ultimate in safe sex, since minds, however "juiced" to overflowing, aren't the same as real bodies. But what happens when the female intermediary is removed from the fantasized tableau? We get a glimpse of such a possibility in the conclusion of the letter, in which Flaubert tells Bouilhet all about the sodomitical practices of his Egyptian companions:

> Dear fellow how I'd love to hug you—I'll be glad to see your face again. . . . At night when you are in your room and the lines don't come, and you're thinking of me, and bored, with your elbows on the table, take a sheet of paper and write me everything—I devoured your letter and have reread it more than once. At this moment I have a vision of you in your shirt before the fire, feeling too warm, and contemplating your prick. [86–87]

Whatever one may want to argue about Flaubert's tone or his "true" sexual preference, this letter inscribes the body of a *homosexual* rather than merely homosocial desire—mental "vesicants" have been replaced by warm "pricks." Nonetheless, the framework in which Flaubert encases this masturbatory scenario presupposes a relation of writing to sexuality as potentially disabling as that which generates Darley's crisis of masculinity in the *Quartet.* For Flaubert must first represent the homoerotic reverie as that which takes place when "the lines don't come," when Bouilhet is "bored" with his poetry and abdicates pen for prick: So too the homoerotics of the *Quartet* literally take place between the lines, precisely because the exotic otherness of sexual "perversion" is figured as the threat of erasure, the negation of artistic vitality or "sap." Thus, in his journal Flaubert will use nonreproductive sexual play as a metaphor to express his despair at not having yet achieved his writing goals: "Where is the heart, the verve, the sap? . . . We're good at sucking, we play a lot of tongue-games, we pet for hours: but—the real thing! To ejaculate, beget the child!" (199). However, against this phallocentric model of narrative creation, in which the pen is the penis only if the desire is heterosexually productive, the substance of the narrative that Flaubert relays to Bouilhet *simultaneously* speaks another story. For the erotic tableau he unfolds is, first of all, *of* writing—"take a sheet of paper *and write,*" he enjoins Bouilhet—and, second, on Flaubert's part it has taken the *form* of writing: "At this moment," he *writes,* "I have a vision of you . . ." That which takes place between the lines, as in Durrell's case, or when the lines don't come, as in Flaubert's, writes itself into the text nonetheless, engendering a discourse of "foreign otherness" that is already inscribed its denial. In the case of the *Alexandria Quartet,* the *sheer effort* of Darley's attempt to construct a nonperverse, "productive" model of sexuality and narrativity, underlining the extremity of the masculine anxiety that at once drives and undercuts his story, ends up only clearing space for the play of the desires it (in both senses of the term) writes out. Meanwhile, Darley corresponds expectantly with Clea in Paris, and Clea replies in kind, serenely awaiting a consummation that never comes; and in the gap between these two lovers, one the constructed mirror projection of the other, exists an other "other" that will not disappear from this text's mappings and remappings of the problematic terrain of male desire.

## Notes

An earlier version of this essay appeared in "Displacing Homophobia," a Special Issue of the *South Atlantic Quarterly* 88, no. 1 (Winter 1989): 73–106.

1. R. T. Chapman, "Dead, or Just Pretending? Reality in the *Alexandria Quartet,*" *Centennial Review* 16 (Fall 1972): 412.
2. "The central topic of the book is an investigation of modern love," Durrell states in an explanatory "Note" at the beginning of *Balthazar* (n.p.). The series was initially published by E. P. Dutton, in the following order: *Justine* (1957), *Balthazar* (1958), *Mountolive* (1959), and *Clea* (1960). I will be citing the Pocket edition of the *Quartet* (New York, 1961), throughout. Page references will be included in my text, along with the first initial of the volume unless the context makes it clear.
3. *Lawrence Durrell–Henry Miller: A Private Correspondence,* ed. George Wickes (New York: Dutton, 1963), 4–5. Durrell repeats the phrase "man-size" twice in his letter.
4. Ibid., 5.
5. Durrell to Miller, April 1937, ibid., 90.
6. Morton P. Levitt, "Art and Correspondences: Durrell, Miller, and The *Alexandria Quartet,*" *Modern Fiction Studies* 13 (Autumn 1967): 302.
7. Durrell has been mocking the English tendency to self-deprecation, which, he jokes, he can do as well as any, and then gives this example: "I part my hair in the middle, adjust the horn-rimmed lenses and settle like a Catholic homosexual at the master's feet" (Wickes,

*Durrell–Miller,* 89); he seems to remain blissfully unaware of the parallels that might be drawn between this image and his expression of literary discipleship that follows.

8. Durrell to Miller, Spring 1944, ibid., 189, 190.
9. Ibid., 189–90; italics added.
10. See Eve Kosofsky Sedgwick, *Between Men: English Literature and Male Homosocial Desire* (New York: Columbia University Press, 1985).
11. Lawrence Durrell, *The Big Supposer: A Dialogue with Marc Alyn,* trans. Francine Barker (1972; New York: Grove, 1974), 130. As Jane L. Pinchin pithily comments in "Durrell's Fatal Cleopatra," *Modern Fiction Studies* 28 (Summer 1982), apropos this world of male camaraderie, "Prostitutes, for Durrell, . . . are places men go to play with one another" (231).
12. Jane Lagoudis Pinchin, *Alexandria Still: Forster, Durrell, and Cavafy* (Princeton, NJ: Princeton University Press, 1977), 174.
13. G. S. Fraser, *Lawrence Durrell: A Study* (London: Faber, 1968), 19. See also Pinchin's comments in "Fatal Cleopatra," for an acute exegesis of the way in which women become pawns in what is an essentially homosocial world of male bonding; writing in 1982 before Sedgwick coined the term "homosocial," Pinchin comes to very similar conclusions as those advanced in *Between Men.*
14. I borrow this term from Edward Said, *Orientalism* (New York: Random House, Vintage Books, 1978), where it appears in the title of sec. 2, chap. 1.
15. The impress of modernist aesthetics is most directly felt in Durrell's first major novel, *The Black Book* (1938); see also his *Key to Modern British Poetry* (1952). In the prefactory Note to *Balthazar* he makes explicit his own innovative agenda: "I have turned to science and am trying to complete a four-decker novel whose form is based on the relativity proposition. . . . The first three parts . . . are to be deployed spatially . . . and are not linked in a serial form. They interlap, interweave, in a purely spatial relation. Time is stayed. The fourth part alone will represent time and be a true sequel" (n.p.).
16. Said, *Orientalism,* 1, 56, 188, 190. For some representative nineteenth-century Western views of Egyptian and Near Eastern "exoticism," see Edward William Lane, *An Account of the Manners and Customs of the Modern Egyptians* (1836), Lucie Duff Gordon, *Letters from Egypt* (1865), and William Makepeace Thackeray, *Notes on a Journey from Cornhill to Cairo* (1844). On homosexual practice, see Sir Richard Burton, "Terminal Essay," *Thousand and One Nights,* vol. 10 (1885–88), T. E. Lawrence, *Seven Pillars of Wisdom* (1926), and, more recently Allen Edwardes, *The Jewel in the Lotus: A Historical Survey of the Sexual Culture of the East* (New York: Julian Press, 1959), esp. chap. 7: "Sexual Perversion: Matter of Taste," 199–262. Durrell's position vis-à-vis colonialism is relevant here. Although he claims, "I don't give a damn about British Empire," he allows himself to be labeled a "colonialist," having been born and raised in India in a family whose Anglo-Indian roots go back three generations. See Joan Goulianos, "A Conversation with Lawrence Durrell about Art, Analysis, and Politics," *Modern Fiction Studies* 17 (Summer 1971): 164–65.
17. Said, *Orientalism,* 103, 187.
18. Ibid., 188.
19. Flaubert to Bouilhet, Jan. 15, 1850, in *Flaubert in Egypt: A Sensibility on Tour,* trans. and ed. Francis Steegmuller (Chicago: Academy Chicago Press, 1979), 83–84; italics added. Further references to this volume—a compilation of Flaubert's travel notes and letters—will be cited in the text.
20. See, for example, Flaubert's juxtaposed commentary of public phallic rituals and the boy massaging his thigh in a Turkish bath (ibid., 62–63), his accounts of the advances of a lecherous old masseuse (85) and of Max being "jacked off" in the ruins (86), more forays to the baths "alone" (89), the attempt of one of the sailors to bugger himself in public and his crew's "*tutti* of cudgelings, pricks, bare arses, yells and laughter" on the Nile cruise (127), the minute description of young Mohammed's "charmingly modeled" torso, with

"firm young biceps . . . and belly uncovered" (133–34), the "nice little black boy" at Es-Sebu'a (146), and the "charming" youth at Philae (150). Of Flaubert's declaration that he has "consummated that business at the baths," Steegmuller notes the elaborate extremes to which Jean-Paul Sartre has gone in his study of Flaubert, *L'Idiot de la famille,* to prove all this homosexual jesting is merely that—locker-room banter. As Steegmuller notes with delicious understatement, "Other writers differ from Sartre on this question" (204).

21. Alexandria is not just or simply the Other, because its historical position as conduit between East and West renders it at once familiar *and* foreign to its Western visitors. This fact radically complicates the Orientalist's goal (and makes a simplistic application of Said's formula impossible), for it means that Alexandria can never be totally differentiated and appropriated, since it is also part of the Western consciousness. Hence the impossibility of Darley's attempt to reduce the city's exoticism to mere theatrical spectacle, as I describe shortly.

22. Durrell's evocation of Justine is similar to Said's description of Western visions of the Orient as "passive, seminal, feminine, even silent and supine" (*Orientalism,* 138).

23. Here my terminology evokes Teresa de Lauretis's description of narrative desire as an oedipal and male-gendered activity in *Alice Doesn't: Feminism, Semiotics, Cinema* (Bloomington: Indiana University Press, 1984), 109, in which woman is doomed to serve as a marker or obstacle, like the Sphinx, in a story of heroic quest that is never her own. Although the answer to the Sphinx's riddle is, of course, "Man," de Lauretis associates the Sphinx (like the Medusa) with a largely disempowered but still threatening matriarchal goddess culture: hence the degree to which she, in her "monstrous" womanhood, represents to male perception what Freud labeled "the riddle of Woman."

24. Alice Jardine, *Gynesis: Configurations of Woman and Modernity* (Ithaca, NY: Cornell University Press, 1985), 33–34, 42. For more on Durrell's existentialism, see Chet Taylor, "Dissonance and Digression: The Ill-Fitting Fusion of Philosophy and Form in Lawrence Durrell's *Alexandria Quartet,*" *Modern Fiction Studies* 17 (Summer 1971): 167–79.

25. On this specular logic of the same, see Luce Irigaray, *Speculum de l'autre femme* (Paris: Minuit, 1974). Punning on the French homme (man) and the Latin *homo* (same), she labels patriarchy's economy of desire as *hom(m)osexualité;* despite the unconscious homophobia in Irigaray's formulation, it usefully describes the swerve in Durrell whereby what might be called the "hom(m)oerotic" desires generated by masculine specularization ironically open the floodgates to a "homoerotics" of desire in the more usual sense of the term.

26. Justine, for instance, looking at her multiple reflections in a store's mirrors, suggests to Darley that fiction should aim for the same sort of "multi-dimensional effect . . . a sort of prism-sightedness" (*J* 16).

27. I am greatly indebted to David Wingrove, whose superb seminar paper "Dance of the Black Dominos: Narrative and Sex-Roles in Durrell's *Balthazar*" (April 1985) inspired me to return to Durrell in the first place, for making this connection (4–6), as well as for his comments on the roles that Scobie, Clea, and Narouz play in bringing Darley's repressions to the surface of the narration.

28. Much less humorously, Scobie's perspective captures the unthinking mentality that allowed for the Western appropriation and exploitation of racially "other," hence inferior bodies, male or female. As Sedgwick notes in reference to Sir Richard Burton's linking of pederastic habits with racial inferiority, "the foreign siting, in imperialist literature, makes the image of [sodomy] more articulately available" (*Between Men,* 193). Durrell's few documented personal comments on Egyptian sodomy also reflect this tendency. Writing to Miller from Alexandria, he sardonically comments that "Love, hashish and boys is the obvious solution to any one stuck here for more than a few years" (May 23, 1944, in Wickes, *Durrell–Miller,* 190) and, returning to this theme several months later, adds, "One could not continue to live here without practising a sort of death—hashish or boys or food" (Aug. 22, 1944, ibid., 195). For this colonialist, the practice of sodomy (enjoying

"boys") becomes the metaphoric equivalent, or symptom, of a slackening of the will, a giving in to sensual surfeit and suffocating enclosure. This response parallels the threat that Darley feels homosexuality poses to his artistic productivity in the *Quartet.* It is telling that as soon as Durrell has expressed this "death-threat" in the August 22 letter, he proceeds to tell Miller about the "wonderful novel on Alexandria" he has just conceived, "a sort of spiritual butcher's shop with girls on the slabs" (ibid., 196). The narrative sequence of this letter thus suggests that underlying the inspiration of the *Quartet* as a heterosexist fantasy of girls as meat-to-be-devoured is the fear of sodomy as an ultimate kind of indulgence in passive pleasure (like drugs, food) that spells "a sort of death" to the self. This overwriting of "boys" by "girls" as objects to be consumed (food, meat) parallels, in reverse, Scobie's overwriting of female sexuality with pederastic pleasures.

29. Note the sexualized language that Darley uses to describe Narouz's taming of this (female) horse: "Two hours later, Narouz brought her back, glistening with sweat, dejected, staggering. . . . he himself was deliriously exhausted, dazed as if he had ridden through an oven. . . . But he was happy underneath it all—indeed radiant. . . . Nothing could finally tire that powerful body—not even the orgasm he had experienced in the long savage battle" (*B* 82).
30. Sander L. Gilman, "Black Bodies, White Bodies: Toward an Iconography of Female Sexuality in Late Nineteenth-Century Art, Medicine, and Literature," *Critical Inquiry* 12 (1985): 212, 221, 229. In addition to Flaubert's several references (*Flaubert in Egypt,* 85, 203), the conflation of "ugly" visage and desirability occurs in du Camp's description of the "former bardash" Khalil, one of the crew members, who is "rather ugly, with a shifty look," but does, "in fact, have a charming behind" (225).
31. Sigmund Freud, *Three Essays on the Theory of Sexuality,* trans. James Strachey (1905, rev. 1910, 1915; New York: Basic, 1962), 13–14, 37–38.
32. In hindsight one realizes that this scene has been briefly represented in *Justine,* where Darley describes entering a prostitute's lighted booth "to wait my turn" (166)—the same phrase used in *Balthazar.*
33. My thanks to David Wingrove for uncovering this imagistic connection.
34. Alan Warren Friedman, *Lawrence Durrell and the Alexandria Quartet: Art for Love's Sake* (Norman: University of Oklahoma Press, 1970), 148. Upon this "necessary sacrifice," Friedman continues, Darley "sheds his unmanly timidity" (149).
35. Pinchin, "Fatal Cleopatra," 235, citing Theodore Reik.
36. To view Clea as sexually incomplete until her seduction by a man overlooks the sexual experience she has earlier shared with Justine: Only from a partial viewpoint is she a "virgin" at the time of Amaril's seduction. As Pinchin wittily puts it, "Amaril and Darley, male doctor and writer . . . make a good woman of Clea [by] curing her of her homosexuality and her virginity" (ibid.).
37. I borrow the phrase "writing couples" from Alice Jardine's "Death Sentences: Writing Couples and Ideology," in *The Female Body in Western Culture: Contemporary Perspectives,* ed. Susan Suleiman (Cambridge, MA: Harvard University Press, 1985), 84–96.